The Choreopolitics of Alain Platel's les ballets C de la B

Dance in Dialogue

Series editors: Anita Gonzalez, Katerina Paramana and Victoria Thoms

The interdisciplinary book series *Dance in Dialogue* critically examines the relations between performance and dance with other disciplines. It fosters interdisciplinary approaches, cross-disciplinary exchanges and conversation as a mode of knowledge production. The series aims to offer new ways of interrogating the relationship of performance and dance – in its broadest conception to include the body, the embodiment and the choreographic – with other disciplines as well as with political, cultural, social and economic issues and contexts. Throughout the books, these relationships with performance and dance are created, presented and theorized.

We seek to challenge the ways in which scholarship has traditionally been represented and disseminated, critically explore the dialogical relationship between theory and practice, and foster the ethos of collaboration, dialogue and political engagement that is needed for vibrant knowledge production both within and outside of academia. We encourage experimentation in publication format and research developed through innovative forms of collaborative and collective working across different modes of disciplinary and interdisciplinary inquiry and dissemination.

To realize this vision, the series offers two distinct publication formats via its two strands:

In Conversation
A collection of short books that present radical thinking emerging from curated conversations between the body(ies)/performance/dance/choreography and another discipline, area of research, field of knowledge or practice on topical artistic, cultural and political issues. Written by leading thinkers (artists and scholars) who critically explore the insights different areas of knowledge and practice offer to one another, as well as the affordances, potentials and implications of these insights for the contemporary world, these approximately 40,000-word books typically develop out of international conversation events and are published within approximately a year afterwards.

Moving forward
A collection of cutting-edge and forward-thinking, full-length monographs and edited collections that challenge understandings of the body(ies)/performance/dance/choreography and its (their) relation to political, cultural and socioeconomic issues and contexts, foster dialogue and interdisciplinarity and critically explore the relationship between theory and practice.

Other titles in the series

In Conversation titles:
Performance, Dance, and Political Economy
Edited by Katerina Paramana and Anita Gonzalez
Dance, Architecture and Engineering
Adesola Akinleye

Moving Forward titles:
FALLING through dance and life
Emilyn Claid

The Choreopolitics of Alain Platel's les ballets C de la B

Emotions, Gestures, Politics

Edited by Christel Stalpaert, Guy Cools and
Hildegard De Vuyst

BLOOMSBURY ACADEMIC
LONDON • NEW YORK • OXFORD • NEW DELHI • SYDNEY

BLOOMSBURY ACADEMIC
Bloomsbury Publishing Plc
50 Bedford Square, London, WC1B 3DP, UK
1385 Broadway, New York, NY 10018, USA
29 Earlsfort Terrace, Dublin 2, Ireland

BLOOMSBURY, BLOOMSBURY ACADEMIC and the Diana logo
are trademarks of Bloomsbury Publishing Plc

First published in Great Britain 2020
Paperback edition published 2021

Copyright © Christel Stalpaert, Guy Cools, Hildegard De Vuyst and contributors, 2020, 2021

Christel Stalpaert, Guy Cools, Hildegard De Vuyst and contributors have asserted
their right under the Copyright, Designs and Patents Act, 1988, to be
identified as authors of this work.

For legal purposes, the Acknowledgements on p. xvi–xvii constitute an
extension of this copyright page.

Cover design: Charlotte Daniels
Cover image © Mirjam Devriendt

All rights reserved. No part of this publication may be reproduced or transmitted
in any form or by any means, electronic or mechanical, including photocopying,
recording, or any information storage or retrieval system, without
prior permission in writing from the publishers.

Bloomsbury Publishing Plc does not have any control over, or responsibility for,
any third-party websites referred to or in this book. All internet addresses given
in this book were correct at the time of going to press. The author and publisher
regret any inconvenience caused if addresses have changed or sites have ceased
to exist, but can accept no responsibility for any such changes.

A catalogue record for this book is available from the British Library.

Library of Congress Cataloging-in-Publication Data
Names: Stalpaert, Christel, editor. | Cools, Guy, editor. | Vuyst, Hildegard de, editor.
Title: The choreopolitics of Alain Platel's les ballets C de la B : emotions, gestures, politics / edited by
Christel Stalpaert, Guy Cools, and Hildegard De Vuyst.
Description: London ; New York : Bloomsbury Academic, 2020. | Series: Dance in dialogue | Includes
bibliographical references and index. | Summary: "Les Ballets C de la B was founded by Alain Platel in
1984. Since then it has become a company that enjoys great success at home and abroad. Over the
years, Platel has developed a unique choreographic oeuvre. His motto, 'This dance is for the world and
the world is for everyone', reveals a deep social and political commitment. Through the three topics
of emotions, gestures and politics, this book unravels the choreopolitics of Platel's Les Ballets C de
la B. His choreopolitics go beyond conveying a (political) message because rather than defending one
opinion, Platel is more concerned about the exposure of the complexity within the debate itself. Highly
respected scholars from different fields contribute to this book to provide an interdisciplinary perspective
on the intense emotions, the damaged narratives, and the
precarious bodies in Platel's choreographic oeuvre"– Provided by publisher.
Identifiers: LCCN 2019043933 | ISBN 9781350080010 (hardback) | ISBN
9781350080027 (epub) | ISBN 9781350080034 (pdf) | ISBN 9781350080041
Subjects: LCSH: Platel, Alain–Criticism and interpretation. | Platel,
Alain–Themes, motives. | Ballets C. de la B. | Choreographers–Belgium.
| Ballet companies–Belgium. | Ballet–Political aspects–Belgium. |
Ballet–Social aspects–Belgium.
Classification: LCC GV1786.B222 C46 2020 | DDC 792.8–dc23
LC record available at https://lccn.loc.gov/2019043933

ISBN:	HB:	978-1-3500-8001-0
	PB:	978-1-3502-3357-7
	ePDF:	978-1-3500-8003-4
	eBook:	978-1-3500-8002-7

Series: Dance in Dialogue

Typeset by Integra Software Services Pvt. Ltd.

To find out more about our authors and books visit www.bloomsbury.com
and sign up for our newsletters.

Contents

List of Figures	ix
Notes on Contributors	xi
Series Editors' Preface	xv
Acknowledgements	xvi

1   Introduction *Christel Stalpaert, Guy Cools and Hildegard De Vuyst*   1

Part One   Multiple Dramaturgies

2   A Dramaturgy of Stuttering *Guy Cools*   19
3   'An Experiment in Democracy': Alain Platel's Collaborative Dramaturgy *Katalin Trencsényi*   32
4   Alain Wins a Prize *Hildegard De Vuyst*   61

Part Two   Emotions

5   Being Alone Together: Alain Platel and the 'Disturbance of Violent Relatedness' in *La Tristeza Complice* (1995), *pitié!* (2008) and *tauberbach* (2014) *Ann Cooper Albright*   69
6   Desire amongst the Dodgems: Alain Platel and the Scene of Seduction *Adrian Kear*   86
7   Alain Platel's Quest for Embodied Salvation: A Musical Perspective on *C(H)ŒURS* *Francis Maes*   99
8   Skin Tests: Views on *nicht schlafen* *Claire Besuelle*   115
9   Platel Is a Barbarian *Hildegard De Vuyst*   136

Part Three   Gestures

10   *Bernadetje*, Catastrophes and Gestures *Erwin Jans*   145
11   Choreic Gesture: Virtuosic Angularity, Alterkinetic Dance in Platel's *Out of Context – for Pina* *Kélina Gotman*   155
12   Staging the Precarious: Vulnerability and Sexual Identity in Alain Platel's *Gardenia* *Miriam Dreysse*   178

13 *tauberbach*, a Diagrammatical Reading: The Body between Self and
Language *Piet Defraeye* 189
14 Schizophrenia and Resistance: On *tauberbach* *Jeroen Donckers* 206

Part Four Politics

15 Mourning a Europe in Crisis: les ballets C de la B's *En avant,
marche!* (2015) *Lourdes Orozco* 215
16 Troubled Pasts and Presents, Differential Futures: Alain Platel's
Choreopolitics with les ballets C de la B *Christel Stalpaert* 230
17 Offspring *Hildegard De Vuyst* 251

Index 259

Figures

1.1	Poster for *Bonjour madame, comment allez-vous aujourd'hui, il fait beau, il va sans doute pleuvoir, etcetera*, 1993	6
1.2	*Bonjour madame, comment allez-vous aujourd'hui, il fait beau, il va sans doute pleuvoir, etcetera*, 1993	7
2.1	Gabriela Carrizo and Ghani Minne Vosteen in *Iets op Bach*, 1998	22
2.2	Mélanie Lomoff and Lisi Estaras in *vsprs*, 2006	25
3.1	Dorine Demuynck and Alain Platel during the rehearsals of *Out of Context – for Pina* in dance studio S3, Ghent 2009	33
3.2	Excerpt from the production book of Alain Platel, made during the creation of *nicht schlafen*, Ghent 2016	42
3.3	Excerpt from the production book of Alain Platel, made during the creation of *nicht schlafen*, Ghent 2016	43
3.4	Excerpt from the production book of Alain Platel, made during the creation of *nicht schlafen*, Ghent 2016	44
3.5	Excerpt from the production book of Alain Platel, made during the creation of *nicht schlafen*, Ghent 2016	45
3.6	Excerpt from the production book of Alain Platel, made during the creation of *nicht schlafen*, Ghent 2016	46
4.1	Hildegard De Vuyst in Teatro Comunale di Ferrara, during tour of *Badke*, 2016	61
5.1	Rosalba Torres Guerrero, Mathieu Desseigne Ravel, Emile Josse, Elie Tass and Lisi Estaras in *pitié!*, 2008	74
5.2	*La Tristeza Complice*, 1995	76
5.3	Koen Augustijnen and Ronald Burchi in *La Tristeza Complice*, 1995	78
6.1	An Pierlé, Titus De Voogdt and Lies Pauwels in *Bernadetje*, 1996	88
6.2	An Pierlé in *Bernadetje*, 1996	89
7.1	Daisy Phillips and Quan Bui Ngoc during rehearsals of *C(H)ŒURS* in dance studio S3, Ghent 2010.	108
7.2	Romeu Runa, Lisi Estaras and stand-in choir during rehearsals of *C(H)ŒURS* in dance studio S3, Ghent 2009.	110
8.1	David Le Borgne and Elie Tass rehearsing for *nicht schlafen* in dance studio S3, Ghent 2016	117

8.2	Scene, *nicht schlafen*, in Jahrhunderthalle, Bochum 2016	117
8.3	Cast during rehearsals of *nicht schlafen* in dance studio S3, Ghent 2016	120
8.4	Romain Guion and Dario Rigaglia during rehearsals of *nicht schlafen* in dance studio S3, Ghent 2016	120
10.1	Lies Pauwels, Gert Portael and Yassin Pycke in *Moeder en Kind*, 1995	147
10.2	Natacha Nicora and Frederik Debrock in *Allemaal Indiaan*, 1999	147
11.1	Romeo Runa, Emile Josse, Hyo Seung Ye, Elie Tass, Kaori Ito and Ross McCormack during rehearsals of *Out of Context – for Pina* in dance studio S3, Ghent 2010	163
11.2	Mélanie Lomoff, Elie Tass, Romeu Runa and Mathieu Desseigne Ravel during rehearsals of *Out of Context – for Pina* in dance studio S3, Ghent 2010	164
12.1	Danilo Povolo in *Gardenia*, 2010	182
12.2	Vanessa Van Durme and Richard Dierick in *Gardenia*, 2010	183
13.1	Romeu Runa, Elsie de Brauw, Ross McCormack, Bérengère Bodin, Elie Tass and Lisi Estaras during rehearsals of *tauberbach* in dance studio S3, Ghent 2013	191
14.1	Elsie de Brauw and Romeu Runa in *tauberbach*, Münchner Kammerspiele, Munich 2014	206
15.1	The Heroes Band and cast of *En avant, marche!* at Sadler's Wells, London, 2016	219
15.2	Gregory Van Seghbrouck, Wim Opbrouck, Griet Debacker and KMV De Leiezonen at NTGent, Ghent 2015	222
16.1	Bouton Kalanda, Russell Tshiebua and Costa Pinto during rehearsals of *Coup Fatal* in KVS Brussels, 2014	234
16.2	Tister Ikomo, Angou Ingutu and Serge Kakudji during rehearsals of *Coup Fatal* in KVS, Brussels, 2014	236
16.3	*Badke* in KVS, Brussels, 2013	244
17.1	Christine De Smedt, Hans Van den Broeck, Pascale Platel and Koen Augustijnen in *Mussen*, 1991	252
17.2	Christine De Smedt in *Untitled 4*, 2010	253
17.3	Sidi Larbi Cherkaoui and Akram Khan in *Zero Degrees*, 2005	254

Contributors

Claire Besuelle is currently a PhD candidate researching presence, gesture and motion in the creative process of contemporary performers in theatre and dance pieces, including Alain Platel's. She is a former student in theatrical studies at the École Normale Supérieure in Lyon, and a graduate from L'École du Jeu, a professional training school for actors. After writing a master's dissertation about solo performances in contemporary creation, she was awarded a scholarship for conducting her PhD research at the École Doctorale Sciences de l'Homme et de la Société (Villeneuve d'Ascq, Nord). Her research dialogues with her own practice as a performer, with L'Inverso-Collectif and Love Labo. She is also currently training in Cinetography (Laban's system of writing movement) at the Conservatoire National de Musique et de Danse in Paris.

Guy Cools is a dance dramaturge. Recent positions include Associate Research Professor at the research institute Arts in Society of the Fontys School of Fine and Performing Arts in Tilburg and Postdoctoral Researcher at Ghent University, where he finished a practice-based PhD on the relationship between dance and writing. He has worked as a dance critic and dance curator. He now dedicates himself to production dramaturgy, contributing to work by choreographers all over Europe and Canada such as Koen Augustijnen (BE), Sidi Larbi Cherkaoui (BE), Danièle Desnoyers (CA), Lia Haraki (CY), Christopher House (CA), Akram Khan (UK), Arno Schuitemaker (NL) and Stephanie Thiersch (DE). He regularly lectures and publishes and has developed a series of workshops that aim to support artists and choreographers in their creative process. His most recent publications include *The Ethics of Art: Ecological Turns in the Performing Arts*, co-edited with Pascal Gielen (Valiz, 2014); *In-Between Dance Cultures: On the Migratory Artistic Identity of Sidi Larbi Cherkaoui and Akram Khan* (Valiz, 2015) and *Imaginative Bodies: Dialogues in Performance Practices* (Valiz, 2016), a series of published, live interviews with major contemporary artists which Cools curated from 2008 until 2013 for Sadler's Wells, London. With the Canadian choreographer, Lin Snelling, he developed an improvised performance practice *Rewriting Distance* (see www.rewritingdistance.com) which focuses on the integration of movement, voice, and writing. Cools lives in Vienna.

Ann Cooper Albright is Professor and Chair of the Department of Dance at Oberlin College, as well as a dancer and a 2019 Guggenheim Fellow. Combining her interests in dancing and cultural theory, she teaches a variety of courses that seek to engage students in both practices and theories of the body. Her latest book, *How to Land: Finding Ground in An Unstable World*, offers a new look at embodiment that treats gravity as an organizing force for thinking and moving through our twenty-first-century world. Her other books include: *Engaging Bodies: The Politics and Poetics of Corporeality* (2013), which won the Selma Jeanne Cohen Prize from the American

Society for Aesthetics; *Modern Gestures: Abraham Walkowitz Draws Isadora Duncan Dancing* (2010); *Traces of Light: Absence and Presence in the Work of Loie Fuller* (2007); *Choreographing Difference: The Body and Identity in Contemporary Dance* (1997). She is co-editor, with Ann Dils, of *Moving History/Dancing Cultures* (2001) and, with David Gere, of *Taken By Surprise: Improvisation in Dance and Mind* (2003). Albright is founder and director of *Girls in Motion*, an award-winning afterschool programme at Langston Middle School, and co-director of *Accelerated Motion: Towards a New Dance Literacy in America*, an NEA-supported website that facilitates active learning and the exchange of teaching strategies and resources to support educators who teach dance studies as a humanistic discipline. She is also a veteran practitioner of Contact Improvisation and has taught workshops throughout the USA and abroad. The book, *Encounters with Contact Improvisation* (2010), is the product of one of her adventures in writing and dancing and dancing and writing with others.

Miriam Dreysse teaches theatre and performance studies at the Universität Hildesheim. From 2009 until 2013, she was Professor of Theatre Studies at the Universität der Künste Berlin. She studied at the Institute for Applied Theatre Studies at the University of Giessen and worked there as an assistant professor from 1997 to 2007. She has written numerous publications about contemporary theatre and performance art and about gender in theatre, performance and popular culture. Her publications include *Szene vor dem Palast: Die Theatralisierung des Chors im Theater Einar Schleefs* (1999), *Experts of the Everyday: The Theatre of Rimini Protokoll* (with Florian Malzacher, 2008), and *Sicherheitslos: Prekarisierung, die Künste und ihre Geschlechterverhältnisse* (with Linda Hentschel and Kerstin Brandes, 2012). Her most recent publication, entitled *Mutterschaft und Familie: Inszenierungen in Theater und Performance* (2015), deals with the representation of motherhood and family in contemporary theatre.

Hildegard De Vuyst started her career as a dance critic and editor at theatre magazine *Etcetera*. From 1994 onwards she worked as a dramaturg, mainly with choreographer Alain Platel and his company, les ballets C de la B. In 2001, De Vuyst started working for the Royal Flemish Theatre of Brussels (KVS) with the aim of reconnecting the theatre to the city of Brussels. Since 2006, she has coordinated PASS (Performing Arts Summer School), an initiative of KVS, les ballets C de la B and the A. M. Qattan Foundation, which consists of a long-term artistic exchange with a new generation of Palestinian performing artists. This process led to the creation of productions like *Keffiyeh/Made in China* and *Badke*. De Vuyst got more and more involved in the practice of intercultural dramaturgy, giving workshops in Kinshasa, Sydney, London. In 2016, she joined les ballets C de la B in order to build a residency programme and followed former KVS director Jan Goossens to the Festival de Marseille.

Piet Defraeye is a performance studies scholar and director. He teaches at the Drama Department at the University of Alberta. He is also connected to the Wirth Institute for Austrian and Central European Studies. He does mainly comparative research in contemporary performance. He has a particular interest in Austrian theatre and has published on contemporary German, Austrian and Romanian theatre, among other themes. Apart from an ongoing focus on strategies of provocation for the stage, he is presently conducting a large research project on the figure of Patrice Lumumba, the first prime minister of Congo, assassinated during his first year in office, as he appears in a variety of cultural discourses, including plays, popular culture, paintings, poetry and novels. Defraeye has been a resident guest professor at several universities (Louvain, Innsbruck, Munich, Antwerp).

Jeroen Donckers is a Belgian psychotherapist, who works with children, young adults and adults. Referring to the work of the French psychoanalyst Maud Mannoni, Donckers has a particular attention for the potential of language, art and literature in helping children with behavioural problems to express themselves. Donckers has developed a particular vision for the connecting potential of art and books, allowing for the psychotherapist's language and the particular (so-called disturbed) language of the patient to encounter one another. In *Psychologische Perspectieven*, he has written about his psychotherapeutic practices and recalls the particular potential of books by Fernando Pessoa in allowing a patient of his to articulate the 'inarticulatory'.

Kélina Gotman is Reader in Theatre and Performance Studies at King's College London. Her work is interdisciplinary, drawing from dance, critical studies of science and medicine, history, philosophy and cultural theory. Her book on dance manias in nineteenth-century medical literature, *Choreomania: Dance and Disorder* (Oxford University Press, 2018) describes the emergence of the 'choreomania' ('dance mania') diagnosis in Europe and the colonial world. Her research on zoanthropy, including lycanthropy and tarantism, *Essays on Theatre and Change: Towards a Poetics Of* forms part of a larger project on ethnofiction, translation and theatre.

Erwin Jans worked as a dramaturg at several important theatres in Belgium and Holland. He is currently working as a dramaturg at Toneelhuis (Antwerp, Belgium). He teaches on theatre and drama at the Artesis Hogeschool Antwerpen where he also does research on the history of the dramatic text. He writes extensively on theatre, literature and culture. Major publications include *Interculturele Intoxicaties: Over kunst, cultuur en verschil* (2006). He was co-editor of an anthology of Flemish postwar poetry *Hotel New Flandres* (2008). Together with philosopher Eric Clemens he wrote an essay on democracy that was also translated in French (2010). Last year he published an anthology of the dramatic work of the Flemish playwright and director Tone Brulin (2017).

Professor Adrian Kear is Programme Development Director, Performance Arts, at Wimbledon College of Arts, University of the Arts London, UK. Prior to joining Wimbledon College of Arts, Kear was Professor of Theatre and Performance at Aberystwyth University (2007–18), serving as Head of the Department. His books include: *Thinking Through Theatre and Performance* (with Maaike Bleeker, Joe Kelleher and Heike Roms, 2019), *Theatre and Event: Staging the European Century* (2013); *International Politics and Performance: Critical Aesthetics and Creative Practice* (with Jenny Edkins, 2013); *On Appearance* (with Richard Gough, 2008) and *Psychoanalysis and Performance* (with Patrick Campbell, 2001).

Francis Maes is Senior Lecturer in Musicology at Ghent University, Belgium. He is the author of a textbook on Russian music history, published by the University of California Press, and a contributor to the *Cambridge Companion to Shostakovich*. His other research interest lies in opera and music theatre, which resulted in book on contemporary opera staging, *Opera behind the Screens of the Emotion* (in Dutch). His current research focuses on the study of the operatic aesthetics of Dimitry Tcherniakov and Ivo van Hove.

Lourdes Orozco is Associate Professor in Theatre Studies at the School of English at the University of Leeds, UK. Her research deals with contemporary Western European performance practices with special focus on the material conditions of performance and its relationship with politics, ethics and identity. She has co-edited two special issues of *Contemporary Theatre Review* on Catalan theatre and on Flemish theatre that embrace different aspects of the making and producing of theatre in these regions as well as dealing with theatre's interaction with politics and national identity issues. Her recent research focuses on the intersections, dialogues and connections that theatre and performance studies has – or has the potential to have – with two other research areas: animal studies and children studies. This research resulted in the publication of *Theatre and Animals* (2013). With Jennifer Parker-Starbuck, she edited *Performing Animality: Animals in Performance Practices* (2015). She is currently working on her second animals in performance monograph, forthcoming with Methuen.

Christel Stalpaert is Professor of Theatre, Performance and Media Studies at Ghent University, Belgium, where she is Director of the Research Centres S:PAM (Studies in Performing Arts and Media) and PEPPER (Philosophy, Ethology, Politics and Performance). Her main areas of research are the performing arts, dance and the new media at the meeting point of philosophy. She has contributed to many journals such as *Performance Research*, *Text & Performance Quarterly*, *Contemporary Theatre Review* and *Dance Research Journal* and edited works such as *Deleuze Revisited: Contemporary Performing Arts and the Ruin of Representation* (2003), *No Beauty for Me There Where Human Life Is Rare: On Jan Lauwers' Theatre Work with Needcompany* (with Frederik Le Roy and Sigrid Bousset, 2006), *Bastard or Playmate? Adapting Theatre, Mutating Media and the Contemporary Performing Arts* (with Rob Vanderbeeken, 2012) and *Unfolding Spectatorship: Shifting Political, Ethical and Intermedial Positions* (with Katharina Pewny and Jeroen Coppens, 2016). She is editor in chief of *Documenta*.

Katalin Trencsényi is a dramaturg and researcher, based in London. Her areas of specialization are contemporary theatre and performance, new dramaturgy, dance dramaturgy, multi-modal play development, and European director's theatre. As an independent dramaturg, Katalin has worked with the National Theatre, the Royal Court Theatre, and Soho Theatre, amongst others. She has taught dramaturgy internationally: including Australia, Canada, Russia and the USA. From 2015 to 2019 Katalin worked as a tutor at the Royal Academy of Dramatic Art (RADA). Katalin is the author of *Dramaturgy in the Making: A User's Guide for Theatre Practitioners* (2015), editor of *Bandoneon: Working with Pina Bausch* (2016), co-editor of *New Dramaturgy: International Perspectives on Theory and Practice* (2014), and an editor of the global theatre portal, TheTheatreTimes.com.

Series Editors' Preface

The *Dance in Dialogue* book series critically explores the intersections between dance, performance and other disciplines. It fosters interdisciplinary approaches, cross-disciplinary exchanges, and conversation as a mode of knowledge production. Supported by the Society for Dance Research and Bloomsbury Academic, the book series will challenge the ways in which scholarship has traditionally been represented and disseminated and offer new ways of interrogating dance and articulating its concerns and relation to other disciplines and to the cultural and socio-economic context in which it is created, presented and theorized.

To realize this vision, *Dance in Dialogue* offers two distinct publication formats via its two strands:

In Conversation: Dance and …
A collection of short books that emerge from curated conversations between dance (in its expanded sense of the body, embodiment, and the choreographic) and another discipline, area of research, field of knowledge or practice on topical issues. Written by leading thinkers who critically explore how the one area of knowledge and practice offers insight into the other, these approximately 40,000-word books typically develop out of international conversation events and are published within approximately a year after them.

Moving Forward
A collection of cutting-edge and forward-thinking full-length monographs and edited collections that challenge understandings of dance and the body or bodies, foster dialogue and interdisciplinarity and critically explore the relationship between theory and practice.

We seek to foster the ethos of collaboration and dialogue needed for the vibrancy of knowledge production within and outside of academia. The series will encourage research developed through new forms of collaborative and collective working across different modes of disciplinary and interdisciplinary inquiry and dissemination.

> Dance as
> Materiality,
> Embodiment,
> Spaces,
> Temporalities.
> Dialogue as
> Contention
> Relation
> Dissensus
> Exchange
> Dance in Dialogue
>
> Anita Gonzalez, Katerina Paramana, Victoria Thoms

Acknowledgements

It all started with our observation that a lot had been published about Alain Platel and les ballets C de la B abroad, more than in Belgium and Flanders. It was Guy who first raised the idea to publish a book on Alain Platel's choreographic work with les ballets C de la B. Considering the scholarly attention he received worldwide, an edited volume was the appropriate format. It goes without saying that a sincere thank you goes to all the authors who attributed to this edited volume. Coming not only from different countries but also from different fields, they provided an interesting wide and interdisciplinary perspective on the choreographic oeuvre of Alain Platel.

Today, we are very proud to announce the first academic publication and chronological overview on the whole choreographic work of Alain Platel. We joined forces as a team of editors to obtain a valuable academic as well as a dramaturgical perspective, providing insight in the artistic process as well as the dance performances of les ballets C de la B.

In the Bloomsbury Academic team, we found an appropriate partner who respected our choices. Thank you Meredith Benson, for the trust and the enthusiasm in guiding us along the editing process.

This job couldn't be done without the help of some crucial helping hands. A special thanks goes to Sophie van den Bergh. She is a very intelligent scholar, who is also gifted with the most refined editing skills. With endless patience, she took care of the reference system and the final editing of the book, a task not to be underestimated. In fact, we would like to take this opportunity to thank all researchers at the research centre S:PAM (Studies in Performing Arts and Media) at Ghent University. They are a wonderful crowd, never hesitant to lend a helping hand. Their sparkling dynamism creates a stimulating research environment.

Another person of invaluable value throughout the editing process is Nele Dhaese from les ballets C de la B. It was Nele who kept an amazing bird's-eye view on the immense archival material of the company. She also provided the captions for the photos and meticulously checked all the names of the performers and the dates of premiere. She teamed up wonderfully well with Sophie for the photo editing.

The photographers also deserve to be mentioned in these acknowledgements. They agreed with the copyright arrangements without hesitation and obviously shared our enthusiasm for the Platel book.

We would also like to thank Alain Platel himself. He was informed about the plans for this book from the very beginning, but he never interfered with the editing process. Not that he was careless. On the contrary! The twinkle in his eyes revealed his enthusiasm. His silent trust felt as a gift and was the stimulating undercurrent of the whole book project. In the end, he even agreed to publish parts of his production diaries, which truly makes this book a unique contribution to dance studies.

Christel Stalpaert
Guy Cools
Hildegard De Vuyst

1

Introduction

Christel Stalpaert, Guy Cools and Hildegard De Vuyst

Different from a lot of his generational peers, until now no publication existed that brings together the critical discourse on the work of Flemish choreographer Alain Platel and his les ballets C de la B. There are several reasons for this. For one thing, Platel himself always resisted the canonization of his work and often preferred a more informal discourse of personal contacts or letters sent to him publicly or privately. Another reason is that the diversity of his work has attracted an equally diverse critical discourse that not only crosses the borders of the art disciplines – theatre, dance, music theatre and opera – but also wanders into fields such as psychoanalysis or queer studies. As editors of this book, we wanted to fill this gap and bring together a diversity of points of view. Most of the articles included have been commissioned for this volume, but some have been republished because of their iconic nature.

We believe that art criticism (even scholarly and academic) should not only reflect on the work it discusses but that it should also attempt to translate some of its formal characteristics into the language and registers used. As such, this volume brings together not only a diversity of topics but also experiments with a diversity of stylistic approaches and text formats.

The three editors have been privileged witnesses of the full thirty years of Platel's career from the early 1980s until today, with different levels of proximity. Hildegard De Vuyst has been Platel's dramaturg for more than two decades, and in 2016 she joined the company as coordinator of the residency programme Co-laBo. Guy Cools has dialogued with Platel's body of work as a critic, as its presenter and co-producer and as the dramaturg of some of Platel's 'offspring'. Theatre scholar Christel Stalpaert teaches at the university theatre department in Ghent, Platel's home turf. As a result of this proximity, the texts in the book oscillate between a subjective point of view that allows us to offer unique insights in Platel's thoughts and working methodologies and a critical distance that allows us to look at different aspects of his work, applying a broad range of critical theories. We hope that the polyphony of voices will guide the readers in Platel's universe and have them (re)discover both its diversity and complexity.

The identity politics of the Flemish Wave

Alain Platel founded les ballets C de la B in 1984 with a group of like-minded friends and colleagues. As such, he is part of the first generation of artists, together with Anne Teresa De Keersmaeker, Wim Vandekeybus, Jan Fabre, Jan Lauwers, Josse De Pauw, Jan Decorte, Eric De Volder, Guy Cassiers, Ivo van Hove, Luk Perceval and Arne Sierens, who were hyped as the Flemish Wave in Flanders, Belgium. The theatre-makers conquered the Netherlands; the dance-makers conquered the international dance stages from the 1980s onwards. The notion of 'Flemish Wave' was a construction of identity politics, created by marketing departments and the media, picked up by culture politics and originally also endorsed by the artists themselves. In their contribution to the book *Europe Dancing: Perspectives on Theatre Dance and Cultural Identity*, the Flemish sociologists Pascal Gielen and Rudi Laermans argue that the 'Flemish wave' rhetoric was a conscious, discursive strategy of this new generation of artists to eventually obtain more financial support. Claiming a regional 'authenticity' was only one side of that discursive strategy. These choreographers were simultaneously legitimized by a careful inscription in an existing, international dance canon.

> In our view, the crucial link in the success story of Anne Teresa De Keersmaeker, Jan Fabre, Wim Vandekeybus or, more recently, Alain Platel was the powerful combination of selective references to internationally acknowledged 'models' or 'styles' with an international recognition as original choreographers by leading festivals and foreign critics. The latter was a pivotal argument in the struggle against the long-standing dominance of the ballet tradition in Flanders, especially around the mid-1980s.[1]

The acknowledgement of a common Flemish identity clearly had a strategic dimension, and from the 1990s onwards it was picked up by the official cultural politics. Even if most artists of the Flemish Wave continued to assert their 'Belgitude' and their solidarity with the other regions, they could not completely escape being used as 'cultural ambassadors' for a growing, Flemish, nationalist identity.

At the same time, each of these choreographers continued to develop a unique, personal signature, embedded in an even more locally specific context. With PARTS, Anne Teresa De Keersmaeker recreated her version of Maurice Béjart's Mudra, investing her own symbolic capital in educating the next generation of dance artists and by doing so establishing Brussels as one of the epicentres of the contemporary dance scene at the turn of the millennium.

As a result, Flanders and Brussels have become attractive living and working places for foreign dancers and choreographers, who often came to work with one of the choreographers mentioned above. Dance critic Pieter T'Jonck reflected on these recent developments in contemporary dance in Flanders as 'the best measure to evaluate the quality and the international character of the Flemish dance'. He concludes, 'the diversity of new choreographers proves that the nomination of "Flemish Dance" has less and less to do with the nationality of choreographers and dancers, and more and more, or even exclusively with where the dance has been created, that is in Flanders'.²

Alain Platel put his home town Ghent on the international dance map. Its history as an anarchistic opposition to the dominant powers of both emperor and church resembles his own rebellious attitude, while its contemporary, urban landscape became a major source of inspiration for his scenic universes. Using his daily walks and bike rides through Ghent as a creative input, Platel has developed a unique choreographic oeuvre, faithfully following his motto, 'this dance belongs to the world and the world belongs to everybody'.

Alain Platel's choreopolitics

Against the reductive identity politics of the 'Flemish Wave' construction, we propose in this book the concept of choreopolitics, originally used by dance scholar André Lepecki in 'Choreopolice and Choreopolitics; or, The Task of the Dancer' (2013). By introducing the concept of choreopolitics in dance studies, Lepecki redefined choreography and released it conceptually from imperative, normative or 'policed' constructions of movement, such as the identity politics described above, which narrow down a complex and multiple artistic identity to only one of its aspects. Drawing on Jacques Rancière's political philosophy, one could say that choreopolicing is concerned with controlling movements, with channelling and directing movements in a confined space, while choreopolitics is more concerned with redistributing habitual and legitimate ways of moving in time and space. It takes part in 'the indetermination of identities, the delegitimation of positions of speech, the deregulation of partitions of space and time'.³ Following Hannah Arendt's observations on freedom, Lepecki considers choreopolitics a way 'to move politically', 'as expressions of freedom'.⁴ 'Arendt's fragment persists, resonates, unsettles, stirs. Its afterlife expresses and beckons a challenge and a provocation that are both political and kinetic – in one word "choreopolitical" – a challenge we must answer … of imagining and enacting a politics of movement as a choreopolitics of freedom.'⁵

Platel meets Arendt's challenge to move politically in his consistent open way of choreographing. He does not consider it to be 'an art of command'.⁶ As Lepecki observed, this choreopolicing is a system of command that 'implements, needs, produces, and reproduces whole systems of obedience'.⁷ Rather than having his dancers and performers obey his commands, Platel has 'learned to wait. Which in turn gives people the confidence to participate in the creative process.'⁸ Platel is not a movement controller. As his dramaturg Hildegard De Vuyst phrases it in this edited volume, 'he consistently refuses to be the great watch-maker who has the cogs perfectly under control'. To put it in Lepecki's words, Platel's choreopolitics with les ballets C de la B always remains 'an open movement, not of commands and their implementation (as in policies), but a movement of the political itself – crisscrossing the multitude, converging divergences, aimed at freedom'.⁹

On a conceptual level, the consistent openness in Platel's choreopolitics also tackles (political) issues concerned with notions of identity, gender and nation(ality). However, Platel's art is not political in its message, nor in the identities it stages or the feelings the performance invokes concerning social and political questions. Political art is not the area of the pamphleteer. For Rancière, 'the "fictions" of art and politics are ... heterotopias rather than utopias'.[10] Platel's choreopolitics with les ballets C de la B is hence to be considered as more than conveying a (political) message. Rather than defending one opinion, Platel is more concerned with the exposure of the complexity within the debate itself.

In order to show that complexity, but also to offer the reader tools to untangle it, we have organized the contributions in this book around four interrelated topics: its multiple dramaturgies, the emotions it consciously evokes, the precarious bodies and gestures it represents and its more overt politics of damaged narratives and inclusiveness. These four themes are necessarily interwoven. The way in which Platel organizes his company and his creative process; the priority he continues to give to an emotional response and reception of his work; and the types of bodies and gestures he gives prevalence to are all equal parts of his choreopolitics, as much as any more overtly political content or message.

Rather than vainly attempting an exhaustive description of Platel's body of work, each chapter zooms in on one or a couple of productions that are particularly relevant for the topics under scrutiny. In each of the four sections of the book, the texts are loosely organized so that the discussed productions give some sense of the chronology of the whole oeuvre.

Multiple dramaturgies

The first part, Multiple Dramaturgies, gives an insight into Platel's collaborative and creative working methods in which he follows a 'decentred dramaturgy'. In this working method, he shares the responsibility of his work with all his collaborators, in the first place his dancers. In his contribution, dramaturg Guy Cools observes how Platel's artistic trajectory evolved from working with untrained amateur performers to highly trained, specialized, professional performers whose virtuosic control of their own bodies is used to embody the hypersensitivity and often lack of control of damaged bodies, such as one often finds in psychiatry.

Using as a main source, next to the work itself, the many public interviews he did with Alain Platel, Cools first considers Platel's viewpoint and working method all through the 1990s, for such as *Bonjour madame, comment allez-vous aujourd'hui, il fait beau, il va sans doute pleuvoir, etcetera* (1993), *La Tristeza Complice* (1995) and *Iets op Bach* (1998). Drawing on a public talk with Platel at Sadler's Wells in 2011, he focuses on the aesthetic and political vision behind the works he created in the first decade of the twenty-first century: *Out of Context – for Pina* (2010) and *Gardenia* (2010), two very distinct but related works, while throwing sideways glances at *vsprs* and *pitié!* He unfolds his notion of a dramaturgy of stuttering to touch upon the particular poetics of their gestures.

Katalin Trencsényi further unfolds Platel's open choreopolitical way of working as 'collaborative democracy'. Drawing on interviews that she did with the ensemble, Trencsényi presents and analyses not only the performers' creative process but also the dramaturgical collaboration between Alain Platel and Hildegard De Vuyst. This contribution first places Platel's particular way of collaborating with dramaturgs in a historical context, referring to Pina Bausch's Tanztheater and to the wider development of dance dramaturgy as developed by, amongst others, Marianne Van Kerkhoven.

Platel and De Vuyst share a process-oriented way of working. Trencsényi introduces the notion of the 'dramaturg-as-translator', after Walter Benjamin's *The Task of the Translator*, to describe the labour of the dramaturg in negotiating between different companies, between different media (music, dance and theatre) and between individuals in group dynamics. Platel's choreopolitics here comes to the fore in the body-politics of the performers, echoing Van Kerkhoven's notion of the macro- and the micro-dramaturgy.

Zooming into some productions, such as *Out of Context – for Pina* (2010) and *nicht schlafen* (2016), Trencsényi further traces the development of the ensemble's 'unruly' collaborative dramaturgy. This 'unruly' dramaturgy dares to take risks, not only in its choice of dancers but also in mixing different movement vocabularies. Of particular interest is Platel's *Blickregie*; this watching together generates a particular mode of co-creating that Trencsényi connects with a particular politics and ethics of democracy.

Dramaturg Hildegard De Vuyst has a special place in this edited volume. Since their first collaboration, *La Tristeza Complice* (1995), she has not only accompanied all of Platel's creations as a production dramaturg but she has also substantially contributed to the discourse that accompanies the work. She does so in her own, unique voice, which, similarly to Platel, not only rationalizes but also follows her own gut feelings. Throughout this book, she is given the opportunity to articulate the underlying ideology of Platel's choreopolitics from an insider's dramaturgical perspective.

In her first contribution, Hildegard De Vuyst puts Alain Platel's early choreographic work in its context. The text is presented as a historical document, as it was a speech on the occasion of the seventh Prix Europe Nouvelles Théâtrales that was awarded to Alain Platel in Taormina (Italy) on 8 April 2001. It observes how les ballets C de la B arose out of the wasteland of a non-existing contemporary dance landscape in 1984 and how it experienced its international breakthrough only in 1993 with *Bonjour madame*. De Vuyst considers Platel's early work, consisting of two trilogies, as a consistent oeuvre. The first trilogy – *Moeder en Kind*, *Bernadetje* and *Allemaal Indiaan* – deals with conflicts in a family context. The second trilogy, *Bonjour madame*, *La Tristeza Complice* and *Iets op Bach* – deals with semi-public spheres in which stories meet and clash. Already in these early works, she observes Platel's refusal to reconcile opposites: 'Platel's world is not neatly divided into sheep and wolves; a man is also a woman, and nothing can ever be only beautiful. He embraces the contrasts and brings extremes together', she writes in her contribution. De Vuyst also detects Platel's open choreopolitical way of working, giving his dancers 'a lot of freedom (and hence a lot of responsibility)'.

Figure 1.1 Poster for *Bonjour madame, comment allez-vous aujourd'hui, il fait beau, il va sans doute pleuvoir, etcetera*, 1993. Poster design by Patricia Rau.

Figure 1.2 *Bonjour madame, comment allez-vous aujourd'hui, il fait beau, il va sans doute pleuvoir, etcetera*, 1993. © Chris Van der Burght.

Emotions

In the second part, we shift from the internal working processes to the reception of the work. We focus on how Platel's choreopolitics deliberately aim at an emotional response and reception by the audience and how this reveals a complexity of often contradictory value systems in which the audience has to constantly reposition itself. The emotional response Platel aims at does not want to avoid but to stimulate a reflective attitude towards the spectator's own responsibility. The musical or 'sonorous dramaturgy' is an essential part of how emotions are being triggered. Soundscapes, sound bites and bits and pieces of quotations and utterings are important when it comes to the construction of meaning, but the treatment of microphones or the electronic transformation and manipulation of voices and sounds is equally vital to the work's visceral impact.

Dance scholar Ann Cooper Albright discusses three evening-length works performed by les ballets C de la B: *La Tristeza Complice* (1995), *pitié!* (2008) and *tauberbach* (2014), with respect to the particular conjunction of theatrical representation and kinaesthetic experience. Drawing on Hans-Thies Lehmann's notion of 'energetic theatre' and John Berger's profound and poetic short essay on Rembrandt's paintings, she explains how scenes of survival and displacement in Platel's choreographic work provide a corporeal space for 'being alone together', requiring a particular 'way of seeing' the other. Drawing on the social and political implications of the relationship between performers and audience members, she refers to the complex connections between one's self and an 'other', surprisingly creating, in fact, a cooperative manner of being together in the theatre. Central in this way of being together is the notion of 'being touched by the work' and as such taking up a response-ability towards it.

In his chapter, Adrian Kear zooms in on one particular scene in Platel's oeuvre: the scene of seduction in *Bernadetje* (1996). The performance reconfigures the logic of theatre as a locus of seduction, entangling the spectator in a particular emotional journey. *Bernadetje* links the historical traumatic experience of the revelation of the conspiracy of silence surrounding the Belgian child-abuser and murderer Marc Dutroux to something like the historical significance of abuse as the silenced experience of childhood's traumatic reality. Implicating the audience of *Bernadetje* in the visceral power of seduction, this performance opens up the question of responsibility in this matter. Instead of merely giving in to the overwhelming experience of seduction, the spectator is invited to bear witness to the culture of abuse as a shared, complicit but nonetheless collective responsibility, much in the same line as Bertolt Brecht desired a theatre experience to be a matter of ongoing incredulity. Platel's choreopolitics again – on a conceptual level – exposes the complexity within the debate itself. Rather than uncovering a crime, drawing a clear line between the abuser and the abused, the spectators find themselves amidst conflictual extremes, finding meaning through a profound response-ability. The sensibility to be developed on behalf of the spectator is a state of constant vigilance, of devoted attentiveness and response-ability on the spot.

Music has a strong overwhelming and emotional appeal. It has the power to stimulate strong emotions with us. Platel's choreographic work with les ballets C de la B is marked by its multifaceted relationship to music. Three of his major productions took their lead from canonical classical composers, starting with the iconoclastic *Iets op Bach* (1998), with the dancers translating the emotions of the music in raw and unsettling ways; to Mozart in *Wolf* (2003), in which the continual juxtapositions of sublime music and earthly reality are striking; to Platel's commentary on the 'indignados' movement in *C(H)ŒURS* (2012), through orchestral and choral pages by Wagner and Verdi. In line with his refusal to maintain cultural divides, Platel mixes high and low musical registers. Bach meets Prince in 'What If God Was One of Us'; Monteverdi borrows 'Tears in Heaven' from Eric Clapton; Mozart meets Céline Dion; Ravel's *Bolero* meets Marlene Dietrich. Platel deliberately plays with these different levels of recognition. As such, there is also a particular connection of body and mind. The music pieces into which Platel's choreopolitics with les ballets C de la B unfold are not neutral. They all have been conceived in a very precise musicological context. Even when they are transposed to a dance performance that abstracts their original setting, they continue to carry a cluster of hermeneutical associations.

This is especially the case for *C(H)ŒURS*, which was created in response to a request by Gerard Mortier, at the time director of the Teatro Real, the Madrid Opera House. The audience of *C(H)ŒURS* hence not only consisted of dance lovers but also of operagoers. The alignment of contemporary dance with Wagner and Verdi struck musicologist Francis Maes as a frantic moving back and forth between corporeal and cognitive stimulae. This paradoxical call on the spectator's mind and body touches upon another paradox at work in *C(H)ŒURS*: that of the individual and the community in revolutionary times. The choral numbers in the operas of Verdi and Wagner often depict, as Platel declares, a group in actions of revolt. However, the dancers' slogans on demonstration banners interfere with the recitation of texts by the French writer Marguerite Duras about the validity of the individual and the injustice that governs the habit to subsume people under fixed collective categories. *C(H)ŒURS* is not a naive ode to revolt. Maes' musicological reading of *C(H)ŒURS* unravels the complexity at work in the performance.

In her contribution, Claire Besuelle similarly approaches the dancing-fighting body in *nicht schlafen* (2016). The body engaged with fighting and dancing is not a heroic figure following a dramatic narrative, disappearing in a character. Rather, Platel's poetics of fight follows 'a musical dramaturgy'. Parallel to the collective singing as polyphony, in which the individual voice is never erased, the materiality of the dancing-fighting body is not erased in favour of the development of a character in a drama. In this musical dramaturgy, not a character, but the dancer's skin is the main dramaturgical motif. This skin is not merely covered with costumes; it acquires response-ability in touching 'a protective layer' as in a mutual dialogue. This mutual touching also relates to other skins, in the touching of the other dancers' skin. In *nicht schlafen* the dead skin of the horse sculptures onstage (designed by visual artist Berlinde De Bruyckere) adds another dimension to this aesthetics of touch, tackling the cultural divide between human and non-human matter, between dead and living material.

The aesthetics of touch works not only on the level of touch, as a caress, but also on a conceptual level, referring to the touching in wonder. The French philosopher Luce Irigaray refers to this touching in wonder as a thinking of the body that is not defined by genus and species. The body should not be understood in terms of its superficial characteristics such as form, functions and kind, or race, gender and identity (something which does happen through the 'mapping' of the distant gaze). Following a musical logic, rather than a dramatic one, the performance also inaugurates a particular relation with the spectator's body, providing space for the sensorial and the dynamic, the emphatic and kinaesthetic. Moreover, the performances that lie at the heart of this book avoid the self-evident, commonplace discourse of those bodies considered to have the talent to perform, the right to speak and hence to have their voices amplified. These performances give voice to bodies that are suppressed in society. They dismantle common sense notions of sex, age and identity and transgress current trends connected with the social meaning of beauty, age and gender. They do so by performing and presenting the articulatory potential of the body and its skin. In that way, they leave room for the dissensus between the demands of reason, the faculties of imagination and our emotional responses.

We conclude this second section on emotions with another time capsule by Hildegard De Vuyst, a speech she delivered at a colloquium for the occasion of Platel's honorary doctorate at the University of Artois, in March 2014. In it she reacts to the sometimes overtly antagonistic attitude in critical discourse to the way Platel consciously seeks to evoke emotions and which was coined 'emo-terrorism' by sociologist Rudi Laermans. Inspired by Martha Nussbaum's observations in *Upheavals of Thought*, De Vuyst perceives emotions as forms of thinking. They are bodily and mentally connected. Precisely by moving away from binary oppositions such as body and mind, low and high culture, superficiality and depth, beauty and ugliness, De Vuyst outlines how perceiving Platel's choreographic work is not a case of pure bodily sensations, lacking any critical reflection. Instead, the spectator is part of a widespread mutation in perception, leading towards a different way of having experiences and creating meaning, as formulated in Alessandro Baricco's widely acclaimed essay *I barbari*.

Gestures

In the third part, we zoom in on the diversity of bodies and gestures that Platel highlights in his work. Several chapters in this section refer to Agamben's 'loss of gesture' and the renegotiation between what is considered normal or abnormal, resulting from this loss. Platel's preference of mixing different bodies and gestures further 'democratizes the aesthetics of dance'. Undoubtedly, Platel's choices are very much influenced by his studies as a remedial educationalist and his early work experiences with children with a disability. During his studies he was inspired by the work of Fernand Deligny, who found communication and meaningful interaction (in his observations of autistic children) where others could only see lack and failure. Deligny's example invited Platel to observe carefully and to look out for the minor gesture. Dancers such as Romeu Runa, Ido Batash or Lisi Estaras have such a specific connection with these small, nervous or spastic gestures that they are invited to build whole sections of choreography for the dancers to perform synchronously, a distinct feature of classical corps de ballet, impossible to accomplish with this resilient material resisting sameness and synchronicity.

After an introduction on the collaboration between theatre-maker Arne Sierens and Alain Platel for the trilogy *Moeder en Kind* (1995), *Bernadetje* (1996) and *Allemaal Indiaan* (1999), dramaturg Erwin Jans observes some key scenes in the performance *Bernadetje*. He indicates that the political engagement of the performance lies in the continuous shifting between *gestus* and hieroglyph. Borrowing the terms from Bertolt Brecht and Antonin Artaud respectively, Jans outlines the artistic strategies of contemporary (postdramatic) political theatre. Jans also refers to Giorgio Agamben's readings of Gilles de la Tourette (1857–1904) and Jean-Martin Charcot (1825–93) in order to operationalize a particular political reading of catastrophic gestures in the choreographic work of Alain Platel.

Drawing from the medical humanities, history, philosophy (Giorgio Agamben) and cultural theory, theatre scholar Kélina Gotman discusses Alain Platel's *Out of Context – for Pina* (2010) and the particular 'dis-abled' gestures onstage. This chapter suggests that we find, perhaps paradoxically, in the aesthetic repetition and transformation presented by these choreographies, a form of aesthetic spectralization: an expansive shift in gestural languages onstage which, rather than trade in stillness or excess, banality or balletic virtuosity, recuperates a different order of polymorphic gesture in the everyday. The polymorphic space of gestural recuperation that Platel's work showcases expands the kinaesthetic regime of the arts, allowing us to rethink representations of gestural ownership, agency and alterity. Gotman calls this expanded realm the alterkinetic: one that embraces the smooth and the spasmodic, as well as the sudden and involuntary. She uses the term 'alterkinetic' in contrast to the distinctly medicalized term 'dyskinetic' (disorder of motion) to signal a performative and aesthetic recuperation of dyskinetic gestures in dance and dance theatre. With the polymorphic, polyvalent gestures characteristic of the alterkinetic landscape, a resurgence of movement appears onstage that is neither strictly classical in its virtuosic minimalism and romantic narrativism nor baroque in its curvatures, its proliferation of lines; nor is it 'against' or 'with' dancing but presents instead a plastic space of discursive para-regimentation, one that operates a *détournement*, we might say, of the anti-balletic prejudice.

Using Judith Butler's concept of 'life at risk', theatre scholar Miriam Dreysse observes from a gender perspective how Platel's *Gardenia* (2010) makes us more sensitive to the risks of the 'queer' life of others and engages us in a non-violent ethics. *Gardenia* features transvestites and transsexuals aged between sixty and seventy years old. Dreysse investigates to what extent the performance communicates the precariousness of life that establishes the ongoing tension of a non-violent ethics. In the fragility of their live performance, the performers draw attention to the voyeurism inherent in the act of looking and thus critique the position of the spectator and the theatrical situation as a whole.

Theatre scholar Piet Defraeye conducts what he calls a diagrammatical reading of Platel's *tauberbach* (2014), burrowing into its paradigms, syntax and compositional grammar. He considers Platel's compositional syntax as one of associative and pivotal conjunction as well as disengaging and unravelling apposition. Next to the music (a deaf choir), it is mostly the gestural language that invites the spectator into *tauberbach*'s peculiar geography because we acutely recognize this language as a system that we must respond to. Referring to Agamben and Emmanuel Levinas, Defraeye investigates how gesture in Platel's *tauberbach* sets in motion an ethical dynamic precisely because it is the ultimate embodiment of a primordial discourse that cannot be refused.

Defraeye's chapter is also a formal exercise in layering the complexity of the references Platel's work uses. Defraeye has his core analysis of *tauberbach*'s gestural language of failure dialogue with encyclopaedic fragments, which give more detailed information on some of the production's creative sources.

Jeroen Donckers, a psychotherapist and spectator, wrote Alain Platel a letter in which he expresses how much he was touched by the performance of *tauberbach* (2014) and how he recognizes in the gestures of the dancers those of his patients and ultimately also his own. Jeroen Donckers observes how *tauberbach* testifies to the unspeakable, unrepresentable or unimaginable. This contribution explores the ways in which the symptoms of different kinds of so-called mental disturbances – such as schizophrenia and aphasia – in fact contain articulatory potential, to be expressive of 'unspeakable' violent or traumatic events. The pain to which *tauberbach* bears witness is too big for words. It is only in the intensity of the dancing bodies and in the uncomfortable silences that the spectator can start fathoming the depths of the unrepresentable and irrevocable past.

As such, Donckers' letter also sheds new light on the importance of language in Freud's analytic setting and on the importance of eloquent speech in people's struggle for power, superiority and distinction. In his political philosophy, Rancière outlined how rhetoric belongs to the realm of the police. It is the art of the discussable.

Art becomes politics precisely by distancing itself from eloquent speech and the rhetoric of the word. Platel's choreopolitics exercises the politics of the inexpressible, featuring stumbling, stuttering and falling bodies. Their 'distortions of language' are not negations of language, nor postures of negativity.[11] They touch upon the creative urge to express oneself despite the short-circuiting effect of rigid language systems; the pronouncement of the unspeakable not despite but thanks to the blank spaces of silence and stuttering. Silence or 'not-telling' is from this perspective not to be considered – as it is considered in traditional psychoanalysis – 'a dangerous retreat, a failure or the site of continued harm',[12] nor a 'tailing off into silence',[13] but an articulatory potentiality.

Politics

Finally, in the fourth part, we discuss more explicit political themes, which all have to do with how one relates to the 'other': the 'queer body', non-Western cultures ... How to include them in one's work, allowing them to have their own voice? The politically correct answer to that question would probably be to refrain from appropriation, relating to Platel's dominant position as white heterosexual male artist. But Platel's work is based on appropriation: he himself calls his dance 'mongrel-dance', 'bastard dance', because he will ask one dancer to copy a phrase from another dancer, to appropriate the material. Since his dancers usually have different bodies, cultural backgrounds and experiences in training, the dance will be transformed by another body. In the end, nobody can claim the ownership of this dance, transformed in the act of appropriation, disowned and shared, and charged with new meanings and understandings. This process is crucial in Platel's work: appropriation and disowning in one movement. These are also the crucial terms when it comes to his intercultural work or work with 'others'. When the Congolese musicians dress up in the *Sapeurs* section of *Coup Fatal* (2014), they use a well-established and documented cultural form of resistance against the colonial regime: to dress up as whites and show their wealth. Platel (and the musicians) give the *sape* a twist, by avoiding the brand-related show-off and by creating playful variations (a dress made of ties, a plaid skirt accompanied by a pipe in the mouth, etc.) but maintaining the attitude. Platel will never be a defender of identity politics, whether black or Palestinian or queer. De-identifying and messing up (*métissage*) seem to be the only possible ways forward in his eyes.

Theatre scholar Lourdes Orozco proposes an investigation of Alain Platel's *En avant, marche!* (2015) with a focus on what Europe means for Platel and how this idea of Europe feeds and shapes his work. She focuses on the London production of *En avant, marche!* because of the specific socio-political moment in which it was performed, exposing the connections but also the complexity of the European project and the relationship between mainland Europe and the UK. As the author outlines, both community and music frame and propel the piece forward; they are interlinked to produce a piece that simultaneously mourns and celebrates the idea of Europe through the metaphor of brass bands.

Since 2001, les ballets C de la B regularly visits the Occupied Palestinian Territories (mostly Ramallah) or invites Palestinian artists to come to Belgium. In early November 2007, Alain Platel and five dancers travelled to Palestine and worked with young local artists. After the Congolese tour of *pitié!* (2009), Alain Platel collaborated with the Congolese countertenor Serge Kakudji for *Coup Fatal*. Christel Stalpaert returns to Platel's choreopolitics, tracing an interesting shift from (dogmatic) moralism to an ethics of accountability in these performances. Whereas politics is connected with the rhetoric effectiveness of the spoken word and with the realm of the discussable, Platel's dance theatre is political precisely because it outwits the confidence that sides with eloquence and the rhetoric of the spoken word. His dance theatre leaves the spectator stuttering in perception and hence calls for a redistribution of the positions of speech, and the notions of identity attributed to those positions of speech. The performances at times leave the spectators lost for words as they have to let go of dominant social meanings and preconceived notions of race, age and gender. In doing so, the performances also inaugurate a contemporary mode of post-colonial thinking that is not stuck in or paralysed by the past but provides space for imagining differential futures specific to, but not limited to or overdetermined by, the troubled, colonial pasts.

Coda: Platel's offspring

Tracing the influence of Platel's choreopolitics on the people who worked with him and of whom many are established choreographers themselves, would comprise a potential book volume in itself. So, rather than making an attempt at this in a single article, Hildegard De Vuyst concludes this book with another subjective insight into how the internal politics of les ballets C de la B changed throughout the years, supporting other artists than Platel – partially following its own internal needs and desires and partially because of changes in the landscape and cultural politics. De Vuyst describes the different transformations that les ballets C de la B underwent and how Platel used his position as an artistic director to create space for others to develop their artistic and choreographic talents. Dance critic Charlotte De Somvielle observes how 'les ballets C de la B has supported choreographers other than Alain Platel and how this choice was consequently at the forefront of this evolution', which was eventually also picked up by some of the other major Flemish dance companies.[14]

The organization of the book as described above attempts to offer the reader some clues to understanding the multilayered diversity and complexity of Alain Platel's body of work. But when reading the different contributions the reader will notice how all of the above-mentioned themes are interrelated and how the different chapters could have easily been placed in different sections. Rather than an analytical, linear development, this book follows a spiralling pattern, where we sometimes revisit the same themes and productions to deepen our understanding of them.

If asked to summarize the whole book with one word, it would be the notion of 'responsibility'/'response-ability', which almost every chapter in the book mentions in one way or another and which is woven as a constant guiding principle throughout

Platel's choreopolitics: the shared responsibility of a collaborative dramaturgy; the response-ability of the spectators to what they emotionally experience; the responsibility that comes with the inclusion of particular gestures and other bodies and cultures.

A note on the cover of this book

The picture on the cover of this book was taken in Perm in June 2018 by photographer Mirjam Devriendt. The company was invited by Teodor Currentzis for the Diaghilev Festival with the performance *nicht schlafen*. Devriendt was touring with the company as director of photography in preparation of the film *Why We Fight* by Platel, triggered by the fighting scene in *nicht schlafen*. *Breakfast in Perm* is not representative of Platel's work, but he loved the picture for the poetry of ordinary objects assembled and transformed in the eyes of the beholder. And that might just be the quintessence of his work.

Notes

1 Pascal Gielen and Rudi Laermans (2000) 'Flanders: Constructing Identities – The Case of the "Flemish Dance Wave"', in Andrée Grau and Stephanie Jordan (eds.), *Europe Dancing: Perspectives on Theatre, Dance, and Cultural Identity*, London and New York: Routledge, 12–27, at 19.
2 Pieter T'Jonck (2009) 'Hedendaagse dans in Vlaanderen 1993-2009', in Charlotte Vandevyver (ed.), *Dans in Vlaanderen (Concertgebouwcahier)*, Gent: Borgerhoff & Lamberigts, 11–27, at 18.
3 Rancière examines politics from the perspective of 'the distribution of the sensible'; Jacques Rancière (2007) *The Politics of Aesthetics: The Distribution of the Sensible*, trans. Gabriel Rockhill, London: Continuum, 13–14: 'Politics revolves around what is seen and what can be said about it, around who has the ability to see and the talent to speak, around the properties of spaces and the possibilities of time' (13). In Rancière's opinion, artistic practices are political as soon as, by taking a standpoint, they take part in the discursive game of distribution and redistribution of time and space, place and identity. They are political in the sense that they 'are "ways of doing and making" that intervene in the general distribution of ways of doing and making as well as in the relationships they maintain to modes of being and forms of visibility … the indetermination of identities, the delegitimation of positions of speech, the deregulation of partitions of space and time', 13–14.
4 André Lepecki (2013) 'Choreopolice and Choreopolitics: or, The Task of the Dancer', *The Drama Review*, 57 (4): 13–27, 13 and 16.
5 Lepecki, 'Choreopolice and Choreopolitics', 14–15.
6 Forsythe in Mark Franko (2007) 'Dance and the Political: States of Exception', in Susanne Franco and Marina Nordera (eds.), *Dance Discourses: Keywords in Dance Research*, London and New York: Routledge, 17.
7 Lepecki, 'Choreopolice and Choreopolitics', 15.
8 Alain Platel and Hildegard De Vuyst (2008) 'An Interview with Alain Platel about *pitié!*' les ballets C de la B, August. Available at http://www.lesballetscdela.be/en/projects/productions/pitie/extra/an-interview-with-alain-platel/ (accessed 12 September 2018).

9 Lepecki, 'Choreopolice and Choreopolitics', 15.
10 Rancière, *The Politics of Aesthetics*, 41.
11 Luce Irigaray (2002) *To Speak Is Never Neutral*, trans. Gail Schwab, London and New York: Routledge, p. 23.
12 James Thompson (2009) *Performance Affects: Applied Theatre and the End of Effect*, Basingstoke: Palgrave Macmillan, 45.
13 D. Summerfield (2005) '"My Whole Body Is Sick … My Life Is Not Good": A Rwandan Asylum Seeker Attends a Psychiatric Clinic in London', in D. Ingleby (ed.), *Forced Migration and Mental Health: Rethinking the Care of Refugees and Displaced Persons*, New York: Springer, 97–114, at 98.
14 Charlotte De Somviele (2018) 'A Look into Contemporary Dance in Flanders and Brussel', *Contemporary Dance from Flanders*. Available at https://dossiers.kunsten.be/dance/contemporary-dance-flanders-and-brussels (accessed 19 August 2019), 17.

References

De Somviele, Charlotte (2018) 'Contemporary Dance in Flanders and Brussels', *Contemporary Dance from Flanders*. Available at https://dossiers.kunsten.be/dance/contemporary-dance-flanders-and-brussels (accessed 19 August 2019).
Franko, Mark (2007) 'Dance and the Political: States of Exception', in Susanne Franco and Marina Nordera (eds.), *Dance Discourses: Keywords in Dance Research*, London and New York: Routledge, 11–28.
Gielen, Pascal, and Rudi Laermans (2000) 'Flanders: Constructing Identities – The Case of the "Flemish Dance Wave"', in Andrée Grau and Stephanie Jordan (eds.), *Europe Dancing: Perspectives on Theatre, Dance, and Cultural Identity*, London and New York: Routledge, 2000, 12–27.
Irigaray, Luce (2002) *To Speak Is Never Neutral*, translated by Gail Schwab, London and New York: Routledge.
Lepecki, André (2013) 'Choreopolice and Choreopolitics; or, The task of the Dancer', *The Drama Review*, 57 (4): 13–27.
Platel, Alain, and Hildegard De Vuyst (2008) 'An Interview with Alain Platel about *pitié!*' les ballets C de la B, August. Available at http://www.lesballetscdela.be/en/projects/productions/pitie/extra/an-interview-with-alain-platel/ (accessed 12 September 2018).
Rancière, Jacques (2007) *The Politics of Aesthetics: The Distribution of the Sensible*, trans. Gabriel Rockhill, London: Continuum.
Summerfield, D. (2005) '"My Whole Body Is Sick … My Life Is Not Good": A Rwandan Asylum Seeker Attends a Psychiatric Clinic in London', in D. Ingleby (ed.), *Forced Migration and Mental Health: Rethinking the Care of Refugees and Displaced Persons*, New York: Springer, 97–114.
Thompson, James (2009) *Performance Affects: Applied Theatre and the End of Effect*, Basingstoke: Palgrave Macmillan.
T'Jonck, Pieter (2009) 'Hedendaagse dans in Vlaanderen, 1993–2009', in Charlotte Vandevyver (ed.), *Dans in Vlaanderen (Concertgebouwcahier)*, Gent: Borgerhoff & Lamberigts, 11–27.

Part One

Multiple Dramaturgies

2

A Dramaturgy of Stuttering

Guy Cools

I have never seen anybody who can participate so intensely while standing aside.[1]

I have been a privileged witness of Alain Platel's career since the moment I wrote a review of *Emma* as a young dance critic in 1986. As dance curator of the Arts Centre Vooruit in Ghent, Belgium, where I had invited les ballets C de la B to be resident from 1991 to 2002, I observed their growing international success and have remained close to them to the present day. In these thirty years, I have had many private and also public dialogues with Alain Platel, some of which have already been published. For this chapter, I will revisit two of them. The first one was published in the magazine *Nouvelles de Danse* in 1998 and is exemplary for Platel's viewpoint and way of working all through the 1990s, producing works such as *Bonjour madame, comment allez-vous aujourd'hui, il fait beau, il va sans doute pleuvoir, etcetera* (1993), *La Tristeza Complice* (1995) and *Iets op Bach* (1998).[2] The second is the transcript of a public talk I held with him at Sadler's Wells in 2011. It focuses on the aesthetic and political vision behind the works he created in the first decade of the twenty-first century and was first published as part of the body:language series, produced by Emma Gladstone at Sadler's Wells, and then integrated into my book *Imaginative Bodies: Dialogues in Performance Practices* (2016). In revisiting both interviews, I will discuss Platel's vision of the body and how this influences the artistic dialogue with his performers.

The autonomy of the performers

In 1998, I interviewed Platel for a special edition of the dance magazine *Nouvelles de Danse* on composition. In my introduction I pointed out the ambivalence of talking to Platel about a 'technique of composition' since his work often resembled orchestrated chaos and seemed to have been created in a very intuitive way. I resolved the contradiction by using one of my favourite metaphors (which is attributed to Balanchine), that the art of choreography resembles the art of cooking in that it is first and foremost a matter of choosing the right ingredients – that is, the right performers –

and then of combining them in the right order and with the right timing so that they reinforce rather than weaken each other. As a result, most of the interview on his composition technique dealt with his choice of performers and how he accompanies and guides them into his work.

Although les ballets C de la B was founded by Alain Platel, his sister Pascale Platel (an accomplished theatre director) and the video artist Johan Grimonprez in 1984, it was not until 1993 that they auditioned and engaged professional performers for the first time. This was for the creation of *Bonjour madame*. Until then, the 'family' of les ballets C de la B consisted mainly of a group of like-minded friends with very different backgrounds and interests, including a doctor, a history student and a cheese-maker. Platel explains how he selected performers by both looking for individual qualities and also being conscious of the potential group chemistry between them.

> Often when we start a new creation process, there are already a certain number of performers from a previous production, with whom I like to work again. So I am looking for people who are complementary or even completely opposite to the ones I have already chosen. I seem to have a preference for people who show a certain 'gene', who don't want to show off immediately ... I also like people with less defined backgrounds, who are not only happy to dance, but who are also active in other fields.[3]

Platel seems to have a preference for performers who combine a strong idiosyncratic, physical personality with an eclectic range of dance techniques. A type of performer that would not necessarily circulate in the contemporary dance field or show up at auditions, but which amongst others he discovered being a jury member on *The Best Belgian Dance Solos*.[4] One of these 'discoveries' was a young Sidi Larbi Cherkaoui, who afterwards joined the company for *Iets op Bach* and also made his debut as a choreographer under the wings of les ballets C de la B.

Platel's selection process does not always result in a harmonious group process. Mirroring the communication difficulties between choreographer and composer described by Katalin Trencsényi in her contribution to this book (which necessitated the mediation of a dramaturg for the first time), Platel himself acknowledges that the rehearsal process of *La Tristeza Complice* was turbulent, full of difficulties and tensions that remained visible in the actual performance. Platel deliberately did not try to conceal this, as the tangible tensions resonated with the particular emptiness of the scenic space:

> As a result of the tense climate during the rehearsals, I needed an environment and a scenic space that made the public immediately understand that those people who meet in there don't necessarily know each other and don't have any ties between each other. Hence the association with train stations, waiting rooms.[5]

In creating and developing movement material, Platel always gives a lot of autonomy to his dancers and remains an empathic witness whose active gaze both stimulates the performers in their individual research and acknowledges the results of their work.⁶ Platel describes how at the time (the 1990s) he would give all his dancers two challenging tasks: to prepare a whole day of work with the entire group on an aspect that they wanted to research, and to create a solo 'which will be certainly included in the performance and which is better than anything you have created or seen before'.

> It is a kind of shock therapy that I administer, and it works. In the beginning, they are all extremely terrified. They don't know what to do and they postpone all the time the moment where they have to show it. During the rehearsals, they have to present the solo at least three times: the first time completely free, the second time in relation to a certain given, for instance a composition by Bach in *Iets op Bach*. And finally, if everything goes well, the solo reaches its culminating point during the third presentation.⁷

The solo Sidi Larbi Cherkaoui created for *Iets op Bach* is exemplary for this approach. Cherkaoui's solo follows a circus act in which the circus artist Ghani Minne Vosteen drops bowling balls from a height on his naked belly, while being suspended in the air, with only his head and feet resting on two poles. During this spectacular act, Cherkaoui sits silently and introspectively on a chair, seemingly unaware of the turbulence around him. Eventually he stands up, walks to one of the children in the cast to hand her over some knitting material in order to return centre stage to dance his solo on the Bach cantata BWV 82, *Ich habe genug*. The moment Cherkaoui starts dancing, you zoom in on him and all the visual noise around him dies out. His solo consists of a series of extremely virtuosic dance positions, from the straight lifted leg from ballet, which he keeps up until another dancer pushes him over, over alternating splits and backbends while making turns on the floor, to a headstand without arm support. All these positions are already interconnected with an agility and fluency that will become characteristic for Cherkaoui's own choreographic universe. At the end of this solo, Cherkaoui's hands are set on fire, the hands being another major motif in his future work, until eventually another dancer carries off his dead corpse – negotiating death being another recurrent theme for the rest of his career. With his task to create a solo, Platel set off Cherkaoui on his own choreographic journey.

Another favourite creative strategy of Platel is to let the dancers develop phrases and then to pass them on to each other:

> It is a sort of game of transfers which can reach a great complexity. I observe all the time and note down in my journal and on individual cards what interests me in the particular movements of a person, how she walks, laughs or talks – and I feed them this information back on a regular basis.⁸

At this stage, Platel is first and foremost a witness of the creative process of his performers, and he consciously keeps this witness role active onstage, during the performance. In his productions, Platel generally keeps all his performers onstage throughout the whole performance and has them witness each other. As a result, dancers and performers are always watching what other dancers and performers are doing.

Figure 2.1 Gabriela Carrizo and Ghani Minne Vosteen in *Iets op Bach*, 1998. © Chris Van der Burght.

> For me it is both a challenge and a game to keep all the performers on stage the whole time. I think the performance benefits from it. On the one hand, everybody stays engaged all the time, even those who are not directly involved in a scene. They remain witnesses, which reinforces their emotional engagement ... During rehearsals, we often do exercises in that sense: those who don't participate in a particular action look for a position close by and try to sabotage the event or change its trajectory.[9]

Because the spectators see the performers watch each other, their gaze is also directed through the gaze of the performers. In *Postdramatic Theatre*, Hans-Thies Lehmann calls this, in analogy with classical painting, '*Blickregie*' or 'the direction of the gaze': the optic path of the viewer is traced through the gaze of the performer.[10] This gaze entails not only a vision but also a (corporeal) engagement of the spectator.

Ideally, Platel's spectators also become witnesses. In her book *Choreographing Difference*, Ann Cooper Albright tellingly describes how watching *La Tristeza Complice* when it was first presented in New York turned her spectatorship into an act of witnessing: 'For dances like *La Tristeza Complice* ask the audience to be willing to stay with the performance, even when the situation becomes disturbing or uncomfortable. For me, this is when the act of watching transforms into the act of witnessing.'¹¹ She continues to describe how this act of witnessing

> implies a responsiveness, the response/ability of the viewer towards the performer. It is radically different from what we might call the 'consuming' gaze that says 'here, you entertain me, I bought a ticket, and I'm going to sit back and watch' ... In contrast, what I call witnessing is much more interactive, a kind of perceiving [with one's whole body] that is committed to a process of mutual dialogue.¹²

In *Certain Fragments*, the British theatre director Tim Etchells makes a similar claim to distinguish mere spectatorship from the act of witnessing: 'because to witness an event is to be present at it in some fundamentally ethical way, to feel the weight of things and one's own place in them, even if that place is simply, for the moment, as an onlooker'.¹³ By placing himself in the witness role during the rehearsal process, Platel prepares both his performers and his audiences to engage as witnesses as well.

Alterkinetic movements

This ethical call upon the audience grew in Platel's work, as becomes clear in a talk we had, almost fifteen years later. The talk took place at Sadler's Wells in London in January 2011 as part of the body:language series, shortly after the creation of *Out of Context – for Pina* (2010) and *Gardenia* (2010), two very distinct but related works. In *Gardenia*, Platel returned to work with a group of 'semi-amateurs', transsexuals and transvestites, all between sixty and seventy years old, who knew each other from a long time ago when they worked in cabarets. In the body:language talk, Platel discussed in detail how working on *Gardenia* was different from working on *Out of Context – for Pina*, because of the differences of the bodies involved: the highly trained and virtuosic skilled bodies of professional dancers in *Out of Context* versus the aged bodies of amateurs in *Gardenia*, whose only material to create their performance from was their own lived experience of the process of ageing and their struggle with gender and identity norms.

> I did realize at the end of 2010 that these two pieces are linked in a certain way, it is true. But only in a formal way. The other things that happen are much more important for me – the psychology and the way that you meet people, collaborate with them, and what kind of dialogue you find with them. In these respects the pieces were completely different. In *Gardenia*, I worked with a group of amateurs, which I like to do and have done before. They were people who stood at a certain point in their experience of life, quite far in ... they are people who have lived 'a problem' – their homosexuality, coming out, transforming sex and gender, which in the 1970s was much more problematic than it would be today.¹⁴

Platel has a deep respect for the body's archive, be it of a professional dancer or an 'experienced' amateur. In his career he has always oscillated between the real, lived experience of 'amateur' bodies and the virtuosity of highly trained bodies. In *Out of Context – for Pina*, he worked with the same group of professional performers which had, for the first time, remained together for a series of creations: *vsprs* (2006), *pitié!* (2008) and *Out of Context – for Pina* (2010). They had kept going deeper into a process of researching and developing a personal language based on the dyskinetic movements of psychiatric patients. Having studied psychology and pedagogy and having worked in child psychiatric hospitals and a centre for children with cerebral palsy, before launching an artistic career almost accidentally, Platel has always been fascinated with the non-verbal expressiveness and hypersensitivity of the other-abled.

> Talking to and working with people there who had extreme physical problems, I found something that I hadn't been aware of before, something specific that for me had to do with sensibility, and with the fact that the body takes over when you are not able to talk about certain things any longer.[15]

Already in some of his earlier productions, such as *La Tristeza Complice*, Platel was fascinated with the movement vocabulary of certain pathological states such as Tourette's syndrome, in which people start to swear or insult others involuntarily and without any apparent reason, and narcolepsy, where people fall asleep in the middle of an activity. A large part of his continuous movement research has been about how to perform the different dyskinetic movement qualities of psychiatric patients through the professional and highly virtuosic bodies of his dancers. A triggering point was the discovery of an early film by a professor of medicine Arthur van Gehuchten, who began filming patients with neurological disorders as early as 1905. Van Gehuchten used the films for diagnosis, documentation and didactic purposes. Platel discovered the film in an exhibition at the Museum Dr. Guislain, a museum linked to a psychiatric hospital that organizes exhibitions confronting the history of psychiatry with themes of contemporary art. Museum Dr. Guislain is Platel's favourite museum, and a visit to it is an obligatory ritual for the whole group of collaborators in the early stages of a new creation process. For certain productions, such as *vsprs*, Platel explicitly used the film to develop this particular movement vocabulary with his dancers.

> With this group of people I suddenly thought, 'I want to know how they interpret those images.' The people in the images are described as being sick people, but for me that was the last thing I was thinking about. I don't see them as that. I see them as people who are extremely sensitive. When you are very sensitive to life, to things that are happening around you, and you don't know how to express your feelings, I can imagine that you would go into these kinds of extreme behaviours. To my surprise the dancers loved it, they thought it was inspiring, and they recognized something that corresponded to their own vocabulary, their own physical language and their own way of expressing things. But it was also awkward at first, and they had to see it again and again and even had to imitate movements from the film before they could go deeper. What was very surprising for me was that they felt

much more exposed than they had when they had used their own identity, name and background, as we had done in earlier pieces where I had focused more on the cultural and social body. They felt that working with these images – as we did for *vsprs*, *Out of Context* and *pitié!* – was deeper, more personal, and more exposing.[16]

The rehearsals for these performances differed from the more improvisatory rehearsals Platel conducted in the past, where the performers might hit upon gestures and movements by chance, by trying things out themselves, following concrete challenging tasks. In these performances, the images from the film provided a controlling context of the choreographer's design to have the performers move in a particular way. However, these 'spasmodic' movements are not imitated from the film screen. They are not in any way devoid of individual impulses or feelings; the extreme movements are rather 'kinetically translated' into the performer's bodies. They possess 'kinetic weight'.[17]

Out of Context starts with the performers, who are seated amongst the audience in their regular clothes, entering the stage, one by one, undressing until their underwear and picking up one of the horse blankets, which together with some microphone stands are the only props on an empty stage. The literal 'nakedness', which is maintained until the very end when the dancers redress and again leave the stage one by one, highlights the precariousness of their pre-verbal condition. Wrapped in their blankets, they engage first in small encounters which have an animal quality: sniffing each other or lifting their lower legs behind them like horses do. The soundtrack, with noises of farm animals, highlights this pre-human condition.

Figure 2.2 Mélanie Lomoff and Lisi Estaras in *vsprs*, 2006. © Chris Van der Burght.

In her contribution to this book, Kélina Gotman defines Platel's movement vocabulary as alterkinetic, 'in contrast to the distinctly medicalized term dyskinetic (disorder of motion) to signal a performative and aesthetic recuperation of dyskinetic gestures in dance and dance-theatre'. In *Out of Context*, Platel mixes the dyskinetic gestures which have a medical origin with similar movements from pop and hip-hop culture, such as popping and crumping. 'Platel's stroke of choreographic genius', according to Gotman, is the way this 'undermines a hierarchy of gestural types' and dissolves any distinction between abled and disabled, marginal or virtuosic, normal or abnormal, controlled or uncontrolled. For Gotman, this alterkinetic turn is a bacchanalian celebration of excess movement that reacts against 'the exhausted anti-dance paradigm' (as described by André Lepecki in *Exhausting Dance*) and further democratizes the aesthetics of dance by including a wide range of movements and gestures: 'there is no gesture that does not also have an equal right to the stage'.

Platel's motivation for recreating the alterkinetic movements of psychiatric patients resonates with the ideas the American philosopher Elaine Scarry expresses in *The Body in Pain: The Making and Unmaking of the World*. Describing the how and why of torture practices in conflicts such as the Gulf Wars, Scarry writes: 'Physical pain does not simply resist language but actively destroys it, bringing about an immediate reversion to a state anterior to language, to the sounds and cries a human being makes before language is learned.'[18] It is this pre-verbal language expressing sorrow, pain and despair – emotions evoked primarily when we are confronted with death – that Platel seeks to recreate onstage. For this he requires virtuosic bodies which are able to totally embody this language without being physically affected by it or emotionally losing themselves in this process of kinetic translation. The latter remains a tightrope balancing act, as Platel's recollection of the final scene and its impact on its performer illustrates:

> At the end of the performance one of the performers always asks the audience to raise their hands, and you see – whoosh! – all these people who raise their hands, which is already very touching. When they do it, he then asks, 'Who wants to dance with me?' In general nobody comes forward, but there are places where people do. I think it is an extremely courageous thing to do, to come to the front of the stage not knowing what is going to happen. Once, in Portugal, not only one person came but forty!
>
> But there was one moment that I will never forget and that was at the Théâtre de la Ville in Paris: when Romeu [Runa] asked, 'Who wants to dance with me?' nobody answered, and all of a sudden there was a guy, twenty years old or so, and he shouted, 'Of course I want to dance. Why do you sit there? How is it possible that you remain in your seats? I am from Iran. I'm a refugee from Iran. I've just arrived in France, and in my country it is forbidden to dance!' All of a sudden, this performance, which was not meant to be directly political at all, became extremely political. The guy came on stage, and he cried a lot. Romeu took him in his arms, danced with him a little bit and then put him back in the audience. Afterwards, when it was finished, I looked for Romeu but couldn't find him – he

had disappeared, until I found him behind the curtain crying his heart out. It is confronting when something like that happens, a magic moment.[19]

Platel's research into alterkinetic movements and his conscious decision to recreate them onstage deviates from traditional dance aesthetics and sometimes creates the illusion that his dancers really suffer in the process of embodying these movements. Consequently, his work has received mixed response by both audiences and critics, who have often struggled to recognize and understand his intentions. It disturbs Platel to be confronted with interpretations of his work that attribute his artistic choices to the desire to shock through transgression.

> I have often been confronted with the question, 'Do you want to shock people?', which I find disturbing to hear, because the answer is, 'Of course not.' I don't know many artists who really want to shock, especially in the performing arts. But to confront myself and an audience with images that are sometimes difficult to cope with – yes! I am equal with the audience in this sense, because I feel as uncomfortable as the people who are watching it.
>
> In the rehearsal space I am dealing with something special: with performers who want to perform – to expose themselves on stage, which is a very strong thing to do. I personally don't understand, I would never dare to do it. What I try to do is to create an atmosphere where people feel safe to expose themselves, to show us what they want to show. I think they sense very quickly that I would never abuse them – I would never use an image just because it is interesting or shocking or whatever. I will only do it when, first of all, there is a need to, and also if they want to do it, and they are not suffering. You can't perform a piece 150 times knowing that someone is suffering.[20]

In her contribution to this book, Ann Cooper Albright discusses how Platel's performances 'call upon a very different engagement with the audience'. Referring to Hans-Thies Lehmann's 'energetic theatre' and John Berger's 'corporeal space', she argues that Platel's work 'prioritizes touch and feeling rather than seeing' and primarily aims at the audience to be 'moved', which she defines as 'both an emotional and visceral responsiveness to the world'. It is this being moved, 'an intertwining of somatic feeling and political urgency', that turns the passive spectator into an active 'with-ness', invited to encounter the 'other' and the 'other-abled' with respect.[21]

The collective body

Parallel to his exploration of the idiosyncrasies of individual bodies, Platel has also always had a keen interest in the collective body. His early studies in psychology not only inspired his discoveries of alterkinetic movements but also meant that the relationship between the individual and the group would become one of his most central themes. 'My pieces always deal with a group of people who just arrived somewhere and while they linger there a bit longer, certain things happen.'[22] In an interview with the

German dance critic Renate Klett, Platel acknowledges the usefulness of courses he took in group dynamics and group psychology: 'They are the most important tools for someone who works with groups,' whereas in his early works the focus was on individuals, from *vsprs* (2003) onwards it shifted to the group itself.[23]

> I have always made pieces in which the 'I' is at the centre, in the shape of the individuality of strong personalities. Now I would like to see how 'I' can be absorbed into 'we'; how we arrive at greater solidarity. I think people have a greater need to be part of a community than to have individual freedom.[24]

Platel's renewed focus on the group is again triggered by a personal experience. Since 2001 he has regularly travelled to Palestine to work with local performers. 'I don't think it is a coincidence that the moment when I was confronted with this idea of community, of being together, happened when I visited an occupied territory.'[25] Platel's interest in the dynamics within a group and the thematic desire of the individual to belong to a community finds it strongest expression in his exploration of the chorus both as a visual and musical metaphor.

In 2001, Platel was invited by the organization Artangel in London to stage a concert for the Roundhouse, a circus-like arts venue in Camden. The resulting piece, *Because I Sing* (2001), brought together very different amateur choirs ranging from gay to Marxist, from Jewish to deaf and to Maori. Each choir presented its own repertoire and by doing so also its own identity as a community. They were placed on different galleries around the audience, which stood in the middle of the circular space. The spatial dramaturgy highlighted the diversity of the city of London. In 2006, Platel repeated this experience with *Uit de Bol* (2006) for the reopening of the KVS, the Flemish National Theatre in Brussels. This time collaborating with musician Fabrizio Cassol, the visual and musical dramaturgy again highlighted both diversity and unity as the various choirs marched off into the city like Olympic delegations, singing a canon that kept their different musical timbres alive.

Platel's exploration of the chorus culminated with C(H)ŒURS (2012), created for the Teatro Real in Madrid. The opera chorus of more than seventy singers was joined by ten dancers from les ballets C de la B to perform a selection from the repertoire of Verdi and Wagner. With this piece Platel actualizes the historical ambiguity of the music, which celebrates nineteenth-century Italian and German nationalism, within the context of today's political landscape and with clear references to the Occupy movement, the Indignados and the Arab Spring: 'The search for a greater collectivity without the loss of individuality, for politics without the loss of intimacy, for eloquence through stuttering, this is the search of C(H)ŒURS.'[26]

A dramaturgy of stuttering

In the music video 'Theme from Turnpike' by the Belgian rock band dEUS, two men walk through the streets of Paris, engaged in a conversation.[27] The older one is the American actor Seymour Cassel; the younger one is a former les ballets C de la B performer and now film actor, Sam Louwyck, who demonstrates some of the early alterkinetic movements he picked up from working with Platel. The effect is one of the body physically stuttering.

In a public dialogue at the annual congress of German dramaturgs in Hanover in January 2017, the German playwright Wolfram Lotz explained how he developed his award-winning writing style out of his own experience of stuttering, which he defines as the struggle 'to regain language against the resistance of the body'. He continues to describe how for him stuttering is the ideal dramaturgical process and conflict:

> Language presents itself. It is however not clear if the words can be uttered, there is a conflict between the body and speech. I know what I want to say, but the medium isn't able to exteriorize it: the kind of nightmarish structure at micro level: everything is clear, but nothing works.[28]

Using as a reference Deleuze's *He Stuttered*, Christel Stalpaert discusses and analyses in *The Creative Power in the Failure of Word and Language* the qualities of stammering and stuttering in contemporary dramaturgy. The challenges to physically articulating one's thoughts make the stutterer more aware of 'the value of words' and his speaking 'a creative urge'. It also demands from the viewer or listener a heightened awareness, automatically turning their spectatorship into witnessing. 'The performance that leaves me stuttering has in other words also an ethical dimension. It is a finger exercise in tactile experience, in exploratory meeting and in creative thinking.'[29]

Stalpaert concludes her essay on corporeal dramaturgy, 'Becoming the Outside Body, Implicated in the Life of Others' with a similar valorization of stuttering: according to her, it calls 'upon the ontological state of instability of a work of art, upon a receptiveness to the fragility of voice or body which, in its fragility, invites the spectator to acquire a greater responsibility to acknowledge otherness'.[30] Her statement perfectly sums up Platel's dramaturgy of stuttering. Through it, he invites the audience to become 'with-nesses', to be 'moved' by and take responsibility for the instability and the fragility of the stuttering bodies, whether individually or collectively, onstage.

Notes

1 Michiel Mertens on Alain Platel in the les ballets C de la B publication, *Objets Trouvés, Sujets Trouvés*, Gent, 1991.
2 In this interview I focused mainly on the dance theatre productions he created with his own company les ballets C de la B and less on the theatre triptych *Moeder en Kind* (1995), *Bernadetje* (1997) and *Allemaal Indiaan* (1998), which he created in collaboration with playwright and theatre director Arne Sierens and which was produced by Victoria.
3 Guy Cools (1998) 'Entretien avec Alain Platel', *Nouvelles de Danse*, 36–7: 220–9, 221. This quote and the following from the same interview are my own translations from French.
4 *The Best Belgian Solos* was a project originally produced by Victoria, which Platel initiated and curated between 1995 and 1997 and which was afterwards copied in other international contexts, amongst others at the Euro-Scene Festival in Leipzig.

5   Cools, 'Entretien avec Alain Platel', 222.
6   See also how the dancer Mélanie Lomoff describes their collaboration in Trencsényi's essay.
7   Cools, 'Entretien avec Alain Platel', 225.
8   Cools, 'Entretien avec Alain Platel', 225–6.
9   Cools, 'Entretien avec Alain Platel', 228.
10 Hans-Thies Lehmann (1999) *Postdramatisches Theater*, Frankfurt: Verlag der Autoren, 297.
11 Ann Cooper Albright (1997) *Choreographing Difference: The Body and Identity in Contemporary Dance*, Middletown, Conn.: Wesleyan University Press, xxii.
12 Cooper Albright, *Choreographing Difference*, xxii.
13 Tim Etchells (1999) *Certain Fragments*, London and New York: Routledge, 17.
14 Guy Cools (2016) *Imaginative Bodies: Dialogues in Performance Practices*, Amsterdam: Valiz, 141–2.
15 Cools, *Imaginative Bodies*, 142.
16 Cools, *Imaginative Bodies*, 143–4.
17 Christel Stalpaert (2010) 'On Poet-Dancers and Animal-Thinkers: The Bodily Capacity to Read and Make Sense of Unjointed Time and Intensive Space in Wayn Traub's *Maria Dolores* (2003)', *Text and Performance Quarterly*, 30 (4): 356–73, 364.
18 Elaine Scarry (1985) *The Body in Pain: The Making and Unmaking of the World*, Oxford: Oxford University Press, 4.
19 Cools, *Imaginative Bodies*, 147–8.
20 Cools, *Imaginative Bodies*, 146.
21 Her ideas resonate strongly with Hildegard De Vuyst's contribution to this book on the 'emotheatre' of Platel.
22 Renate Klett (2007) *Alain Platel: Gespräche mit Renate Klett*, Berlin: Alexander Verlag, 44. My translation from German.
23 Klett, *Alain Platel*, 19.
24 Alain Platel in the programme brochure of *vsprs*. My translation from Dutch.
25 Cools, *Imaginative Bodies*, 145.
26 Hildegard De Vuyst in the programme brochure of *C(H)ŒURS*. My translation from Dutch.
27 See dEUS, 'Theme from Turnpike' (from *In a Bar under the Sea*), available at https://www.youtube.com/watch?v=0ctOyryYhaI (accessed 19 August 2019). Platel was not involved in the production of the dEUS video, but it is just one more illustration of his far-reaching influence, outside of his own body of work.
28 Wolfram Lotz and Harald Wolff (2017) 'Stottern und stammeln in der Kunst', *Dramaturgie: Zeitschrift der dramaturgischen Gesellschaft*, 2: 39–43, 39. My translation from German.
29 Christel Stalpaert (2010) 'The Creative Power in the Failure of Word and Language: On Silence, Stuttering and Other Performative Intensities', *International Journal of Literary Studies*, 45 (1): 77–93, 90.
30 Christel Stalpaert (2014) 'The Distributive Agency of Dramaturgical Labour and the Ethics of Instability: Becoming the Outside Body, Implicated in the Life of Others', in Katharina Pewny, Johan Callens and Jeroen Coppens (eds.), *Dramaturgies in the New Millennium. Relationality, Performativity, and Potentiality*, Tübingen: Gunter Narr Verlag, 97–110, 107.

References

Albright, Ann Cooper (1997) *Choreographing Difference: The Body and Identity in Contemporary Dance*, Middletown, Conn.: Wesleyan University Press.

Cools, Guy (1998) 'Entretien avec Alain Platel', *Nouvelles de Danse*, 36-7: 220-9.

Cools, Guy (2016) 'The Political Body. A Conversation with Alain Platel', in *Imaginative Bodies: Dialogues in Performance Practices*, Amsterdam: Valiz, pp. 137-52.

Etchells, Tim (1999) *Certain Fragments*, London and New York: Routledge.

Klett, Renate (2007) *Alain Platel: Gespräche mit Renate Klett*, Berlin: Alexander Verlag.

Lehmann, Hans-Thies (1999) *Postdramatisches Theater*, Frankfurt: Verlag der Autoren.

Lepecki, André (2006) *Exhausting Dance: Performance and the Politics of Movement*, London and New York: Routledge.

Lotz, Wolfram, and Harald Wolff (2017) 'Stottern und stammeln in der Kunst', *Dramaturgie: Zeitschrift der dramaturgischen Gesellschaft*, 2: 39-43.

Scarry, Elaine (1985) *The Body in Pain: The Making and Unmaking of the World*, Oxford: Oxford University Press.

Stalpaert, Christel (2010) 'The Creative Power in the Failure of Word and Language: On Silence, Stuttering and Other Performative Intensities', *International Journal of Literary Studies*, 45 (1): 77-93.

Stalpaert, Christel (2010) 'On Poet-Dancers and Animal-Thinkers: The Bodily Capacity to Read and Make Sense of Unjointed Time and Intensive Space in Wayn Traub's *Maria Dolores* (2003)', *Text and Performance Quarterly*, 30 (4): 356-73.

Stalpaert, Christel (2014) 'The Distributive Agency of Dramaturgical Labour and the Ethics of Instability: Becoming the Outside Body, Implicated in the Life of Others', in Katharina Pewny, Johan Callens and Jeroen Coppens (eds.), *Dramaturgies in the New Millennium: Relationality, Performativity and Potentiality*, Tübingen: Gunter Narr Verlag, 97-110.

3

'An Experiment in Democracy'

Alain Platel's Collaborative Dramaturgy

Katalin Trencsényi

Thinking about the dramaturgy of dance is probably as old as dance itself, yet the role of the dance dramaturg as a professional occupation only emerged in the late twentieth century.[1] What brought about the existence of a separate professional working in a dialogue relationship with a choreographer was the emergence of collaborative, interdisciplinary processes in the field of dance. The first officially acknowledged dance dramaturg was Raimund Hoghe, who worked with Pina Bausch and the Tanztheater Wuppertal between 1979 and 1989.

Bausch was a pioneer in marrying dance and theatre and in giving her dancers a crucial role in the process. Bausch's search for new means of expression, and the 'necessity' she felt when working together with differently trained artists (dancers, actors and singers) led her to develop a new method of working.[2] In order to set out on this new path, it was necessary for Bausch to relinquish the role that was expected from her as a choreographer or director: claiming the knowledge of the end product at the beginning of the process.

During this creative process, instead of teaching pre-developed movement phrases, Bausch asked her ensemble members personal questions related to the subject of the new piece, and from their responses (writings, images and improvisations) to these generative questions she gradually developed the new dance-theatre piece, using collage technique in creating the work's dramaturgy.[3]

Alain Platel considers the late Pina Bausch as one of his main influences:

> Pina made me and many people in the 1980s believe that anyone can make performances. That you just have to do some things, and then you make a collage from the material that you find in the studio, and you should not be a professional dancer. But the more I work, the more I understand that this is only the surface, of course. I think she installed a way of working that many people would try to copy. The main thing is that she asks questions, and then she asks people to improvise. And with whatever she sees, she tries to make constructions.
>
> Pina had a particular way of observing people, and making choices. And with these choices she made a performance. This was her signature.[4]

Bausch's presence lingers in les ballets C de la B's headquarters in Ghent, Belgium. The show the ensemble was working on at the time of the German choreographer's untimely death in 2009 was immediately renamed as *Out of Context – for Pina*. This is the only piece that, following the dancers' request, will remain in the ensemble's repertoire as long as possible. 'It is a way for them to meet once a year and to see how they get older in a performance', says Platel.⁵ This idea of a dancer maturing together with the piece they created, and performing it many years after the premiere is very true to Bausch's spirit, whose dancers (for instance, Dominique Mercy) remained part of the cast sometimes for decades.

The respect for Pina Bausch not only shows in the dedication of a performance but also in Platel's way of working. The creative process depends on observing his performers and making choices. This is not always the easiest way to go, as the collaborative method leaves behind secure foundations:

> I think what I share with Pina (that's what we talked about when we first met) is the fact that she was not afraid to be very afraid when she worked … Like, this afternoon it was very frightening: I saw all the solo works made by the dancers but I don't know what to choose or what to do because it is an enormous task. So you have to keep on looking, looking for a long time and try to figure out how you can put together these ingredients by emphasizing the personality of the dancers. You don't have a tried and tested recipe.⁶

Figure 3.1 Dorine Demuynck and Alain Platel during the rehearsals of *Out of Context – for Pina* in dance studio S3, Ghent 2009. (Photographer unknown.)

Unruly dramaturgy

Apart from Maurice Béjart's ensemble, Ballet du XXième Siècle (residing in Brussels at the Théâtre Royal de la Monnaie from 1959 to 1987), contemporary dance as an art form did not exist in Belgium until the mid 1980s. Around this time, a number of artists emerged simultaneously, who, without any state funding, began to create new work that, as dance critic Pieter T'Jonck notes, 'appeared to start from scratch with every new production, to repeatedly ask the question of what the [social] meaning of dance could be, or from where it could emerge'.[7] Here the audience too found itself in a radical new position, instead of 'consuming meaning', notes dramaturg Jeroen Peeters, they were encouraged to 'take up their part of the responsibility', and 'negotiate the realm of meaning'.[8] The 'choreographers of the first hour', the emerging pioneers who then largely shaped and influenced the contemporary dance scene in Flanders and beyond were: Jan Fabre, Anne Teresa De Keersmaeker (Rosas), Alain Platel (les ballets C de la B) and Wim Vandekeybus (Ultima Vez).[9]

Trained as a remedial educationalist, Platel throughout his career refused to tread worn paths. When he founded les ballets C de la B in 1984, together with his sister Pascale Platel and his friend Johan Grimonprez, they created performances with professional and amateur artists. The establishment of the company was first a joke – a response to his former college teacher's challenge to Platel's dislike of Béjart's work.[10] Even the name of the ensemble ('les ballets C[ontemporaines] de la B[elgique]') is poking fun at Béjart's 'pompous Ballet of the 20th Century'.[11]

This rebellious gesture – questioning and sometimes ridiculing the values of the establishment – can also be observed in Platel's attitude to disturb the accepted aesthetic values and political assumptions on the stage. The bravery for provocation and disobedience manifests itself on many levels of the ensemble's micro- and macro-dramaturgy. For example, this can be observed in the choice of the dancers, who because of their physical features, age or unusual personality would not necessarily comply with the norm of classical dance ensembles. It is notable that there are no female dancers in the group who would fit the description 'classical beauty'; on the contrary, the women in les ballets C de la B look rather unconventional and manifest an exceptional inner strength, rebelliousness or fragility. The same daring attitude can be recognized in ignoring aesthetic conventions as to what is 'allowed' in art and performance: for instance, bringing a toddler on the stage (*lets op Bach*, 1998) or even dogs (*Wolf*, 2003).

This 'unruly dramaturgy' can also be observed in the rougher aesthetics of les ballets C de la B performances that use a mixture of free improvisation and choreographed movements, and often embrace chaos in structuring the piece. Hybridity characterizes Platel's aesthetic of mixing various movement vocabularies (for instance, everyday gestures, classical ballet and contemporary dance) or turning to movement vocabularies 'that are usually banned from dance: dystonia, dyskinesia, movements that are not of normal muscle tone or are tense, verging on the outer side of taboo'.[12]

With his choice of music, Platel also employs hybridity by contrasting classical music with popular culture or folk music, and mixing noises, sounds and words in his performances. This fusion or *métissage* is an important aesthetic and political statement for Platel, who disregards aesthetic rules, roles and boundaries when creating a performance:

> I never make dances, I just work with the material. The material is not a written text or a book – I work with the material that I see, then I just place them and play with them. I like to work with people who like to move. And in that sense people call me a choreographer. But whether it is theatre or dance or opera, this is really not something I am thinking of. This is also a question Pina Bausch raised fifty years ago. That performances are all these things together. I don't make any distinctions any more.[13]

Dance dramaturgy, emerging in the rehearsal room or dance studio, demands a different kind of dramaturgy than the production dramaturgy that was developed in twentieth-century Regietheater, that operated with pre-existing material (the play text), a given structure (the dramaturgy of the play) and a concept that was often formed before the rehearsals began. These conditions and ingredients were not applicable for the work that took place in the dance studio. In fact, some of the premises and vocabulary of traditional text-based, production dramaturgy seemed to be defunct in these new circumstances.

The first dance dramaturgs in Flanders, such as Marianne Van Kerkhoven, were professionals who moved from theatre towards dance in the 1980s. T'Jonck notes how Van Kerkhoven, 'through her pioneering contribution in the early work by Rosas ... underpinned pieces such as *Bartók/Aantekeningen* by tirelessly questioning the production process and enhancing it with additional material such as texts or film', positioning the work 'in a broader context'.[14] With Van Kerkhoven's and her colleagues' input the profession of dance dramaturgy evolved and solidified itself in Flanders in the 1990s.[15]

It was Van Kerkhoven who coined the term 'new dramaturgy' to establish a new theoretical and critical discourse. In her understanding, new dramaturgy was referred to as a process-oriented method of working:

> [a] quest for possible understanding, [where] the meaning, the intentions, the form and the substance of a play arise during the working process ... In this case dramaturgy is no longer a means of bringing out the structure of the meaning of the world in a play, but [a quest for] a provisional or possible arrangement which the artist imposes on those elements he gathers from a reality that appears to him chaotic. In this kind of world picture, causality and linearity lose their value, storyline and psychologically explicable characters are put at risk, there is no longer a hierarchy amongst the artistic building blocks used.[16]

From its establishment in 1984, les ballets C de la B operated as a collective, working together and sharing responsibilities with performers and, eventually, a dance dramaturg. They reached international fame as a collaborative contemporary dance theatre ensemble by the early 1990s, as a result of the reception of their 1993 production

Bonjour madame, comment allez-vous aujourd'hui, il fait beau, il va sans doute pleuvoir, etcetera. This international success helped the company to become a major force on the contemporary Flemish performance scene, and with the relative financial stability that came with the government of Flanders' 1993 Performing Arts Decree, further possibilities opened up for les ballets C de la B.[17]

In 1995, the ensemble embarked on a collaboration with LOD Muziektheater, a Ghent-based production company for opera and music theatre, in order to create a new piece. The agreement between the two organizations for *La Tristeza Complice* (1995) was that the concept and the direction would come from Platel, les ballets C de la B would bring the dancers and the designer (William Phlips) to the new piece, and LOD would provide an accordion orchestra, a composer (Dick van der Harst), and a dramaturg (Hildegard De Vuyst).

From a pragmatic point of view, securing a dramaturg for a work that uses 'adaptation' (Platel's intention was to rewrite Purcell's music for the dance piece) seems reasonable. However, one cannot avoid sensing the political implications of the appointment: imposing a dramaturg on a production, who is (to quote theorist André Lepecki) 'desired by the producers in order to fill in a lack or a perception of a lack of knowledge or information'.[18]

Having started her career as a dance critic, De Vuyst was working full time for LOD as their dramaturg, a role that was fairly new for her too. (She took it up in 1994.) At the time, she considered her role was to provide a 'reflection content' to the theatre director's work.[19] Until this point, Platel had never worked with a dramaturg before. He heard about the role but thought it was for text-based theatre and had no idea how he could benefit from collaborating with a dramaturg on a contemporary dance production. It was a mutual challenge for both of them during the creative process to work out 'what to do with each other' and 'what to be for each other'.[20] Platel remembers: 'And that is a very good start, in fact, I realized. Because instead of "meeting the function", it was meeting a person, and then we had to find out what her job could be, and how I could communicate with her – it is something that emerged in the moment.'[21] The 'arranged marriage' turned out to be mutually beneficial. De Vuyst thought that the extensive amount of time they spent together on their first production contributed greatly to the development of their particular and close dramaturgical collaboration. But she also felt that it was her role in helping to resolve a conflict that arose between the composer and the director-choreographer that was an eye-opener for Platel. Platel's intention was to rework Purcell's music for a dance piece. At the core of the conflict was a misunderstanding about the composer's role in the production. De Vuyst recalls:

> The deal was that Dick van der Harst would write his composition and use Purcell's music as an influence. However, when Alain listened to the new composition, he was disappointed, because what he found interesting and important in Purcell's baroque music was lost in the new piece. Then I somehow managed to convince Dick to respect the baroque basis and create an 'adaptation', rather than compose a new piece of music. I think at that delicate situation during our collaboration Alain understood how a dramaturg may be useful.[22]

In the sense of being a negotiator, De Vuyst fulfilled the implicit political role that she was assigned. However, it was not only De Vuyst's diplomacy but also her role as a 'translator' in the process that was valuable: 'Within the conflict I just tried to formulate for the composer on the one hand and for Alain on the other hand what the other was actually dealing with, so a translation of different logics that they were in.'[23]

The experience proved to be a milestone in Platel and De Vuyst's ongoing collaboration, for both parties involved. De Vuyst recalls how the interaction with Platel changed her view of the dramaturg's role:

> In the discussions with Dick van der Harst in the context of his adaptation of Purcell for *La Tristeza Complice*, I was confronted for the first time with your [Alain Platel's] ideas about it: how does that affect you? I have never forgotten that first discussion. I have always borne it in mind: on the one hand you have the independence of the artist but you also have to communicate with the audience. It is all about building bridges between the two.[24]

Beyond the intellectual, artistic and political similarities, and fluid communication, there is also an intuitive, trusting connection between Platel and De Vuyst. It is first and foremost a friendship, a dynamic relationship that is not fixed to predefined roles but that changes and evolves over time, which makes their professional relationship function so well. De Vuyst remarks that their secret is the secret of any well-functioning relationship: 'We make each other better, stronger, more eloquent, more understanding, and more performant.'[25] Having worked together for over twenty years, they are still genuinely curious about each other's thoughts, listen to each other with great attention, and they can still surprise each other. Platel says:

> I still discover things about Hildegard with delight. That she likes this or she would say that. But certainly and consciously I am sure that she is the person who helps me to bring things together. When she says: 'I see this – do you want to communicate this or not? Do you think it is necessary to have this text in it?' – then I can ask a lot of questions.[26]

The dramaturg-as-translator

The metaphor of dramaturg-as-translator finds its origin in Walter Benjamin's essay, 'The Task of the Translator'[27] and is also recognized in Bertolt Brecht's *The Messingkauf Dialogues*.[28] It was further developed and adapted for an intercultural context by Ric Knowles and most recently rethought for movement dramaturgy by Katherine Profeta.[29] In this context, 'translating' means a dynamic process, moving between different cultural systems and embedding one (with its marked differences) into another, thus the task of the dramaturg being 'to effect the reverberation of one type of structure across another'.[30] This dynamic translating role, negotiating between different knowledge systems, suits the job description of the dramaturg of les ballets C de la B, since the ensemble's work builds on the hybrid aesthetics of intercultural work. Moreover, Platel's casting choices reflect the race, age and gender diversity of a contemporary Western European society. He notes, 'If you talk about the world, you have to represent it well.'[31]

The different knowledge systems do not only concern translating between different cultures or disciplines such as music and dance theatre; they also imply translating the relationship between the individual and a community into body-politics. De Vuyst notes:

> Physical theatre and choreography for me is speaking, communicating with the body, through the body, through physicality. I think it is very important these days, and it is hyper important in mixed communities, where people talk various languages and embody different cultures. Potentially, with all the dominance of visual information it could allow to reach out to more people than, say, a repertoire theatre using words and language.
>
> Your choices can be extremely political: what kind of bodies do you put on stage, who is represented and who is not, what kind of movements do you make, do you need dancers to be formally trained or not, etc. In a globalized context it is the body that you have as a platform for communication and resistance.[32]

Since the plot-driven narrative structure is mostly absent in this physical theatre, De Vuyst understands dramaturgy (using Tim Etchells's metaphor) primarily as 'doing time'.[33]

> Because it is live art, it means you can only go linear. Since the work you are presenting advances in time, that means you can use that to your advantage: there is certain information the audience doesn't know at the beginning, that you only reveal in the middle, etc. As you have a certain development in time, you build up expectations, that you either satisfy or frustrate. Dramaturgy is the working of time in a piece: it is the beginning, the middle and the end.[34]

There is more to this notion of 'doing time', however, than the fitting of temporal coordinates in a dramatic structure. As the performance is unfolding over time, regardless of whether it contains a plot or not, it suggests a 'narrative', a journey for the audience, even in a postdramatic context, warns De Vuyst. Any moving along the linearity of a performance demands a dramaturgy, even if there is no plot: 'Dramaturgy is the narrative that is underneath everything – whatever context we are in. People who watch or take part in a performance are "interpreting machines": they imbue narrative to it. So as a theatre-maker it is better to be conscious about it.'[35] Dramaturg Katherine Profeta calls this 'soft narrative understanding'.[36] In her book *Dramaturgy in Motion*, Profeta explores the notion of the narrative in post-mimetic performance, bringing awareness to 'the storied nature of perception',[37] acknowledging the activity of the brain creating a 'back story' from the temporality of actions. The consequence for a performance is that, by seeing events over time, the audience will create a pattern and will assign meaning to that pattern, which will be read as some sort of narrative. For instance, a chain of events can be regarded as progression or recurrence, colouring even abstract movements with emotions. De Vuyst is aware of this 'soft narrative understanding' as the dramaturg's responsibility in the rehearsal room when thinking about the structure of a dance piece.

Another translation that belongs to the dramaturg's task forces is the translation between the rehearsal process and the world at large:

> I am someone who pays attention to the process, structures, bigger entities, so my work is also related to the larger context and particularly the institutional context in which the work is made. Is it directed by one person or is it a co-creation? What is involved? I am analysing the power structures that are present in the work process. And this perspective is larger than the dramaturgy of a piece.[38]

De Vuyst here (similarly to Van Kerkhoven, who created these terms,[39] or Eckersall[40]) makes a distinction between micro- and macro-dramaturgy. Whereas micro-dramaturgy focuses on the dramaturgy of a performance or its dramaturgical process, macro-dramaturgy is a larger system that takes into consideration the artist, the company, the theatre, its place in the community and other social and political factors. Obviously the micro- and macro-dramaturgies are intertwined, and can influence decisions on both levels.

Platel's working process

Stage 1: Marking out the area of investigation[41]

Platel's process is one of collaborative creation: 'I am someone who can install a trustful atmosphere in the studio, then waits. And then, I know that I compose with all the material that I see. But always in dialogue with my collaborators.'[42]

The inspiration for a new piece can come from anywhere, says Platel. In *nicht schlafen* (2016), the starting point was the music of Gustav Mahler and the book *The Tumbling Years* by Philipp Blom, commissioning Ghent-based contemporary artist Berlinde de Bruyckere as a set designer, and a cast of nine dancers.[43] In *C(H)ŒURS* (2012), it was the research into the meaning of freedom through the choral scenes of Verdi's and Wagner's operas that intrigued Platel. In *vsprs* (2006), the starting point was the exploration of ritual and sacrifice. All these themes, Platel remarks, are a variation on his main question about examining the relationship between the individual and society.

> I can recognize that in my works I am circling around certain themes: the tension between how to remain an individual, a person with a character and an identity, and blend with a group. Another theme is how people have a very personal way to express themselves physically and how this physical expression becomes an individual language. A lot of my work is about death and how to deal with that. Recently it is also about ... perhaps one can call it lust for life: how this urge to live can become a form of rebellion. It is not necessarily to be on the barricades, but just by wanting to live, you can become a rebel.[44]

Platel does not have a permanent ensemble. He finds his collaborators, 'fellow travellers/*companions de route*',[45] through workshops or mutual interests, and these relationships last as long as both parties benefit from it: from the period of one production to even decades of working together (as in the case of dancer and director Lisi Estaras). The dancers who are selected at castings are invited to participate in a weekend workshop with les ballets C de la B at their Ghent base. These workshops are preliminary to the creative process but are not unrelated to it. While Platel is testing some ideas about the new piece, it is also an opportunity for the dancers to familiarize themselves with the atmosphere in les ballets' studios, their way of working, to get to know each other, to begin to develop their group dynamic, and to see how they respond to Platel's method. Dancer Mélanie Lomoff was selected at an audition in Paris. She recalls the ensuing workshop experience in Ghent in 2005:

> I remember the organized lunch, people coming and cooking, and I appreciated the state of mind behind the work. I think at that time Alain and the composer Fabrizio Cassol already had thoughts about the music and using Monteverdi's *Vespers*, so we tried some things. Alain immersed us in improvising: he gave us various tasks and watched how we responded.[46]

Based on these preliminary workshops, Platel finally invites the people who are then contracted for the creation of the new piece, and with this a three- to four-month journey together begins. Lomoff recalls:

> Alain didn't say much about why he chose me, and that's what I appreciate in working with him. For me this was a question that sometimes came into my mind during the process, because he saw me at the audition in my pointe shoes, but during the work we never did things like that; I started from zero with him. This gave me lots of space to surprise myself and him.[47]

During this first stage of the work the ideas are still flexible; everything is still open and possible. At this stage, De Vuyst is only present in the dance studio sporadically; nowadays she is less involved in the preparation, she trusts in Platel's choices.

Stage 2: Developing and forming the material

Once the team is put together, the work on the new production continues with a period of collaborative research of 'gathering the material'.[48] During this time the members of the ensemble immerse themselves in the theme of the piece, and the dancers begin to create movements that respond to it. The possibilities seem endless; everything is full of potential. In the dance studio Platel creates an atmosphere where the dancers 'feel good about themselves',[49] thus they are confident and feel secure to experiment with the material, and feel encouraged to come up with ideas, further develop them, and challenge themselves. Everybody's input is valued.

Platel facilitates this phase of the work by assigning the dancers specific tasks during the studio time and providing them with other creative stimuli: reading books, watching videos, collecting images, listening to music, having discussions or even organizing 'field trips'. These ideas are then translated into actions, 'always starting from the physicality and the personality of the dancers':

> What do they want to show and share, what kind of dances they want to make, and what kind of dances they make when I ask them certain kind of questions. And from this material at certain points we'll grow, little by little, the piece and develop the dramaturgy of the piece.[50]

The work is discussed and sometimes repeated. De Vuyst is in and out of rehearsals, consciously trying not to interfere with the dancers' activities but discussing emerging themes or possible directions with Platel. At this stage, Platel deliberately avoids communicating these emerging scenarios with the dancers because he wants them to 'still feel free to bring in lots of different material'.[51]

Platel's calm and benevolent personality is a very important requirement for this kind of collective search for the piece. He is an important reference point for the dancers when they share something with the group. Lomoff recalls:

> Like a sketch, the piece took shape day by day. And because we had a long time for the work, it became much more subtle, deep and matured. It gave us a lot of confidence and calmness during the process, that we felt that we were not in a rush.
> I learnt a lot during this time. How you can question your emotions and your body. How you can feed your work with research. How you can improvise or transpose a new vocabulary of movement into your existing one. For me it was thinking another way and working another way.[52]

The attention that Platel pays to his dancers, and the respectful nurturing of their offerings into a whole may stem from his past as an educator. Crucially, Platel considers this an important choice with political and ethical implications:

> It's like an experiment in democracy and in how to live together. It is something I take care of a lot here at les ballets C de la B. There are moments of tension. Of course. But I am talking about respect. And I am less afraid of the possibility that in the end we have a performance that I am not happy with, than having a piece that the dancers would not be happy about; and they would have to tour with it for a year and feel miserable inside. It's an obsession for me that I feel that everybody is confident and comfortable in the performance.[53]

During the creative process, Platel keeps a journal, a so-called 'production book' – a combination of writings, cut-outs, photos, hand-drawn pictures and schemes jotting down the choreography. Here he meticulously preserves information on what they did at that day's rehearsal, documenting his research and thoughts on the work, important moments from the dancers' exercises, as well as events that happened during the working process which had an effect on their lives. For instance, during the making of *nicht schlafen* in 2016, the Brussels bombing took place. Newspaper cut-outs, emails of encouragement and sympathy the ensemble received after the attack found their place in the production book.

This documentation of the process is crucial, since Platel's aim in free searching together with the ensemble is to find and construct potent images for the stage.[54] These images then are meticulously composed and adjusted with precision up to every detail. All the collaborators (designers, composers, dramaturg, etc.) are around and watch the work emerge. The set, the design, the lighting, the dramaturgy and the music are taking shape during this period as a response to the dancers' work in the studio. De Vuyst notes:

> At this stage Alain and I don't spend much time with each other. We are watching together. Once a week before the rehearsal we sit and talk with Alain, and once after the rehearsal we stay and talk with the composer. I'm withdrawing a lot from the conversations with the dancers. On the other hand, I'm so into it and trusting the process, and when necessary, because something is really confusing or troubling me, I'll step in. Until then why would I? I enjoy watching it. But I think it's important to follow up, how things are, where things come from. And you also need to understand issues with the dancers. In order to be aware.[55]

Composer and long-time collaborator Steven Prengels explains that when developing a new piece for les ballets C de la B, the working process is a mixture

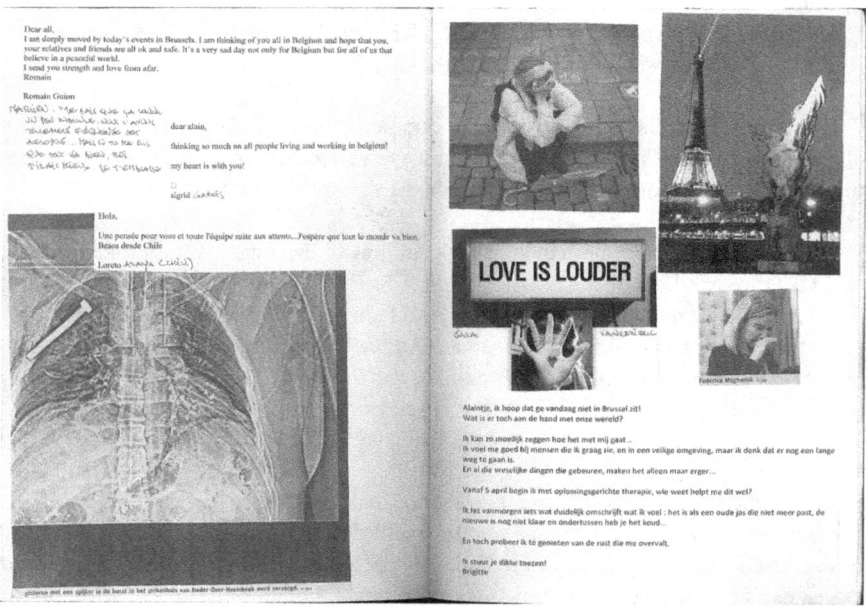

Figure 3.2 Excerpt from the production book of Alain Platel, made during the creation of *nicht schlafen*, Ghent 2016. (Image courtesy of Alain Platel.)

'An Experiment in Democracy' 43

Figure 3.3 Excerpt from the production book of Alain Platel, made during the creation of *nicht schlafen*, Ghent 2016. (Image courtesy of Alain Platel.)

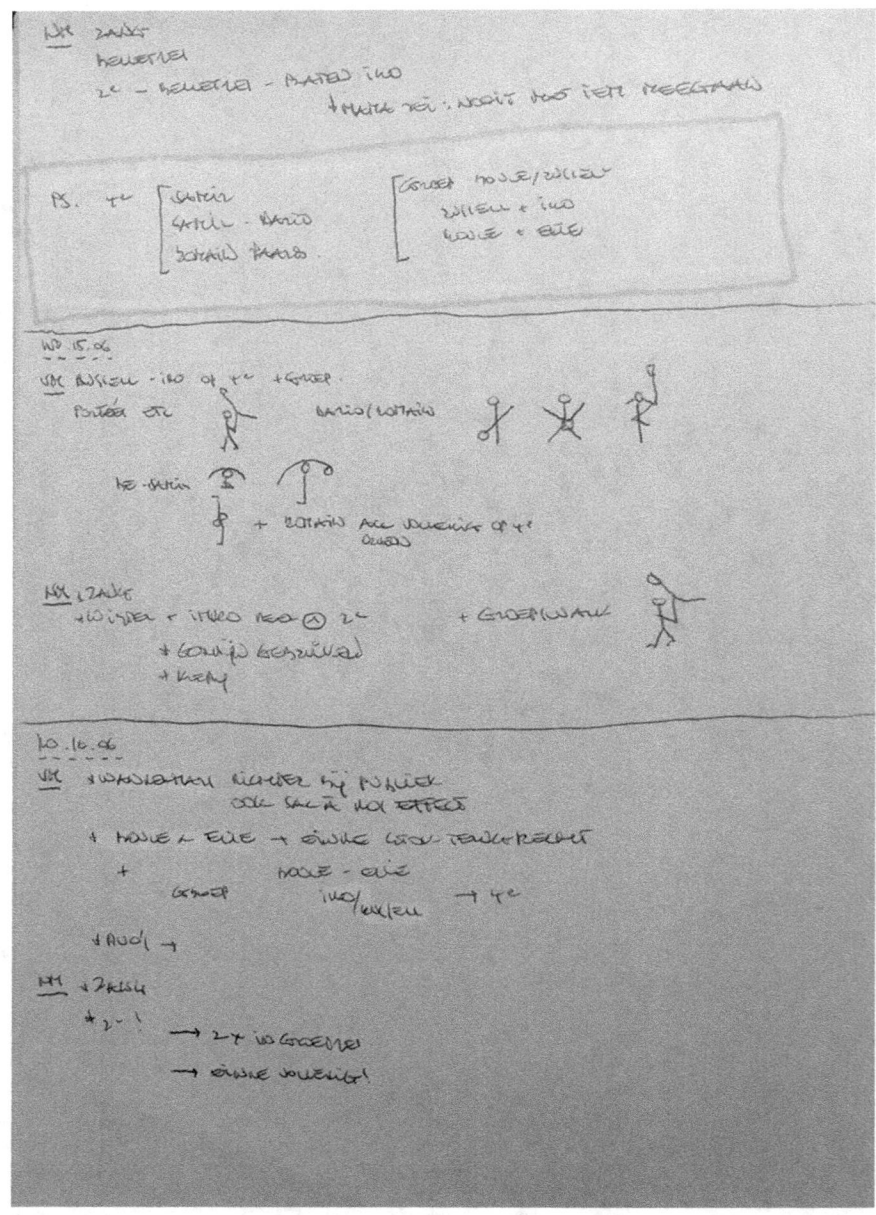

Figure 3.4 Excerpt from the production book of Alain Platel, made during the creation of *nicht schlafen*, Ghent 2016. (Image courtesy of Alain Platel.)

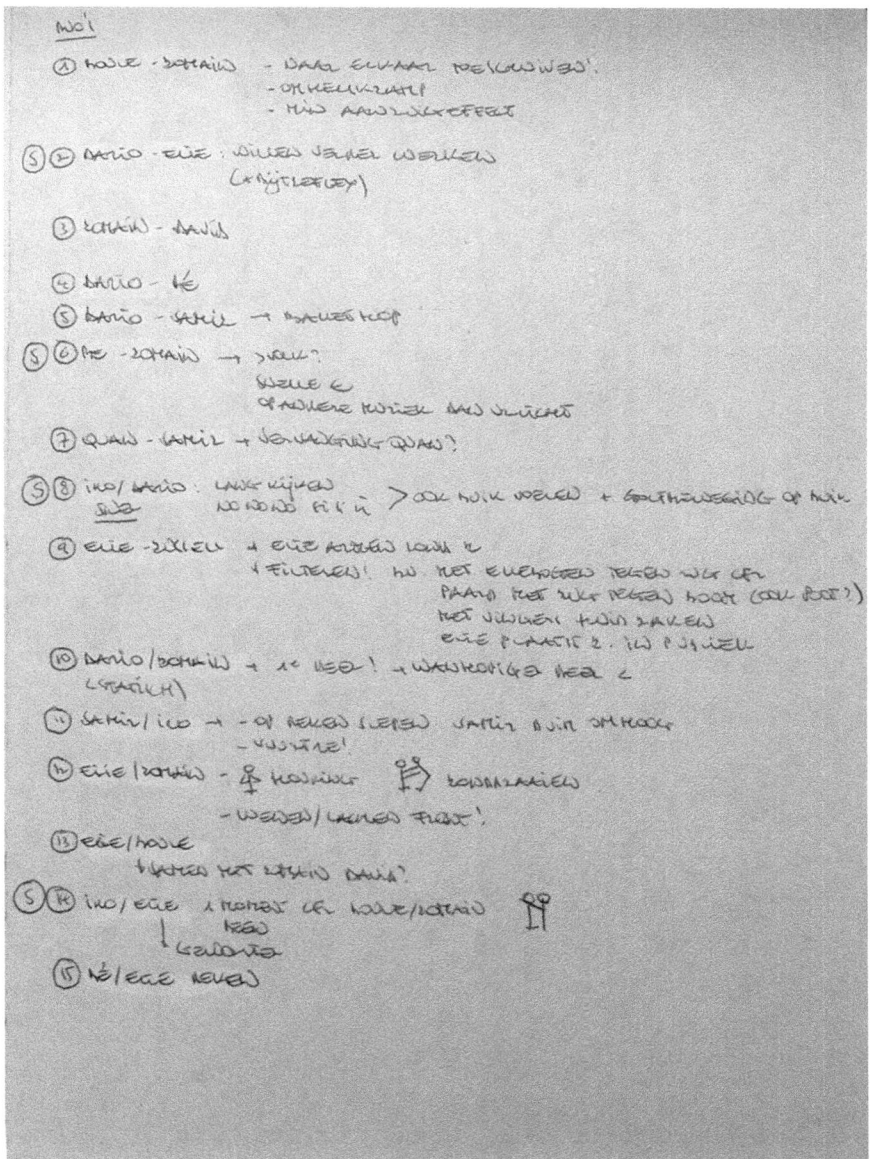

Figure 3.5 Excerpt from the production book of Alain Platel, made during the creation of *nicht schlafen*, Ghent 2016. (Image courtesy of Alain Platel.)

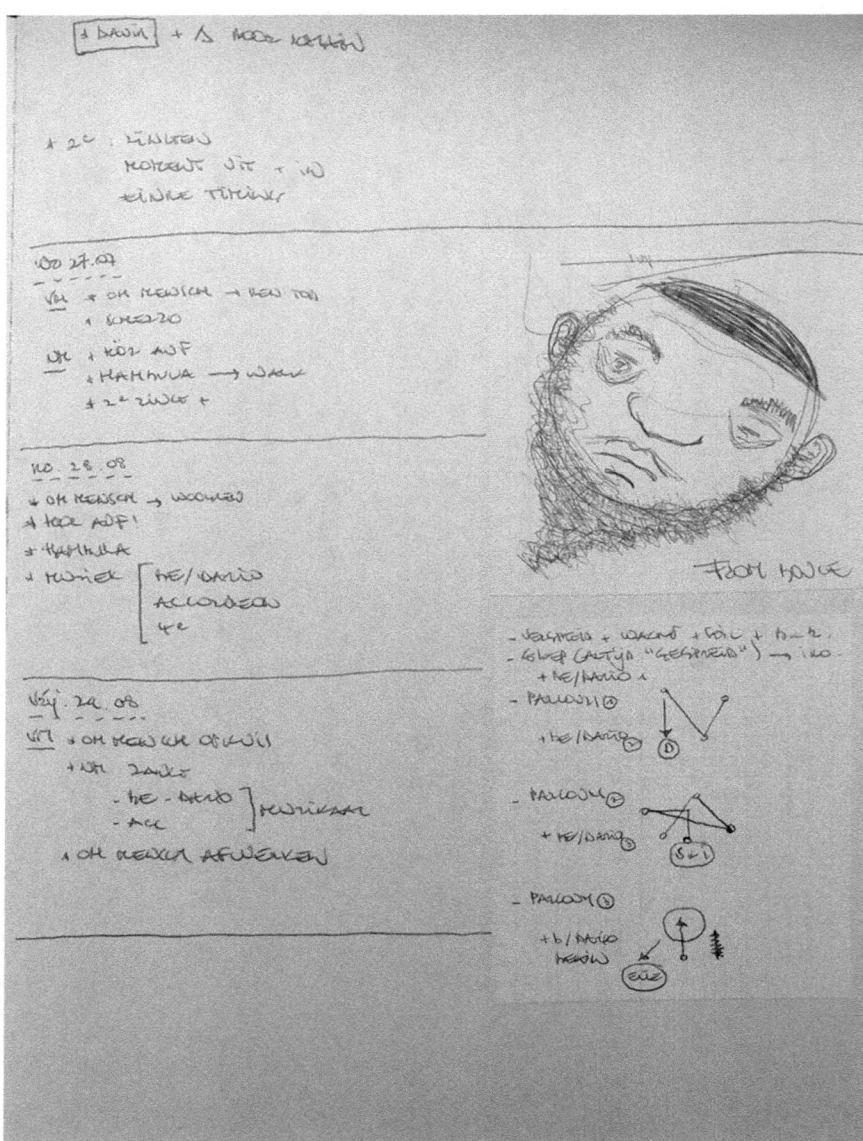

Figure 3.6 Excerpt from the production book of Alain Platel, made during the creation of *nicht schlafen*, Ghent 2016. (Image courtesy of Alain Platel.)

of instinctive responses to the material that they chose to focus on, followed by an evaluation and critical thinking about the response: 'My soundscapes [for *nicht schlafen*] did not emerge from a preconceived plan to take Mahler's collage techniques to the limit but from the creative interaction with Alain and the dancers during rehearsals. I tried to organically respond to what everyone came up with during the improvisations.'[56]

The feedback and ideas are then put back into the piece, to further inform the development, which is then again discussed, and so on. This applies not only to the music but to every area of the performance. They are developed through a dialogue between the ensemble's creative mode (that is visceral, kinetic and often instinctive) and analytical mode (where critical, aesthetic, technical, practical and ethical issues are thought through and discussed), and enriched by the research and findings that arise from the exercises Platel gives to the dancers.

In this open, organic process of growing the piece, with all the members of the creative team in the rehearsal room almost every day, Platel does not present himself as the one who possesses all the knowledge. 'Alain surrounds himself with co-creators', notes Prengels.[57] 'The boundaries are gone, and you are not limited to your "area of expertise" only.'[58] For example, Prengels testifies of how in *En avant, marche!* (2015) he made suggestions for the choreography and how he danced in that piece as well as conducting the band performing onstage.[59]

Although Platel's approach to music consists of creating a collage, he often focuses on one particular composer or genre.[60] The fabric of this musical collage is made in collaboration with a contemporary composer (Platel mainly works with Fabrizio Cassol and Steven Prengels), who not only adapts the chosen pieces of original music but also composes smaller new pieces that fit seamlessly within the body of the main work. The original musical scores are deconstructed, enriched and reconstructed, contributing to the dramaturgical development of the production. However, the composer's work in les ballets C de la B goes beyond mere translation, adaptation or enrichment of the original score. The composer is also responsible for creating and cultivating a soundscape for the performance. This includes not only music but also various recorded sounds and sound effects that are part of the rich aural landscape of the piece.[61] The composers at les ballets C de la B are for that matter responsible for the sonorous dramaturgy of the new piece.[62] In that sense, the role of the composer is also dramaturgical, that is, to develop the new piece's aural architecture.

The sonorous dramaturgy is developed in close collaboration with the dancers. As such, Congolese dancers Russell Tshiebua and Boule Mpanya were involved in composing a piece of music that was included in *nicht schlafen*. Platel (who worked with them previously in *Coup Fatal* in 2014), was very impressed with the way 'they sing Pygmy music with their very own polyphonic and rhythmic complexity.'[63] He notes: 'Even from the outset of the preparations for *nicht schlafen*, I could imagine some sort of counterpoint between this African music and the adagios of Mahler.'[64]

In recalling how they composed the song, Tshiebua observes how they had to discover Mahler, as they had never heard about him before. This exploration of 'finding a way to combine his world with my world' came close to the experience of 'how we accept and deal with each other ... and offer space to the other'.[65] As an artist, Tshiebua believes that our ability to negotiate with each other's values and create a 'mixture' has implications for the future of our society too.⁶⁶

The musical collage dramaturgy of *nicht schlafen* was conceived of in a similar mode of encountering the other. Prengels observes how they could only create a new musical landscape for the performance in response to Mahler, by respecting Mahler's logic of composing.

> The architecture of Mahler's music is like a cathedral, you can't interfere with its logic and mathematics and proportions randomly without spoiling and destroying the whole thing.
>
> Creating the music for *nicht schlafen* was like creating a symphony, a new logic, but using Mahler's way of composing. We stuck to a very clear and limited amount of choices to keep it as pure as possible. The question we asked before we made a choice was: what is adding something to what you are trying to say with the piece.⁶⁷

During this second stage, the costume design is developed in close collaboration with the team. Fabric artist and costume designer Dorine Demuynck, who has a decade-long history of working with les ballets C de la B, testifies of this collaborative dramaturgy with two choreographers of the ensemble: Lisi Estaras and Alain Platel.

> A few months before the start of the rehearsals, Alain tells me what the new piece will be about, and he gives an idea of the direction for the clothes by showing me some pictures for inspiration. In the rehearsal studio there is also a 'mood board' – a wall with pictures to which everybody can contribute to or gain inspiration from.⁶⁸

At the beginning of the work, as a starting point, Demuynck always brings into the rehearsal room her stock of clothes that she collected from various second-hand shops. She watches the dancers' costume choices during the rehearsals and tailors her offers at the next rehearsal to those choices as a response. Demuynck likes reusing second-hand clothes for several reasons: for her there is an ethical and ecological reason for not getting or making something new that will be disposed of later. Besides, she is attracted to the fact that those 'pre-loved' clothes already have a history, a hidden narrative that they 'bring' with themselves into the rehearsal room. And finally because: 'The second-hand clothes are coming from different countries of the world, so they also contain their own typical cultural style.'⁶⁹

Responding to the work in the rehearsal room, Demuynck also keeps an eye on the piece as a whole (she imagines it as a painting, a picture) and makes her costume adjustments accordingly (in terms of shades of colours, for instance). Some of the adjustments are practical: for the fight scene at the beginning of *nicht schlafen*, the dancers needed clothes from fabrics that could be easily ripped and shredded and be replaced for every performance. Other choices have aesthetic considerations: the colours of the clothes she offered for *nicht schlafen* contributed to the muted colour scheme of the performance, thus visually expressing the feelings the performance tried to evoke.

Stage 3: Re-evaluating the work, reshaping the material

From the search for physical expressions of the thoughts and feelings that arose during the previous stages of the work, the new piece slowly and organically emerges. Its possible vocabulary (movements, sounds and colours) evolves, as well as its 'units' (shorter solo or group scenes that are devised and developed) that will become the performance's building blocks. The third phase of the process is when these small units are pieced together (and further shaped), and thus the new piece's architecture is created.

This is the stage where Platel (following Pina Bausch's method) takes every small unit that has been developed and labelled, writes them on laminated cards and, by laying out and arranging those cards, works out the piece's overall dramaturgy. Earlier in their career, De Vuyst used to join Platel in this process; nowadays, Platel does it alone, and later, during rehearsals, De Vuyst will comment on the construction if she feels it necessary.

This collage dramaturgy uses fragments – an eclectic mixture of 'high' and 'low' culture, colliding different styles and moods, contrasts, and layering (having simultaneous actions on the stage) – and assembles them together, creating a narrative that is no longer plot-ridden but follows an inner logic and rhythm.[70] Prengels recalls how in this stage of the assembling process, the musical dramaturgy for *nicht schlafen* was like painting: 'to add some lights here and there as a final touch'.[71]

When examining the dramaturgy of les ballets C de la B's performances, we can find that they are structured from 'blocks'. All the blocks are labelled by a trigger word – this helps the dancers remember the 'soft narrative', the dynamic progress or the quality of the block. The length of these blocks can vary. For instance block 'No. 2' at the end of *nicht schlafen* is 22 minutes long: an entire movement of Mahler's Symphony No. 2.

There are two types of blocks to be distinguished: blocks where the choreography – even if it is seemingly chaotic – is tightly and meticulously composed, and blocks wherein the choreography is improvised. This was a new departure for Platel, explains De Vuyst, that in *nicht schlafen*, for the first time during his career, he relinquished his directorial control and allowed the performers to shape two scenes live (the opening fight and the closing, celebratory dance) entirely freely during every performance.[72] The improvised blocks, however, are not completely impromptu, inasmuch as there is a mutual agreement about the theme and the duration of the improvisation, the quality of the movements, the feeling that the given block is about to convey, i.e. the 'rules' for the dance within that unit. It is the shift in the music or soundscape that marks the beginning and the end of each block: the timing of movement and music is interrelated. The arrangement of these blocks (the dramaturgy of the piece) is developed by playing with balance and counterbalance between the flowing and fixed units.[73]

De Vuyst explains that during the working process, dramaturgically there are two frameworks to follow: a smaller and a larger one. The larger one is the major trajectory and theme of the piece that gradually grows and evolves. She and Platel discuss this a lot during the work, 'but the bigger framework is not necessarily the theme that is given to the dancers to make something out of it'.[74] The other is a much smaller and simpler framework that consists of the daily exercises that Platel does with the dancers. These two frameworks continuously evolve and 'grow into each other during the rehearsals'.[75] Platel gives an example from the work on *nicht schlafen*:

> One of the dancers, Ido, had a very strange and unique way of making movements, an idiosyncratic way of using the ballet vocabulary. It was often based on very small, ordinary, flapping movements. You can't understand it, and there is no logic or a clear aesthetic to it: it is chaotic, but I really like it. So I asked him to make something for the group. Because I know that certain movements if you let them perform in synchronization with other people, especially when they are very strange, then the effect becomes bigger and it is really amazing to watch. So I saw this group choreography that they learnt with Ido, and I thought, what if we combine this with one of the Mahler laments ['Adagietto' from *Symphony No. 5*], which is a very deep, emotional, sentimental, nostalgic song about humanity. Then when you put the two together, it is that through this contrast, somehow in a very strange way, they reinforce each other. The movements have more impact on the music, and the music becomes so important. It is like a very strange, beautiful marriage. And maybe this is the kind of procedure that I use very often.[76]

Lomoff recalls a similar experience as a dancer during this stage of the work:

> You as a dancer-interpreter forget about the bigger picture, because you are so focused on the process, you can't remember all the improvisations you have done, you have a memory of certain moments only; and suddenly you hear their conversation and begin to see that there are 'strings' going in certain ways around these improvisations, creating a network with each other. And from this 'ping-pong'-style interaction between Alain and Hildegard, in a few days they created quite a consistent part of the performance.[77]

This stage of the process can be difficult for the dancers (letting go of one's own material, finding out about their role in the performance); that's why Platel makes sure that they are treated respectfully. De Vuyst explains:

> Alain is very generous and really takes care of the material that people give him. He places it in such a way that the dancers can actually shine in it, and it can become meaningful. It's not a painless process. It is unavoidable when you have to put things in a certain order or length. But in the end of the process, I think, the dancers recognize their material, that it is genuine, and they feel that it's been validated, given value by how it's used in a bigger piece.[78]

In this assembling process, Platel is reluctant to discard material that the dancers developed previously, so he tries to find a place for all of them, unless it really has no place in the work. Platel says: 'Not to throw away things means you have to discover the meaning of things by letting them coexist, to put them next to each other.'[79]

During the assembling process, Platel and De Vuyst always allow room for the material that is 'too good to throw away but you don't know what it can be'.[80] This collection of material goes into the 'recycling bag', their virtual storage place (kept in the rehearsal recordings as well as in their memories) which they return to when putting the piece together: when they feel that in order for transition from phrase 'A' to phrase 'C' they need some bridging material, to link the two. Platel and De Vuyst have developed a skill of swiftly finding in the 'recycling bag' the material that can be fitted between those phrases. Platel says:

> Despite the fact that her presence in the rehearsal studio is lighter than it was, say, twenty years ago, Hildegard is an even more important reference than before. Because there is a little bit of distance, so every time she comes into the studio, there is something that has happened, there is something to look at. I often refer to her role as my mirror. Because she describes what she is seeing, and asks me if this is what I wanted to achieve. Which is different from somebody who would come and interpret immediately what happens. Hildegard is not giving quick suggestions. She just describes what happens. And that for me is a very important experience to confront my work with in this way. Because then I can think like: 'Is this the effect of what happens on stage? And if it is – do I want it or not?'[81]

When giving feedback, the focus on what the piece communicates ('What is this telling about us today? What are we communicating by doing that?') remains the dramaturg's main concern, according to De Vuyst.[82] Her communication with Platel is like an evolving, layering process – that sometimes does not even require the dramaturg talking, only being present, watching and listening. Platel says:

> The relationship over the years has blossomed into a very complex way of communicating. For instance, I discovered that by telling Hildegard what happens in a scene, I can already realize whether it's interesting or not, without her seeing it. Or when she is here in the rehearsal studio and watches something, I can feel whether we should continue working on it or not. It's not necessarily because if she doesn't like something that I will give up. On the contrary! It might just stimulate me to try to find out how I can convince her, because I saw something that is quite important, and has a potential but perhaps needs further development. And I trust the fact that she will never say something to please me personally.[83]

Stage 4: Watching together – the audience as dramaturg

During the fourth and last phase of the work, Platel assigns an important dramaturgical role to the audience: the piece is finalized with the spectators' help. This is not something the ensemble advertises or directly asks, but they invite viewers from very early on and use these first spectators' experiences for direct and indirect feedback, 'watching with them', to find out how the piece in the making is received by the viewer, what works and what needs changing.[84] Platel says:

> I find it very important that you don't lose the audience. I can accept when people see something in my shows that they disagree with, and they leave. But if they left

> for the wrong reason, because they are bored – that's very bad. There are many moments in the performance where if you don't correct the spacing and timing, you can lose the audience. When I started to do things, I wanted to shake up people, not to shock perhaps but to be controversial. I got over this by now. Today I think of the audience as a friend that you take for a walk together.[85]

The introduction of the audience to the new piece is slow, gentle and is carefully controlled by the ensemble's producer. The end of the second stage of the work (creating material) is marked by a strictly private, in-house showing. At this time, the order of the 'building blocks' is often random or only preliminary. The aim for this showing is some sort of stock-taking, watching the new material together and seeing what emerges from it – and what connections can be made during the next phase that will focus more on structuring the material. At this showing the piece is very fragile – it is more of a draft than a completed work – yet the first complete run gives the creators an opportunity to begin to look at the work from a distance.

At the end of the showing there is no organized or official feedback session, only informal conversations sharing first impressions and thoughts. The work (in the case of *nicht schlafen*, after a couple of weeks' summer break) continues, and when the piece starts taking shape, more 'public' run-throughs are planned. The invitees now are people close to the ensemble: family members, friends, trustworthy colleagues – although there is an emphasis on having a variety of viewers with 'different connections'.[86] The number is still kept small: twenty to thirty people at most. De Vuyst says:

> Alain works as a choreographer from the perspective of the audience. From day one of the work he offers feedback as an audience member, what he feels and what he sees, and how to work on that relationship with surprises. The aim with these early showings is to have a shared experience with the piece. We all know we have our favourite moments and personal taste, but when you are watching it with others, you are forced to watch it differently, you have to step out of your private relationship with the piece. You take the feedback, but sometimes just feel the audience's response, when the attention drops, when people start to move. You don't have to talk so much afterwards.[87]

As the show grows stronger and the ensemble becomes more confident in performing it to an audience, these semi-public work-in-progress presentations become more regular, reaching to two to three showings a week for the final few weeks of the work. A low-key pre-première showing closes the months of work, often celebrated with a party. This ends an important stage of the work: from now on the piece is ready to meet the world.

Decentred dramaturgy

In an interview with Marie Anezin, Platel confirms that he considers his artistic strength lies in him being an 'outsider' to the dance world:

I think that what helps me is that I am neither a choreographer nor a dancer; it means that I really depend on what the artists feel like offering. I work with this material there; I won't transform it or change it to my language, I only have what my eyes regard.[88]

This 'regard', which consists of waiting patiently for something to emerge, recognition, contemplation, analysis, focus and testing, is Platel's main dramaturgical tool, his 'camera', the lens through which he sees and frames the dancers' work. Its perception and sensitivity has changed over the years – so has the dramaturgy of Platel's pieces. While in the past there was a narrative, a plot (or multiple stories) featuring recognizable characters in les ballets C de la B's pieces such as in *Bonjour madame* ... (1993), *La Tristeza Complice* (1995), and *Iets op Bach* (1998), this has changed since *vsprs* (2006). De Vuyst explains:

With *vsprs*, a big shift happened in the dramaturgy of the pieces. After *vsprs* our pieces became not the reflection of the outside world but an inner experience, and you had trajectories that were related to ecstasy or trance or rituals or to memory – a whole other territory, which was much more like an internal voyage. The pieces are built up like an experience that we go through with an audience, for which we use the dramaturgy of a ritual.[89]

De Vuyst observes that her work as a dramaturg has changed over the decades; she is taking a more relaxed, more withdrawn role now than before:

I feel that this withdrawal is very conscious. I'm trying to intervene less and less, and letting go, and see what's coming up. That's part of what I've learnt from Alain through his genuine love and appreciation towards the performers. Before, I was much more rigid, structured, a control freak. And now I know from experience that you discover all the amazing things that happen, if you just give people space. For me this has been an incredible learning process. I feel that the less I do, the better it will be for the piece. Because it means all these unexpected, not projected, not intended things can resurface – and Alain really recognizes their potential. And the way he puts things together usually is very, very fine. So I'm there for adjustments only, to remind him that we already did this in another piece, or when I recognize something with the procedure, or if I think that we should further develop a scene, because we can challenge ourselves even more.[90]

The type of dramaturgy that De Vuyst here describes has been present since the evolution of the role of dance dramaturg and is very characteristic for new dramaturgical processes. It can be labelled as 'decentred dramaturgy'.[91] This gentle, decentred dramaturgy is very different from the active role of the Brechtian production dramaturg; it is almost the inverse of that interfering activity. It is a meditative and mindful role, an intense and felt presence, one that is devoid of effort or striving for action. An empty state of mind: open, silent, fully aware and relaxed. The dance dramaturg's presence in the rehearsal room might be described as an 'alert state of silence'.[92] They are open and very sensitive to the work happening in the rehearsal room, but their presence is not intrusive. Yet, this observation causes a 'disturbance in the system being observed',[93] and the end product, the performance, benefits from this slow and gentle interaction with the system by the dramaturg. In an earlier essay I called this 'observer effect' the 'Copenhagen interpretation' of new dramaturgy, borrowing the term from quantum physics.[94] This means accepting that in the performance-making process, just like in quantum physics (to quote science writer John Gribbin), 'the very act of observing a thing changes it, and that we, the observers, are in a very real sense part of the experiment'.[95]

Taking into consideration the translation between the micro- and macro-dramaturgy, the dramaturgical creative process also has a political and ethical quality: it allows for a democratic collaboration to unfold. Christel Stalpaert calls this the 'distributive agency of dramaturgical labour'.[96] This mode of collaboration 'blurs the division between reflection and creation, between theory and practice and inaugurates a dramaturgical constellation in a Benjaminian sense of the word'.[97] Sandra Noeth reflects on this possibility 'to think about dramaturgy not primarily as a form-giving instrument, but rather as a shared practice of encounter. The question of how community is created and whether we can still today say "we" alongside the "I".'[98]

This dramaturgical way of working has two consequences. The first is that the piece's dramaturgy throughout the process is unstable and is in flux. The other consequence is that the role of the dramaturg becomes a facilitating role often performed by several members of the ensemble, crossing disciplinary boundaries:

> It means opening up a divided, usually temporary space of negotiation and the creation and reflection of the evolving act of tracking the diverse traces of what is emerging. It does not mean not making decisions. It is much rather about the shouldering of responsibility with respect to the politics of decision-making.[99]

With that we have returned to the political function that has been assigned to dramaturgy since its inception (most obviously when it comes to Brecht and his aim of using dramaturgy as a tool for change of society, but it can also be traced back to Lessing's aim of striving to create a national theatre and nurturing national identity). Yet, in the case of dance dramaturgy and new dramaturgies, this is a very different political role: through the creative process that opens up a shared space for negotiations, it is about maintaining democracy. For which we have a profound need today more than ever.

Coda

Alain Platel: It is so evident that I can't imagine that you, Hildegard, wouldn't be there any more.
Hildegard De Vuyst: Don't you sometimes need a new dialogue?
AP: I worked with someone, it was really nice, but it feels to me that I have to give more information and explanation to them than to you. It's a lot of things that

is happening between us, and sometimes you surprise me. The way you look at things and how you translate them into movements is still valid and valuable.

HDV: It's the history we share, and our references, and memories. You still push me, and I feel, perhaps not a lot, but I can still challenge you. And as long as this happens, this is a live relationship.

Notes

1 For more on the development of dramaturgical thinking in dance, see Katalin Trencsényi (2015) 'Dance Poetics: The History of Dramaturgical Thinking in Dance', in *Dramaturgy in the Making: A User's Guide for Theatre Professionals*, London: Bloomsbury Methuen Drama, 195–209. For more on the development of the role of the dance dramaturg, see Katalin Trencsényi (2015) 'Dance Dramaturgy: The Development of the Role', in *Dramaturgy in the Making: A User's Guide for Theatre Professionals*, London: Bloomsbury Methuen Drama, 210–25.
2 Pina Bausch (2007) 'What Moves Me', speech on the occasion of the Kyoto Prize award ceremony in 2007, Pina Bausch Digital Archive.
3 For more on Hoghe's work as a dance dramaturg and Bausch's method of developing a piece, see Katalin Trencsényi (2016) 'Introduction: What Is the Point of Bandoneon?' in Raimund Hoghe, Ulli Weiss and Katalin Trencsényi (eds.), *Bandoneon: Working with Pina Bausch*, London: Oberon Books, 6–70.
4 Alain Platel, in Alain Platel and Hildegard De Vuyst (2016) interview by Katalin Trencsényi, 23 May 2016, Ghent.
5 Platel, email message to author, 11 October 2016.
6 Platel, in Platel and De Vuyst, interview by Trencsényi, 23 May 2016.
7 Pieter T'Jonck (2016) Contemporary Dance from Flanders (1980–2016)', *Contemporary Dance from Flanders*. Available at http://dossiers.kunsten.be/dance/contemporary-dance-flanders-1980-2016 (accessed 19 August 2019).
8 Jeroen Peeters (2010) 'Heterogenous Dramaturgies', *Maska*, 1 September.
9 T'Jonck, 'Contemporary Dance from Flanders'.
10 Judith Mackrell (1999) 'Horror That Started as a Joke', *The Guardian*, 7 December; Sanjoy Roy (2010) 'Step-by-Step Guide to Dance: les ballets C de la B', *The Guardian*, 5 May 2010.
11 T'Jonck, 'Contemporary Dance from Flanders'.
12 Hildegard De Vuyst (2010) Interview by Katalin Trencsényi, 25 November, Brussels.
13 Platel, in Platel and De Vuyst, interview by Trencsényi, 23 May 2016.
14 T'Jonck, 'Contemporary Dance from Flanders'.
15 Maaike Bleeker (2003) 'Dramaturgy as a Mode of Looking', *Women and Performance*, 13:2 (26): 163–72, at 164; Myriam Van Imschoot (2003) 'Anxious Dramaturgy', 13:2 (26): 57–68, at 65.
16 Marianne Van Kerkhoven (1994) 'On Dramaturgy', *Theaterschrift*, 5–6: 18–20.
17 T'Jonck, 'Contemporary Dance from Flanders'.
18 Lepecki in Scott deLahunta (2000) 'Dance Dramaturgy: Speculations and Reflections', *Dance Theatre Journal*, 16 (1): 20–5, at 24.
19 De Vuyst, interview by Trencsényi, 25 November 2010.

20 De Vuyst and Platel (respectively), in Platel and De Vuyst, interview by Trencsényi, 23 May 2016.
21 Platel, in Platel and De Vuyst, interview by Trencsényi, 23 May 2016.
22 De Vuyst, in Platel and De Vuyst, interview by Trencsényi, 23 May 2016.
23 De Vuyst, interview by Trencsényi, 25 November 2010.
24 De Vuyst in Alain Platel (2006) 'Conversation with Hildegard De Vuyst', in Hildegard De Vuyst (ed.), *les ballets C de la B*, Tielt: Lannoo, 134–6, at 135.
25 De Vuyst, email message to author, 28 June 2016.
26 Platel, in Platel and De Vuyst, interview by Trencsényi, 23 May 2016.
27 Walter Benjamin (1999) 'The Task of the Translator. An Introduction to the Translation of Baudelaire's Tableaux Parisiens', in *Illuminations*, London: Pimlico, 70–82. First published 1923.
28 Bertolt Brecht (2002) *The Messingkauf Dialogues*, London: Methuen. First published 1963. Although Brecht doesn't state it explicitly, from his essay it is clear that the role of the dramaturg in Brecht's 'thaëter' is that of a translator-adapter who would play an important part in the director's interpretation and staging process and be an active agent in transforming the work (for instance moulding and shaping an existent play) for the 'scientific age', i.e. rendering it to the target culture's and society's current needs.
29 Ric Knowles (2011) 'Calling off the Border Patrol: Intercultural Dramaturgy in Toronto', in Ramón Rivera-Servera and Harvey Young (eds.), *Performance in the Borderlands*, Basingstoke: Palgrave Macmillan, 161–81; Katherine Profeta (2015) *Dramaturgy in Motion: At Work on Dance and Movement Performance*, Madison, Wisc.: University of Wisconsin Press, 181–7.
30 Profeta, *Dramaturgy in Motion*, 187.
31 Platel, in Platel and De Vuyst, interview by Trencsényi, 23 May 2016.
32 De Vuyst, in Platel and De Vuyst, interview by Trencsényi, 23 May 2016.
33 Tim Etchells (2009) 'Doing Time', *Performance Research*, 14 (3): 71–80.
34 De Vuyst, in Platel and De Vuyst, interview by Katalin Trencsényi, 23 May 2016.
35 De Vuyst, nterview by Jake Orr, 1 June 2012, London.
36 Profeta, *Dramaturgy in Motion*, 52.
37 Jahn, quoted by Profeta, *Dramaturgy in Motion*, 52.
38 De Vuyst, interview by Trencsényi, 25 November 2010.
39 Marianne Van Kerkhoven (1994) 'The Theatre Is in the City and the City Is in the World and Its Walls Are of Skin', State of the Union Speech at the 1994 Theater festival, Brussels. Available in English translation at http://sarma.be/docs/3229 (accessed 19 August 2019); Marianne Van Kerkhoven (1999) 'Van de kleine en de grote dramaturgie', *Etcetera*, 68 (17): 67–9. In the English translation of Van Kerkhoven's 1994 essay they are referred to as minor and major dramaturgy; however, these terms are problematic, as they implicitly contain a value judgement, hence in recent English discourse the terms 'micro-dramaturgy' and 'macro-dramaturgy' have been used instead.
40 Peter Eckersall, in Peter Eckersall, Paul Monaghan and Melanie Beddie (2014) 'Dramaturgy as Ecology: A Report from the Dramaturgies Project', in Katalin Trencsényi and Bernadette Cochrane (eds.), *New Dramaturgy. International Perspectives on Theory and Practice*, London: Bloomsbury Methuen Drama, 20–2, although he uses the term 'theatre-ecology' instead.
41 For the description of the various phases of the process, I use the stages dramaturg Mira Rafalowicz indicated in her essay about her work with Joseph Chaikin; Mira

Rafalowicz (1978) in 'Dramaturgs in America: Eleven Statements', *Theater*, 10 (1): 15 – 30, at 27–9. These four stages (for the sake of a clear, logical argument in this chapter) will be separated and will follow a linear order; however, in reality, the working process is more organic, and these phases of the work overlap and sometimes happen simultaneously.

42 Marie Anezin (2016) 'L'Interview: Alain Platel', *Journal Ventilo*, 12 December. Translation by the author.
43 Platel, email message to author, 10 February 2017.
44 Alain Platel in Alain Platel and Hildegard De Vuyst, Interview by Katalin Trencsényi, 23 August 2016, Ghent.
45 Anezin, 'L'Interview: Alain Platel'.
46 Mélanie Lomoff, Interview by Katalin Trencsényi in Skype, 5 August 2016.
47 Lomoff, interview by Trencsényi, 5 August 2016.
48 Platel, in Platel and De Vuyst, interview by Trencsényi, 23 May 2016.
49 Mackrell, 'Horror That Started as a Joke'.
50 Platel, in Platel and De Vuyst, interview by Trencsényi, 23 May 2016.
51 Platel, in Platel and De Vuyst, interview by Trencsényi, 23 May 2016.
52 Lomoff, interview by Trencsényi, 5 August 2016.
53 Platel, in Platel and De Vuyst, interview by Trencsényi, 23 May 2016.
54 Anezin, 'L'Interview: Alain Platel'.
55 De Vuyst, in Platel and De Vuyst, interview by Trencsényi, 23 May 2016.
56 Alain Platel and Steven Prengels in Jan Vandenhouwe (2016) 'Music for a Broken World: A Conversation with Alain Platel and Steven Prengels on Mahler, Pygmy Music and Bach', les ballets C de la B, August. Available at www.lesballetscdela.be/en/projects/productions/nicht-schlafen/extra/text-jan-vandenhouwe (accessed 29 August 2019).
57 Steven Prengels, interview by Katalin Trencsényi, 23 August 2016, Ghent.
58 Prengels, interview by Trencsényi, 23 August 2016.
59 Prengels, interview by Trencsényi, 23 August 2016.
60 In *Wolf* (2003), it is Mozart. In *vsprs* (2006), it is Monteverdi's *Vespers for the Blessed Virgin*. In *pitié!* (2008), it is Bach's *Matthew's Passion*. In *C(H)ŒURS* (2012), it is Wagner and Verdi's choir music. In *tauberbach* (2014), inspiration is drawn from Artur Żmijewski's *Tauber Bach* (Bach's choral music sung by deaf people). In *En avant, marche!* (2015), it is marching brass-band music. And in *nicht schlafen* (2016), it is the symphonies of Mahler.
61 For instance, to counterbalance the strong and heavy music of Mahler and Bach in *nicht schlafen*, the breathing sounds of small, sleeping animals, recorded by artist K49814, were added to lighten up the soundcape.
62 The term 'sonorous dramaturgy' originates from Eugenio Barba; Eugenio Barba (2010) *On Directing and Dramaturgy: Burning the House*, London and New York: Routledge, 40–4. The term then was further developed by Kai-Chieh Tu, 'Sonorous Dramaturgy: Part I', *The Theatre Times*, 5 December 2016.
63 Platel in Vandenhouwe, 'Music for a Broken World'.
64 Platel in Vandenhouwe, 'Music for a Broken World'.
65 Russell Tshiebua, Interview by Katalin Trencsényi, 23 August 2016, Ghent.
66 Tshiebua, interview by Trencsényi, 23 August 2016.
67 Prengels, interview by Trencsényi, 23 August 2016.
68 Demuynck, email to author, 8 February 2017.
69 Demuynck, email to author, 8 February 2017.

70   Platel in Vandenhouwe, 'Music for a Broken World'.
71   Prengels, interview by Trencsényi, 23 August 2016.
72   De Vuyst, interview by Trencsényi on Skype, 10 May 2019.
73   More on the fixed and flowing elements of a performance, see Carroll, quoted in Katalin Trencsényi (2016) 'Storytellers: The Factory's Dramaturgy', *TDR/The Drama Review*, 60 (3): 39–63, at 56.
74   De Vuyst, in Platel and De Vuyst, interview by Trencsényi, 23 May 2016.
75   De Vuyst, in Platel and De Vuyst, interview by Trencsényi, 23 May 2016.
76   Platel, in Platel and De Vuyst, interview by Trencsényi, 23 May 2016.
77   Lomoff, interview by Trencsényi, 5 August 2016.
78   De Vuyst, in Platel and De Vuyst, interview by Trencsényi, 23 May 2016.
79   Platel, in Platel and De Vuyst, interview by Trencsényi, 23 August 2016.
80   Platel, in Platel and De Vuyst, interview by Trencsényi, 23 August 2016.
81   Platel, in Platel and De Vuyst, interview by Trencsényi, 23 May 2016.
82   De Vuyst, in Platel and De Vuyst, interview by Trencsényi, 23 May 2016.
83   Platel, in Platel and De Vuyst, interview by Trencsényi, 23 May 2016.
84   Platel, in Platel and De Vuyst, interview by Trencsényi, 23 May 2016.
85   Platel, in Platel and De Vuyst, interview by Trencsényi, 23 August 2016.
86   Platel, in Platel and De Vuyst, interview by Trencsényi, 23 August 2016.
87   De Vuyst, in Platel and De Vuyst, interview by Trencsényi, 23 August 2016.
88   Anezin, 'L'Interview: Alain Platel'.
89   De Vuyst, in Platel and De Vuyst, interview by Trencsényi, 23 May 2016.
90   De Vuyst, in Platel and De Vuyst, interview by Trencsényi 23 August 2016.
91   Eckersall, 'Dramaturgy as Ecology', 23–4.
92   B. K. S. Iyengar. (1988) *Yoga Vrksa: The Tree of Yoga*, edited by Daniel Rivers-Moore, Oxford: Fine Line Books., xii.
93   John Gribbin (1998) *In Search of Schrödinger's Cat: Quantum Physics and Reality*, London: Black Swan, 121.
94   Katalin Trencsényi (2016) 'Introduction: What Is the Point of Bandoneon?' in Raimund Hoghe, Ulli Weiss and Katalin Trencsényi (eds.), *Bandoneon: Working with Pina Bausch*, London: Oberon Books, 6–70, at 58.
95   Gribbin, *In Search of Schrödinger's Cat*, 160.
96   Christel Stalpaert (2014) 'The Distributive Agency of Dramaturgical Labour and the Ethics of Instability: Becoming the Outside Body, Implicated in the Life of Others', in Katharina Pewny, Johan Callens and Jeroen Coppens (eds.), *Dramaturgies in the New Millennium: Relationality, Performativity, and Potentiality*, Tübingen: Gunter Narr Verlag, 37–110.
97   Stalpaert, 'The Distributive Agency', 100.
98   Sandra Noeth (2011) 'Protocols of Encounter: On Dance Dramaturgy', in Gabriele Klein and Sandra Noeth (eds.), *Emerging Bodies: The Performance of Worldmaking in Dance and Choreography*, New Brunswick, NJ: Transaction Publishers, 247–56, at 253.
99   Noeth, 'Protocols of Encounter', 254.

References

Anezin, Marie (2016) 'L'Interview: Alain Platel', *Journal Ventilo*, 12 December.
Barba, Eugenio (2010) *On Directing and Dramaturgy: Burning the House*, London and New York: Routledge.

Bausch, Pina (2007) 'What Moves Me', a speech by Pina Bausch on the occasion of the Kyoto Prize award ceremony, The Pina Bausch Archive. www.pinabausch.org/en/pina/what-moves-me (accessed 29 August 2019).

Benjamin, Walter (1999) 'The Task of the Translator: An Introduction to the Translation of Baudelaire's *Tableaux Parisiens*', in *Illuminations*, London: Pimlico, 70–82. First published 1923.

Bleeker, Maaike (2003) 'Dramaturgy as a Mode of Looking', *Women and Performance: A Journal of Feminist Theory*, 13:2 (26): 163–72.

Brecht, Bertolt (2002) *The Messingkauf Dialogues*, trans. John Willett, London: Methuen. First published 1963.

De Lahunta, Scott (2000) 'Dance Dramaturgy: Speculations and Reflections', *Dance Theatre Journal*, 16 (1): 20–5.

De Vuyst, Hildegard (2010) Interview by Katalin Trencsényi, 25 November, Brussels.

De Vuyst, Hildegard (2012) Interview by Jake Orr, 1 June, London.

De Vuyst, Hildegard (2019) Interview by Katalin Trencsényi on Skype, 10 May 2019.

Etchells, Tim (2009) 'Doing Time', *Performance Research*, 14 (3): 71–80.

Eckersall, Peter, Paul Monaghan and Melanie Beddie (2014) 'Dramaturgy as Ecology: A Report from the Dramaturgies Project', in Katalin Trencsényi and Bernadette Cochrane (eds.), *New Dramaturgy: International Perspectives on Theory and Practice*, London: Bloomsbury Methuen Drama, 18–35.

Gribbin, John (1998) *In Search of Schrödinger's Cat: Quantum Physics and Reality*. London: Black Swan.

Iyengar, B. K. S. (1988) *Yoga Vrksa: The Tree of Yoga*, edited by Daniel Rivers-Moore, Oxford: Fine Line Books.

Knowles, Ric (2011) 'Calling off the Border Patrol: Intercultural Dramaturgy in Toronto', in Ramón Rivera-Servera and Harvey Young (eds.), *Performance in the Borderlands*, Basingstoke: Palgrave Macmillan, 161–81.

Lomoff, Mélanie (2016) Interview by Katalin Trencsényi on Skype, 5 August.

Mackrell, Judith (1999) 'Horror That Started as a Joke', *The Guardian*, 7 December.

Noeth, Sandra (2011) 'Protocols of Encounter: On Dance Dramaturgy', in Gabriele Klein and Sandra Noeth (eds.), *Emerging Bodies: The Performance of Worldmaking in Dance and Choreography*, New Brunswick, NJ: Transaction Publishers, 247–56.

Peeters, Jeroen (2010) 'Heterogenous Dramaturgies', *Maska*, 1 September. Available at http://sarma.be/docs/1325 (accessed 19 August 2019).

Platel, Alain (2006) 'Conversation with Hildegard De Vuyst', in Hildegard De Vuyst (ed.), *les ballets C de la B*, Tielt: Lannoo, 134–6.

Platel, Alain and Hildegard De Vuyst (2016) Interview by Katalin Trencsényi, 23 May, Ghent.

Platel, Alain and Hildegard De Vuyst (2016) Interview by Katalin Trencsényi, 23 August, Ghent.

Prengels, Steven (2016) Interview by Katalin Trencsényi, 23 August, Ghent.

Profeta, Katherine (2015) *Dramaturgy in Motion: At Work on Dance and Movement Performance*, Madison, Wisc.: The University of Wisconsin Press.

Rafalowicz, Mira (1978) 'Dramaturg in Collaboration with Joseph Chaikin, New York' in Jonathan Alper, Andre Bishop, Oscar Brownstein, Ann Cattaneo, Barbara Field, John Lahr, Steve Lawson, Jonathan Marks, Bonnie Marranca, Mira Rafalowicz, Douglas Wager, 'Dramaturgs in America: Eleven Statements', *Theater*, 10 (1): 15–30, at 27–9.

Roy, Sanjoy (2010) 'Step-by-Step Guide to Dance: les ballets C de la B', *The Guardian*, 5 May.

Stalpaert, Christel (2014) 'The Distributive Agency of Dramaturgical Labour and the Ethics of Instability: Becoming the Outside Body, Implicated in the Life of Others', in Katharina Pewny, Johan Callens and Jeroen Coppens (eds.), *Dramaturgies in the New Millennium: Relationality, Performativity and Potentiality*, Tübingen: Gunter Narr Verlag, 97–110.

T'Jonck, Pieter (2016) 'Contemporary Dance from Flanders (1980–2016)', *Contemporary Dance from Flanders*. Available at http://dossiers.kunsten.be/dance/contemporary-dance-flanders-1980-2016 (accessed 19 August 2019).

Trencsényi, Katalin (2015) *Dramaturgy in the Making: A User's Guide for Theatre Professionals*, London: Bloomsbury Methuen Drama.

Trencsényi, Katalin (2016) 'Introduction: What Is the Point of Bandoneon?' in Raimund Hoghe, Ulli Weiss and Katalin Trencsényi (eds.), *Bandoneon: Working with Pina Bausch*, trans. Penny Black, London: Oberon Books, 6–70.

Trencsényi, Katalin (2016) 'Storytellers: The Factory's Dramaturgy', *TDR/The Drama Review*, 60 (3): 39–63.

Tshiebua, Russell (2016) Interview by Katalin Trencsényi, 23 August, Ghent.

Tu, Kai-Chieh (2016) 'Sonorous Dramaturgy, Part I', *The Theatre Times*, 5 December. Available at https://thetheatretimes.com/sonorous-dramaturgy-part-i (accessed 29 August 2019).

Vandenhouwe, Jan (2016) 'Music for a Broken World: A Conversation with Alain Platel and Steven Prengels on Mahler, Pygmy Music and Bach', les ballets C de la B, August. Available at www.lesballetscdela.be/en/projects/productions/nicht-schlafen/extra/text-jan-vandenhouwe (accessed 29 August 2019).

Van Imschoot, Myriam (2003) 'Anxious Dramaturgy', *Women and Performance: A Journal of Feminist Theory*, 13:2 (26): 57–68.

Van Kerkhoven, Marianne (1994) 'On Dramaturgy'. *Theaterschrift*, 5–6: 9–35.

Van Kerkhoven, Marianne (1994) 'The Theatre Is in the City and the City Is in the World and Its Walls Are of Skin', State of the Union Speech at the 1994 Theatre Festival, Brussels. Available in English translation at http://sarma.be/docs/3229 (accessed 19 August 2019).

Van Kerkhoven, Marianne (1999) 'Van de kleine en de grote dramaturgie: Pleidooi voor een "interlocuteur"', *Etcetera*, 68 (17): 67–9.

4

Alain Wins a Prize

Hildegard De Vuyst

Figure 4.1 Hildegard De Vuyst in Teatro Comunale di Ferrara, during tour of *Badke*, 2016. © Samaa Wakeem.

This text is a historical document, a speech on the occasion of the seventh Prix Europe Nouvelles Théâtrales that was awarded to Alain Platel in Taormina (Italy) on 8 April 2001. It observes how les ballets C de la B arose out of the wasteland of a non-existing contemporary dance landscape in 1984, and how it experienced its international breakthrough only in 1993 with Bonjour madame, comment allez-vous aujourd'hui, il fait beau, il va sans doute pleuvoir, etcetera.

Nothing about this Mr Platel is what it seems. Who would suspect that behind the French-sounding first name Alain and surname Platel one would find a Flemish man from Ghent? A giant of the international dance world? I have seen him dance at a party once or twice. But I haven't seen him create a choreography for the past five years. Ah, so he's a director! But all the material comes from his actors, or his dancers. Or at least that's what he himself says. And what are we to think of the flag his company sails under: les ballets C de la B, which stands for Les Ballets Contemporains de la Belgique, which doesn't dance ballet, let alone contemporary ballet, and isn't a Belgian institution either. What has he done to deserve this prize? Has this shady character created a repertoire that future generations can get their teeth into? Has he devised a new formal language in dance or theatre, launched new working processes that will fuel generations to come? Has he established a solid institute, mobilized a well-oiled ensemble? In short, has he done anything that will stand the test of time? No. And yet I am still glad he has received a prize.

Company

We know about the heroic beginnings. Nineteen eighty-four. Anne Teresa De Keersmaeker, Jan Fabre and others exposed the wasteland of dance in Flanders. All at once everyone imagined they were a dancer. It wasn't very long after punk, when you only had to know two chords. It was enough to bash about on an oil drum. In Ghent, the collective Les Ballets Contemporains de la Belgique was set up. Amateurs. Friends. Acquaintances. With a desire to do something. As volunteers, after work in the evening. Some members put their own money into the collective, if they had any. Others worked with an exemption from signing on. The curious concoctions of folklore and performance art soon found several fanatical backers. With varying success until 1991, but then Platel left. The collective was based too much on his input. By looking for other settings to work in, he obliged the other members to take action in their own right. In addition, he felt the need to broaden his horizons and gain professional experience (Speeltheater, LOD, Nieuwpoorttheater, Victoria). Hans Van den Broeck took his place, and later Koen Augustijnen and Christine De Smedt too. Les ballets became a pool of choreographers who each followed their own course.

In 1993, Platel had his international breakthrough with *Bonjour madame*. A large group to work with (nine men and one woman), the first scraps of baroque music (at that point still on cassettes), the mixing of children and adults, amateurs and professionals, the plastic bags. A first taste of the powerful style he was later to develop, alternately with les ballets and the Victoria youth theatre company in

Ghent, and alternately alone and in a duo with the writer Arne Sierens. His six productions in six years (for the sake of convenience I'm not mentioning Sierens' fantastic play *Mouchette*, directing amateurs from the village where he was born) make up a consistent oeuvre that roughly speaking comprises two trilogies. *Moeder en Kind*, *Bernadetje* and *Allemaal Indiaan* are about the family as a private biotope from which to break free, and *Bonjour madame*, *La Tristeza Complice* and *Iets op Bach* dealt with semi-public biotopes where stories converge.

What followed was a dramatic turn: Platel announced that he would quit. I suspect that he had to call a halt to the whole international circus in order to regain his sense of need as a theatre-maker. So as not to get stuck on the treadmill or regurgitate the same methods. To recharge his batteries, so as not to become fossilized. In the meantime, the pressure on the available resources at les ballets increased. When more requests to make productions came from such as Sam Louwyck, Ghani Minne Vosteen, Sidi Larbi Cherkaoui et al., it was a matter of pushing and shoving for a place. Les ballets increasingly looked like a production company, a dovecote where one laid one's egg. Another dramatic turn: although Platel stopped making productions, he took up the post of artistic director of les ballets for the first time. Together with his chums, he drew a line under the past, under the accomplishments and privileges. All the choreographers left the organization. Les ballets rethought and redefined itself on the basis of a deep-rooted desire for anarchy. The question that most occupied Platel was not 'How do we rake in as much as possible, how do we keep as much as possible for ourselves?' but 'How can we loosen things up again?' In my view, he should receive this theatre prize for this reason alone, because he consistently refused to become an institution.

If not that, what?

At first sight, he does very little as a director and choreographer. It looks as if his creations emerge from his own mind only to a very limited extent. Little has been established by the time rehearsals start – there is no plan. He's always embarrassed about it. There is of course always a lot more, one hopes and suspects, but Platel deliberately withdraws to leave room for the unexpected and the uncontrived. He guards against giving his fantasies away too early. He first lets things come, elicits, angles for what the dancers absolutely want to say. So the substance of the productions derives from the dancers and/or actors. Let us be clear: this method is not new. The way the performer's own personality penetrates the production, with their history, all their baggage, is now as old as the hills. Just think of his great love, Pina Bausch; she too is already over sixty.

What is more, this freedom the performer has must also be qualified; Platel is subtly and summarily manipulative. But there has to be more than this, because there are numerous imitators (from improvisation to montage/collage) who adopt roughly the same methods but who are far beneath him in stature. It's a small distinction that makes a world of difference. He is truly interested in the other; he puts his trust in people (you don't have to try to gain it), gives them freedom (and therefore the accompanying responsibility), does not judge (or at least not too quickly), is not bothered about stylistic purity nor bad taste, throws nothing away and lets time work to his advantage. He stimulates (so that people transcend themselves; many give their best performances under Platel) and lastly takes final responsibility for the ultimate result. Even though he often says that in the course of the process he doesn't know where he's going, you nevertheless feel that with him your material is in good hands.

Although this autonomy of the performer is in part mythologized in the production, it is no less real. In the sense that no one avoids the question 'What do you really want to do?' If you were now given the one chance in your life to do what you want to do, what would you do? And this question acts as a slow poison that permeates far beyond the performance. You constantly confront yourself with your responsibility for your own life. In this sense it is not abnormal that so many ex-Platel dancers do their own productions. (I'm not saying anything about their quality.) Even those in auxiliary positions such as the technicians, the promotional staff, the tour manager and so on do not escape this confrontation. Life will never be the same again. There is no way back. In my view, Platel should receive this theatre prize for this reason alone, because he consistently refuses to be the great watchmaker who has the cogs perfectly under control: le prix des Nouvelles Transformations Vitales.

Nouvelles Réalités Théâtrales

And then there's the work itself. There are so many clichés about the productions that we are fed up with them. 'The street put on stage.' A slice of life. Misunderstandings. People probably say it's the simultaneity of contradictory information. Clashing worlds. Children/adults. Amateurs/professionals. It is never either/or. Platel's world is not neatly divided into sheep and wolves; a man is also a woman, and nothing can ever be only beautiful. He embraces the contrasts and brings extremes together. And/and. At the same time. There is no winner or loser in this, let alone any notion of reconciliation. (This is the clash, the sustained conflict as an inexhaustible source of wealth; if the story does after all have to have a moral, and this for someone who prefers to avoid conflict.) So this is what one calls vibrating life, the street, reality. However, it is not realism but at best hyperrealism or magic realism or something else. In any case it is a lie. But it is composed and given rhythm, structured and transformed in such a way that we recognize reality in it better than in reality itself. What is remarkable is that Platel is receiving this theatre prize for innovation, whereas as far as I'm concerned it's not a matter of anything new. My assertion here is that what Platel does is not a beginning but an ending. It is a synthesis of the two most important movements in the living arts of the twentieth century: Brecht (reflection, critique, detachment, politics, commitment) and Artaud (physical, subconscious, hysteria, madness, visceral). Platel has had no training in theatre or dance. Initially he did not even have any professional ambitions in the disciplines of dance or theatre. It makes you think when someone who had never heard of Brecht or Artaud brings about this synthesis.

And yet Platel is also consciously engaged in Nouvelles Réalités Théâtrales. They are not to be found in his productions but in the responsibility he takes with regard to the dance world. When he began, there was hardly any frame of reference; of all the major Flemish contemporary choreographers (De Keersmaeker, Vandekeybus, Fabre, Platel), only one had any training in dance. There was no old guard to be swept aside. But in the meantime they have in their turn become points of reference, the old guard to be eliminated (which in Platel's case is particularly difficult because he is rarely authoritarian). So the standard that newcomers in Flanders currently have to match is exceptionally high. To this is added the extreme commercialization and the pressure of the market: as a result of which the new cannot simply present itself; it has to be produced, formatted and marketed – the danger being that young people are immediately picked up by theatre directors and immediately dumped again after the first disappointment, with the result that they are soon worn out. The luxury of messing around for ten years as Platel did in the 1980s is no longer possible. (And it was messing around, believe me.) But remember: young artists are not the victims of a perverse system but want nowadays to conquer the market as quickly as possible, get to the front of the pack, cash on the nail.

Here's a brief quote from Platel:

> It may have something to do with my Catholic upbringing, but restrictions and obstacles can be useful when you want to achieve something. In that way you get to know your personal motivation. After almost ten years of work, people brought me to the attention of the authorities and after that I received a subsidy. But in those first ten years I was able to try out a whole lot of things. Too much support for new initiatives shifts it towards the material aspect.

This is why the question that currently occupies him the most is 'How do you give yourself room again without going back to the past?' How can you offer alternative or subversive formats to stand up to the pressure of the market? As far as I am concerned, this theatre prize should be given to Platel for this reason alone, not for the Nouvelles Réalités Théâtrales of the past, but those of the future.

Part Two

Emotions

5

Being Alone Together

Alain Platel and the 'Disturbance of Violent Relatedness' in *La Tristeza Complice* (1995), *pitié!* (2008) and *tauberbach* (2014)

Ann Cooper Albright

The space is strewn with piles of clothing, creating a crazy-quilt mix of bright colours, whites and darks. The reds, orange and bright blues stand out of the random collage of fabric that resembles a field of wildflowers. Despite its brilliant visual texture, however, the setting itself seems claustrophobic, a *huis-clos* where time is meaningless since no one is going anywhere anytime soon. It is a place where waiting has become such a part of being in the world that no one remembers what they are waiting for. A woman walks around, mumbling to herself as she moves through her garden of cast-off shirts and pants. Abruptly she stops, galvanized by an internal obsession. 'Must stay in control!' she shouts to no one in particular before going back to her sorting and resorting.

The space is littered with cast-off clothing and blankets, a crazy-quilt assortment of fabric strung up from building to tree and back. Most of the clothing is faded, but a bright red or yellow flashes like poppies on the edge of a highway. The setting feels claustrophobic – this narrow lane squeezed between one building and another, a place where waiting has become a way of life and decisions (when to leave, where to go) impossible. A woman moves nervously around, looking for something she has lost, muttering to herself. She freezes for a moment, listening and attentive to the possibility of danger, but then resumes her search.

These two descriptions of scenarios are almost identical; and yet one is a staged production, the opening scene from *tauberbach*, a 2014 production by Alain Platel and les ballets C de la B, and the other occurred just a few months ago right outside a friend's apartment building in Athens, Greece. The parallels were striking, but their implications diverge significantly. After all, one is a theatrical representation and the other carries the weight of real life. Nonetheless, they both insist on a reckoning with the forces of fate and implicate us in questions of individual agency and the social conditions that shape our world today. Whether onstage or in the street, it is challenging to watch this disintegration of life yet hard to turn away.

Staging the intersections of life and art

In the three decades that Alain Platel has been creating movement-theatre pieces with his artistic collaborators in les ballets C de la B, he has forged a reputation for crafting a 'poor theatre' (his term) in which performers evoke misfits, outcasts and the mad who either ramble aimlessly around the stage or propel themselves here and there in violent fits and starts. Often they fight, scratch and claw one another before returning to a distracted, vaguely catatonic state. Depending on their aesthetic proclivities, critics have either lauded Platel's creations as essential reflections on the human condition or wondered why on earth he insists on staging the 'everyday dramaturgy' of social dysfunction that we can often see on the street just outside our window. It is true that in much of his work performative virtuosity seems to be defined by surviving rather than thriving in the midst of the physical and psychic challenges built into les ballets C de la B's ninety-minute theatrical extravaganzas. Even the most laudatory reviews underline the sense of exhaustion in the audience as well as the performers by the end of the show.

I am interested in the space between what some critics describe as a 'being subjected to' and what others see as 'emotional truths' in these performances. In the writing that follows, I address this particular conjunction of theatrical representation and kinaesthetic experience across several of Platel's major theatrical projects. Although my examples are not meant to be encyclopaedic or exhaustive, I believe that they do point to themes that thread throughout his two decades of work with les ballets C de la B. But first, let us return to the two scenes with which I began this chapter to comprehend both the mutual aesthetic influences, as well as critical differences, between life and art. *Tauberbach* was inspired, according to Platel, by a Brazilian documentary about a woman who chose to live by a dump next to one of the favelas in Rio de Janeiro. Perhaps this sensibility of individual will in the midst of difficult circumstances accounts for the intriguing sense of personal agency that the actress, Elsie de Brauw, exhibits as she moseys around the stage, picking up a vest here, trying on a shirt over there and sorting through various articles of clothing, occasionally finding a treasure within (look, a hairbrush!). With a certain understated bravado, this queen of the dump has adapted admiringly to her circumstances. She seems completely unfazed by the appearance and disappearance of the other members of the cast, who grow from the layers of discarded clothing like carnivorous plants sprouting out of some fertile soil, periodically wilting back down into the piles of multicoloured fabric. Her mumblings maintain a low background frequency that erupts from time to time into a full-blown hysterical fit.

The first time this outburst occurs is when she arrives downstage in front of a mike hanging from the rafters. Her language becomes increasingly urgent as her voice spills into her body in waves of spasms. In this moment, words leave the realm of meaning and become the current of energy that floods her voice as it expands to highs and lows and eventually opens up into a loud and sustained guttural sound. At this point in the performance, she is joined by the off-stage male voice (considerably distorted), and they blend together in a kind of bizarre harmony, a duet of vocal dissonance that carries at the same time a slight edge of competition. The sounds emitted are not harmonious in the classical sense, but they do suggest a vocal togetherness that is echoed later in the sound score, which was based on recordings of deaf people singing Bach. Emotionally spent and pissed off, the central character suddenly slams the mike suspended in front of her and immediately the orchestra begins to play.

Much has been made of Platel's compelling and frequently ironic use of classical music (often baroque) in his avant-garde productions. Even when the music is transposed onto more contemporary instruments, the tempered classical style provides an aural backdrop that helps to mitigate the interpersonal tensions that develop within each piece. *Tauberbach* is a telling example of Platel's and his musical director's (in this case, Steven Prengels') use of music to pull the performance back from the brink of chaos. Time and time again, as events erupt onstage or situations unravel and everyone goes off in their own direction, the musical accompaniment asserts itself not to comment on, nor to reinforce the action (or distraction) onstage, but rather to simply assert the existence of a parallel universe. It is similar to how a sunset can be stunningly beautiful, even if you have just heard some terrible news.

The musical accompaniment is just one of the obvious differences between stage and life; smell is another. Even if *tauberbach* has some grounding in real life, its consequences are radically different than the scene that took place outside of my friend's apartment over the course of a long month in the early spring of 2017. When the Congolese immigrant first took up residence outside of her apartment building, my friend (who lives on the first floor but works in another city during the week) offered him hot soup and several blankets. Others in her Exarchia neighbourhood (known for its socialist, not to mention anarchistic, tendencies) did the same. As time passed, however, his affairs (literally and figuratively) began to spread out until he was taking up a good portion of their block. Eventually, he was joined by another refugee, a woman from Eastern Europe (possibly Polish or Romanian), whom he (reportedly) began to pimp in the local square. In addition to the stench of human waste, there were intense middle-of-the-night episodes capped by scenes of violence, her crying and wailing, his yelling, and neighbours complaining. My friend felt increasingly helpless about the situation. It got to the point where she could not open her front windows and took to walking around the block the other way to avoid the worst of the smells and street debris. Two days before I showed up to visit, the street squatters left, and the folks on the block took up a collection to pay another immigrant, an Albanian woman, to clean up the mess with a good dose of chlorine.

These scenes of survival and displacement – of being alone together – provide the contemporary background for some of Platel's dramaturgy, but, as the above examples demonstrate, they are not equivalent. A whole lot more is at stake when the lives of real, dispossessed people are implicated. If we are not to assume, as one reviewer does, that Platel is just cashing in on the latest fad of politically correct poverty porn, we need to unpack more thoroughly the confluence of life and body, gesture and performance, representation and experience at stake in his work. That is to say that we need to attend to the multiple levels of meaning, both symbolic and kinaesthetic, that intertwine, creating what Hans-Thies Lehmann (quoting Jean-François Lyotard) describes as 'energetic theatre': 'This would be a theatre not of meaning but of forces, intensities, present affects ... Energetic theatre would be theatre beyond representation – meaning, of course, not simply without representation, but not governed by its logic.'[1]

Ways of seeing

One of the best descriptions of how this kind of 'energetic theatre' operates on the level of bodies – those of the performers as well as those of the audience members – comes, ironically, from an art historian. In an extraordinarily profound and poetic short essay on Rembrandt's paintings, art critic John Berger traces the differences between the artist's drawings and his paintings, particularly the late portraits. Whereas in his drawings Rembrandt is a master of proportion, in his paintings this realistic perspective is radically altered. Berger asks, 'Why in his paintings did he forget – or ignore – what he could do with such mastery in his drawings?' Alluding to the historical context of Rembrandt's time, Berger suggests, 'He grew old in a climate of economic fanaticism and indifference – not dissimilar to the climate of the period we are living through. The human could no longer simply be copied … the human was no longer self-evident; it had to be found in the darkness.'[2]

Berger searches for a particular language to address what is not directly visible in Rembrandt's painting and postulates that 'something else – something antithetical to "real" space must have interested him more.'[3] Vital yet elusive, palpable yet not immediately visible, this 'something else' present in Rembrandt's work is defined by Berger as a 'corporeal space'. By distorting a part or parts of the bodies he was painting, Rembrandt was able to give them what Berger calls a 'special power of narration'. Tellingly, this corporeal space is incompatible with architectural, measured space. It is connected to energy, not geometric lines. Berger writes, 'corporeal space is continually changing its measures and focal centres, according to circumstances. It measures by waves, not metres. Hence its necessary dislocations of "real" space.'[4]

In order to give his readers a sense of the different orientations of this corporeal space, Berger charges us to 'leave the museum' and go the emergency room of a hospital. It is there, Berger insists, that we will find

> [t]he space of each sentient body's awareness of itself. It is not boundless like subjective space: it is always finally bound by the laws of the body, but its landmarks, its emphasis, its inner proportions are continually changing. Pain sharpens our awareness of such space. It is the space of our first vulnerability and solitude. Also of disease. But it is also, potentially, the space of pleasure, well-being and the sensation of being loved.[5]

For Berger, this corporeal space can be felt by touch more clearly than it can be seen by sight, which is why it is the space that caring nurses occupy more often than (rationally) diagnosing doctors. '[O]n each mattress, within each patient, it takes a different form.'[6]

I am intrigued by Berger's notion of a corporeal space, as it requires another 'way of seeing' to register its potency. In the context of Alain Platel's work, I want to explore how this corporeal space prioritizes touch and feeling rather than seeing, shifting the traditional subject–object dynamic of these performative exchanges. I believe that it is significant that Platel uses these exact terms ('touch' and 'feeling' rather than vision and awe) to talk about the audience's reception of the extreme physicality in the performances of les ballets C de la B. Of course, I am talking not only about the social and political implications of the relationship between performers and audience members or apartment dwellers and street squatters but also of the complex connections between one's self and an 'other'.

Many people have commented on Platel's obsession with representing marginalized figures in our society, what Renate Klett describes as 'losers in a world of winners'. While one writer positions Platel as belonging to 'a generation of European theatre-makers who believe the big issues and emotions of the "human condition" can just as easily be evoked and portrayed through the "ordinary" life of "everyday" people', another labels one performance 'a senseless spectacle of revolting regression'.[7] Clearly there is something in Platel's work that gets under people's skin. To understand how and why this is the case, we need to shift from our usual focus on the performers' mimetic characterization, attending instead to the energetic currency of their corporealities. I define corporeality here as an intertwining of sensation and perception where the body remains anchored as the central scope of awareness. With this in mind, I want to propose that Platel is less interested in the representation of these 'misfits' (authentic or not) and more interested in sharing with his audiences the somatic dimensions of their idiosyncratic and physical experiencing of the world. This shift in theatrical framing insists that we in the audience also change how we attend to the actions onstage. I argue that we need to give up our desire to see a coherent narrative or theatrical development and instead allow ourselves to be moved – both literally and figuratively – by their situation.

From spectator to witness

My discussion of audience reception of Platel's work hinges on the reverberations of that last word, 'moved' – the meaning of which splits across the psychic and physical to encompass both an emotional and a visceral responsiveness to the world. There is, I believe, something very vital in both *La Tristeza Complice* (1995) and *pitié!* (2008) that leads the audience from passive spectators into the role of active witnesses, raising the stakes of our viewing experience. Being moved by a performance represents an intertwining of somatic feeling and political urgency that characterizes these works. As I have argued in another context, to witness a performance suggests a response-ability, which includes both an ability to respond to the events onstage and a sense of being implicated in their outcome.[8] In what follows, I explore the ways in which Platel's devised movement-theatre structures an affective relationship with the audience that engages neither a direct psychological identification with the protagonist(s) onstage nor a conventional notion of physical empathy but rather prioritizes other kinds of exchanges, bringing attention to corporeality as encompassing somatic embodiment as well as cultural representation.

In order to use corporeality as a category of reception, it is crucial to think beyond the most obvious dramaturgies of vision, text and music and describe a kinetic texture that affects the audience's bodily sensibility. That is to say, we need to learn to appreciate the elusive contours of somatic meaning. Although embodiment is enjoying a renaissance in contemporary cultural theory these days, it is most often elided with

Figure 5.1 Rosalba Torres Guerrero (left) and from the bottom to the top (right): Mathieu Desseigne Ravel, Emile Josse, Elie Tass and Lisi Estaras in *pitié!*, 2008. © Chris Van der Burght.

discussions of affect. I want to resist this well-trodden path, however, and branch off into a territory that is not as clearly charted by conceptualizing feeling as the practice of sensing (I am feeling) rather than the object of possession (I have feelings). Keeping the verb fully active without letting it settle into the stable structure of a noun not only helps us to resist the psychological construction of an interior self so endemic to discourses of affect but also disrupts any easy equation of physical corporeality with social identity.

In his survey of contemporary theatre practices, *Postdramatic Theatre*, Hans-Thies Lehmann maps out the contours of an international range of contemporary performance work that both confuses and refuses any simple distinctions between theatre as strictly focused on a text and dance as movement-based performance. Throughout his book, Lehmann catalogues the many aesthetic and ideological differences between mimetic dramas, where the script is the clear priority for the staging and more experimental productions in which the frame of realistic representation is disrupted. 'Wholeness, illusion, and world representation are inherent in the model "drama"; conversely, through its very form, dramatic theatre proclaims wholeness as the model of the real.'[9] One of the major differences that Lehmann outlines in his survey is the difference for the audience between the experience of watching a traditional narrative in which the final scene almost always stages a resolution before 'the end' of the script and that of witnessing the multilayered, often conflicting and unresolvable aspects of much contemporary performance work. While his discussion of these performance elements is descriptive rather than prescriptive, Lehmann insists that there is a fundamentally different audience dynamic within postdramatic theatre. This is not just a question of a new style of staging but rather a new conception of what constitutes the performance experience. He writes, 'it becomes more presence than representation, more shared than communicated experience, more process than product, more manifestation than signification, more energetic impulse than information.'[10]

Within the context of Platel's work, this corporeal presence circulates between the bodies onstage and those in the audience; but those relationships of power and exchange are rarely predictable. This is not to suggest, however, that they are entirely subjective either. Audience members and performers can share the process of feeling together without necessarily imbuing that experience with the same meaning. My task here is to incorporate a critic's sensibility within a theoretical inquiry such that I both describe onstage events and conceptualize their impact without assuming a normative, universal audience reaction or a completely random series of individual responses. Corporeality brings our attention to a heightened receptivity that is never only intellectual or even strictly emotional but is also always rooted in a bodily awareness. The performative situations set up by les ballets C de la B are compelling, but not easily digested or articulated. Thus, Renate Klett suggests:

> Platel's universe of filth and glory can't be recounted, only *experienced*. It needs the climate, the music, the sweat. It needs eyes filled with dance and desperation, or someone cowering on a railing eating an apple. Every triumph can plunge into disaster, and every limit can teach one how to fly.[11]

Even though the scenes are chaotic and the action is more often than not intense, I think it is worthwhile to actually do a close reading of what transpires onstage in order to comprehend more fully the ambiguous and inter-corporeal nature of Platel's theatrical worlds.

Sharing sorrows

The lights brighten on a single man in the centre of the stage. He is playing a little ditty on a plastic recorder, the kind they hand out in elementary schools. Finished, he drops the instrument, and a series of twitches overtake his previously calm demeanour. His face zips to one side, his arms jut out to the other. The spasms spread through his torso like Tourette's syndrome on speed. An adolescent boy enters to face him, trying to hold onto his hand as it flops on the end of his increasingly spastic arm. After several attempts, the boy succeeds in grabbing an arm and with the force of his whole weight manages to calm first one arm and then the other. He reaches towards the man's face, holds onto it and waits for his touch to penetrate underneath the nervous twitches. It is a sweet moment of transformation, an inverted gesture of maternal care, as his tactile attention to the man smooths his erratic behaviour. Moments later, however, the boy walks over to the man again and wallops his backside with his foot, jumpstarting the twitches all over again.

Thus begins *La Tristeza Complice*, an early production (1995) that set the tone for much of les ballets C de la B's international reputation. The title is most often translated as 'the shared sorrow'. Set in a waiting area with plastic chairs around the perimeter and scaffolding on one side, *La Tristeza Complice* features the peculiar neurosis or individual despair of each vagrant character as they enter the space one by one. We see a crazed man in his underwear careening through the space on one roller blade, at times gliding gracefully and at other times limping around the stage. Then there enters the tall, lanky (not very convincing) drag queen who is precariously balanced on her heels as she fights off the taunts and abuse of the two boys circling her like angry bees. More characters enter the fray, including a singer who is dressed in an old-fashioned black skirt and buttoned-up shirt, and whose soprano voice punctuates the performative angst with operatic airs of loss and love. Then there is the rope and noose dangling from one corner, triggering unpleasant premonitions of events to come.

Much of the time, these awkward characters try their best to show off, frantically performing one trick after another in a desperate attempt to impress the spectators,

Figure 5.2 *La Tristeza Complice*, 1995. © Chris Van der Burght.

including everyone standing around onstage. For instance, there is the snake charmer who descends dramatically from a rope to perform a mesmerizing sequence of transformations with a small rug. This magic carpet first helps him fly around the stage and then becomes a matador's cape which he deftly manipulates in a series of grandiose gestures that are, frankly, impressive and entertaining. The audience laughs, relieved that they can enjoy this virtuosic display of fluid movement and bodily ease. Soon, the rug becomes a skirt as this figure ventures downstage and begins to vamp for the audience with a shimmy here and a seductive look there. But this is a fleeting moment of pleasure, as are all the displays of physical virtuosity. Acrobatics, club dancing (including a weirdly spastic style of voguing) and circus tricks usually devolve into crazy rants whose words are important less for their literal meaning and more a vocalization of a psychic state of disorientation. It is not what they say that is important (mostly they are swearing in several different languages) but rather how they voice their struggles that matters. Most often in *La Tristeza Complice*, the human voice carries the emotional intensity that can be strikingly absent from the disconnected bodies. A reviewer of the September 1995 premiere in Ghent, Belgium, offers the following observation:

> Contrast, opposites, dissonances: these are the key words for a choreographer who couldn't care less for streamlined, harmonious structures. Platel's creations have neither a middle point nor a high point. On the contrary, they invariably fluctuate between extreme rowdiness and utmost apathy. *La Tristeza Complice* looks the most like a ramshackle, jolting roundabout of more or less crippled characters. Crippled, because every dancer, though each in a highly individual idiom, shows the daily insanity of a degenerate, hostile, intolerant or, in one word, ugly world.[12]

Towards the end of *La Tristeza Complice*, there are two existential solos. First the dragqueen figure and then one of the women come onstage by themselves. They both seem lost and at a loss. This feeling comes from the fact that they turn, take a few steps, then turn again, but never seem to arrive anywhere satisfactory. Each gesture begins with a moment of energy, a sense of hope (maybe this time ...), but inevitably their arms fall limply to their sides. In the woman's solo, her legs similarly lose energy, buckling underneath her like a young colt's limbs. She gets up, takes a few steps, and they give out again. But this is not the cheerful children's story of the little train who tried and tried and finally succeeded. It is not clear if these figures are completely apathetic or if they have simply tried and failed too often to even bother to commit themselves to making the effort any more. What I find disconcerting in this moment is the fact that these solos never develop, neither person achieves anything close to redemption or realization, and they limp off-stage leaving the audience in a state of animated suspension, waiting for a resolution that never comes. Once again, John Berger's words are surprisingly apt. In the midst of a discussion of the late eighteenth-century artist Géricault's painting, Berger writes:

> Anyone who has been beside a friend beginning to fall into madness will recognize this sense of being forced to become an audience. What one sees at first on the stage

is a man or a woman alone, and beside them – like a phantom – the inadequacy of all given explanations to explain the everyday pain being suffered. Then he or she approaches the phantom and confronts the terrible space existing between spoken words and what they are meant to mean. In fact, this space, this vacuum is the pain. And finally, because like nature it abhors a vacuum, madness rushes in and fills the space and there is no longer any distinction between stage and world, playing and suffering.[13]

In *La Tristeza Complice*, the audience is forced to witness how representation (including the safe distinctions between reality and the stage) becomes evacuated – how the physical components of madness or dysfunction or alienation affectively take over the performers until the spaces between doing and being collapse.

During an interview about the making of *La Tristeza Complice*, Platel comments, 'Here we're involved with the noise, the imperfect, the hesitation.'[14] I would add to that list a deep sense of existential dis-connection, a 'being alone together' as the project's press release suggests. In this theatrical no-person's land, interpersonal connection inevitably morphs into confrontation (for instance, that first scene between the man and the boy) as the performers ride the edge between aggression and empathy. In one section, the drag-queen figure repeatedly attacks a woman's body with his mouth. There is a striking moment when he grabs her hair and pulls it off. It takes the audience a second to register that it was a wig, that this is theatre and that we did not just witness a violent scalping. Pulling and picking at her skin and her clothing, he seems at once

Figure 5.3 Koen Augustijnen and Ronald Burchi in *La Tristeza Complice*, 1995. © Chris Van der Burght

abusive and yet also desirous of becoming her. Watching a white man touch a black woman in such an abusive and insistent manner is very difficult to witness because of the racial and sexual politics implicated in this scenario. Nonetheless, these politics are complicated by the fact that this man was wearing a bra and lipstick as well as the fact that he had earlier been the object of sexual harassment by other men. In addition, the woman endures the whole event while doggedly singing a slow folk ballad. This sense of ambiguity between love and hate, desire and rejection, is always implicit in each contact, each touch between the characters onstage.

In the midst of all this loneliness, however, there are several extraordinary moments of physical communion – a dancing or singing together – that functions as a group lamentation, pulling the cast together despite their separate circumstances. This enactment of their 'shared sorrow' echoes the musical melancholy provided in turns by the soprano and the ten accordion players. These moments most often arise from the kinaesthetic dynamics of the movement itself rather than from any specific dramatic connection. The physical energy is contagious, and when one person begins a rhythmic, repetitious stamping combination (reinforced by the upbeat folk music), the others are drawn in to their dance. Sometimes this exchange of energy becomes destructive, but at other times it suggests a kind of curious connection, a sharing of something even besides sorrow. One memorable moment occurs about halfway through the performance when suddenly there are five people lying down, curled to one side. In a simple, sweet gesture, a woman gets up to give a pillow to the drag-queen character who did not have one. Once everyone is lying down with pillows (reminiscent of a kid's sleepover), they begin a unison sequence of movements that are wonderfully fun and funny. Using the pillows as support for their heads, they play with the inverted possibilities of their bodies. Butts in the air, their limbs flying in various coordinated directions, they move like mini-puppets in a fair sideshow.

One reviewer comments on this kind of ludic inversion: 'There is, therefore, in a strange way, a feeling of optimism in the performance. Once in a while its mopiness undergoes a sudden surge of life, a moment of madness into which everyone throws themselves regardless. This gives us a strange reversal, showing this sad world suddenly, apparently, to be very warm, attractive and free.'[15] Similarly, I find these moments to be powerful and compelling, particularly during scenes when the characters followed the intensity of a movement exchange so long that its disturbing qualities began to transform into a communal ritual. In *La Tristeza Complice*, these moments of 'communitas' are fleeting and never resolve into a deeper, more lasting connection. Indeed, they tend to be the exceptions that prove the rule that we are essentially and existentially alone, even when together.

pitié!

By the time he created *pitié!* in 2008, however, Platel substantially shifted the dynamic of being alone together. In this two-hour operatic extravaganza based on Bach's *St Matthew Passion*, redemption is to be found in the touch of another.

The warm amber lights brighten gradually, revealing a three-part tableau with the richness of detail and saturated colours of an old oil painting. Even if an audience member did not realize that this work was inspired by Bach's sacred oratorio, they might well be reminded of the exquisitely rendered religious iconography such as the Grunewald Altarpiece in Colmar, or any of the many marvellous depictions of the Last Supper from Renaissance painting. Seated around a table are three figures dressed in black: two women and a young man who will sing the role of Christ. The opposite side of the stage features another, more contemporary, world. Here a group of people wear a motley assortment of T-shirts and sweat pants and sit side by side on a long bench as if waiting to be called into the doctor's office. Above both scenes is the third part of the tableau, a raised platform with the musicians and a separate enclosed area draped with what looks like animal hides. Everything is still for a moment, giving the audience the time to study the symbolic details: an axe, a cup, a rope, the veils of mourning.

As the small chamber orchestra of strings and brass strikes up a jazzy rendition of Bach's music, our attention is soon drawn to the minute movements of one dancer's fingers twitching, then a tilt of his head. These isolated gestures begin to spread through his body, leading him into the open space at the centre of the stage. What follows is an extraordinary display of physical agility. Part circus, part capoeira, part spastic and involuntary gesture, his movements seem to surprise him, as if they were passing through his body on the way to somewhere else. He folds and unfolds into a series of handstands and other inversions, switching earth for sky. At one point he vaults onto the table, caressing the head of one of the women before stealing (briefly) her sunglasses. The music is folksy and energetic, and his awkward dancing carries a sense of playfulness even as his body parts loosen beyond his control.

Soon, a woman approaches to face him and begins to undress him and then herself. Naked except for their underwear, they grab one another's skin like a handle, pulling on the flesh of their partner for support as they lean away from one another. At another moment, she steps on the soft part of his belly as he is lying on the ground, walking slowly (and painfully) to his ribcage and then his shoulders. The audience responds to this extraordinary and potentially abusive act with a collective shudder. Finished, she turns and helps him up as if nothing unusual had transpired. This image of being painfully connected yields to the pleasure of an embrace, as the kinetics of connection and dis-connection flicker through their awkward physical entanglements.

This duet is the first of a series of pas de deux that weave through the piece's larger narrative structure. Each duet is unique in its combination of dysfunction and connection. For instance, the next duet between a short man and a tall one ends in a straight-armed embrace that encompasses both comic and tragic dimensions. These couplings span a continuum of touch that moves from aggressive to intimate and back again. In these moments, the surface of the body – the tactile sensibility of skin – vibrates between being an armour against the outside world and being the soft connective tissue that receives another's touch.

In his review essay on *pitié!* ('Human Failure and Humane Exhaustion: The Passion of Alain Platel'), Ryan Platt locates this 'wistfully ephemeral intimacy' in the vulnerability of the human condition, what he describes as a 'shared surface of compassionate relation'. He traces how throughout this restaging of Christ's (com)passion 'an instant of grace' is conferred by the 'reassuring touch of another'. 'Predicated upon the universality of the flesh – or rather, the skin – the corporeal experience of such contact is real, but remains an analogy, which can only achieve symbolic unity.'[16] Although *pitié!* is much more obviously symbolic than many of Platel's previous works, it is nonetheless important to recognize that the corporeal engagement of the performers moving together provides a kinaesthetic counterpoint that is just as essential to the work's currency, even if it is less immediately obvious. Touching, embracing, holding hands, supporting one another, this is the tactile dimension that draws on the audience's own physical responsiveness, one that spills beyond the mimetic dimensions of its representational context.

As a cello begins to play and one of the sopranos begins a soulful aria, the entire cast of dancers, ten in all, begin their first unison sequence. Bending over at the waist, heads almost brushing the floor, they slowly take off their shirts, revealing a contoured landscape of skin, muscle and bone. Arms folded around their heads, these figures transform into otherworldly creatures as they slowly progress towards the audience like a herd of strange but dignified beasts. It is a strikingly beautiful image, made all the more compelling as the two other singers join voices and hands around the table. Here, Platel's stage world turns from material to symbolic, from secular to sacred, from flesh to image. Soon the whole cast is singing and moving into a larger tableau, forming a living painting that crystallizes for a moment before morphing into another and then another scene, like a slow-motion rendering of the life of Christ through abstract motion. This representational structure is both highlighted and made ironic by the large and tacky Christ figure emblazoned on the male singer's shirt. The narrative is never clear, but images of someone falling backwards, arms held out their sides, or momentary glimpses of a *pieta* as one person melts into another's arms before slipping down to the floor conjure the threads of this biblical story in which suffering is the root of compassion and the voice of the Christ figure vibrates between suffering and redemption.

Being singular plural

In the same year that Platel staged *La Tristeza Complice* and spoke of 'being alone together', the French philosopher Jean-Luc Nancy wrote a book entitled *Being Singular Plural* (*Être singulier pluriel*, 1995). The first and longest of six essays also carries that title and places these terms next to one another ('in a single stroke, without punctuation, without a mark of equivalence, implication. Or sequence') to mark the ontological connection (together) as well as the cultural disjunction (alone).[17] In the introduction to this series of writings, Nancy describes the historical context for his writing as a 'theatre of bloody conflicts among identities'. He proceeds to list a devastatingly global array of ethnic conflicts, civil wars and contemporary genocides, including those among Serbians, Croatians and Bosnians in the former Yugoslavia, and that between the Tutsis and the Hutus in Rwanda. He writes, 'These days it is not always possible to say with any assurance whether these identities are intranational, infranational, or transnational; whether they are real, mythical, or imaginary; whether they are independent or "instrumentalized" by other groups who wield political, economic, and ideological power.'[18] The ellipses here are telling, for they indicate at once the urgency of his inquiry and the difficulty of its address.

In these essays, Nancy displaces the traditional philosophical take on consciousness as the foundation for selfhood (Descartes's (in)famous *Cogito, ergo sum*) and instead posits our being in the world as a being with one another in the world. This 'with-ness' is primarily bodily, and he calls on us to recognize the ways in which it operates in our lives. However, Nancy specifies that this sense of 'with' is not simply an additive measure, like 1 + 1 = 2. Rather, it is the plurality of we 'others' that serves as the ground from which any sense of individuality emerges. For Nancy, this 'with' establishes 'neither a collective subject nor 'intersubjectivity' but is the space between people, a singular dis-identification that acknowledges both our mutual proximity and the labour of crossing over. As a word, 'with' crosses over between self and other as well as between relation and opposition, giving us a perspective on the frictions between belonging and difference, singular and plural in a way that is remarkably similar to the world staged by Platel in his theatrical work.

Towards the end of *Being Singular Plural*, Nancy brings the focus of his language from existential positioning to the materiality of our connective tissue. 'Beings touch', he writes, 'they are in con-tact with one another.'[19] In a number of his writings, Nancy invokes touch (con-tact) as a metaphor for reading, a play of movement and (e)motion that exceeds boundaries, as well as a connection that awakens our capacity for love; 'proximity is the correlate of intimacy'.[20] And yet he cautions us that 'feeling together' is not the same as 'being one'. 'Togetherness and being-together are not equivalent'.[21] 'Being-together' implies a process, a working process, maybe even a work-in-process. Working with, feeling with, being with, these actions require a willingness to experience proximity (if not intimacy). But there are no guarantees that we will succeed. In the middle of listing the civil wars raging in the world in the mid 1990s, Nancy declares:

> What I am talking about here is compassion, but not compassion as a pity that feels sorry for itself and feeds on itself. Com-passion is the contagion, the contact of being with one another in this turmoil. Compassion is not altruism, nor is it identification; it is the disturbance of violent relatedness.[22]

This last phrase – 'the disturbance of violent relatedness' – is wonderfully evocative of Platel's stage worlds in which individuals are alternately aggressive and violent with one another but where their 'relatedness' is always part of the kinaesthetic texture of the *mise en scène*. Unlike *La Tristeza Complice*, the twenty-first-century work *pitié!* resolves this push and pull between compassion and resistance with a final denouement of tactile interconnection. As the lights slowly fade, the performers walk up to one another and embrace one another for a long theatrical moment, allowing their flesh to touch and be touched in a responsive and receptive manner – a true com-passion.

Throughout *pitié!*, Platel depicts the roots of Christ's compassion as a mutual suffering (pathos) with another. Most explanations of this word include the modifier 'deep', suggesting a powerful affect that has somatic implications, just like Berger's notion of corporeal space. Invariably, compassion is seen as a force – it moves us to act. One element of that force is empathy, which is similar to, but not synonymous with, compassion. Empathy also suggests a certain kind of physical disposition. In her memoir of suffering and love, *The Faraway Nearby*, Rebecca Solnit identifies the root of empathy as 'path'. 'Empathy is a journey you travel ... the information travels toward you and you meet it halfway, if you meet it.'[23] Like a compass, empathy is what we use to navigate our journeys together – our co-path. Kinaesthetic in its nature, empathy maps the geography of com-passion onto our bodies, registering its affect in our connective tissue. This is one of the foundations of expressive dance, which Platel evokes when he remarks in an interview: 'I sometimes feel like I am going back to the essence and origins of dance: a personal, collective and physical way to express the emotional layers we're carrying with us.'[24]

In his review essay focused on *pitié!*, Platt highlights this sensibility when he recognizes that Platel 'relies on dance as a means of expression'. He writes: 'Frequently using contact improvisation, his manifestly modern idiom emphasizes guts (i.e., the solar plexus), ground, and gravity.'[25] Unlike the modernist concept of kinaesthesia in dance as a universal idiom (most fully articulated in the work of the mid-twentieth-century dance critic John Martin), however, I would argue that Platel's use of corporeality acknowledges differences in perception even while engaging our bodily sense of 'relatedness'. His notion of 'pity' in *pitié!* is much more attuned to Nancy's sense of compassion – a feeling together. Thus, I find this interconnection of feeling and being onstage best captured by dance scholar Deidre Sklar's notion of 'empathic kinesthetic perception'. In her essay, 'Five Premises for a Culturally Sensitive Approach to Dance', she notes:

> empathic kinesthetic perception suggests a combination of mimesis and empathy ... Whereas visual perception implies an 'object' to be perceived from a distance with the eyes alone, empathic kinesthetic perception implies a bridging between subjectivities. This kind of 'connected knowing' produces a very intimate kind of knowledge, a taste of those ineffable movement experiences that can't be easily put into words.[26]

Platel's performances navigate the space between life and art, representation and experience, in ways that call upon a very different engagement with the audience. My discussion of Berger's 'corporeal space', Lehmann's 'energetic theatre' or Nancy's 'disturbance of violent relatedness' is an attempt to expand how we might think about the circulation of embodied energies in these performances. I am interested in the less theorized and often invisible exchanges of somatic and cultural meaning that affect us in ways that we find hard to articulate and conceptualize. The examples of Platel's work presented here deploy theatrical elements of text, image and motion often confound our usual ways of seeing and compel us to be moved by our witnessing of the dramas of touching and feeling between the performers onstage. Splitting across the corporeal registers of language and gesture, the performances by les ballets C de la B discussed in this chapter take us beyond ourselves, leading the audience to develop new response-abilities towards what is happening onstage.

Notes

1. Hans-Thies Lehmann (2006) *Postdramatic Theatre*, London and New York: Routledge, 37–8.
2. John Berger (2001) 'Rembrandt and the Body', in *The Shape of a Pocket*, New York: Pantheon Books, 105.
3. Berger, 'Rembrandt and the Body', 106–7.
4. Berger, 'Rembrandt and the Body', 109.
5. Berger, 'Rembrandt and the Body', 107.
6. Berger, 'Rembrandt and the Body', 107.
7. See Guy Cools (2001) 'Intercultural Storytelling: A Voyage around the Theater World of Alain Platel', *Parachute*, 102: 102–13; and Ryan Platt (2010) 'Human Failure and Humane Exhaustion: The Passion of Alain Platel', *PAJ: A Journal of Performance and Art*, 32 (1): 90–6.
8. See the introduction to Ann Cooper Albright (1997) *Choreographing Difference: The Body and Identity in Contemporary Dance*, Middleton, Conn.: Wesleyan University Press.
9. Lehmann, *Postdramatic Theatre*, 22.
10. Lehmann, *Postdramatic Theatre*, 85.
11. Renate Klett (2006) 'Nothing Happens, and Yet Everything Does: The Theater of Alain Platel', *Theater*, 36 (1): 162–5, at 164. Emphasis added.
12. Frank Pauwels and Mieke Versyp (1995) 'Bittersweet Lament', *De Gentenaar*, 2 October.
13. John Berger (2015) *Portraits: John Berger on Artists*, ed. Tom Overton, London: Verso Press, 211–12.
14. Peter Anthonissen (1995) 'My Work Is as Cheerless as the World around Me', Belang van Limburg, 26 September, in les ballets C de la B's press packet from 1995.
15. Pieter T'Jonck (1995) 'Sad World with a Gleam of Hope', *De Standaard*, 22 September, 8.
16. Platt, 'Human Failure', 95.
17. Jean-Luc Nancy (2000) *Being Singular Plural*, trans. Robert D. Richardson and Anne E. O'Byrne, Stanford, Calif.: Stanford University Press, 37.
18. Nancy, *Being Singular Plural*, xii–xiii.
19. Nancy, *Being Singular Plural*, 96.
20. Nancy, *Being Singular Plural*, 79.
21. Nancy, *Being Singular Plural*, 60.
22. Nancy, *Being Singular Plural*, xiii.
23. Rebecca Solnit (2003) *The Faraway Nearby*, New York: Viking Press, 195.
24. Alain Platel and Lou Cope (2010) 'Looking Inward, Outward, Backward and Forward', *Contemporary Theater Review*, 20 (4): 416–20, at 420.
25. Platt, 'Human Failure', 94.
26. Deidre Sklar (2001) 'Five Premises for a Culturally Sensitive Approach to Dance', in Ann Dils and Ann Cooper Albright (eds.), *Moving History/Dancing Cultures*, Middletown, Conn.: Wesleyan University Press, pp. 30–2, at 31–2.

References

Albright, Ann Cooper (1997) *Choreographing Difference: The Body and Identity in Contemporary Dance*, Middletown, Conn.: Wesleyan University Press.

Berger, John (2001) 'Rembrandt and the Body', in *The Shape of a Pocket*, New York: Pantheon Books, 105–11.
Berger, John (2015) *Portraits: John Berger on Artists*, edited by Tom Overton, London: Verso Press.
Cools, Guy (2001) 'Intercultural Storytelling: A Voyage around the Theater World of Alain Platel', *Parachute*, 102: 102–13.
Klett, Renate (2006) 'Nothing Happens, and Yet Everything Does: The Theater of Alain Platel', *Theater*, 36 (1): 162–5.
Lehmann, Hans-Thies (2006) *Postdramatic Theatre*, London and New York: Routledge.
Nancy, Jean-Luc (2000) *Being Singular Plural*, trans. Robert D. Richardson and Anne E. O'Byrne, Stanford, Calif.: Stanford University Press.
Platel, Alain, and Lou Cope (2010) 'Looking Inward, Outward, Backward and Forward', *Contemporary Theater Review*, 20 (4): 416–20.
Platt, Ryan (2010) 'Human Failure and Humane Exhaustion: The Passion of Alain Platel', *PAJ: A Journal of Performance and Art*, 32 (1): 90–6.
Solnit, Rebecca (2003) *The Faraway Nearby*, New York: Viking Press.
Sklar, Deidre (2001) 'Five Premises for a Culturally Sensitive Approach to Dance', in Ann Dils and Ann Cooper Albright (eds.), *Moving History/Dancing Cultures*, Middletown, Conn.: Wesleyan University Press, pp. 30–2.

6

Desire amongst the Dodgems

Alain Platel and the Scene of Seduction

Adrian Kear

> *We must demand that theatre, to use [Artaud's] image, should affect us as music affects snakes, by a shudder that strikes us first in the belly and runs through our whole body.*[1]

Perhaps it should come as no surprise that, as a psychoanalytic theorist of performance, André Green should conjure an image of auditory seduction to illustrate his desire for the theatrical encounter to bring about an experience of bodily captivation. The implication seems to be that the sensory impact of performance should be equivalent to that of an irresistible embrace, producing nothing less than passionate abandonment in the face of love's all-consuming presence. The language of theatre operates, in this formulation, as a metonymic extension of the rhetoric of seduction – a formalized system for the generation of affect and the circulation of emotion. Its overarching ambition and effect are therefore, Green suggests, to sway the audience with the visceral power of seduction (to which one might add, ideological persuasion). But the overwhelming experience of going to the theatre is, for me – amongst others – one of severe disillusion or disappointment. All too often the actuality of the event fails to deliver, as though theatre itself cannot live up to the 'idea of theatre' it seeks to actualize and extend, cannot sustain either its own promise or the demands and expectations placed upon it. It invariably seems a letdown. Occasionally – rarely – theatre's capacity to produce the exceptional is reaffirmed, however, through an encounter with live performance that is experienced subjectively as a matter of primal importance. Such an 'event' might be figured as an irruption of theatre's potentiality – to interrupt its context, to disrupt social stability, to disturb the spectator's sense of equanimity – that maintains itself nonetheless within those countless disheartening, frustrating, head-shaking performances it appears to be set apart from. This would suggest that the experience of theatre *bona fide* is not simply contingent on aesthetic quality but also on the 'chance' production of affective communicability. To be 'moved' by a piece, to be shocked, stimulated, exhilarated, amused or horrified is, in effect, to have a 'gut-reaction' to it: a visceral as well as intellectual experience 'that strikes us first in the belly then runs through our whole body'.

Although such experiences are infrequent – and intermittent – they serve to reacquaint the spectator with the phenomenal possibilities of theatre, to renew our belief in its enduring matter and import, to reignite our love affair with it. Or at least they begin to. For in reality the immediacy of the theatre experience, the quality of its happening-to-you, necessitates that the analysis of what occurs in that moment follows afterwards, *après coup* (after the fact). Being struck by the theatre event, or by a fragment of it, strikes me as being an appropriate starting point for interrogating theatre's affective dynamics. Indeed, returning to the scene of a sensate encounter and reinterpreting from memory an embodied experience of aesthetic 'shudder' might provide a method for extending our understanding of the impact of performance across a range of critical and conceptual registers, not least the psychoanalytic. With this in mind, I'd like to revisit a show I saw several years ago, *Bernadetje* (*Little Bernadette*), which was also my introduction to the Belgian theatre company Victoria and the work of the director and choreographer Alain Platel. This performance was for me 'exemplary' for a number of reasons, not least because watching it made me feel physically sick. I attempt to explain why in what follows, analysing in the process this production's remarkably persuasive investigation and reconfiguration of the logic of theatre as a locus of seduction.

I came across *Bernadetje* almost accidentally, during its brief tour to Britain in October 1997, supported by Artangel and the Centre for Performance Research. Although this piece was in fact the second part of a theatrical trilogy – its sister works being *Moeder en Kind* (1995) and the internationally acclaimed *Allemaal Indiaan* (1999) – there appeared to me to be something singular about the production's impact, form and methodology. Platel, in conjunction with Arne Sierens, had collaborated with the young people of the Victoria youth theatre company to fashion an event of extraordinary insight and intensity. This is not to say that the show was a thing of great beauty or technical quality but rather to indicate that it forged a powerful connection, experientially, between what took place inside the theatre and that which conditioned its appearance, culturally. More specifically, as I aim to show, *Bernadetje* was exceptional in the way that it linked the traumatic experience of recent cultural history – the revelation of the conspiracy of silence surrounding the Belgian child-abuser and murderer Marc Dutroux – to something like the historical significance of abuse as the silenced experience of childhood's traumatic reality. In so doing, it effectively opened up the enduring questions of responsibility, ethics and agency that haunt not only contemporary theatre in Europe but also European culture, politics and social identity. And by implicating the audience in this nexus, more importantly, by grounding it in the concrete situation of the theatrical seduction, it went some considerable distance to producing something akin to performative testimony to the historical significance of abuse as the very site and substance of subjectivity.

But this is to anticipate the argument to come somewhat precipitously. Let us return to the performance in its materiality as a theatre event, beginning again with its staging in London in 1997 at the then recently reopened Roundhouse in Camden. The conversion into a theatre venue of this enormous, cavernous building (a former engine shed famous for being the construction site of Stephenson's first *Rocket*), seemed intended as an audacious provocation to the companies invited to perform there. Its empty shell appeared more suited to housing a rave party than to accommodating theatrical scenery, to the consumption of ecstasy than the construction of dramaturgical intimacy. Yet the contradiction was potentially generative in that it offered the opportunity to conceive of theatre space outside of the limitations imposed by 'black-box' dimensions and proscenium conventions. A truly site-specific performance might have been able to make interesting use of these alternative possibilities, but *Bernadetje* was remarkable largely for its unique modification of them. Installed within the vast hulk of the Roundhouse was a fully functioning dodgem car track, whose shiny magnetic surface, rigid steel edges, and meshwork electric canopy created a metallic grey caged environment – both real and fictional – for the show. Lit by fluorescent strip lights suspended from the gantry, this quasi-formal space-within-a-space echoed the shape and structure of a studio theatre, albeit a fantastically playful one. Hovering above the back of the stage, and illuminating its recess, was a large neon sign written backwards: 'Lourdes'.

This appeared to attempt to situate the materiality of the stage environment within a nominated diegetic context, to confer the onstage theatrical activity (which consisted largely of riding the dodgems) with narrative coherence and credibility. The giant caption, placed 'retrospectively', as it were, seemed to signify the stabilization of the meanings in play in the performance itself – rendering it a 'modern version' of the epiphany story of Bernadette of Lourdes.[2]

Figure 6.1 An Pierlé, Titus De Voogdt and Lies Pauwels in *Bernadetje*, 1996. © Kurt Van der Elst.

Bernadette's ecstatic vision was in this case translated into a group of teenagers' obsessive occupation of a fairground attraction, a metaphorical 'place of pilgrimage for young people, a place of awakening adulthood' and site of seduction.[3] The narrative of transformation was at least in part, however, lost in translation – possibly because the Flemish and English were barely audible, let alone comprehensible. The emphasis instead was on the place itself, on the material environment of the dodgem track and the activity contained within it. This consisted of the adolescent actors literally 'playing' in the performance space, driving the dodgems frenetically and performing their enjoyment with a vibrancy and vitality suggestive of an altogether different source of theatrical energy. The performers were clearly not 'acting' in a conventional sense – 'playing characters' – but rather were 'playing themselves'; playing themselves 'playing' (however seriously). Their unadulterated enthusiasm for the tasks undertaken was clear to see – the pleasures taken by the young company in their essentially hermetic expressive repertory reflecting back to the audience the vicarious cause of our own eviscerated entertainment, leaving us both elated and disappointed at not being able to join in. Such preclusion of participation, moreover, appeared central to the construction of an explicitly voyeuristic spectatorial relationship, in which the audience became increasingly aware of their own investment in the theatrical occasion. As Platel knowingly remarks, 'You can see [the set] as a dance floor, a centre with its periphery, in which a game of watching and being watched is played out.'[4]

One scene in particular seemed to mark this double movement, rupturing the drama's circular interiority with a direct address to the audience of discomforting

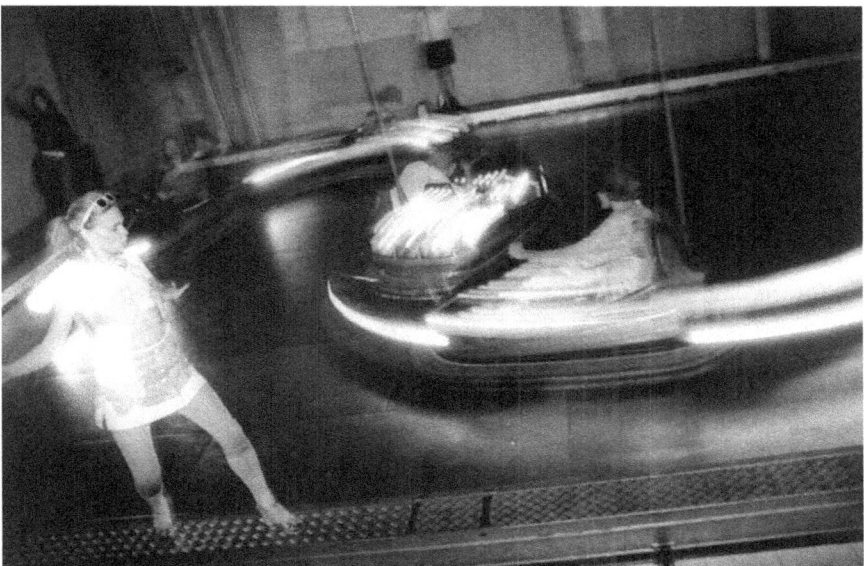

Figure 6.2 An Pierlé in *Bernadetje*, 1996. © Kurt Van der Elst.

familiarity. As the dodgem cars continue to circumnavigate, a young woman writhes, enraptured, to the sound of Prince's 'Cream'.

One of the boys joins her at the front of the stage, removes his T-shirt, and embraces her violently. The dodgems stop suddenly, as if in protest at this intrusion of up-front sexuality (or the tokens having run out prematurely), and the scene shifts into an even more explicitly sexualizing display of adolescent bodies and juvenile exhibitionism. Each of the teenage performers in turn sashays across the stage, from back to front, flashing a piece of their flesh to the audience in a more or less formalized 'catwalk' routine. This is undertaken with such calculated abandon, such intentional insouciance, that it demands to be read as significant.

The clearly coded revealing (and concealing) of these young people's bodies is fairly obviously directed towards the explication of the structural relations of the viewing contract. The activity onstage is designed to reference the spectator's activity off stage, to index, so to speak, their implication in its performance of apparent, if ambiguous, knowingness. The audience would seem to be situated by it as the agents of a disturbingly paedophilic gaze, whose look – like that of the man in dark glasses continuously loitering around the edge of the show – sexualizes the performers' activity. In this reading, the sublimated energy of the performance, which might otherwise be seen as a displacement of adolescent sexuality, is offered back to the audience as a new form of sexual activity.[5] The 'catwalk' display thus appears to offer the spectator what he 'really' wants to see – and it is a 'he' quite specifically; the trope works exclusively within a strictly gendered visual economy – but in such a way that it can no longer be looked at innocently. The reversal of expectation makes explicit the scopophilic grounds of the relation, rendering the remainder of the performance so 'charged' that the audience cannot continue to just watch sitting comfortably. It is as if the theatre event introduces the reversal of the process of sublimation as its critical activity, performing the production of 'new excitation' and 'new energy' as evidence of the traumatizing effects of the imposition of adult sexuality.[6] Perhaps this is one way the show sought 'to hit the public: from side to side, from the back, and full frontal', making us conscious of our otherwise unconscious desiring machinery.[7] I for one was discomforted by the implication – I felt sick to my stomach and incredibly angry at the production – and wanted to resist my interpellation into its perverse visual economy. But rather than reject its troubling argumentation, I decided to investigate further the logical dynamics of its intervention.

The burning questions I wanted to address concerned what might be called the ethics of performance in this theatrical representation. To what extent were the adolescent actors aware of what it was they were doing? Did they have ownership of the *mise en scène*, or was it subject to a calculated and controlling directorial strategy? In short, what were the relations of authorship and agency at play within the compositional process of this company? Platel maintains that the work emerged directly from collaboration between himself, Sierens, and the performers, with the latter responsible for the generation of material and the former its selection, editing and arrangement. He suggests that there was considerable input from the young people themselves in making the catwalk scene from their own experience and expressive resources, 'although I'm not sure if they're aware of the effect of this showing off on all of the audience'.[8] But is it reasonable to expect them to be, given that the relations of power between stage and auditorium are here imbricated in the difference between childhood and adult matrices of interpretation and intelligibility? Do the performers need to understand (or be oblivious to) the 'argument' of the show in order to perform it effectively? As Platel explains, the volatility of theatre as a signifying practice militates against 'using these elements very consciously', relying instead upon unconscious representations for their immediacy and improvisational vitality.[9] But their translation into performance produces a different order of intentionality and therefore demands further interrogation of the questions of representation and responsibility.

The shift of context from rehearsal room to auditorium automatically engenders an alteration of intersubjective relation: theatre does not just take place in front of me; it addresses itself to me in my very subjectivity. As the psychoanalytic theorist Jacques Lacan writes of what he calls the 'other scene' of language (its unconscious register), 'the signifier is what represents the subject *for* another signifier'.[10] Although the syntax here is difficult, the sense is nonetheless clear: signification carries within it a veiled 'content' or subjective encoding. The spectator of that 'other scene' is not necessarily the actual spectator but its representation – 'another signifier' if you like – that is nonetheless addressed by the subject within the circulation and exchange of signifiers that forms representation's economy. Hence, in the language of performance, the theatre, 'before signifying something, signifies *for* someone'.[11] The concrete situation of the theatre event thereby draws attention to the material fact of audience, to the others gathered there whom it reaches as address. For sure, the meanings generated within a production might mean more, or other, than they were supposed to – creating an affective supplement or subjective remainder that destabilizes any simple conception of theatre as purposive communication – yet at the same time they continue to function in the mode of representation (of something for someone). This is not to say that such an effect of intersubjectivity cannot be manipulated or created intentionally but rather that signification is never a unidirectional transaction or unique responsibility.

In the case of *Bernadetje*, it is tempting to read the disturbing affect of the catwalk scene as an effect of this dynamic ambiguity. With recourse to Lacanian interpretive procedures, we can demonstrate that the performers are simply 'acting out' a quintessentially hysterical theatrical relation. This functions, on the one hand, as a representation of the process of 'imaginary' identification – the identification with an image in which the actors appear desirable to themselves – and, on the other, as a simulation of the structure of 'symbolic' identification, in which the actors identify with the very place from which they are observed, the place from which they appear to themselves as desirable. As Mikkel Borch-Jacobsen explains in his analysis of the performative elements of psychoanalysis, the subjective principle of hysteria is inimically theatrical:

> In a word, the hysterics would stage themselves. They would separate themselves from themselves by adopting the point of view of the spectator, of that other for whom they played as actresses. Or again, they would put themselves in representation in order to better see themselves 'in front' of themselves, from the exterior, through the gaze and speech of recognition of the other – of all the others assembled [there].[12]

In this role-playing, then, it is clear that 'imaginary' identification is already anticipated by 'symbolic' identification, and that the image is always formed 'on behalf of a certain gaze in the Other'.[13] That the gaze considered here is gendered and sexualized provides the basis for the parade of gender and sexuality on the catwalk. Its conventions form the theatrical language through which the performers seek to offer 'themselves' to the Other as the objects of its desire – a desire that necessarily exceeds the boundaries of the context of its articulation. The discomfort felt by the audience probably derives from being positioned in this locus of absolute otherness, as the material embodiment of a primarily 'ecstatic', self-reflexive address. And as the analysis of hysteria suggests, the transference involved in conflating the Other with the other ('all the others') assembled in the audience can have profoundly destabilizing effects.

By the same token, however, the function of such 'acting out' might be seen as a short-circuiting of representation, providing a form and framework for the direct expression of experience or 'passion' that is not motivated by conscious, deliberative consideration.[14] This is confirmed in *Bernadetje*'s subsequent choreography: as the catwalk gyrations continue, the young woman who had been embraced at the outset of the action drives a dodgem around the track manically, watched menacingly from behind the screen of dark glasses of the onstage 'paedophilic' adult male. As the scene grows in intensity, he jumps into the car with her and tries to repeat the passionate embrace that initiated the sequence. She fights him off, and the scene comes to a sudden halt with this violent interruption, the dramatic timing of which draws attention to the adult's intrusive misreading of the space of teenage play. This momentary standstill forces a concomitant instant of recognition: the meanings and values imposed by the interpretations of adult spectatorship are not necessarily coextensive with the 'intentions' of adolescent display. The anticipation and invocation of grown-up desire in the form of the gaze is not the same thing as an invitation to a certain perverse 'grown-up' after all. The onstage adult, for one, superimposes the fantasy with his reality and misrecognizes himself as the intended addressee of the catwalk scene, collapsing in the process the distance – the difference – between material and psychic reality. The dramaturgy of his nauseating intervention makes manifest the performance's profoundly ethical revelation of the temporal and spatial fissure between adult and childhood frameworks of understanding, a hermeneutic hazard which these adolescent actors are at once trying to illustrate and to navigate, to occupy and eschew.

Their enactment of the circular movement between imaginary and symbolic identification thus appears, in the first instance, to substantiate the abusive process of sexual subjectivation and its associated deflection of the metonymy of desire into the vicissitudes of ideology. However, it is worth remembering that the materiality of performance reminds us of the radical disjunction between utterance and enunciation, between the fact of saying something and the certain 'something' meant by the thing said. The performance of the gap between them is in effect what marks the politics of the 'hysterical' revelation in *Bernadetje*, leaving the audience assessing the space between the performers' articulation of desire and its concomitant encoding in specific movement, speech and gesture. The demand placed upon the spectator is therefore not 'Find me desirable!' but an invitation to reject this request because it is a mere refraction of reality, a distortion of the truth. The truth of its 'meaning' rather resides in probing further the problem of desire's perverse translation into 'the metonymy of the discourse of demand',[15] by asking aloud the counter-intuitional question 'What is it you are saying by saying this?'[16]

As the adolescent actors reveal bits of their bodies it should be increasingly clear that the seeming autonomy and transparency of 'the body' does not itself authorize any simple reading of their gestures as self-referential or self-evidently 'autobiographical'. Rather, their movements might be seen to signify enigmatically – enigmatic being Jean Laplanche's conception, following Lacan, of the signifier that has been divested of its signification 'without thereby losing its power to signify to'.[17] The performers' presentation of a clearly mimetic expressive activity further suggests that the catwalk scene points towards, or allegorizes, something else in the significatory relays of its address. Enigma and allegory appear closely related, for, as Fredric Jameson has noted in his closely argued study of the theatre-thinking of Bertolt Brecht:

> Allegory consists in the withdrawal of the self-sufficiency of meaning from a given representation. That withdrawal can be marked by a radical insufficiency of the representation itself: gaps, enigmatic emblems, and the like: but more often ... it takes the form of a small wedge or window alongside a representation that can continue to mean itself and seem coherent.[18]

So by both existing within yet moving outside of *Bernadetje*'s otherwise hyper-realistic aesthetics, by simultaneously disrupting and drawing attention to its adroit illustration of adult–adolescent relations and dynamics, the mimetic 'interruption' of the catwalk scene at once appears to mark and to mask the materiality and historicity of its signifying practice. One after another a succession of young people come forward and reveal to the audience a point on their skin (elbow, nipple, lips, thigh, chin …), offering it as a 'wedge or window' into the significance of what they are themselves demanding. As has been seen, the mimetic endows the sign with a certain historicity, and its placement on the body appears to ground it in subjective reality. Indeed, it might even possible to speculate what, in the present scene, it is a signifier of exactly, but its function is rather, I would suggest, to keep open the possibility of it signifying to its own materiality.

The theatrical allegory would here seem to function in relation to its 'other scene' in a way akin to Jameson's description of it as 'a reverse wound, a wound in the text' – or its embodied fabric, the skin, which 'can be staunched or controlled … but never quite extinguished as a possibility'.[19] Laplanche would argue that the presence of an enigmatic signifier on the surface of the skin is evidence enough of the scene's indexical structuring, pointing analysis away from the level of the 'symbolic' and back towards its material ontogenesis. The catwalk scene in *Bernadetje* can thereby be seen as a refraction of the relations embedded in the foundational scene of seduction. This 'other scene' operates as the traumatic site of the 'implantation' of adult sexuality into the child, of its incorporation into an at least partially sexualized sociality.[20] This 'implantation', Laplanche argues, takes place by 'fixing' signifiers to the psycho-physiological 'skin' of the subject – signifiers produced by the adult's necessarily inappropriate 'address' to the child:

To address someone with no shared interpretive system, in a mainly extra-verbal manner: such is the function of adult messages, of those signifiers which I claim are simultaneously and indissociably enigmatic and sexual, in so far as they are not transparent to themselves, but compromised by the adult's relation to their own unconscious, by unconscious sexual fantasies set in motion by his relation to the child.[21]

In his schematization, which differs decisively from Lacan's, the adult's message forms the first part of the sequence through which the unconscious is formed in the subject as the product of material practices and intersubjective relations. It is a 'message' precisely because it means something to the subject – something more or less 'meant' by the sender – and, equally importantly, because it represents someone to an other – 'the subject for another signifier'. Its implantation in the skin of the infant, whose unconscious agency as yet remains undifferentiated, leaves it exposed to the child's first active attempts at 'translation'. As translation is impossible without a shared interpretive system, there is a concomitant 'partial failure of translation', which is only resolved by the activation of repression. This system then forms for Laplanche the generalized structure of 'seduction' – message, translation, partial failure of translation – which introduces the unconscious into the infant as 'an alien inside me, and even one put inside me by an alien'.[22] For Laplanche, the theory of seduction 'affirms the priority of the other in the constitution of the human being and of its sexuality. Not the Lacanian Other but the concrete other: the adult facing the child'.[23]

This returns us, then, to the concrete theatrical situation, to the adult facing the child in the spectatorial relation. My gut reaction at being addressed directly by the 'enigma' of the catwalk scene has its discomfiture confirmed by subsequently coming to understand it as a representational condensation of the dynamics of childhood seduction. Its mimetic quality points to this anteriority while at the same time being unable to signify it directly. The scene works across the spatial fissure and temporal delay between what is played out before us and the inaccessible 'other scene' buried within it, repeated and replaced by the movement of allegory. The other to which it is addressed is, almost certainly, 'the other of seduction, the adult who seduces the child' rather than the much more vague and fictional Other of Lacanian symbolic determinacy.[24] The scene's affective temporality operates according to the logic of 'deferred action' – Freud's *nachträglichkeit*, which Laplanche translates as 'afterwardsness' – that ensures that the actual affective experience of the traumatic 'other scene' is felt only in the echo of its apparent reoccurrence or repetition on a later, metonymically linked, occasion. In *Bernadetje*, adolescence itself seems to signify the space of developing understanding, during which the matter of what has been 'signified to the subject' is opened through conceptual 'afterwardsness'; the time frame enabling the retranslation and reinterpretation of the enigmatic message being mapped onto the time of emergent sexuality in such a way that the subject becomes capable of reprocessing the message's 'meaning' and at least partially cracking the code of its intelligibility. 'Growing-up' would appear therefore to entail realizing onstage what grown-ups do and have done off; but for the adult spectator implicated in the scenic structure of this mimesis of seduction, the 'deferred action' of psychoanalytic understanding offers little comfort or redress. Situated in one moment as the agent of a perversely sexualizing gaze, the audience is invoked in the next to bear witness to its traumatic effects. In offering an affective 'renewal of the traumatic, stimulating aspect of the childhood enigma', the choreography of *Bernadetje* simultaneously positions the audience as both object and source of the adult message – as the adult facing the child (in the theatrical reality) and the child faced by the adult (in the stimulated 'memory' of unconscious fantasy).[25] Compromised by their own unconscious's historicity, the audience member is drawn into occupying the three roles in the seduction scene sequentially – adult, child and witness – each played out as the effect of a certain 'afterwardsness'.

In *Bernadetje*, the structure of seduction is at once clarified and condensed by the spatial and temporal organization of the theatrical scene. However, it also emerges that the catwalk has been watched intently not only by the adults in the audience and the onstage 'paedophile' but by a small child downstage left, carrying a teddy and wearing a white communion dress. That the scene might function for her primarily as an enigmatic message is made self-evident when she dumps the teddy, takes centre stage from the rest, and is transformed into a miniature 'rave' dancer. With arms and head pumping in ecstatic excess, she herself appears as the embodiment of 'Little Bernadette'. The neon sign spelling 'Lourdes' flashes blue and red above her as she boogies away, energetically performing a bodily translation while at the same time incorporating seduction's core theatrical relation: the scene witnessed is not just 'innocently' observed; it is offered, proffered, presented to the subject who receives its 'message' as a direct, almost physical address. In other words, it comes loaded with intent. The child translates the meaning of these scenes as best it can, which, given that the adult always 'says' more than they mean, necessarily leaves a residual, untranslated element: the obscure, sexual, enigmatic content of the message.[26] So, as the little girl in *Bernadetje* mimetically translates the adolescent movements into the 'new energy' of a further sublimated *mise en scène*, are we to interpret her dance as a similarly precocious display of prodigious sexuality? Perhaps, but not yet, surely; not by seeing through our glasses darkly with an abusive 'adult' gaze; but by recognizing that the space and time she is in is incompatible with our own. Without such a distinction, seduction slides into abuse, which may very probably be what the enigmatic signifiers in the body of the theatrical fantasy in fact reference, materially.

This would appear to be the stance adopted by Platel in his choreography: one that requires the audience 'to think, and to position themselves in relation to what is happening'.[27] In *Iets op Bach* (1999), for example, he produces an even more graphic literalization of the sexual socialization performed by seduction. A prepubescent teenage girl – a tweenie you might say – with a bandaged eye and NHS specs sits, downstage right, worshipping a poster of the boy band Westlife. Behind her a sweaty, bald-headed, bare-chested male dancer feels himself up and calls her over. She refuses to budge. He is joined instead by an adult female dancer, who sits herself down on his lap; as they embrace, he looks directly towards the child, making it clear that the scene is given to her to be seen. Later, she replaces the woman on his knee, squirming uncomfortably as the implicit message is literalized as an explicit molestation. She runs away back to the poster shrine, against which she is then pinned by the man's aggression as he implants his violent 'message' in the form of Chinese star-darts thrown around the contours of her skin. The incomprehensibility of the adult's message, its incommensurability with the world of childhood could not be illustrated more provocatively. The theatrical literalization of seduction is, for sure, disturbing to see, but then so is the recognition that abuse is, perhaps, inimical to its representational currency. Hence, Platel maintains that

> when people feel uncomfortable seeing certain scenes in my performances, then I just have to tell them that I feel uncomfortable myself. And so, for example, when you relate as an adult to how young people look and behave, I can only say I feel uncomfortable too ... I can describe it, and I understand it more and more, but it's still very upsetting, sometimes. So it's more about putting your demons on-stage than about feeling I'm going to give you a lesson in how to watch, how to think.[28]

The ethics of performance in these productions would therefore seem to depend upon our ability to read them as representations – albeit representations cross-cut by material relations. When the above scene in *Iets op Bach* triggered a police enquiry in Belgium after complaints from the audience in London, it could not have been altogether surprising: for this show, along with *Bernadetje*, appears to be bearing witness to the culture of abuse that is represented, almost literally, as our shared, complicit but nonetheless collective responsibility. The after-effects of encountering this in the theatre experience should be then, as Brecht was keen to remind us, a matter of ongoing incredulity.

Acknowledgements

Thanks are due to the Centre for Performance Research and Artangel for the use of their archives. The author gratefully acknowledges the support of the AHRB. This chapter was originally published in Joe Kelleher and Nicholas Ridout (eds.) (2006) *Contemporary Theatres in Europe*, London and New York: Routledge, 106–19. Reproduced with permission of the publishers.

Notes

1 André Green (1979) *The Tragic Effect: The Oedipus Complex in Tragedy*, Cambridge: Cambridge University Press, 9.
2 Bernadette Soubirous (1844–79) is renowned for receiving a series of 'visitations' from 'Our Lady of Lourdes' in Lourdes, France, around the time of her first communion in February 1858. She first appeared to Bernadette on the banks of the river Gave, wearing a pristine white dress, and revealed to her the nearby stream that was the source of the holy spring, telling her to drink from it and bathe in it too. Bernadette returned the place every day for a total of seventeen days, she claimed in a letter to a friend, and received instructions from the Virgin to build a chapel at the site of the spring. The shrine of Lourdes, as it became, has since received over 200

million visitors seeking redemption and curative restoration from its blessed waters. Bernadette, the patron saint of poverty, piety and sickness (as well as shepherds and teenagers) and herself an incomparable beauty, was beatified in 1925 and canonized in 1933: 'The more I am crucified, the more I rejoice.' See www.catholic-forum.com/saints for more information.
3   Alain Platel, *The Times*, 2 October 1997.
4   Alain Platel and Arne Sierens, *Bernadetje* press release, 1997.
5   Timothy Murray (2001) 'Scanning Sublimation: The Digital Poles of Performance and Psychoanalysis', in Patrick Campbell and Adrian Kear (eds.), *Psychoanalysis and Performance*, London and New York: Routledge, 47–59, at 50.
6   Jean Laplanche (1992) 'The Kent Seminar', in *Jean Laplanche: Seduction, Translation, Drives*, ed. John Fletcher and Martin Stanton, London: ICA, 32.
7   Platel and Sierens, *Bernadetje* press release, 1997.
8   Adrian Kear (2002) 'Seduction and Translation: Alain Platel in Conversation', *Performance Research*, 7 (2): 39–40.
9   Kear, 'Seduction and Translation', 40–1.
10 Jacques Lacan (1970) 'Radiophonie', *Scilicet*, 2/3, cited in Mikkel Borch-Jacobsen (1993) *The Emotional Tie: Psychoanalysis, Mimesis and Affect*, Stanford, Calif.: Stanford University Press, 20. Emphasis added.
11 Jacques Lacan (1977) *Écrits: A Selection*, London and New York: Routledge, 82. Emphasis added.
12 Borch-Jacobsen, *The Emotional Tie*, 95.
13 Slavoj Žižek (1989) *The Sublime Object of Ideology*, London: Verso, 106.
14 Borch-Jacobsen, *The Emotional Tie*, 144.
15 Jacques Lacan (1992) *The Ethics of Psychoanalysis: The Seminar of Jacques Lacan*, Book VII, London and New York: Routledge, 293.
16 Žižek, *The Sublime Object of Ideology*, 111.
17 Jean Laplanche (1989) *New Foundations for Psychoanalysis*, Oxford: Blackwell, 45.
18 Fredric Jameson (1999) *Brecht and Method*, London: Verso, 122.
19 Jameson, *Brecht and Method*, 122.
20 Jean Laplanche (1976) *Life and Death in Psychoanalysis*, Baltimore, Md.: Johns Hopkins University Press, 46.
21 Jean Laplanche (1999) *Essays on Otherness*, ed. John Fletcher, London and New York: Routledge, 79–80.
22 Laplanche, *Essays on Otherness*, 65.
23 Laplanche, *Essays on Otherness*, 212.
24 Laplanche, *Essays on Otherness*, 72.
25 Laplanche, *Essays on Otherness*, 224.
26 Laplanche, *Essays on Otherness*, 156–9.
27 Platel in Kear, 'Seduction and Translation', 48.
28 Platel in Kear, 'Seduction and Translation', 48.

References

Borch-Jacobsen, Mikkel (1993) *The Emotional Tie: Psychoanalysis, Mimesis and Affect*, trans. Douglas Brick and others, Stanford, Calif.: Stanford University Press.

Green, André (1979) *The Tragic Effect: The Oedipus Complex in Tragedy*, trans. Alan Sheridan, Cambridge: Cambridge University Press.
Jameson, Fredric (1999) *Brecht and Method*, London: Verso.
Kear, Adrian (2002) 'Seduction and Translation: Alain Platel in Conversation', *Performance Research*, 7 (2): 35–49.
Lacan, Jacques (1977) *Écrits: A Selection*, trans. Alan Sheridan, London and New York: Routledge.
Lacan, Jacques (1992) *The Ethics of Psychoanalysis: The Seminar of Jacques Lacan*, Book VII, ed. Jacques-Alain Miller, trans. Dennis Porter, London and New York: Routledge.
Laplanche, Jean (1976) *Life and Death in Psychoanalysis*, trans. Jeffrey Mehlman, Baltimore, Md.: Johns Hopkins University Press.
Laplanche, Jean (1989) *New Foundations for Psychoanalysis*, trans. David Macey, Oxford: Blackwell.
Laplanche, Jean (1992) 'The Kent Seminar', in *Jean Laplanche: Seduction, Translation, Drives*, ed. John Fletcher and Martin Stanton, London: ICA.
Laplanche, Jean (1999) *Essays on Otherness*, ed. John Fletcher, London and New York: Routledge.
Murray, Timothy (2001) 'Scanning Sublimation: The Digital Poles of Performance and Psychoanalysis', in Patrick Campbell and Adrian Kear (eds.), *Psychoanalysis and Performance*, London and New York: Routledge, 47–59.
Žižek, Slavoj (1989) *The Sublime Object of Ideology*, London: Verso.

7

Alain Platel's Quest for Embodied Salvation

A Musical Perspective on C(H)ŒURS

Francis Maes

Alain Platel created *C(H)ŒURS* in response to a request by Gerard Mortier, who was at the time director of the opera of Madrid, the Teatro Real. He suggested basing a production of contemporary dance on the music of Giuseppe Verdi. This initiative can be understood as a significant manifestation of Gerard Mortier's endeavour to update the experience of opera. After the end of his tenure as artistic director of the Salzburg Festival, Mortier pleaded for an even more radical liberation of opera from its historical constraints, perhaps even extending these ideas to the very institute of high art. This idea went much further than Mortier's artistic policy at the prestigious festival in the hometown of Mozart. He founded the democratic Ruhrtriennale in 2002 for precisely that reason. One of the first manifestations of his new direction was his request to Alain Platel to produce something in homage to Mozart. The result was the successful production of *Wolf* (2003). When Mortier took over the leadership of the venerable Teatro Real, he searched for opportunities to align modern performance art with the core of the operatic tradition. He reasoned that the wedding of contemporary dance with the most iconic composer of the repertoire would demonstrate the validity of Verdi's music for contemporary society better than more routine interpretations of his operas: 'Alain Platel possesses the art to transmit great music to new audiences and to young people. I have proposed to him to work on the emotions created by the music of Verdi'.[1] Platel's team included the dramaturg Jan Vandenhouwe and sound designer Steven Prengels. During the preparations for the performance, Mortier suggested to Platel and his team to broaden the scope of the musical influence, to include excerpts from the operas of both Verdi and Wagner.

C(H)ŒURS received its premiere in the Teatro Real on 12 March 2012, at a time when the Indignados movement was very active in the Spanish capital. Indignados means the indignant and is the term for a protest movement that arose in reaction to the excesses of capitalism and a failing globalization. The Indignados movement followed a period of revolt, called the Arab Spring, in 2010. Within this context, the production was readily interpreted as a commentary on the revolutionary events of the time. Platel encouraged this interpretation by declaring that he was mainly drawn to the choral numbers in the operas of Verdi and Wagner. He felt these sections often depicted a group in actions of revolt. In an interview with Michaël Bellon of 2013, he stated: 'in many works by Verdi and Wagner, one has the feeling that the chorus represents the people, a people often in revolt, by the way. That made them into an echo of the protest movement that one could see right then in the streets.'[2]

To a certain extent, the production could indeed be read as an exercise on the dynamics of revolutionary movements, of group behaviour and of political protest. This aspect of the production is most obvious in the scenes in which the chorus is split into different action groups, in which the group members write down their slogans on banners. The effect of these actions is questioned, however, through the voice of the French writer Marguerite Duras. In fragments taken from her *Autoportrait*, Duras speaks about the value of the individual and the injustice that governs the habit of subsuming people under fixed collective categories.[3] She sharply condemns collective ideologies like Marxism and nationalism as forms of injustice to the individual. By quoting her statements, Platel indicates that his interest is vested more in the relationship between the individual and the collective than in the revolutionary act itself. The revolutionary reading of the performance is certainly not the only perspective on the performance that is possible. A closer look at the musical selection from Verdi and Wagner may provide a starting point to develop a broader interpretative framework.

Alain Platel had accumulated considerable experience in handling classical music before he took on Verdi and Wagner. In 1998, his provocative *Iets op Bach* was his first take on a canonical composer. In 2003 followed the production on Mozart, *Wolf*. With Fabrizio Cassol, Platel worked on the *Vespro della Beata Vergine* by Monteverdi under the title *vsprs* (2006). Next in line was *C(H)ŒURS* (2012). In all these productions, Platel reacted to music as if from the perspective of an outside observer. He always took an intuitive approach to these musical works, reacting to the features that appealed to him at face value. He never approached these classical pieces with the a priori knowledge of an informed listener. The strength and the appeal of his work on classical music is the result of this sense of wonder, of a spontaneous reaction to the appeal of specific musical ideas. During the creative process, the dancers too had a strong influence on the final shape of the production. The final result was always the outcome of a highly collaborative creative process.

Work on *C(H)ŒURS* was somewhat atypical for les ballets C de la B. Since the production included the collaboration of the standard forces of a large opera house, such as an orchestra in the pit and an opera chorus onstage, the musical plan had to be fixed well in advance. During the actual creative process, the only room for flexibility left resided in the final touches on the soundscapes, connecting the opera excerpts.

An interpretation of the relationship between Platel's choreographic universe and the music of *C(H)ŒURS* could be based on two radically divergent perspectives. On the one hand, it could consider the music as an *objet trouvé*, a pure-sounding edifice on which Platel projected his visions. According to the sound designer Steven Prengels, the treatment of the pieces in their own right as manifestations of pure music was precisely the point of departure of the entire undertaking. According to Prengels, the music had to be there for its immediate appeal, without any consideration of the function it may have had within its original context. The music was stripped of its historical meaning. The semiotic baggage was wiped off. Stripped of its original meaning, Verdi and Wagner were viewed as a clean slate on which new meaning could be projected.[4]

Another interpretation could start from the perspective of the original context and meaning of the pieces. Whatever the intentions of the makers, an art form that originated in a specific historical context is likely to carry some historical weight. A complete obliteration of historically constructed semiotic meaning may be illusory. Musical works are likely to carry something of their original function with them, even if they are radically transposed to new contexts. A considerable part of the audience for *C(H)ŒURS* – especially in its original run at the Teatro Real – would have consisted of seasoned opera lovers. They would have recognized the original significance of pieces from *La Traviata* or *Lohengrin*. However hard the makers may have tried to impose a neutral perspective on these pieces, it remains unlikely that the entire audience would experience them in this manner. Opera lovers would readily associate Wagner's pilgrim's chorus with the Tannhäuser legend, or the music from *La Traviata* with the touching fate of Violetta, the famous courtesan dying from tuberculosis in 'that crowded desert which is called Paris', as she puts it herself. The music carries enough gestural content to tie it unequivocally to the cultural dynamics of the nineteenth century, even for spectators without former knowledge of opera. Spontaneous connotations with the highly charged and rhetorical forms of expression of nineteenth-century romanticism would remain hard to miss. This observation alone should suffice to legitimize attention to the original meaning of the pieces in any effort to come to terms with a production like *C(H)ŒURS*.

The two perspectives mentioned – the music in its essence of pure-sounding energy on the one hand, and music as carrier of historically determined semiotic significance, on the other – echo a debate that has been ongoing in musicology since Carolyn Abbate's foundational publication on the tension between the drastic and the gnostic in musical understanding.[5] In the drastic experience, she understands all the effects of music in actual performance, both on the performer and on the listener. The gnostic is her term to cover the diverse efforts required to read music hermeneutically, to invest musical structures with conceptual meaning. Applied to the musicological interpretation of Platel's *C(H)ŒURS*, this drastic approach would seem to be useful in elucidating the relationship between Platel's extended choreographic language and the music on which it is based. In a balanced musicological approach, however, the gnostic has to be taken into account as well. The pieces onto which Platel has grafted his extraordinary visual language are not neutral in content. They all have been conceived in the very precise context of a drama or a religious service, as is the case for Verdi's *Messa da Requiem*. Even transposed to a dance performance that turns them into musical *objets trouvés*, they continue to carry a cluster of hermeneutical associations.

Platel appears to be conscious of this dualism in music as an experience in its pure form and as tied to expectations and previous knowledge. Both sides of the coin are present in this statement: 'When I realize a piece, I always try to find what speaks to people in a specific music. What do people know or recognize and how can I use this music in an alternative way? That "recognition" guarantees a direct emotional link, which in this case I find extremely important for this piece.'[6]

In Platel's vision, the two poles seem to come together. By deliberately using the musical selection in a way that contradicts expectations, he creates a space in which the music can communicate directly to listeners, transcending the hermeneutical confines of its original setting. On the other hand, Platel plays with the genre of opera in *C(H)ŒURS*. Contrary to previous productions based on classical music (*Iets op Bach* and *Wolf*), Platel abandoned his habit of dissociating the stage imagery radically from the visual associations that are traditionally connected with Bach or Mozart. In those performances, Bach is heard in the visual environment of an asylum, Mozart in the chaotic underground culture of the contemporary banlieues. The radical dissociation of the performance from the visual sensory stimuli based on the music's cultural associations was no longer a defining trait of *C(H)ŒURS*. Platel tailored this performance to the context and institutional conditions of an opera house. There is an orchestra in the pit, a genuine conductor, a chorus and a ballet onstage. The absence of historical costumes does not place the production outside contemporary operatic practices. Historical verisimilitude in setting and costumes is no longer an issue in contemporary opera. *C(H)ŒURS* is a work for and of the opera house without repeating the operatic routines from the past. The result transcends the historical confines of the institution in a most radical way.

How revolutionary?

Gerard Mortier tended to use the revolutionary argument in his efforts to explain the relevance of the operatic classics for contemporary audiences. He stated that Verdi and Wagner wrote these pieces in the context of the revolution of 1848. While it is correct to argue that Verdi and Wagner were involved with revolutionary processes, the pieces used by Platel do not necessarily carry revolutionary import – even if one considers Wagner's active role in the 1849 Dresden uprising. Mortier slightly misses the point when he states 'Verdi and Wagner played a role in the revolution of 1848. This music that has become so popular in our ears has a revolutionary history.'[7]

In Platel's selection, no piece has unequivocal revolutionary bonds. Verdi's *Nabucco* (1841) may come to mind as a piece obviously linked to the Italian Risorgimento. In reality, the symbolical association of *Nabucco* with the Risorgimento movement occurred later than the time of its conception and premiere. The famous chorus 'Va pensiero' achieved its iconic status of the unofficial hymn of Italians only later during the period of post-Risorgimento consolidation. Wagner's *Tannhäuser* (1845) can only be understood as revolutionary in a very individualized sense, in so far as it depicts the internal existential struggle of the individual in opposition to societal conventions and pressure. Verdi's *Macbeth* (1847) and Wagner's *Lohengrin* (1850) do have a sharp political edge, but they are hardly revolutionary. Both operas are concerned with defeating tyrants and usurpers. However, the outcome for the crisis is still sought in the reinstatement of the legitimate ruler as the representative (unequivocally so in *Lohengrin*) of God's order.

All the other pieces in the selection are dated later than the revolutionary years of 1848 and 1849. Verdi's *Messa da Requiem* (1874) is a post-Risorgimento statement. Through the commemoration of a representative of the Italian genius, the writer Alessandro Manzoni in this case, the *Messa da Requiem* was planned to strengthen the civic awareness of the citizens of the new Italian state. Wagner's *Die Meistersinger von Nürnberg* (1868) is decidedly the most problematic piece when evaluated within the nationalist turmoil of its age. Wagner's opera recognizes the importance of the people as the foundation of national values but more in a spiritual than in an active sense. Although the opera ends with a festive, even jubilatory note, the disturbing implication is that would-be rulers may manipulate that spiritual essence to their advantage.[8]

The chorus *Patria oppressa* from Verdi's *Macbeth* comes closest to representing revolutionary action. In the original opera, the piece forms the starting point of Shakespeare's iconic scene in the forest of Birnam. Conducted by Macduff, the chief adversary to the usurper Macbeth, the Scottish protesters camouflage themselves with the trees of the forest. Later, Macbeth will be under the impression that the forest itself is moving towards his castle, signalling his death according to the mysterious prophecies of the witches. By reducing the scene to the initial choral number alone, Platel does not include this revolutionary action into the plot of his danced production, only the passive voice of grief of a crowd in mourning.

The famous chorus of the Hebrew slaves, 'Va pensiero' from Verdi's *Nabucco*, belongs to the same category. The historical process of the Risorgimento, the nineteenth-century unification of Italy, has invested this choral number with huge symbolic power. The piece in itself, however, is a lament, a nostalgic elegy on a vanished world. At the time of the opera's premiere in Milan, it did not make an appeal that was likely to disturb the Habsburg authorities.[9]

The other choral numbers in the selection do not portray people in revolt at all. In the excerpt from Wagner's *Lohengrin*, the armies of Brabant salute their king. The choruses from Wagner's *Tannhäuser* are songs of praise of pilgrims returning from their journey to Rome. In the crowd scene from the third act of Wagner's *Die Meistersinger von Nürnberg* the chorus represents a collective voice. However, the content of their song is not revolutionary, but laudatory. In the original plot, the citizens of Nürnberg salute their beloved mastersinger Hans Sachs by breaking into his most iconic song. The other pieces are sacred – Verdi's *Messa da Requiem* – or instrumental, such as Wagner's preludes to *Lohengrin* and the third act of *Die Meistersinger*, and Verdi's first and third act preludes of *La Traviata* (1853).

When using the music as the point of departure for reading C(H)ŒURS, the content of the pieces necessitates an interpretative framework that will move beyond the idea of the revolutionary. Considering the production as a dialogue of contemporary dance with nineteenth-century operatic classics, with both mediums equally contributing to the construction of meaning, other categories come in sight, such as the sacred, the political, the emotional and the role of the body.

Probing the sacred

The first piece of music that is heard in *C(H)ŒURS* is the *Dies irae* from the *Messa da Requiem* by Giuseppe Verdi. This is an iconic piece of sacred music, representing humanity's apocalyptic awe in the face of the inescapable. Verdi's massive treatment of the Last Judgement tableau forms the *nec plus ultra* in the representation of the *terribilità* of existence, complete with the notorious *grand cassa* depicting the splitting of the face of the earth.

The use of this particular piece of sacred music in the opening scene of *C(H)ŒURS* is no coincidence. The first part of *C(H)ŒURS* has a definite sacred overtone. Verdi's *Messa de Requiem* is followed by the mystical prelude to Wagner's *Lohengrin*, a depiction of the descent of God's grace on earth through the vessel of the Grail. The pilgrim's choruses from *Tannhäuser* are sacred too. The production employs the actual pilgrim's chorus, chanted by the pilgrims on their way back from Rome, and the chorus of the younger pilgrims that bring the good news about Tannhäuser's salvation. The overarching theme in this musical selection seems to be salvation. The sacred continues in the *Wach auf* chorus from *Meistersinger*. This is a chorale on a historical text from the pen of Hans Sachs, the sixteenth-century Meistersinger on whose biography Wagner modelled his fictional character. The hymn celebrates Luther's Reformation. Verdi's *Va pensiero* is strongly associated with the Italian Risorgimento but also fits within this sacred theme. The text is closely modelled on the words and images of Psalm 137, the famous expression of the desire of the Hebrews to return to Jerusalem during their Babylonian exile.

However, the choreographic treatment of the first musical number immediately defies expectations. The choreography onstage does not duplicate the massive force of Verdi's *Dies irae*. One single dancer in a white dress is seen from the back. As the dancer keeps the head down, the character's gender is not immediately apparent. The only movement that corresponds to the rhythm of the music is made by the hands, which are visible above the shoulders of the dancer. The choreography reduces the movement to the tiniest possible dimensions, a choice that modifies the perception of the massively orchestrated music. Instead of focusing on the terror of the apocalyptic moment, the choreography presents a vision on the individual, crushed under the terror conveyed in the music. The opening makes clear that Platel will focus on the tension between the individual and the force of the masses. This is not conveyed through the semiotic meaning of the music but through the energy of the sound in itself. The very sound of a huge chorus immediately suggests a group in collective action. The stage picture, however, focuses on the vulnerability of the individual.

When Verdi introduces the trumpets of the apocalypse, which sound from afar, as if from the four quarters of the earth, and gradually come close in a shattering climax, the dancer slowly pulls up his dress to reveal his naked backside. In combination with the apocalyptic music, the image comes close to the iconic *Ecce homo* from Christian iconography, the ultimate graphic representation of human vulnerability. The music stops after its climactic chord and gives way to a soundscape in which sounds of trumpets and cheering masses secularize the previous image and tie it to the dynamics of group behaviour.

The choreographic approach to Wagner's *Lohengrin* prelude is the opposite of the minimalist approach to Verdi's *Dies irae*. From a musical perspective, the prelude is carefully composed to introduce the idea of the sacred as a defining agent of the drama that will unfold. All the details of the musical texture are carefully chosen to represent the descent of God's grace on earth. To achieve this aim, Wagner focuses more on texture than on melody or rhythm. The prelude is one of the finest examples of music that couples the unfolding of time to spatiality, as if sound is moulded into a spatial sonorous object. This quality anticipates Wagner's more extensive elaboration of 'time becoming space' in *Parsifal* (1882), his other music drama on the subject of the mystical Grail. In its musical essence, the effect of the *Lohengrin* prelude is based on the coupling of tiny movements in the musical texture within the slow unfolding of musical time. The effect on the listener could be likened to the visual observation of the unmoving surface of a lake, made lively through the wrinkling of the water.

The music is constructed as one gradual expansion and reduction of a basically static texture, with just enough melodic and rhythmic movement at the surface to keep the textural unfolding interesting for the listener. Alain Platel, however, radically alters the impression the music generates. His choreography initiates from melodic details as its starting point. The dancers respond to the vibrating details of the music with large and energetic bodily movements, especially the two dancers at the back. They are surrounded by a girl on the front of the stage, and by a couple in the background, all dressed in white. The gradual expansion of the texture is paralleled with an augmentation of the group of dancers to five. At the entrance of the brass instruments, three women in red take the platform with broad, almost ecstatic gestures. The movement of the dancers continues when the music returns to its ethereal starting point and fades away.

Platel's approach to the prelude is as drastic as can be. Through his focus on the energy of the melodic movement, he unravels the carefully constructed sacred image. It is a fine example of how Platel's approach defies expectations and broadens the semiotic space in which the music operates.

As the piece continues, the dancers suddenly drop a piece of cloth that they had been holding in their mouth. At that moment, it becomes clear that they had been carrying their underwear. They start to put it on but are severely hindered by a continuous trembling of the muscles. These uncontrolled movements are part of Alain Platel's gestural vocabulary, which was also used in his production of *vsprs* (2006). Platel understands this type of movement as more than a mere depiction of bodily dysfunction:

> It is a language that I explore since *vsprs* of 2006 and which might reveal things about that type of feelings for which we do not find words ... Perhaps, these brutal movements, which some even qualify as spasmodic – which I do not like to hear – are symptomatic for things we are confronted with in our societies.[10]

The act of putting on underwear becomes almost an insurmountable undertaking. The body has to fight its constant uncontrolled movements. The act is coupled with the pilgrim's chorus from Wagner's *Tannhäuser*. The hymn starts a cappella. The continuous movement of the dancers contradicts the measured melodic shape of the music but draws attention to the sonority of the choral singing in itself. As soon as the orchestra sets in, the movements appear to move along with the markedly rhythmical accompaniment. In the context of the opera, the figuration in the violins was designed as an expression of exaltation for the pardoned pilgrim's souls, but in Platel's vision they become associated with the uncontrolled bodily tremors of the dancers.

In the performance, the pilgrim's chorus is connected to the hymn of the younger pilgrims, which in Wagner's original work occurs later in the third act of *Tannhäuser*. In the plot, the hymn marks the moment of Tannhäuser's salvation. Young pilgrims from Rome proclaim the miracle of the flowering of the pope's staff as God's sign for Tannhäuser's pardon. The accompaniment is constructed as a continuous motion in triplets in the woodwinds, a choice that is meant to give the music its characteristic radiance. The fight of the dancers against their bodily tremors continues during this second chorus, and during the general jubilation with which Wagner brings his opera to a close.

Platel's treatment of the music of *Tannhäuser* takes its cue from the accompaniment rather than from the melodic structure or phrasing. However, his interpretation of these accompaniment figures contradicts their original function only at first glance. In Wagner's concept, they convey the joy of the soul in the assurance of salvation. In Platel's vision, the quest for salvation becomes tangible in a radically embodied way. Salvation is deprived of its religious meaning and understood in the broadest sense as the act of overcoming hindrances. Whether we would read them as purely physical or as a metaphorical indication of societal pressures, the perception of Platel's radical embodiment of the struggle remains the same. The victory over hindrances is represented by the effort of the mind to gain control over the body. The shriek that follows the music of *Tannhäuser* marks the attainment of a new freedom of action. The group's cry leads to a repetition of the music of the *Dies irae* as if it were an extension of their scream.

The political turn

The chorus becomes visible in the background onstage and takes over from the dancers with the choral setting of Hans Sachs' master song *Wach auf* from the third act of Wagner's *Die Meistersinger von Nürnberg*. 'Wake up, it is almost day' is the first line of the choral song. Platel takes this as a rhetorical appeal to revolt. In its original context, the song does not have that function. The crowd strikes up the song to greet and praise its composer Hans Sachs. The song is a hymn to Luther and the renovating force of his Reformation. In *C(H)ŒURS*, the song is deprived of its original meaning. The action onstage takes its cue only from the initial words. It turns the *Wach auf* into a wake-up call for activism.

The physical presence of the chorus onstage marks the moment in which group dynamics take over from the individualized emotions of the dancers. Verdi's *Va pensiero* from *Nabucco* represents a further stage of development in the search for a collective voice. During the singing, the dancers stand or perform with their mouths open. They mainly move to the rhythm of the accompaniment. On the prolonged final chord, the singers join the dancers in their movements of the arms. Dancers and singers then put their fist into their mouth as an indication that they are silenced by force.

At that moment, one realizes that Verdi's iconic choral song is, in fact, about voice. *Va pensiero* is an elegy, a genre of poetry and music that is distinguished by its ability to give voice to complex feelings, mostly of grief and loss. The book of psalms from which the words are moulded is also precisely that: an early literary masterpiece that gives a voice to complex and disturbing feelings. The glory of Verdi's choral song lies precisely in its ability to turn emotion into melody. The abrupt silencing of dancers and singers at the end of the elegy emphasizes this quality in retrospect.

The soundscape that comes immediately after the *Va pensiero* makes clear that the voice is silenced by the power of the demagogue. In the montage, this force is represented in an iconic way by the use of the recorded voice of the Belgian politician Bart de Wever during his victory speech at the federal elections of 2010, with its undisguised reference to the *Triumph des Willens* of early Nazism through the Latin slogan *Nil volentibus arduum*: 'Nothing is hard for the willing'. The dancing crowd turns into an active collective force now, stamping their feet, clapping their hands rhythmically, yelling, and hurling their shoes – as a reference to the Arab Spring revolts.

After this intense moment of revolt, the stage is emptied for the gradual development of Wagner's martial music for the third act greeting of King Heinrich in *Lohengrin*, an operatic 'pomp and circumstance of glorious war' if ever there was one. A woman in a red dress dances ecstatically to the sound of the fanfares. Two children observe her. A dancer drags the children away. The dancer in a white dress – the one who had opened the performance – lies on the ground and tries to stand up with difficulty. After the choral acclaim to King Heinrich, he manages to stand up and starts singing. The individual tries to recover his own hesitant and fragile voice. To this aim, Platel employs the music of the king's address to the armies of Brabant, but stripped from its words and turned into a wordless vocalization. The dancer, who had personified the *Ecce homo* moment at the outset of the production, represents once more the fragility of the individual in the midst of turmoil and agitation.

The following section returns to the non-normative bodily struggling for acceptance, in all its failure and imperfection. Dancers fall, roll off the steps and lie on the ground. The beginning of the music of Wagner's third act prelude from *Die Meistersinger* has a brooding quality. It underlines an image of helplessness. In Wagner's concept, the first musical idea of the piece stands for Hans Sachs's meditation on the source of evil in the world. The ensuing chorale marks the renewal of his faith in life through the strength of his religious conviction. The festive brass chorale replaces these dark musings with their representation of the light of faith. The process is first coupled onstage by the efforts of the dancers to overcome their lethargy, and then their bodily tremors. The dancers seem to deal with uncontrolled bodily movements as a reaction to the

Figure 7.1 Daisy Phillips and Quan Bui Ngoc during rehearsals of *C(H)ŒURS* in dance studio S3, Ghent 2010. © Chris Van der Burght

texture of the brass chorale. The soaring passage in the high violins is coupled with heavy gesticulation. The second chorale in the brass is also accompanied with highly energetic bodily movements. The music ends unresolved. The dancers look around in bewilderment, and depart.

On individuality and love

The image of the dancers striving for freedom of movement, with their trembling, uncontrolled bodies, is coupled to a statement by Marguerite Duras about the value of individuality. No two persons are alike. Every form of collective generalization is poor. Simplistic generalizations lead to fascism, racism and Marxism. Even millions of people doing the same thing does not mean that people are alike.

The speech gives way to an act of social organizing. Groups are formed and changed. People make up slogans and write them down on placards. Two children show a banner with the words *Revoluciones devoran a sus hijos*: 'Revolutions devour their children'. The words are taken up immediately in the funeral image of two groups, carrying away the corpses of two children. The music feels appropriate for the occasion. Verdi's chorus *Patria oppressa* from *Macbeth* deals with the sorrow of people under oppression. In its original context, the chorus sets the scene for Macduff's aria deploring the death of his children through the hands of the tyrant. The text of the chorus refers to the imagery of a mother losing her children in its appeal to the fatherland: 'You do not have any longer the sweet name of a mother, since you have been converted into a grave for your children.' The fatherland has become a place of orphans and widows. The entire chorus conveys immobility in the face of collective grief. The dancers convey this feeling as well as they endeavour, once again, to regain their bodily freedom. The gesture of the fist in the mouth suggests oppression. Platel uses the rhythm of the pizzicato strings to highlight the bodily ticks.

The noisy soundscape gives way to a fragment from the third-act exchange between Violetta and Alfredo from Verdi's *La Traviata*, as if sounding from afar. It is Alfredo's promise to Violetta of the renewal of life in the face of her imminent death from tuberculosis. The dance includes the movements of a couple that seeks to comfort each other with their embrace. Wagner's hymn to the evening star from *Tannhäuser* starts in the background of the mind. Wolfram's hymn is also a plea for salvation, although of a more mystical nature than Violetta's plea to overcome her illness through the forces of love. In the course of the aria, couples search and find each other. When Platel shifts from a political grouping to a more individual constellation of lovemaking, the orchestra takes over the instrumental postlude, with its wonderful melody in the cellos and with an accompaniment by the harp. The chorus enters the stage from behind. The dancers continue their lovemaking. The chorus extends the movement of the music. They rattle their fingers on the wood of the stage. They move and breathe rhythmically. When the chorus lies down on the ground, only one dancing couple remains upright.

The words by Marguerite Duras speak about the universality of death and the democracy inherent in human mortality. To this background, the couple of a man and a woman perform a sensual pas de deux, first to the sound of the speech, then to the tones of Verdi's third act prelude from *La Traviata*. Coupled to the music, the *pas de deux* becomes almost classical, if not in style then in impact. The deliberate variations on the classical style – such as the woman lifting the man instead of the more typical lift of the female ballerina by the male dancer – even strengthen the connotation with classical dance. Verdi's instrumental preludes to *La Traviata* represent the fragility of the individual soul. The delicate tone, made by the use of spare textures and fragile violins *con sordino*, points to the most intimate and solitary feelings. In this fragility, a couple of lovers find each other.

The following scene contrasts with the previous one in the depiction of a wild dance unaccompanied by music. The soundscape gives a hint of a march in the background. The chorus lies on the ground. Their hands are red. For the first time, a vocal soloist sings live onstage – apart from the dancer who sang a wordless vocalization to King Heinrich's address in *Lohengrin* in his untrained but dramatically adept voice. At this moment, a professional soprano expresses fear and gives a voice to a plea for salvation through the tones of the *Libera me* from Verdi's *Messa da Requiem*. The piece is shortened. The montage makes the soprano solo connect immediately to the choral

Figure 7.2 Romeu Runa, Lisi Estaras and stand-in choir during rehearsals of *C(H) ŒURS* in dance studio S3, Ghent 2009. © Chris Van der Burght

fugue that occurs later in the piece. In the course of Verdi's *Messa da Requiem*, the fugue represents the certainty of faith in the face of individual anguish. Its abstract qualities hint towards a doctrinal answer to the fears of the soul. In the final movement of the Verdi *Requiem*, however, this doctrinal voice fails to be entirely convincing. The fugue culminates in a dramatic plea for salvation, followed by the subdued recitation of the prayer. The music ends on a major chord, but not in an emphatic way. The conclusion of Verdi's *Requiem* comes close to a giant question mark in the face of human destiny.

The comparably formalized dance on the *Libera me* which seems to freeze at times in beautiful abstract gestures, could be taken for the veritable endpoint of the emotional process developed during the entire production. The anguish expressed at the beginning has reached a subtle, if not very definitive, conclusion. The rhetorical force of the music guides the viewer towards such a perception. However, the performance is not entirely over. The last piece of music could be heard as a postlude, since it is not accompanied by actions other than the slow retreat of the dancers and the undressing of some dancers and chorus members. The retreat is coupled to a routine movement of the red hands of the chorus members, a movement that is linked to the accompaniment to the melody of Verdi's first act prelude to *La Traviata*. Again, Platel does not base bodily gestures on the melody but rather on the figures of the accompaniment. The effect of the final tableau derives from the combination of the compulsive, ritualized gestures of the hands with the soothing lyricism of Verdi's melody.

Opera and embodiment

The operatic system of the nineteenth century is to a great extent derived from the principle that musical and bodily movements could parallel each other. This system was already in place in the eighteenth century. The semiotic function of the dance rhythms and their hierarchy in the musical dramaturgy of Mozart is widely recognized, as are the roots of the mimetic function of bodily gesture in eighteenth-century comic opera.[11] In the nineteenth century, this system of meaning developed into new directions, but the mimetic function of the music remained largely intact.[12] In this sense, opera has been characterized as an art of overstatement, in which bodily and musical gestures double each other.

Romantic opera enlarged the expressive means of musical dramaturgy with the representation of inner states beyond the classifiable emotions of eighteenth-century dramaturgy. Feelings like anger or joy could be linked to corresponding bodily states or behaviour, as is largely the case in the semiotic system of eighteenth-century opera. The soul's quest for salvation, however, does not have a counterpart in bodily movement. Although nineteenth-century visual art and theatre tended to couple the expression of the spiritual quest to exalted bodily gestures, the highly spiritual treatment of the music often suggests otherwise.

For a dance production that takes the extension of emotional gestures of music into movement as its point of departure, it may come as a surprise that most pieces in the musical selection do not correspond to a gestural mimetic category. Several excerpts used by Alain Platel in C(H)ŒURS seemed to originate from a more spiritual standpoint rather than from a kinaesthetic perspective. The most obvious examples are the hymn to the evening star from *Tannhäuser*, or the third act prelude to *Die Meistersinger*. Verdi also sought to extend his musical vocabulary as far as possible in the expression of the innermost soul in the two preludes to *La Traviata*. The chorus of the returning pilgrims in *Tannhäuser* similarly represents the exaltation of the soul through the coupling of ritualized singing with the radiance of the accompaniment. The highly rhythmical figures that underline the phrases of the chorale point to overwhelming inner joy. The rhythmical figuration in the hymn of the younger pilgrims serves as a musical equivalent to a visual suggestion of shimmering light.

As a result, Alain Platel's approach of basing bodily gestures on the figures of the accompaniment is highly significant. His gestural translation of the rhythmical figuration into nervous tremors radically alters their function. Contrary to Wagner's original work, which expressed salvation received, the dance embodies the quest for salvation at its most basic and tangible level. Nevertheless, the two systems of meaning are related to each other. At the end, salvation becomes tangible through the image of the recovery of bodily freedom to move, even though these movements remain undisciplined and unattractive by conventional standards.

The passage is characteristic for Platel's dialogue with the music. By basing movement on the musical figuration of the accompaniment, he forges links between dance and music that are both musically justified and unexpected. Musical details may be coupled to broad and energetic bodily movements, as in *Va pensiero* or the *Lohengrin* prelude, while the massive violence of Verdi's *Dies irae* is confined within the tiniest dimensions of the gestures of the hand and fingers. Most choral numbers selected for the production are of the passive type. They do not represent a group in action but rather a moment of passive contemplation or mourning. It is significant that Alain Platel presents most action of a revolutionary nature in between the musical numbers. Only in the *Meistersinger* chorus does he derive gestures of contestation and protest from the phrasing and the sheer sonority of the choral texture.

Questions about group dynamics and individuality lie at the basis of the concept of *C(H)ŒURS*. However, the performance moves beyond the political and the revolutionary bonds. The dynamics of human collectives are demonstrated as part of the quest for existence. The dimensions of the personal and the collective, of the individual and societal pressure, are closely connected. Reading the performance through the perspective of the music suggests that salvation is the key concept. Most musical pieces are about salvation in one form or the other, either in the personalized spiritual, or in the collective, societal sense.

The quest for liberation culminates in the ultimate plea of Verdi's *Libera me*. In Platel's production, this quest is conveyed in a radically embodied way. His piece does not lead towards a transcendent end point, but his expressive system does allow for a suggestion of a partial solution to the pressing questions. The first solution is in love, conveyed through the relatively classical *pas de deux* on Verdi's *La Traviata*. The second occurs during the *Libera me*, where abstract gestures acquire an almost tableau-like quality, underlining the search for the stability in faith that is expressed in the music. At these moments, the choreography acquires a measure of control in an abstract shape that is deliberately eschewed in the preceding scenes.

In *C(H)ŒURS*, the drastic and the gnostic intertwine in the perception of the music. The choreography does not only react to the direct emotional appeal of the music. It also engages with the poetic and symbolic content of the original musical pieces. The way it deals with these mental concepts, however, is strikingly physical. In his work with the dancers, Platel situates the quest for salvation in gestural extremes that lie beyond typical norms of behaviour. The chorus members participate to a certain extent in the choreography, but their gestural language stays closer to the standard physicality of ordinary life. Both types of physicality complement each other. As nineteenth-century opera oscillates between the realistic portrayal of behaviour and the representation of the strivings of the soul, Platel's production uses irregular physicality as an extension of the standard behaviour in order to express what cannot be put into words. These two poles underline the interconnectedness of the rational and the irrational in dance; just like it was one of the defining features of the semiotic system behind nineteenth-century opera.

'Salvation' is a term laden with much historical weight. In the context of nineteenth-century opera it was associated with the sacred and with a theological vision of the human soul. In the secularized setting of Alain Platel's *C(H)ŒURS*, the quest for salvation becomes more tangible through a radical transposition of the search for deliverance to embodied experience. The need to cope with tics, spasms, bodily dysfunctions or involuntary behaviour becomes an expression of the quest for deliverance. It can be argued that this embodiment is far more tangible and difficult to cope with than the soul-searching of operatic characters like Violetta or Tannhäuser. Alain Platel represents this quest both on the level of individual experience as on the societal scale of groups in protest against all kinds of societal ills. On both levels, *C(H)ŒURS* eschews the promise of a radical breakthrough, an optimistic view on utopian transcendence. At best, the dancers and singers arrive at moments of adaptation, control and partial deliverance. Societal salvation is situated in the acceptance of imperfection. In Platel's world view, that is precisely what we can and should hope for. In the representation of this realistic, and seemingly unassuming, perspective lies the overwhelming emotional force of the performance. It is also the key to the humanistic core that lies at the basis of Platel's confrontational choreographic language.

When it comes to the relationship between the drastic and the gnostic in Platel's response to the music, the former is the most apparent. *C(H)ŒURS* demonstrates that choreographic movement could indeed turn the perception of music on its head. When movements are derived not from the main melody but from textural qualities or musical figures of the accompaniment, the music is perceived in a thoroughly different way. Foreground becomes background, and vice versa. Platel's spontaneous approach defies expectations but has the strength to reveal the energy of music in other ways. The listener is forced to experience the music anew in its basic quality of movement in sound. This drastic approach does not mean, however, that the gnostic interpretation is entirely absent. Platel does not directly invest in the images or concepts that the music conveyed in its original context. However, the residue of historical meaning remains present in the background of the perception. The concept of salvation is stripped of its ideological and religious connotations but makes for a meaningful dialogue with the representation of the search for bodily control and the struggle of the individual for recognition in the face of collective forces. The music provides more than a collection of *objets trouvés*. In dialogue with the dance and the stage action, it contributes to the elaboration of an intriguing semiotic space in which the embodied emotions of the present interact with a residue of historical experience.

Notes

1   'Alain Platel, explique Mortier, a l'art de transmettre la grande musique vers de nouveaux publics et vers les jeunes. Je lui ai proposé de travailler sur les émotions créées par la musique de Verdi'. From an interview with Guy Duplat (2012) '*C(H)ŒURS* d'Alain Platel', *La Libre Belgique*, 24 January.
2   'Dans nombre d'œuvres de Verdi et Wagner, on sent bien que le chœur représente le peuple, un peuple souvent en révolte d'ailleurs. Cela formait comme un écho aux mouvements de contestation que l'on pouvait alors voir dans les rues.' Michaël Bellon (2013) 'Les Séductions du Choeur: Alain Platel entre Verdi et Wagner', *Agenda: Uit in Brussel/Vos sorties à Bruxelles/Out and about in Brussels*. 1391: 10–11.
3   Excerpt from a series of radio interviews, made between 1952 and 1991, and issued in the series of recordings Les Grandes Heures INA/Radio France under the title *Marguerite Duras: le ravissement de la parole*. See https://presse.ina.fr.
4   Personal communication. My sincerest thanks to Steven Prengels for sharing this information with me.

5   Carolyn Abbate (2004) 'Music: Drastic or Gnostic?', *Critical Inquiry*, 30: 505–36.
6   'Lorsque je réalise une pièce, j'essaie toujours de retrouver ce qui parle aux gens dans une musique déterminée. Qu'est-ce que les gens connaissent ou reconnaissent et comment puis-je utiliser cette musique de façon alternative? Cette "reconnaissance" garantit un lien émotionnel direct, que je trouve en l'occurrence extrêmement important pour cette pièce.' Michaël Bellon, 'Les Séductions du Choeur', 10–11.
7   Guy Duplat, 'C(H)ŒURS d'Alain Platel'.
8   The point has been made, most vividly, by Karol Berger in his chapter on '*Die Meistersinger von Nürnberg*: Politics after Tristan', in: Karol Berger (2017) *Beyond Reason: Wagner contra Nietzsche*, Oakland, Calif.: University of California Press, 2017.
9   For an extensive commentary on the piece and its historical significance, see Roger Parker (1997) '*Va Pensiero* and the Insidious Mastery of Song', in *Leonora's Last Act: Essays in Verdian Discourse*, Princeton, NJ: Princeton University Press, 20–41.
10 'C'est un langage que j'explore depuis *vsprs* en 2006 et qui peut révéler des choses sur ce type de sentiments pour lesquels on ne trouve pas de mots. La danse a toujours joué un rôle à cet égard. Jadis, on voyait dans la danse ces mouvements langoureux et alanguis que l'on trouve un peu ridicules de nos jours, mais qui, alors, étaient peut-être pertinents. D'une façon similaire, peut-être que les mouvements brutaux que certaines personnes qualifient même de spastiques – ce que je n'aime pas entendre – sont symptomatiques de choses auxquelles nous sommes confrontés dans nos sociétés.' Michaël Bellon, 'Les Séductions du Choeur', 10–11.
11 See, for instance, Wye Jamison Allanbrook (1984) *Rhythmic Gesture in Mozart*: Le Nozze di Figaro *and* Don Giovanni, Chicago, Ill.: University of Chicago Press.
12 Mary Ann Smart (2004) *Mimomania: Music and Gesture in Nineteenth-Century Opera*, Berkeley, Calif.: University of California Press.

References

Abbate, Carolyn (2004) 'Music: Drastic or Gnostic?' *Critical Inquiry*, 30: 505–36.
Allanbrook, Wye Jamison (1984) *Rhythmic Gesture in Mozart*: Le Nozze di Figaro *and* Don Giovanni, Chicago, Ill.: University of Chicago Press.
Bellon, Michaël (2013) 'Les Séductions du Choeur: Alain Platel entre Verdi et Wagner', *Agenda: Uit in Brussel/ Vos sorties à Bruxelles/ Out and about in Brussels*, 1391: 10–1.
Berger, Karol (2016) *Reason: Wagner contra Nietzsche*, Oakland, Calif.: University of California Press.
Duplat, Guy (2012) 'C(H)ŒURS d'Alain Platel', *La Libre Belgique*, 24 January.
Parker, Roger (1997) *Leonora's Last Act: Essays in Verdian Discourse*, Princeton, NJ: Princeton University Press.
Smart, Mary Ann (2004) *Mimomania: Music and Gesture in Nineteenth-Century Opera*, Berkeley, Calif.: University of California Press.

8

Skin Tests

Views on *nicht schlafen*

Claire Besuelle

> It embraces me in order to better cut into me. Unless it is the other way around.
> Field notebook, August 2016

The words in my epigraph were the ones that surfaced from among the notes made after seeing *nicht schlafen* for the first time *in extenso*. It remains one of the most faithful ways to convey my experience of the show as a spectator, a bit less than a year – and a dozen performances – later. *Nicht schlafen*, not to sleep. Seeing Alain Platel's show is similar to hearing its title slam: an injunction to vigilance as much as an invitation to life itself. An incessant, sublime and grotesque show; naive, lyrical and cruel, *nicht schlafen* summons the lexical field of the cutaneous, and words always seem to be lacking the amount of flesh necessary to express the complexity of the sensations that surface when one is immerged in this piece.[1] Then, any attempt to write about this experience as accurately as possible results in a meditation on the complex notion of the skin, this porous wall of the living, this touch-based interface of being in the world. As a matter of fact, Alain Platel claims that exploring the gesture of touching the other with all that it implies has been an active part of his work from the beginning and continues to impose itself in a recurrent fashion.[2] *Nicht schlafen* comes within the scope of this major theme – 'the skin' was markedly one of the tasks assigned to the dancers in the early stages of the creation – and yet displays it in a singular way, which I will propose to analyse in these lines.

My chapter seeks indeed to approach the skin as a dramaturgic motif of *nicht schlafen*, by focusing the argument on the fabrication of gestures that make up the piece.[3] Following Susan Leigh Foster, for whom 'any notion of choreography contains, embodied within it, a kinesthesis, a designated way of experiencing physicality and movement that, in turn, summons other bodies into a specific way of feeling towards it', I will start out from the reactions provoked by five characteristic gestures of the show: (1) entering/watching, (2) fighting, (3) singing, (4) uniting and (5) meeting.[4] Each of these descriptions is to be taken as an attempt of 'fictioning'[5] how a dramaturgy of the skin weaves itself 'to the very body and senses of the performer'.[6] The choice of these specific moments is necessarily arbitrary and resolutely subjective but will make it possible to propose in a relatively restricted space a description of the show while accounting for the multiplicity through which the motif of the skin is materialized in the show.

I need here to say a word about the context in which these analytical fictions were elaborated: watching *nicht schlafen* took for me several forms which will all inevitably be summoned here. Having observed part of the creative process underlying the show as a researcher, I attended several phases of its creation in the studio and exchanged with the artistic team before watching it several times as a spectator while it was on tour. The following descriptions and analyses stem from the ongoing interferences between the act of writing what the gesture makes me feel; the light shed by an examination of the genesis of these gestures among those who make them; and the perspectives offered by theoretical references that I have mobilized to deepen certain intuitions. Skin and touch are complex notions whose field of conceptualization in the humanities is more than vast.[7] I have chosen to summon throughout the writing process the female and male authors whom I read during analysing the piece, rather than setting out *a priori* a conceptual framework to my development.[8] Thus a polyphonic text was woven which seeks to stay as close as possible to a practice of the *regard* (look, watch) as defined by François Cheng:

> The combination of *re* and *garder* is rich in connotations. More than the fact of furtively capturing a view, an image, it evokes the repossession or the renewal of something that has been kept (*gardé*) and which demands, at each new occasion, to be developed in its capacity as being. Let's add that the regard also includes the idea of *égard* (consideration, regard); it always incites the person who watches (*regarde*) to get more profoundly engaged.[9]

Superimposing descriptions of gestures that are ever becoming and the way in which they have not ceased to question the body that apprehends them is the very fabric of this text.

Entering and watching

Berlinde De Bruyckere's sculpture lies there, exposed: the dead flesh of two horses, surrounded by the rags of a torn blanket. A spectator, I enter the hall almost at the same time as the dancers, who advance in the halo of light bathing the peaceful disaster. Slowly: their gestures are extremely controlled and quite gentle. Bells resonate in the distance, reminiscent of a tranquil golden age. I enter to watch, they enter to contemplate. To size up the heap, distance themselves from it, examine it for possible signs. One prays. Another smells. Almost all of them have their backs turned to me. Some put down a bundle of worn blankets at the foot of this strange altar then step back, without taking their eyes off the horses. Their eyes lead mine to scrutinize the charnel house of the tangled, offered equine bodies. The verticality of their transfixed

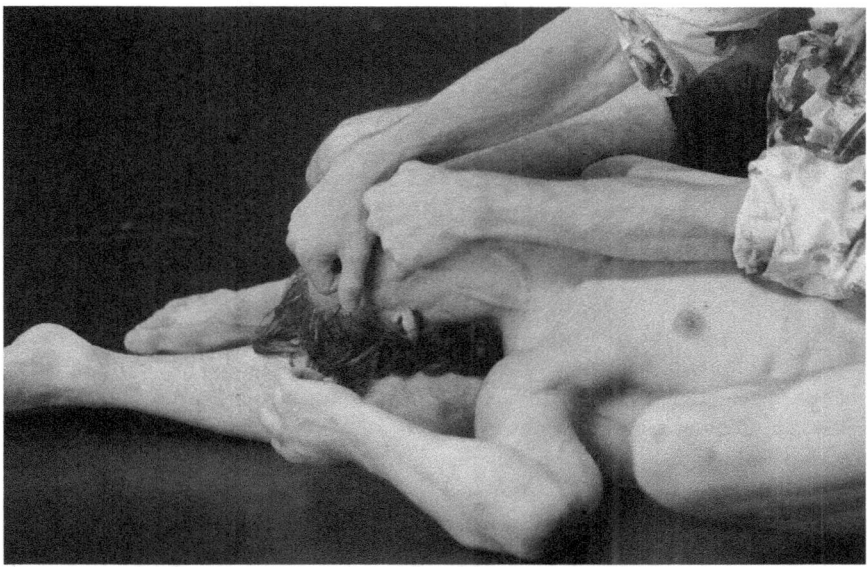

Figure 8.1 David Le Borgne and Elie Tass rehearsing for *nicht schlafen* in dance studio S3, Ghent 2016. © Chris Van der Burght.

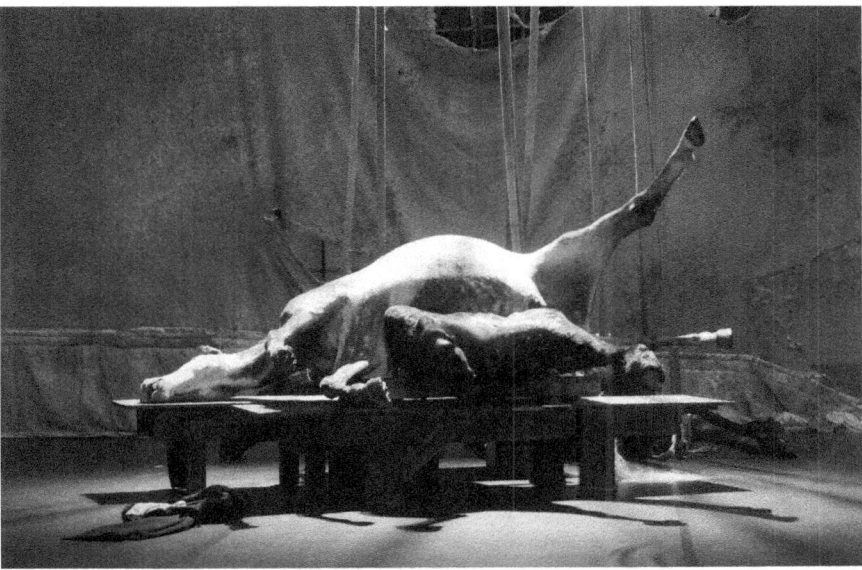

Figure 8.2 Scene, *nicht schlafen* in Jahrhunderthalle, Bochum 2016. © Chris Van der Burght.

silhouettes – all except one – contrasts with the horizontality of these horses abandoned on the floor. Are they gathering their thoughts? Engaging in private prayers? I watch the watchers. Not having access to the expressions on their faces, I watch with them through the minute adjustments of their postures and, by resonances, I feel the others around me watch with me.

The act of entering the hall duplicates the act of entering onstage and at once sets in motion a doubling of the mirror mechanism: I enter, and at once I look at the dancers, who themselves are in the act of entering in order to look at De Bruyckere's sculpture. Yet looking involves a collaboration between visual perception and touch: by seeing, I touch the perceived object from a distance, projecting myself into the visible and completing the visual information with data of a tactile order, such as the roughness of the surfaces, their temperature or their humidity, all bits of information that are perceptible through the skin.[10] The presence of the dancers to their gaze offers an intermediary to the immersion in the tactile resonances of my own, and I progressively adapt to an environment that functions as a sequence of envelopes. Thus, the outsized blanket suspended from the hangers forms the first membrane of a space of which I imagine that it was once closed and protective but whose fluffy character has made way for roughness, its torn fibres having failed to protect anything for a long time. By contrast, as close as possible to the bodies of the dancers, the garment thickens and functions as a protective layer. They are all dressed very warmly, with heavy coats, woollen sweaters, shirts, socks and hats – so many peels that generate a feeling of comfortable warmth but make them look bundled up. Every evening each of the performers must once again select these ill-assorted layers, this moment being the subject of quite particular attention. Romain Guion underlines its importance in his preparatory ritual for the performance: 'It's sometimes a question of minor details that change everything, like the time I take to choose the opening costume. That choice is important; it reflects your mood, your frame of mind on that day and what you want to convey in the show.'[11] A sensible stimulus for my perception, the garment is also a prefatory and foundational support for the performers in their performance.

A similar dynamic is at work in the relation to the flesh of the horses. The sculpture acts as another threshold: depositing the offerings around this unlikely altar opens up the possibility of seeing in it a refuge, a monstrous and paradoxically reassuring hiding place similar to the haunted animal cemeteries of fairy tales. It is probably the most prominent element of this universe in which the tactile prevails: 'rarely has flesh been more ubiquitous ... pallid and waxen like dead flesh, with that translucidity that hints at the muscles, the bared tendons, the fat, and a few pinkish streaks, the vestige of a life under the skin'.[12] Berlinde De Bruyckere works with the skin of dead animals, which she collects then applies to a cast.[13] The dancers witnessed this creative process, an experience which the dancer Bérengère Bodin evokes in these terms: 'When we made the sculpture with Berlinde and the dead horses it was crazy. Facing death directly like that was extremely powerful; it is the tragedy that awaits us all.' A memory that provides material for the interpretation of the dancers. Thus Bérengère Bodin says she makes sure she does not get used to the presence of the horses and makes herself look at them really, with all that this implies: 'It's terrible, when I no longer see them, I don't feel anything. So I have that line during the show: I try to find moments when I can position myself opposite them and let the echoes that are still in me pass before me.'[14] The dancer's words bear witness to the search for a state of presence characterized by a constantly renewed perceptive acuity, and by a willingness to let the affective reminiscences of the story experienced with these horses come up to the surface. Nevertheless, it is a matter of letting oneself be touched by it, and not of creating or fabricating the affect: 'I let what happens happen, certainly without telling myself "Ah, these are dead horses!" Because these are not even dead horses. It is a sculpture made with the skin of a dead horse. There is no need to add anything extra.'[15] We can therefore understand that the dancers are the depositories of an experience that is both intimate and collective and that acts on the quality of the connections which they establish with their environment (both the scenography and the layers of costumes). The gaze of each of them is coloured by these affective and tonic resonances, which my own gaze understands (*comprend*) in return in the etymological sense of the term: it takes (*prend*) them with me. The non-allocation of the memory to a particular manifestation lets it exist in a latent state and enables me to construct a singular relation with the skin of these horses without anything being imposed.

Entering and watching are two gestures that I perform at the same time as the dancers, this simultaneity automatically creating a common space in which I am invited to share a gaze with the dancers, whose tactful restraint neither imposes nor exposes. The permeable and impermeable, solid and fragile dimension of the skin as wall is already at work. Disseminated by the potential spotting of several envelopes that the tactile solicitations linked to the different matters support, the motif is also embodied in a more sensible manner in the tonic and affective dialogue of which the performers are the vectors through the activity of their gaze. Between visible and invisible, the dramaturgy of the skin occurs through several sensory canals that set up the two main semantic senses of touch: the tact(ile) and the affect. Out of this common space – this common skin – other gestures will unfold, which can be seen as explorations of the possible relations to the other.

Fighting

It's still the beginning of the show. The framework of the dreamy contemplation which the exposition seemed to conjure is torn by the irruption of a radical act. The dancer Ido Batash first approaches slowly. His gaze is fixed on Elie Tass – the only one who is not standing and facing the horses but lying on the ground, three-quarters towards the public. Elie Tass's legs are laid out, his chest half-raised, resting on his forearms. Moving in successive jerks, his gaze takes in various points of the space without attaching itself to anything. Batash hardly breathes. Each step weighs on its rectilinear trajectory. In his face and in his eyes, I believe I can perceive each of his thoughts before they have reached his conscience. Hunting, rage, tenderness, desire, madness: I don't know what he wants, he who advances, and everything seems possible. He advances, while Romain Guion and Russell Tshiebua retreat towards the horses and Dario Rigaglia, for his part, hovers at the end of his sinuous and fluid solo. And the rope breaks. Batash suddenly pounces on his target, rushes and grabs hold of him, rolls on the floor with him. The signal unleashes a melee. All of a sudden, the urgency to set about the other is allowed.

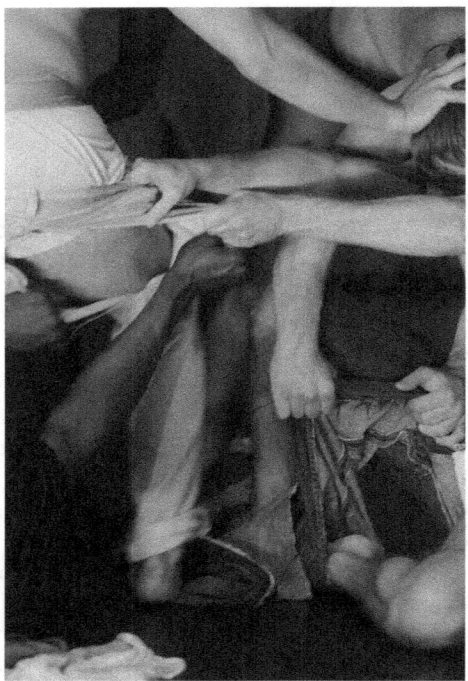

Figure 8.3 Cast during rehearsals of *nicht schlafen* in dance studio S3, Ghent 2016. © Chris Van der Burght.

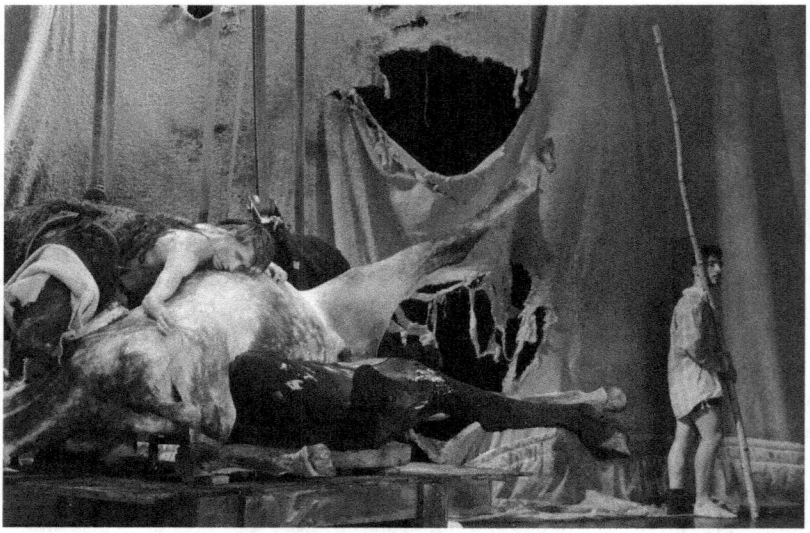

Figure 8.4 Romain Guion and Dario Rigaglia during rehearsals of *nicht schlafen* in dance studio S3, Ghent 2016. © Chris Van der Burght.

From embraces to evasions, the only objective of the melee is to strip the other of his faded finery and to reach the naked flesh. Shivers. The stage is like an arena on which one pushes, pulls and pushes back, using hands, head, feet: what one can, what one finds. Grabbing hold of a leg and biting into a back, dragging the other down in one's fall in order to better weigh down on him and immobilize him. To spit. To shout from the depths of one's guts. The dancers slide, agglomerate and then free themselves to take the space to measure one another, to prepare a new attack. Shoulders are hunched to better serve as rams. I let out a laugh but my eyes are screwed up so as to diminish their window, under the effect of an irrational fear of a blow that would reach me (or a protective reflex to counter a violence I cannot stand). Their breathing becomes short and their eyes wild; the skins appear, gradually reddened, burned, marked. It seems to me that this all-out confrontation could go on for hours, and perhaps I could continue watching them. Following their lost evolutions with the feigned disapproval of a poorly dissimulated pleasure.

This melee lasts about ten minutes, during which the dancers' sole task is to fight and to skin one another. There are no set terms, and neither have the movements been scripted, except for the beginning and end, a (possible) resolution of the fight being introduced by the beginning of the music (the *Adagietto* of Mahler's *Symphony No. 5*). Later, furtive brawls will punctuate the entire show, resurgences of this inaugural madness that will end up turning on itself. This first and long wrestling scene, brutal, violent and explosive, broke radically with the show's opening, as if we had been led up a wrong track. This is all the more striking since it is the first modality of physical contact between the dancers.

These minutes of the performance rest on the investment by the performers in physical actions characterized by their power and combining a constant engagement in their relation to time, to space, to weight and to the conduct of the gesture. The result is a striking reality effect: I can see men struggling for their survival, meeting the violence of the other with violence. Elie Tass compares the scene to an initiation ritual. This refers not only to the global dramaturgy of the show but also to his personal path within it. To him, the fight is indeed a necessary step enabling access to another level of engagement in the show: 'all the physical swelling that takes place there is used to make what we call the "phrases" in a profound way, fully and … yes, the right way'.[16] The scene acts therefore as a threshold influencing the dancers' overall development. The absence of any regulated script imposes an increased vigilance due to the potential physical endangerment of the bodies, intensifying the presence even further. For Bérengère Bodin, 'the opening battle is physically difficult because from the start we are in a borderline situation. We are always on the border between fighting and performing the fight. Either we lapse into something "fake" which we don't like, or we flirt with a risk-taking which sometimes goes quite far.'[17]

Note the mention of the weak link between 'performing' and 'not performing' the confrontation, performing here being understood in the sense of feigning. The pretence rejected here is that of a simulated action that would not fully entail its physical, psychic and affective implications, even though awareness and mastery are necessary for the execution of a scenic action reproducible if not in its details, then at least in its principle. And yet the practical details of inter-corporeity developed in the battle imply perceptive and sensorial dispositions that induce a singular state of being in the world. The acquisition of humankind's erect posture enabled the development of prehension and a perceptive faculty dominated by sight and hearing, the organs of the distal senses, and the development of this posture is key on the physiological, affective and symbolic levels.[18] Here, the erect posture is deconstructed, and, with it, the abolition of the norms characteristic of a social inter-corporeity is consecrated: 'you enter the space of people, people enter your space, in complete violation'.[19] Although the physical actions are not written, their dynamic characteristics involve a motility governed by centres symbolically attached to the domains of the instinctive and pulsional, frustrating the tacit normative framework on which the elaboration of a vision of the human depends, always correlated to a certain hierarchization of the physical centres of the movement.[20] In this regard, the displacement of the function of the hands and mouth are particularly notable. The hand abandons its role as a prehensile organ, the tool of a 'cognitive touch', and is demoted to a supporting function, a claw whose sensibility no longer serves to discriminate but to tear, scratch or push back. Likewise, the mouth no longer serves to talk here, but to spit, bite or shout, the inarticulate and secretion referring to the primary tactile function of the mucous membranes, to the uneducation of a sense of taste that we have learnt to restrict to the (rationalized) intake of food and to the development of sexual activities that belong strictly to the private sphere. Immersing oneself in these actions thus has an influence on the perceptive, motor and affective faculties of the dancers, an element that plays to the fullest in the intensity of the performance by the development of an 'almost visceral' reactivity, in the words of Bérengère Bodin.

The objective of this battle is to strip the other of his clothes, that is, of his skin, his social roles, the normative frameworks that define him. We have moreover seen that this choice of costumes is the locus of an intimate investment on behalf of each of the dancers. This exhibition of the skin sought with an unfeigned determination acts as a limit, all the more so since the confrontation does not seem to have any other goal than stripping the other bare and to reveal his skin, as if it were possible to dig into the other down to the bone to reach the possibility of really touching him. Reddened, marked and increasingly bruised skins as the confrontation rages on, sweating and dripping skins under which we imagine the muscular tension. The taboo of touching, the tacit law of tact in the social organization is unsettled doubly by the exposure of the flesh, which is bruised moreover, and this is not unambiguous. My gaze, too, is unsettled. The reality effect of the action that takes place freezes it between incredulity and excitement. A jubilation emanates from the paradoxical liberty that the dancers allow themselves. The extended temporality causes rhythmic variations that arrive in successive waves, anchoring in a cyclical time this confrontation that no longer seems to have to conclude. This vagueness of time brings into play the limits and refers to the taboos: violence, sexuality, cannibalism.[21] Seeing becomes an impulse in which pleasure and disgust, culpability and excitement blend. Mixed emotions which open up the spectre of the sensible, questioning values and principles by confronting them with the notions of the limit and the norm.

Several dimensions of the motif of the skin come together in the sequence, contributing to the ambivalence of this foundational scene. The kinaesthetic contagion permitted by the engagement of the dancers in the action underlines the exposition of the skin in an erotics of bruising, and thereby works on two facets of my perception. The deaf echo of the simulated pain of the blow, the more acute one of the burn or of the scratch blend with an urge to watch. The duration of the scene questions the fundamental motor of the gesture: what is to be attained in this determination to go and see beneath the skin? What desire is also at work in the flesh of my gaze, which still wants to watch and yet cannot watch any more? The state of embodiment sought by the dancers renders the moment 'emotionally troubling', not for the physical danger that one takes but for the violence that it reveals.[22] Seeing these beings welcome in themselves a capacity for violence acts like a catharsis, as much as it compels a reflexive distance. It is from the impossibility of analysing the complexity of sensations that open up that I am led to question my conception of violence, my relation to the other and to his skin.

Serving as a counterpoint to the radicalness of a melee in which clasping is synonymous with tearing is another crucial gesture of *nicht schlafen*, that involves something almost opposite to the physical envelope: singing.

Singing

Singing is a recurrent gesture in *nicht schlafen*. Its first occurrence takes place at the very beginning of the show, with *Hör auf zu beben* (*Bereite dich zu Leben!*), an a cappella chorus arranged by Steven Prengels and based on the fifth movement of Mahler's *Symphony No. 2*. It is a slow song, with a weighty rhythm, which is drawn out in time and gradually gains in power. Once the dancers have gathered around the horses and looked at them, before the fight, before any other action, the song spreads like a wave. It creates a halo of presence. I only barely perceive the trajectory of the breath that supports the emission of the sound through the chests of the dancers. I hear the singular plural of the voices that merge in the chorus but can only see in chiaroscuro the solitudes of the body-statues pushed from the ground. The presence of the voices has neither a beginning nor an end, and besides it evaporates as surreptitiously as it arrived. Soon after, a second song breaks out. The community evolves in scattered order, long after the battle, and re-enacts the first chorus in a fragmented configuration. As though out in the sun, their hands on their hips, this time the dancers let their bodies be the echo of the fluid melody of the verse *Den Tod niemand zwingen könnt* ('No one can compel death', composition for a cappella chorus by Steven Prengels, based on Mahler's *Symphony No. 2* and Johann Sebastian Bach's *Cantata* BWV 4). The voluptuousness of the song momentarily brings them together and carries me away, just before the blows of the *Scherzo* of Gustav Mahler's *Symphony No. 7* catch up with the dancers to lead them into a wild unison dance. All of a sudden, Boule Mpanya and Russell Tshiebua shout '*Ambula Makasa!*' and all the others answer forcefully.[23] The pygmy melody establishes itself like a game, but, seizing the voices in flight, another intense and percussive pulsation impresses itself in the bodies, pulling them away from the song. The music is Steven Prengels' orchestral composition after the *allegro energico* of the finale of Mahler's *Symphony No. 6* and Strauss's *Kaizer-Walz*. The bells attached to the feet of the dancers support their exultant and sinisterly joyful march, in a frontal line that moves forward ineluctably. The density of this moment flows and dissolves into a second Congolese polyphony which absorbs its echo in the voices.[24]

In his study on the skin, Didier Anzieu emphasizes that the skin cannot refuse sensations, and we can add that it is impossible – with the exception of prostheses and earplugs, for instance – to escape from auditive stimuli and their vibratile waves of contagion.[25] The resonance increases further when the sound comes from human voices which make themselves be heard. As Sophie Herr reminds us, the voice 'takes root in the sensible experience of a body' whose flesh has been traversed, modelled, fashioned by the plasticity of the breath that passes through it. Following the analyses of Roland Barthes, she adds, 'the voice returns the body on itself in an "internal sensuality" while its vibrant force flies out of the body and disseminates the corporal impression in the sound environment.'[26] The voice, as the locus of the intimate par excellence, crystallizes the passage between internal space and external space of the body, escaping the limits of the physical envelope. The voices of the nine dancers constitute sound envelopes which, thanks to the amplifying mechanism of the stage noises (two microphones dangling from the hangers), condense by diffracting them each of their presences in the echo of the singular grain of their voices. Each of these voices blends into the chorus – or perhaps we should here call it a body – and this vocal matter constantly weaves and unweaves itself over the course of the rhythmic, melodic and respiratory qualities that successively found the songs. To continue the metaphor of the voice turning the body over itself, we could say that each of the dancers exposes themselves by giving their voice, and in doing so participates in the creation of a sound material with an inimitable and indivisible grain.

Singing is indeed here first a collective gesture: in the polyphony of the arrangements composed by Steven Prengels, the voices blend by section in a traditional way (soprano, alto, tenor and bass). In the pygmy songs, the form is structured rather around an exchange of questions and answers, the voices of Russell Tshiebua and Boule Mpanya standing out as soloists, always nevertheless supported and carried by the chorus of the seven other dancers. The work of this chorus of voices during the creative process of the piece appeared to me like one of the essential moments in the constitution of the show's dramaturgic universe. As Russell Tshiebua relates: 'Every day after the break, we picked up at 2 p.m. and we would do 15 or 20 minutes of singing. It was simultaneously a meeting with contemporary dance and with Mahler's music: learning these texts in German and these scores, that is how the meeting really took place.'[27] During the touring period, the ultimate preparation phase of the dancers before the show started moreover with a collective vocal warm-up at the end of which the different bits of the show were rehearsed. The necessarily collective dimension of this preparatory time underlines the importance of a process which connects what is intimate and what is common on the level of the very fabrication of the vocal gesture, particularly sensitive in the execution of these choral moments, between communion and exaltation.

This praxis combines also the very substance of the music with heterogeneous origins: baroque polyphonies of Western art music and traditional pygmy songs. If singing a tune means breathing it to incorporate its dynamic qualities, the experience of the song thus inscribes in the very breaths the diversity of the collected musical cultures and plays on the counterpoints. Beyond the collusion, it is a conflagration that takes place, 'one of the things that prove that the future of the world depends on *métissage*', in the words of Russell Tshiebua. The singer admits that he and Boule Mpanya

> didn't think it was going to work and just tried ... in my view, you can feel that it is not a cut and paste ... It's organic. The way we enter into it is magic ... You don't expect this itinerary: we end up there without expecting it or realizing how we got there. And experiencing it each time is magic ... Making Westerners who barely know Africa ... sing organically is magic ... And I'm not a Pygmy either! ... But even if I'm not a Pygmy and them even less so, it sounds – it sounds good.[28]

A work on the very flesh of the sound, we could say, which makes it possible to operate by sutures on the advent of a musical dramaturgy. At the beginning and in the middle of the show, the two classical choirs form a first envelope that shatters into pieces when the pygmy songs break out. Interruptions which will continue to irrupt in the musical fabric itself of the show, resolutely combining various influences and sonorities. It is on the basis of the work of this polyphony that the symbolic and referential dimension of the choice of pieces unfolds, a choice that involves several levels. The historic and socio-cultural plan through the collusion between Western art music and traditional pygmy songs.[29] The aesthetic plan too, the composition of the show inscribing itself by the use of this process in the tradition of the practice of Mahler himself, who used to conjure up a popular musical imagination at the very core of compositions of art music: symphonies, lieder, etc. The phenomenon of weaving and embedding in action in the work of the voices picks up this momentum of agglomeration, which is not like a citation or collage but like a recomposition, a reconfiguration of new melodic arrangements in which the harmonies of a historic, geographic and cultural sphere meet others to create something new.

Playing on the vibratile solicitations specific to vocal music, the content and the forms of the songs convoked here prolong the dialogue between the intimate and the collective inherent to the experience of singing in unison. The polyphonic vocal form functions like a dramaturgic line of the show: it is in the independence of each of the voices (in the dual sense of the voice specific to each singing individual and of the melodic voices carried by the different compositions) that the matter in constant metamorphosis carried by the unison grows dense, becomes diffracted and transforms itself. The meaning brings to the surface the expressive and dynamic qualities of each song and of the in-depth work that binds them together. Prolonging the kinesic experience, the engagement in and through the song densifies the network of tactile solicitations displayed by the piece. It is a common vocal body which comes into being through the diffraction and demultiplication of the bodies of the nine dancers, and this body only materializes itself in a weaving of geographic and cultural spheres. The semantics linked to language is blended in a network of intensities, making the force prevail over the sign, opening new possibilities of being in the world in common.[30] This polyphonic paradigm can moreover help better grasp what is at work in the choreographic composition of the so-called unison passages, prolonging the reflection on the porosity of the bodies.

Uniting

O Mensch. From a scattered, even disparate order, they come together slowly but surely. They suddenly resemble children afraid of the storm, plastic clothes zipped onto their very skin. Nine breaths hung on their intimate depressions. In turn waiting expectantly, stupefied, then suddenly carried away by a small dry frenzy, which gradually gains in amplitude. Absorbed in listening to a murmur to which I do not have access, their only choice is to let things unfold. To collect themselves and to breathe before the next wave. I can find no centre in this paradoxical unison, nothing that can steer my gaze or my perception: I am lost before their absence. And yet they are together. The K-Way clothes rub against the music, fingers pick at the space. Mouths articulate in silence the words pronounced by the singer and the feet knead the floor while the arms revolve around an empty axis. Their eyes wander, look furtively, almost fugitively for something to hold onto. And the palm touches the skull, the hand catches hold of the nose, the interlaced fingers of both hands crush the sternum, touching the heart. Splinters of fear in the eyes. Squeezing around oneself to ensure the tangible existence of a palpitating and living ensemble. Seeking out the depths of what is moving under the carcass.

The beginning of the text by Nietzsche used by Mahler for the night song of his *Symphony No. 3* translates as follows: 'O man! Take heed! / What saith deep midnight's voice indeed? / I slept my sleep –, / From deepest dream I've woke.'[31] The voice of Dagmar Pecková fills the hall like a gentle lamentation in which the dancers come together. The unison is composed according to the founding principle of the 'bastard dance' set up by Platel in his very first creations already: all the performers had to learn a choreographic phrase composed by one or the other without the unison being synonymous with strict homogeneity in the execution of the gesture.[32] Here it is a proposal by Ido Batash working on a heightened proprioceptive awareness that makes it possible to distance oneself from the spatial references which the focalization of the gaze yields.[33] Batash then draws his inspiration from a photograph tacked to the wall of the rehearsal studio, representing two boys in pink short-sleeved shirts and with perfectly combed blonde hair, but eyes staring and frozen, as though lost beyond the lens. The dancer's research drew the attention of the choreographer:

> Alain said something about my face which apparently looked very strange when I was doing it and I wasn't aware of it at all. I wondered what I was doing with my face and my look. In fact I realized that I was simply trying to vague my gaze, not to look at anything or any point, to erase my gaze.[34]

On this basis, the phrase developed rapidly around that singular quality of movement, between hyper-presence and absence. 'How is it to be detached from everything around you, and being not connected at all to your own body?' Batash continues about the quality of the targeted movement.[35] For whoever is watching, seeing the gesture take place without perceiving its anticipation through the gaze and the gravity modulations that accompany the equilibration produces a puppetization effect of the performer's body which restricts one to hypnosis. The relation between the centre and the periphery is constantly frustrated, the dancers seem to be overcome and moved by the movement rather than being its actors. This gives the music an omniscient and almost manipulative function. The passages of silent articulation of the words of the sung text crystallize the erasure effect: the depth of the song and of its harmonics is answered by the empty mastication of a breath that seems to have lost itself.

This particular work of coordination sought and found by Ido Batash is something that each dancer had to seek in themselves by working to be as close as possible to the dynamic qualities of the movement so as not only to reproduce the effect of a state of body but to seek to go back to the source of what builds it up in terms of postural and gestural organization.[36] The unison thus builds itself up on the basis of each of these solitudes working on their own passivity in the action. In the slipstream of the characteristics of the above vocal polyphony, the principle of composition that results in unison starts from the bottom, in a common movement towards a specific quality of presence. Here the principle is accentuated by the dynamic qualities specific to the passage, the erasure being sought paradoxically highlighting the singularity of being at the very heart of the gesture. The technical and aesthetic stake of the execution of the passages during the performance also crystallizes its political dimension. Ido Batash puts it this way:

> In *O Mensch* we have no counts on how we are moving, and the group is following me so I have a huge responsibility to gather the group in some ways. I try to be precise but I don't want to have counts or clear cues in the music. That's another place where things are really alive: you live the process, there is no outcome to complete. These particularly shaky place are where the piece is vibrating very strongly.[37]

It is the capacity to listen to the other, to unite one's own movement to that of the other which is at stake and which takes place each evening in a process where the living takes precedence.

At the level of the gesture, the puppetization effect linked to the coordination described above coexists with a series of manifestations of the body in its most primary aspects. The breath is visibly the primary support of the gesture and the motor of its execution. From this basis, an exposition of the body breathing and suffocating crystallizes in two places. One, when the dancers use their intermingled hands to press down on their sternum, pressing down on the lungs as on bellows; the other, when they block one of their nostrils and describe a large circle with their free arm, inhaling and exhaling synchronously: two fantasy self-resuscitations of the vital functions through a mechanical action. A series of gestures prolongs this physiological presence of the body: furtive self-contacts with the tips of their fingers on the cheek of the open mouth, as though to feel for a decayed molar; the palm of the hand on the hair, to confirm the shape of the skull; down to the final burp which, involving the respiratory system, the diaphragm and the viscera, signals the apogee of the organic manifestation. There is a hiatus here between a particular quality of interpretation which seeks on the level of the *fond du geste* to drive the subject behind their movement while its tracing refers to a form of hypochondriac worry, i.e. the excessive and anguished preoccupation of a subject regarding their health.[38] We then witness the strange exposition of scattered organic manifestations that occur and happen without any coherence, with music as their sole guide. This produces a conflagration between vitality and artificiality, humanity and animality like so many potential becomings of a body-space traversed by affects, constructing in each body an abstract line or an arrangement which reverses the usual relations.[39] The tangible seems to move in the space between the bodies of the performers traversed by the same movement, resonating not without humour in the vibrations of their plastic clothes trembling in the space and picked up by the microphones. 'Of all the sensorial organs, [the skin] is the most vital: we can live and be blind, deaf, stripped of taste and smell', writes Didier Anzieu.[40] Here the work of the absent gesture restricts to a kinesic meditation on the skin as a wall of the living. The skin here seems to scatter itself, to become a matter that would no longer delimitate the entity of the subject, that would no longer fail to block, despite the K-Way. This passage of unison-fusion opens up on a sequence where another possible relation with the other is explored, like an attempt to meet them without being immersed in them.

Meeting

Trois petits tours ... At the end of *O Mensch*, some still seem to float in the trail of the ropes that gently fade, busts abandoned at the back and covered with successive waves. Others gently stand up again. Romain Guion and Elie Tass, for their part, stand up quickly. With their hands on their hips, they paw the ground somewhat randomly. One unzips a K-Way, another makes little flicking gestures: because they spin on themselves, they will end up freeing up the space. None will remain, except them. Then they breathe one another and blow on each other. Prolegomena to a meeting where nothing seems to have to meet. Is it a question of looking for something elsewhere? They push one another in turn in a childish merry-go-round. The hands of Elie Tass trace smoke signs in the air that hypnotize Romain Guion for a moment. Then it's Romain Guion who rests on Elie Tass as though on a low wall, seeking to see above an invisible obstacle. They try to kiss, open their arms, press up against one another. Nothing doing: they fail to find one another. They call one another, sometimes even welcome one another, but fail to meet. An implacable and obscure logic produces a series of directionless events, without a narrative, without a trajectory. Suddenly on the ground, Elie Tass half-reclining, and Romain Guion kneeling on his lap, the two dancers expose one another in a series of intense emotional states which nothing connects, however. Romain Guion takes Elie Tass's pulse, raises his fists to an invisible boxer, laughs so much that tears run down his face, and cries. Elie Tass sneezes, calls for help, converses with ghosts. And then they separate without any warning, crawling on their knees, their legs abandoned on the ground.

The improvisation in the form of a duo was one of the first tasks given to the dancers at the start of the creative process, and, as mentioned in the introduction, these raw materials of the show developed on the meeting with the body of the other, with as their main task: 'the skin'. Two lines are added to the genesis of this duo: the desire to reach the top without managing to get there, associated with the idea of suffocation or asphyxia; and a game on the permanent and rapid succession of very different emotional states. In line with his evolution in the show, Romain Guion calls this moment a first attempt to meet the other without blending with him (whether in the energy of the battle or in the fusion of a unison):

> With Elie, it's the first time that I am meeting a foreign being, another body. This implies not knowing what to do with this body, not knowing how to approach it. There is a certain clumsiness ... All these elements come to the surface when I approach the moment of the duo. But the most important thing ... is that clumsiness. The fact of not knowing where to put my hands, where to put myself.[41]

The insistence on clumsiness via the work on the hands is in itself revealing in the dancers' utterances. The hands are equipped with a large number of receptors, which increase the tactile sensibility, and they are also – this is not unrelated – one of the zones of the body most intrinsically linked to the semic. The duo develops on the displacement of the right gesture, always frustrated and revisited. It marks the reprise of a kinesphere specific to the individual and in which there is no longer any question of immersing oneself. The development of a motricity characterized by the absence of a spatial anchorage point and a dry suddenness in the changes of orientation of the body nevertheless seems to make difficult any form of communication with the other. The dancers asphyxiate one another, swelling up and deflating like balloons, and the suffocation threatens the life of each of these monads without windows not so much through their inability to breathe but through the solitude to which this impossible adaptation to the other and to the environment seems to condemn them. Their erratic gestures are paradoxically mimetic: if they refer to a certain number of everyday and recognizable gestures (feeling the pulse, sneezing, embracing someone), they are nevertheless performed contrary to common sense, breaking the adequacy between the gesture and its context. This inadequacy produces traces that go unheeded: drawings traced in the air that impress themselves on the retina and dissolve in the absence of a conceptual substratum which would make it possible to articulate their inscription in reality. This dissolution of the concept refers implicitly to that of the subject as a unifying function, whose gesture would be supported by a unifying apprehension of reality. A dissolution further emphasized by the work on the expression of the emotions, flying by at full speed without any identifiable cause or effect. The precision of the execution reinforces the dark humour of the situation, generating a laughter that remains stuck in the throat, because it takes note precisely of a 'failure of meaning'.[42] The impossibility of the meeting thus goes through the impossibility of touching. In its aborted attempts to find the way to touch appropriately, the duo exposes the intrinsic link between touch and meaning: when touching is no longer possible, it is the very possibility of meaning, of communication and common construction that seem to be so too. 'Many questions arise today about the way in which we can touch the other. What is the dignity of the other?' asks Alain Platel.[43]

The incongruous leads to the absurd, in the dual literal and philosophical sense of the being acting in a way that is not in accordance with the laws of logic, producing an event that does not let itself be apprehended by a rational interpretation. Yet, in this pocket of resistance, a ferocious vitality manifests itself, all the more sensitive since it seems to expend itself in pure loss. The skin as interface, an instance of relation (in the dual sense of being in contact and being touched by something or someone), is here seized in the dialectic between surface and depth which it crystallizes. 'There is nothing deeper in mankind than the skin': these words of Paul Valéry express the cutaneous as an organ of the feeling of being in the world, of tangibility of the self through the meeting with the other. Platel continues: 'We complain a lot about the way social networks have profoundly altered our way of connecting to the other … We must take the initiative to communicate with someone: using one's mobile phone is obvious, but it's less obvious to go and talk to someone.' Here, what physiologically provokes and suspends the laughter in my throat is the spectacle of an impossibility of touching which refers directly to an impossibility of being: without interaction with the other made possible by meeting the other, no meaning is possible.

The skin. 'An inherent given of both an organic and an imaginary order … a protective system of our individuality as well as a first instrument and place of exchange with the other' – to describe it I will choose the image given by Didier Anzieu of this complex set of organs, at the intersection of the anatomical, functional and affective.[44] A sensitive surface – to touch, pressure, heat, softness, nodal in the crossed functioning of perception and necessary to the development of proprioception, its role in a number of biological functions (breathing, secretion and elimination, digestion, reproduction) finish making it a vital organ. A paradoxical, porous and impermeable frontier, it signals independence as much as necessary interaction, capturing and transmitting essential information to the survival of humanity in its environment while giving the external world characteristic elements on its identity/identities. *Nicht schlafen* takes shape in this complexity of the skin. Surface–interface, presence–absence, interior–exterior, unicity–collectivity, we can inscribe all the gestures displayed by the show in a circulation inside these fields of tension, which it explores to turn them inside out or claims before knocking them over. What am I touching when I touch the other? As Anzieu reminds us, the semantic spectre of the verb, from 'put your hand on' to 'move' also extends from the corporal to the affective. The injunction '*Noli me tangere*', a Christian taboo of touching evoked in the Bible, is constitutive of a Western form of sociality and relation to politics.[45] Not to touch: not to attack, protect (oneself) from the impulse of violence and sexual desire. Not to touch anymore: to get out of the fusional joining and constituting oneself as an individual by means of 'a separate existence'.[46] By embodying, either by carrying in the flesh – that of the dancers, that of horses or my own – the impulse, the contagion, the tearing, the ripping, the exultation, the piece continues to question the limits of the skin. It refers to these 'hypersensitive' bodies, 'receptive to the subtlest exterior stimuli, intensely deformed by the least emotion' described by Evelyne Grossman, and in which she sees a testimony of the contemporary complexity of our relation to the bodies and to the affects that traverse them.[47]

The descriptions-analyses of these five gestures crystallize ways of rendering sensible the motif of the skin in the show, which could take on other shapes and become more complex through other descriptions. The keystone of a dramaturgy of resonance of things through the self, the motif of the skin makes it possible to envisage the orchestration of the piece following the examples of a neuralgic network. The sensitive experience of the dancers is both core and bark, front and back, determining and determined by a set of score-like structures.[48] It is to account for the specificity of this embodied aesthetic that I tried to get as close as possible to those through which the cutaneous motif of *nicht schlafen* becomes crystallized, those who render it sensible, if not visible. The construction of an aesthetic discourse centred on the performance of the performers – performance being here understood as their singular processes of elaboration, maturation and performance of their trajectories in the show – is an uncertain exercise, which involves leftovers and the minuteness of the gaze. And yet it reveals the polyphonic dimension of the construction of the show, whose 'different levels coexist simultaneously and prolong one another in each other, superpose one another and separate one another from one another' reveal themselves, and create a common and singular space of which I would like this text to be like a follow-up, where the affects resonate without ever communicating.[49]

Acknowledgements

My most heartfelt thanks to the entire team of les ballets C de la B for the warm welcome they gave my research approach, without which this chapter would not exist.

Notes

1   This is a tendency that is to be found in writings other than mine, as the title of the text by the show's dramaturg Hildegard De Vuyst so rightly says: 'Les Bienfaits du sous-cutané'.
2   Alain Platel, interview by Claire Besuelle, 18 November 2016, Lille.
3   The expression 'fabrication of gesture' refers here to a methodological posture towards observing and analysing dance that is well synthetized in the introduction of *Histoires de gestes*: 'when we are trying to catch the meaning of a gesture, we are sensitive, consciously or not, to the particular awareness that makes it up [*qui le fabrique*], the way of watching, the way of touching, the quality of listening, the way the movement is initiated, the way the supports are organized as well as the construction of the space by the subject in motion. In other words, we are facing a "motor project" [*projet moteur*] that interprets the world and bears the prints of all the body representations which irrigates social and esthetical behaviours'. Laetitia Doat, Marie Glon and Isabelle Launay (2012) *Histoires de gestes*, Paris: Actes Sud, 18. The structure of this chapter is freely inspired on that way of focusing on one gesture (here, one that appeared characteristic for me in the piece) to develop on what it convey through diverse approaches (here, mainly by the dialogue between aesthetic analysis and a genetical one).
4   Susan Leigh Foster (2010) *Choreographing Empathy*, London and New York: Routledge, 2.

5   I am using the term 'fiction' following the studies of Isabelle Ginot about writing about dance pieces. She stresses the fictional dimension of the relationship between the critic and the piece, claiming that that fictional dimension should be the condition of writing rather than being a marginal or hidden aspect of the texts, which would let one believe in the existence of an objective or truthful object that the text should describe faithfully. Isabelle Ginot (2006) 'La Critique en danse contemporaine: theories et pratiques, pertinence et délires', Département Danse de l'Université Paris 8. This methodological posture is consistent with the phenomenological approach defended by Michel Bernard in his essay 'Esquisse d'une théorie de la perception du spectacle chorégraphique', in Michel Bernard (2002) *De la création chorégraphique*, Paris: Centre National de la Danse, and as well with the pragmatic aesthetic Philippe Guisgand claims in *Les Fils d'un entrelacs sans fin. La Danse dans l'œuvre d'Anne Teresa De Keersmaeker*, Lille: Les Presses du Septentrion, 2008. That is why I assume this text to be resolutely subjective and putting that subjectivity as an epistemological frame.

6   Anne-Marie Guilmaine (2012) 'État de porosité', *Spirale: Arts, Lettres, Sciences Humaines*, 242: 36–7. Available at http://id.erudit.org/iderudit/67978ac (accessed 20 August 2019).

7   Besides the references cited in bibliography, I would cite the work of Alain Berthoz, who in *Le Sens du mouvement* (Paris: Odile Jacob, 1997), shows the importance of touch in proprioception. Coming from a totally different approach, the chapter dedicated to touching in David Le Breton's *La Saveur du monde, une anthropologie des sens* (Paris: Métaillé, 2006) gives an anthropological perspective on the subject. From a more political and philosophical angle one can refer to *Politics of Touch* by Erin Manning (University of Minnesota, 2007). Closer to the performance-arts realm, I would underline the collective publication *The Senses in Performance*, edited by Sally Banes and André Lepecki (London and New York: Routledge, 2007).

8   Didier Anzieu's work *Le Moi-Peau*, Jacques Derrida's reflections on touch, and the notion of flesh borrowed by Luce Irigaray from Merleau-Ponty to express the specificity of the relation between the skin and the tactile, on the interface between interiority and exteriority, the passive and the active, although they are not directly cited, did accompany the writing of this article (references at the end of this article).

9   François Cheng (2006) *Cinq méditations sur la beauté*, Paris: Albin Michel, 108.

10 To follow Merleau-Ponty in his description of the chiasmatic and inter-sensorial functioning of perception, see Maurice Merleau-Ponty (1964), *Le Visible et l'invisible*, Paris: Gallimard, 172–204. Basile Douganis elaborates on that assumption in a chapter entitled 'The Visible as the Tactile: Distal and Proximal', in his study of Japanese corporal practices, *Pensées du corps, la philosophie à l'épreuve des arts gestuels japonais* (Paris: Les Belles Lettres, 2012), 75–80. On the aesthetic field we can cite the approach of Laura Marks in her book *The Skin of the Film: Intercultural Cinema, Embodiment and the Senses* (Durham, NC: Duke University Press, 2000), in which she offers a theory of 'haptic visuality', that is to say a visuality that functions like the sense of touch by triggering physical memories of smell, touch and taste.

11 Roman Guion, interview by Claire Besuelle, 18 November 2016, Lille.

12 Ildiko Dao, *Inferno*, published 23 September 2016 and accessed online 27 December 2016. Available at https://inferno-magazine.com/2016/09/23/alain-platel-nicht-schlafen-la-batie-geneve/.

13 She has been developing this singular process since 2000, when she created the exhibition *In Flanders' Fields* on the First World War. For more details on her work,

see the article devoted to her by Anne Galzi on the website Regard au pluriel. Available at http://www.regardaupluriel.com/berlinde-bruyckere/(accessed 25 July 2017).
14 Bérengère Bodin, interview by Claire Besuelle, 18 November 2016, Lille.
15 Bodin, interview by Claire Besuelle, 18 November 2016.
16 Elie Tass, interview by Claire Besuelle, 27 May 2017, Paris.
17 Bodin, interview by Claire Besuelle, 18 November 2016.
18 As demonstrated in the text by Erwin Strauss (2004), 'La Posture érigée', *Quant à la danse*, 1: 22–41.
19 Samir M'Kirech, interview by Claire Besuelle, 25 May 2017, Paris.
20 Basile Doganis has shown this through his study of the notion of 'centre' in Japanese gestural arts. See *Pensées du corps, la philosophie à l'épreuve des arts gestuels japonais*, Paris: Les Belles Lettres, 2012, 64.
21 It is moreover noteworthy that Georges Bataille, in his work devoted to eroticism understood as an impulse towards a potential lost continuity, devotes to each of these subjects a development. Moreover, his developments around the notion of expense as a production of energy at a pure loss drawing from this very unproductivity the force of its existence and its possibility of affection also seems to us to resonate with the gesture of the struggle as it is put forward here. See Georges Bataille (2014) *L'Érotisme*, Paris: Les Éditions de Minuit; and Georges Bataille (1967) *La Notion de dépense*, Paris: Les Éditions de Minuit.
22 Bodin, interview by Claire Besuelle, 18 November 2016.
23 'Porte tes pieds en avant', by Boule Mpanya, Russell Tshiebua and the cast.
24 'Pygmee Song' by Boule Mpanya, Russell Tshiebua and the cast.
25 Anzieu, *Le Moi-Peau*, 36.
26 Sophie Herr (2009) *Geste de la voix et théâtre du corps*, Paris: L'Harmattan, 15.
27 Russell Tshiebua, interview by Claire Besuelle, 24 May 2017, Paris.
28 Tshiebua, interview by Besuelle, 24 May 2017.
29 An echo that is all the more sensible seeing as the Congo, the birth country of Russell Tshiebua and Boule Mpanya, was a Belgian colony until 1960.
30 To use the distinction made by Michel Foucault in *Surveiller et punir, naissance de la prison* and used by Laurence Louppe in *Poétique de la danse contemporaine* (Brussels: Contredanses, 1997), 48.
31 For a translation, see http://www.lieder.net/lieder/get_text.html?TextId=108214 (accessed 20 August 2019).
32 This principle has been used by many choreographers who have danced with, among others, les ballets C de la B, including Sidi Larbi Cherkaoui, whose work has been the object of studies that name this process 'coherent heterogeneity'. See Claire Dutilleul (2016) 'La Culture propre des pièces de Sidi Larbi Cherkaoui: La notion d'hétérogénéité cohérente dans *Rien de rien*, *Foi*, *Apocrifu* et *TeZuka*', master's thesis, Université Lille 3.
33 Ido Batash, interview by Claire Besuelle, 30 June 2016, Ghent.
34 Ido Batash, interview by Claire Besuelle, 24 May 2017, Paris.
35 Batash, interview by Besuelle, 24 May 2017.
36 As Bérengère Bodin relates, 'Ido's phrase: if we let the body find what are the impulses, the postures, the quality of movement and the relation with the gaze, it will be good.' Interview by Besuelle, 3 June 2016.
37 Batash, interview by Besuelle, 24 May 2017.

38 An expression coined by Hubert Godard, the *fonds du geste* refers to the postural attitude and to the pre-movement (as attitude towards weight and gravity) as the background from which the figure detaches itself, or the drawing of the movement. See Hubert Godard (2002) 'Le Geste et sa perception', in Isabelle Ginot and Marcelle Michel (eds.), *La Danse au vingtième siècle*, Paris: Larousse.
39 As Basile Doganis comments about the thought of Gilles Deleuze, in *Pensées du corps, la philosophie à l'épreuve des arts gestuels japonais* (Paris: Les Belles Lettres, 2012, 102.
40 Anzieu, *Le Moi-Peau*, 35.
41 Guion, interview by Besuelle, 18 November 2016.
42 Mireille Losco-Lena (2011) *Il n'y a rien de plus drôle que le malheur: Du comique et de la douleur dans les écritures dramatiques contemporaines*, Rennes: Presses Universitaires, 23.
43 Platel, interview by Besuelle, 18 November 2016.
44 Anzieu, *Le Moi-Peau*, 25. My emphasis.
45 '*Noli me tangere*' ('Touch me not' or 'Cease holding on to me') is a Latin expression that is a translation of the words spoken by the risen Jesus on Easter Sunday to Mary Magdalene. This Latin expression is found in the Latin translation of the Bible made by St Jerome and known as the Vulgate: John 20.11–18.
46 Anzieu, *Le Moi-Peau*, 173.
47 Evelyne Grossman (2017) *Éloge de l'hypersensible*, Paris: Les Éditions de Minuit, 9.
48 The use of the term 'score' (partition) is to be understood here in the sense of 'generative structure' which Julie Sermon gives it when she tackles the question of the 'score' of the performer: a structure that generates a force, an intensity, an experience, moving scaffolding that underlines the performance by giving the performer a certain number of support, both objective (text, choreographic writing, set, etc.) and subjective or intimate (visions, images, association of ideas, emotions, etc.). In Julie Sermon and Yvane Chapuis (2016) *Partition(s), objet et concepts des pratiques scéniques (20e et 21e siècle)*, Dijon: Les Presses du Réel, Collection Nouvelles Scènes, 216.
49 Doganis, *Pensées du corps*, 167. The philosopher invokes the model of polyphony to get out of the idealist and materialist philosophical dead ends when one approaches the question of the faculties of the human being and their possible description.

References

Anzieu, Didier (1995) *Le Moi-Peau*, Paris: Dunod. First published 1985.
Bataille, Georges (1967) *La Notion de dépense*, Paris: Les Éditions de Minuit.
Bataille, Georges (2014) *L'Érotisme*, Paris: Les Éditions de Minuit. First published 1957.
Bernard, Michel (2002) *De la création chorégraphique*, Paris: Centre National de la Danse.
Cheng, François (2006) *Cinq méditations sur la beauté*, Paris: Albin Michel.
Derrida, Jacques (2000) *Le Toucher*, ed. Jean-Luc Nancy, Paris: Galilée.
Doganis, Basile (2012) *Pensées du corps, la philosophie à l'épreuve des arts gestuels japonais*, Paris: Les Belles Lettres.
Foster, Susan Leigh (2010) *Choreographing Empathy*, London and New York: Routledge.
Foucault, Michel (1975) *Surveiller et punir, naissance de la prison*, Paris: Gallimard.
Glon, Marie, and Isabelle Launay (2012) *Histoires de gestes*, Arles: Actes Sud.

Godard, Hubert (2002) 'Le Geste et sa perception', in Isabelle Ginot and Marcelle Michel (eds.), *La Danse au vingtième siècle*, Paris: Larousse.
Grossman, Evelyne (2017) *Éloge de l'hypersensible*, Paris: Éditions de Minuit.
Guilmaine, Anne-Marie (2012) 'État de porosité', *Spirale: Arts, Lettres, Sciences Humaines*, 242: 36–7. Available at http://id.erudit.org/iderudit/67978ac (accessed 20 August 2019).
Herr, Sophie (2009) *Geste de la voix et théâtre du corps*, Paris: L'Harmattan.
Irigaray, Luce (1984) *Éthique de la différence sexuelle*, Paris: Les Éditions de Minuit.
Losco-Lena, Mireille (2011) *Il n'y a rien de plus drôle que le malheur: Du comique et de la douleur dans les écritures dramatiques contemporaines*, Rennes: Presses Universitaires.
Louppe, Laurence (2004) *Poétique de la danse contemporaine*, Brussels: Contredanse.
Merleau-Ponty, Maurice (1964) *Le Visible et l'invisible*, Paris: Gallimard.
Stalpaert, Christel (2017) 'The Spectator's Reappearance in *Map Me* (2003): Moving Beyond Interpersonal and Technological Immersion', in Christel Stalpaert, Katharina Pewny, Jeroen Coppens and Pieter Vermeulen (eds.), *Unfolding Spectatorship: Shifting Political, Ethical and Intermedial Positions*, Ghent: Academia Press, 85–103.
Strauss, Erwin (2004) 'La Posture érigée', *Quant à la danse*, 1: 22–41. First published 1939.
Valéry, Paul (1933) *L'Idée fixe ou deux hommes à la mer*, Paris: Gallimard.

9

Platel Is a Barbarian

Hildegard De Vuyst

This is a speech Hildegard De Vuyst delivered at a colloquium for the occasion of Platel's honorary doctorate at the University of Artois in March 2014. In it she reacts to the sometimes overtly antagonistic attitude in critical discourse to the way Platel consciously seeks to evoke emotions.

> The motivation for this text is one word. A word that stings. I found it in the theatre review *Etcetera*, which for a long time was the only critical magazine in Flanders dedicated to the performing arts. It first saw the light of day at the same time as a whole generation of theatre and dance practitioners, the famous twentieth-century Flemish Wave, which includes Alain Platel. It should therefore have been the magazine that documented his work, reviewed it, and brought it to the attention of an interested public. But nothing could be less true. *Etcetera*'s archive has been digitized – a wonderful project – which also makes it possible to search for mentions: Alain Platel, sixty-three, versus Anne Teresa De Keersmaeker, 235. Of those sixty-three mentions, many were in advertisements, and there has not been a single one since 2008. Barely two reviews. And one dispute, in which the fatal word that is the reason for my story occurs: the word 'emoterror'.
>
> The dispute, between Rudi Laermans and the late Roel Verniers, was about *Allemaal Indiaan*, a 1999 production by Alain Platel and Arne Sierens, and the criticism about it. Laermans sets the tone with the words of dance critic Pieter T'Jonck, who still writes for the Belgian newspaper *De Morgen*: 'There is a popular belief that art should grab you by the throat, practically knock you out, etc., etc. I don't really believe in that sort of artistic terror. It's different if art catches you unaware, making you look at things from a particular angle and suddenly revealing another facet of reality.'[1] Subsequently, Laermans, sociologist and dance philosopher, says of *Allemaal Indiaan*,
>
> > I expect performances that zoom in on marginal lives ... to portray marginality, show you images that really wake you up because they no

longer fit the dominant or hegemonic picture of "the popular". Basically, the only interesting way to go is metatheatre, staging images that are implicitly or explicitly critical of the prevailing dogma.[2]

And later,

> *Allemaal Indiaan* mimics an everyday anecdotal narrative style, without a trace of detachment or reflection. It works, of course, it is so well known that it seems to be an almost natural way to represent life. Personally, I thought this implicit game of recognition extremely dogmatic, all too easy, cheap even. I don't go to a theatre performance to see (and hear) ordinary, everyday situations confirmed – 'life's a smile and a tear, because …' that type of thing.

And, finally, he concludes, 'The message is, think. Reflect on the reflections that occur to us immediately, that grip us, or whatever.'[3]

That was the critical context we found ourselves in when *Allemaal Indiaan* was made, and that approach is more prevalent today than ever, the idea that reflection, critical detachment, metatheatre, reflections on reflections should be paramount. And this is the dominant discourse of people who are not only critics but who teach, advise on policy and sit on the evaluation committees as well. The result is a lot of dance about dance, conceptual or cerebral performances. Everything but emoterror.

How is it possible that the Flemish cultural media can reject Platel's work, or refuse to acknowledge its existence, as *Etcetera* does, when the public embraces it wholeheartedly – and all over the world at that? After all, Platel has been awarded the Océ Prize, an honorary doctorate in Arras, and the European New Theatrical Realities prize in Taormina. He is ranked by the newspaper *De Morgen* as one of the ten greatest Belgian artists but barely recognized by the live arts sector.

Emoterror is defined by Rudi Laermans as 'art as a successful attack on the nerve bundles'. In the *Etcetera* article concerned, Laermans refers to emotions as purely physical processes, cell reactions.

But to contend with academics, you need other academics. In her book *Upheavals of Thought*, published in 2001, the American philosopher Martha Nussbaum says, 'Emotions are not just the fuel that powers the psychological mechanism of a reasoning creature, they are parts, highly complex and messy parts, of this creature's reasoning itself.'[4] By that line of reasoning, it is pointless to weigh emotion against reason or reflection, since emotion is a specific part of the intellect. Furthermore, Nussbaum has more to say about emotion in art – in music, for example – that is definitely worth reading. She explains in detail how in music emotion is not only at the end of the chain in its reception by the audience, but how the emotion is actually built into the work, not in the content but in the form.

In his much-read book *The Barbarians*, Alessandro Barrico somewhat ironically announces the arrival of the barbarians with signs which, for culture pessimists, are proof of degeneration.[5] According to Barrico, however, they are signs of profound cultural transformation, proof that culture is becoming more democratic, broader, more accessible and superficial, so that attributing meaning becomes a collective skill in the registration and compilation of the mosaic of reality.

> Most people think that art involves complicated information and that you can only understand its deeper meaning, in the sense of the beauty and the truth hidden within it, if you devote lengthy and thorough study to it. So many people give up. Barbarians do not want to live in books. What interests them is the breadth of direct life. They are unaware of the prism of depth through which intellectuals look at culture and the world, and they are not interested in it either. Conversely, it is only intellectuals that complain about the superficiality and commercialization of the new culture. (Remember Laermans's use of 'easy' and 'cheap'?) As a result, there is no dialogue, just a fight based on a stupid principle, depth as opposed to superficies. But imagine that that depth is non-existent, an invention of the Romantic Movement? In that case, beauty and truth lie not in depth but can be found everywhere, and in a different way.
>
> These days, beauty comes in many very different forms, from Lady Gaga's exuberant outfits to the elegance in Wim Wenders' films. There can be beauty in anything, and it is no longer definable. Beauty is the principle of desire, and that can also be the desire for energy and emotion. The problem with the cultural elite today is that it is unable to appreciate this new world's culture of beauty – the intensity, the power and the truth of it. Instead it clings to the optical illusion of depth. That is the drama these days.[6]

These are the words of Alessandro Barrico in *Rekto:Verso*, a Flemish culture review that, not coincidentally, is twenty years younger than *Etcetera* and gives a voice to a new, younger generation. It is both broader and more accessible. We need to reinstate emotion as a way of acquiring knowledge, communicating and interpreting meaning, instead of resisting it as terror. It is all right to cherish superficies, a desire for energy and emotion is a legitimate approach to the arts, unlike meta art, which is cerebral and assumes prior knowledge. Reading Nussbaum and Barrico confirms that.

I have worked as a dramaturg with Alain Platel for nineteen years. We have collaborated on a variety of productions, from *La Tristeza Complice*, *Iets op Bach*, *Wolf* and *vsprs*, to the PASS summer school productions in Palestine and a choir project for the opening of the then newly renovated KVS theatre (2006), to *pitié!*, *Out of Context – for Pina*, *C(H)ŒURS* and *tauberbach*. If I look back at them all, I see that they mainly fall into two types of performance. One of them is based on the representation of a multicultural reality, with a lot of consideration for those who find themselves on the fringes of the world. The other type is more like a journey, an experience of (religious) ecstasy, a trip down memory lane or an initiation. Representation versus experience, the outside world versus the inner world, hyperrealism versus the development of a language of movement, the piling up of cultural friction versus the tracing of a visceral path. But always the beauty of what is considered ugly, in all its aspects. Always a mixture of high and low culture.

Bach was mixed with Prince, Monteverdi with Eric Clapton, Mozart with Céline Dion. Classically trained dancers were mixed with hip-hoppers or circus artists, children, transsexuals, alcoholics, deaf people and even dogs. Trained and untrained. Opera was associated with the street. And always in a language based on musicality, not content. Starting with Severine Krott's monologue in *La Tristeza Complice* about the social services, language was something with a particular sound, a particular colour, that was intended to impart a particular emotion rather than a particular message. By simplifying the meaning and doubling through technical effects, Platel eventually succeeded in making the words vibrate even in *tauberbach*, opening up a world rather than putting limits on it, closing it with words. Basically, he succeeded in bringing language in as poetry.

Consequently, by Barrico's definition, Platel is a barbarian; he prefers associative to difficult and cerebral, opts for experience, shows little respect for repertoire, reconstructs meaning by relating fragments to each other. As a barbarian he does not hesitate to put Wagner and Verdi together in *C(H)ŒURS*, or to imagine the political and the physical together.

Yet every time there is that misunderstanding. That it must be about a slice of life, as if you could just go out into the street and pick up the life you see on the stage. That it is meant to be about the fourth world – because of the costumes, the setting or the characters' ineloquent behaviour, because of the pop culture; that it is about ordinary people or set in Ghent. What goes unnoticed is the extent to which chaos must be through-composed to be read as chaos, the level of complexity, the effect of contrast through juxtaposition. Unnoticed, too, the carefully constructed reality, so precise and detailed that it could be mistaken for an *objet trouvé*.

So, according to Martha Nussbaum, Alain Platel is a composer, someone who, throughout the composition, throughout the course of the performance, orchestrates the emotions. It can be no coincidence that baroque music is his favourite, because it is always based on the orchestration of emotion in line with the doctrine of affections.

Platel's composition is based on contrast, on counterpoint. Take my favourite scene from his work, the women in *Iets op Bach* followed by *Den Tod niemand zwingen könnt*. The image of the Foolish Mothers on the Plaza de Mayo that follows the one of Einat Tuchman wanting to commemorate the assassination of Rabin, assisted by the Cuban Lazara Rosell who has made herself a yoghurt mask; South America, voodoo and Palestine mixed together, liberation struggle and emancipation. But meanwhile the women choke the little girl with the microphone cable they are trying to grab from each other. That combination of genuine outrage and fighting for justice and at the same time being blind to the evil taking place in front of one's eyes. No, actually it is even worse. It is doing evil and forcing the child to take part in a demonstration when she does not want to and is not ready for it. If she says, 'Yo quiero a todo el mundo', she will get a slap in the face as well. And all of the details, the shift from Argentina to Evita (former President Perón's wife) in 'Don't Cry for Me Argentina' to 'Like a Virgin' (because Madonna had played Evita). The shift via the music from the political/personal to the existentiality of mortality in the cantata, no one can overcome death.

The power of juxtaposition, whereby two images that cancel each other out or contradict each other are evoked simultaneously, give rise to conflicting emotions, so that judgement must be suspended. With Platel, an unclear message is not vague but disturbing. 'I flirt with meaning rather than trying to impose it' – it is an old statement that is still valid. The outcome is never simply good or bad. It is both black and white. While it is often said that the audience approaches theatre with a suspension of disbelief (the audience is ready to take everything as true and real), Platel invites the audience to approach it with a suspension of judgement. He invites them to explore the link to the reality of all sorts of behaviour that is considered to be outside the norm. But again, it is not only content or subject, it is about the form. *Gardenia* is constructed as one long slow travesty; *Out of Context* is a ritual you step in and out of; *vsprs* propels you to ecstasy and orgasm; and *tauberbach* is about the possibility of transformation.

In the baroque period, people believed in the healing function of art, in line with the doctrine of affections. To my mind then, Platel is a healer rather than a terrorist. I have probably seen the scene of the weeping women (who are joined later in the scene by the male dancers, until all performers are weeping) a hundred times – and I have wept with them a hundred times. To my surprise, because I did not know that we could share so much sorrow with each other, not only personal sorrow but sorrow for the ways of the world, the missed opportunities, the lost ideals, the dreams that never became reality or the dreams that turned out to be nightmares. *Tauberbach* has this potential to heal: the singing together, the Bach chorale, 4-part harmony as a metaphor for hope; the body as a utopia for when thinking fails. Gone with any kind of identarian discourse – literally putting an end to 'I will not change my being' and offering a (painful) perspective of change. This story of transformation opens up the possibility of our own transformation. That is why it affects us.

The Flemish artistic elite is fixated with dogmatic rules about form which all come down, in the end, to 'purity' and a 'clear line' and waging a rear-guard battle for the autonomy of the arts which, in the guise of criticism and reflection may serve no other purpose than the art itself. Performances or theatre about theatre abound, dance is in many cases a niche for the same old audience of peers, dance for other dancers. If this continues the performance arts will soon have made themselves entirely obsolete. And they will become the objective allies of the politicians who want nothing more than for art to focus exclusively on art, and definitely not on society or politics.

While Platel is democratizing the experience of art, and in that too shows himself to be a barbarian, he is opening it up to a lot of people who thought that art was not for them. Popular never becomes populistic though. For that the imagery is too uncomfortable, the dancing too dystonic – cramps, spasms, tics, you do not win any beauty contests with them. No, despite his immense popularity the work is resistant, and does not lend itself to manipulation by politics or the media. Platel definitely makes us look at things from a particular angle (the critics demand that), but he does not make a straitjacket of it.

I think there is still a lot of ground for the barbarian Platel to conquer. The best is yet to come. The barbarian way in which he treats opera, for example, might just point the way to saving opera. If we fail to force open the repertoire the genre is condemned to death. We have to extract the usable bits (fragments) and put them back together again, not to fit some libretto that simply does not stand up to scrutiny these days but inspired by a different logic, that of the barbarian who draws up his top ten without inhibition and mixes things that, according to the dictates of 'good taste' or history, do not belong together. Or the barbarian way that Platel (and Cassol) suffuse baroque music with Africa in *Coup Fatal*, lots of Congolese musicians who take over 'our' music and give it back to us revitalized. That is the direction the performance arts should take, that is the way to the future. Because however you look at it, Rudi Laermans' criticism is firmly framed within the context of white,

Western art (history). That might well apply to other Flemish art connoisseurs too, but it is no longer the frame of reference of the majority of people in an urban context such as Brussels. I cite Brussels because it is the example I know best. But neither is it the frame of reference in other world cities, where people no longer share a common past but do have to build a common future. The project for that common future will be based on barbarian cultural products trademarked Alain Platel. Theatre will either be emoterror or it will cease to exist. The future belongs to the barbarians.

Notes

1 Rudi Laermans and Roel Verniers (2000–3) '*Allemaal Indiaan*: verhevigde realiteit of emo-terreur?' *Etcetera*, 18 (71): 64–9. Available at http://theater.ua.ac.be/etc/page.py?f=2000-03_jg18_nr71_64-69.xml
2 Laermans and Verniers, '*Allemaal Indiaan*'.
3 Laermans and Verniers, '*Allemaal Indiaan*'.
4 Martha Nussbaum (2001) *Upheavals of Thought*, Cambridge: Cambridge University Press, 3.
5 Alessandro Barrico (2006) *The Barbarians*, New York: Rizzoli Ex Libris.
6 Anna Tilroe (2012) 'Het gelijk van de cultuurbarbaar: Interview met Alessandro Baricco', *Rekto:Verso*, 24 September. Available at http://www.dewereldmorgen.be/artikels/2012/09/24/het-gelijk-van-de-cultuurbarbaar-interview-met-alessandro-baricco (accessed 20 August 2019).

References

Barrico, Alessandro (2006) *The Barbarians: An Essay on the Mutation of Culture*, New York: Rizzoli Ex Libris.
Laermans, Rudi, and Roel Verniers (2000–3) '*Allemaal Indiaan*: verhevigde realiteit of emo-terreur?' *Etcetera*, 18 (71): 64–9.
Nussbaum, Martha (2001) *Upheavals of Thought*, Cambridge: Cambridge University Press.
Tilroe, Anna (2012) 'Het gelijk van de cultuurbarbaar: Interview met Alessandro Baricco', *Rekto:Verso*, 24 September.

Part Three

Gestures

10

Bernadetje, Catastrophes and Gestures

Erwin Jans

This contribution is based on a couple of scenes from the iconic production *Bernadetje* (1996) that Alain Platel made with theatre-maker Arne Sierens, more than twenty years ago. Endeavouring to say something substantial about a rich choreographic oeuvre like Platel's based on only two scenes is not without its risks or even a certain pretention. Nonetheless, I think that the two moments demonstrate a tension that characterizes all Platel's choreographic work. In that tension, I see the influence of Pina Bausch's Tanztheater and traces of the thinking of two of the twentieth century's most important theatre-makers: Bertolt Brecht and Antonin Artaud. With that historical perspective, I will try to reveal something of what drives Platel's work.

Tanztheater

Like many contemporary choreographers, Alain Platel has developed in the broad wake of Pina Bausch's (1940–2009) dance theatre. With productions like *Blaubart* (1977), *Er nimmt sie an der Hand und führt sie in das Schloß, die anderen folgen* (1978), *Café Müller* (1978), *Kontakthof* (1978), *Keuschheitslegende* (1979), *1980: Ein Stück von Pina Bausch* (1980) and *Nelken* (1982), Bausch brought about a profound revolution in European dance in the late 1970s and early 1980s. Her Tanztheater was a radical mix of dance, singing, pantomime, acrobatics, ordinary everyday gestures and theatre. Bausch substituted the straightforward storyline with a collage, or montage, of separate scenes. This review-like structure was held together by an internal non-narrative logic, a sort of stream of consciousness in which repetition and parallel actions played an important role. The universe of Pina Bausch played out somewhere on the border between dream and reality. Hysterical elation and deep melancholy alternated in associative images combining realistic and surrealistic situations. Bausch searched with her dancers for what drove them emotionally. One of her well-known sayings was: 'Mich interessiert nicht so sehr, wie sich Menschen bewegen, als was sie bewegt' ('I'm not so much interested in how people move as in what moves them'). To discover that, she would start rehearsals by asking her dancers questions and giving them assignments. Then, from the resulting improvisations, she would select the raw material for her choreography. The difficult and often aggressive relationship of the dancers with their own bodies and the equally conflictual relationship with the opposite sex was central to this. Both her performances and her work method deeply influenced a whole generation of choreographers and theatre-makers.

For Hans-Thies Lehmann, the development of Tanztheater, from the 1980s onwards, ran parallel to what he calls 'postdramatic theatre'. In the theatre, the text and dramatic development, which had been central to the meaning, were shifted to the margins and replaced by the physical presence of the actors, their charisma, their auras, their capacity to communicate through gestures, their shocking bodily presence. The physicality of the actor became the alpha and omega of the performance, the filter of every psychological and social issue.

> As post-dramatic theatre moves away from a mental, intelligible structure towards the exposition of intense physicality, the body is absolutized. The paradoxical result is often that it appropriates all other discourses. What happens is an interesting volte-face: as the body no longer demonstrates anything but itself, the turn away from a body of signification and towards a body of unmeaning gesture (dance, rhythm, grace, strength, kinetic wealth) turns out as the most extreme charging of the body with significance concerning the social reality. The body becomes the only subject matter. From now on, it seems, all social issues first have to pass through this needle's eye, they all have to adopt the form of a physical issue.[1]

The trilogy – *Moeder en Kind* (1995), *Bernadetje* (1996) and *Allemaal Indiaan* (1999) – which Alain Platel and Arne Sierens staged in the second half of the 1990s, is part of this postdramatic development. The performances derive their dynamics from the constant shift between theatre and dance, between words and movement, and between story and physical presence. Everyday situations and ordinary lives are the main inspiration for this triptych. Both Sierens and Platel are motivated by enormous social sensitivity. They both like to work with non-professional actors and share a fascination for popular culture (film, music, photo albums, etc). The focus in all three productions is on children and young people in a world of dysfunctional (or absent) parents. The setting for *Moeder en Kind* is a living room, for *Bernadetje* a funfair attraction, and for *Allemaal Indiaan* the back of an apartment building. All the characters are ordinary people with a language idiom that is simultaneously poetic and insolently aggressive. The atmosphere of the performances is explosive, erotic, lively and rebellious, stimulated by dancing, singing and pop music. The stage can barely contain the physical energy and the dramatic tensions of the many story lines. The apparent realism and even misery of the stories is transformed into an imaginative world that breaks out of the limits of reality. Lehmann includes *Moeder en Kind* in his book on postdramatic theatre as an example of the way the hyperrealism inspired by television culture can acquire a utopian dimension:

> In the hypernaturalist scene modelled on TV scenes of everyday life a fantastic vision can break forth without commentary or interpretation. Trivial, utopian

Figure 10.1 Lies Pauwels, Gert Portael and Yassin Pycke in *Moeder en Kind*, 1995. © Phile Deprez.

Figure 10.2 Natacha Nicora and Frederik Debrock in *Allemaal Indiaan*, 1999. © Kurt Van der Elst.

images of desire of great intensity emerge. In *Moeder en Kind*, a performance by the Belgian theatre company *Victoria*, the confined lodgings of the sub-proletarians transform into a fairytale-like and crazy pop dreamland where the individual figures express their deepest longings in pop songs and rock music.[2]

Between triviality and utopia, between ecstatic pop music and deep melancholy, between theatre and choreography, the characters work through their traumas – big and small – as they act.

Falling and bumping

Bernadetje is engraved in the memories of its audiences because of its spectacular scenography, a smaller but accurate and realistic reproduction of the bumper cars at a typical Flemish funfair. The dodgem cars stand for the social world of ordinary people and provide the place where young people of both sexes hang out, unlike the merry-go-round and the fishing booth which are mainly visited by parents with small children, or the shooting gallery which is a rather exclusive men's and boys' world. The boasting, exaggeration, flirting, acting tough, the challenges, dates, arguments, techno music and dancing are all part of a place where boys and girls meet each other and test their still immature – or precocious – male and female identities. In that sense, the dodgems are in themselves a form of theatre, a stage on which young people can perform. Strong parent figures who guarantee order and normality are noticeably absent.

That brings me to the two scenes that I want to look at more closely. At a certain moment in the performance, an obviously drunken adolescent boy comes onstage. He staggers, falls and crawls upright again, the movement developing in all its realism. In the context of *Bernadetje*, the drunken boy's fall could be a picture of a youth gone astray without parental supervision. But the boy keeps on falling, not two or three times, but eight, nine, maybe even ten times, transforming his falling into a choreographed and coded movement that no longer speaks of social misery and emotional deprivation. Ceasing to be a representation, it appears to refer only to itself. The 'fall' is saved by its ritual repetition and made graceful.

The same shift happens a bit later, but this time it applies to the whole performance. The resounding music is no longer that of youth culture but the timeless religious music of Bach. The dodgems stop their aggressive bumping into each other and zigzagging to avoid collisions, and one of the scooters starts an almost endless series of circular movements round its axis. On it, five boys begin a choreography. To the music of Bach, they slowly unfold their bodies on the rotating scooter, as a flower opens its petals, so that some of them, bent backwards, almost touch the ground with their heads. Here Bach's music also justifies the associations with pictorial representations of the dead body of Christ. The funfair becomes a church, the catastrophe a harmony. But what exactly happens in these two scenes? In order to understand the transformation of the gestures better, I want to put them in a broader context than that of Pina Bausch's Tanztheater.

The loss of gesture

Giorgio Agamben's statement that 'by the end of the nineteenth century, the Western bourgeoisie had definitely lost its gestures' puts modern dance – and the whole of modern art – in the context of loss, mourning and an attempt to regain those gestures.[3] The dances of Isadora Duncan (1877–1927) and Diaghilev (1872–1929) – as well as Proust's novels, Rilke's poetry and silent film – attempted, in the words of Agamben, 'for the last time to evoke what was slipping through its fingers forever'.[4] For Agamben one of the most important signs of this loss was the scientific interest in everyday gestures, on the one hand, and anomalies, on the other. It is an interest that shifts constantly and negotiates between notions of normal and abnormal behaviour. Agamben cites passages from the work of Gilles de la Tourette (1857–1904) and Jean-Martin Charcot (1825–93). Gilles de la Tourette describes with the utmost detail the movements and interactions of the leg and foot when walking, one of the basic gestures of everyday life:

> While the left leg acts as the fulcrum, the right foot is raised from the ground with a coiling motion that starts at the heel and reaches the tip of the toes, which leave the ground last; the whole leg is now brought forward and the foot touches the ground with the heel. At this very instant, the left foot – having ended its revolution and leaning only on the tip of the toes – leaves the ground; the left leg is brought forward, gets closer to and then passes the right leg, and the left foot touches the ground with the heel, while the right foot ends its own revolution.[5]

In his turn, Charcot describes in the same clinical and detailed manner the uncontrolled and totally incoherent gestures of one of his hysterical patients:

> He sets off – with his body bent forward and with his lower limbs rigidly and entirely adhering one to the other – by leaning on the tip of his toes. His feet then begin to slide on the ground somehow, and he proceeds through some sort of swift tremor ... When the patient hurls himself forward in such a way, it seems as if he might fall forward any minute; in any case, it is practically impossible for him to stop all by himself and often he needs to throw himself on an object nearby. He looks like an automaton that is being propelled by a spring: there is nothing in these rigid, jerky, and convulsive movements that resembles the nimbleness of the gait.[6]

What fascinates me especially is the chiasmus arising from these medical descriptions. On the one hand, when it is described analytically and in detail, the everyday gesture becomes part of a strange and surprising pattern of behaviour. The normal is pushed to the limits of what can be understood and becomes, as a result, almost unrecognizable and abnormal. On the other hand, when it is systematized and categorized, the abnormal, the strange, the insane, the neurotic or psychotic gesture becomes, to a certain extent, understandable and logical within a scientific frame of reference. It is perhaps not exaggerated to suggest that this chiasmus between normal and abnormal, alienation and systematization, is the underlying dynamic of modern theatre in the broad sense of the word. The descriptions above, of the foot walking and of the hysterical body, could be descriptions of movements in (post)modern dance, which transforms and changes both ordinary and unusual gestures through a process of slowing them down, repetition, stylization, magnification, elaboration, and so on. In other words, the catastrophe of gesture and gesture as catastrophe manifest themselves as the Janus head of twentieth-century theatre. The ordinary and well-known appears in a strange light and the bizarre and unusual takes on the appearance of a new form.

Interiority

Gesture, in the sense that Agamben uses it, refers not only to a physical expression, but to the hermeneutics and ethics underlying it as well. This is how Agamben describes the catastrophe of gesture at the end of the nineteenth century:

> An age that has lost its gestures is, for this reason, obsessed by them. For human beings who have lost every sense of naturalness, each single gesture becomes a destiny. And the more gestures lose their ease under the action of invisible powers, the more life becomes indecipherable. In this phase the bourgeoisie, which just a few decades earlier was still firmly in possession of its symbols, succumbs to interiority and gives itself up to psychology.[7]

The loss of gestures and outward symbols caused a withdrawal into an inner world. This withdrawal into an inner life left clearly visible traces in the rise of the modern drama at the end of the nineteenth century, as described by Peter Szondi in his *Theory of the Modern Drama*. Szondi interprets the catastrophe of the bourgeois gesture as a crisis in dramatic structure. In his opinion, it is a crisis of dialogue and intersubjectivity, of language and representation, the ability to understand and then to act. It is the crisis of interpersonal relationships and in that sense the manifestation of a new world image in which the human subject is no longer central. The plays of Strindberg, Ibsen, Chekhov and Maeterlinck deal with this implosion of intersubjectivity and the shift to an inner life that is bedevilled by the unconscious, libidinous passions, the past, memories of anxiety and guilt, feelings of insignificance and boredom, and the awareness of an inability to act.

When We Dead Awaken is the title of one of Ibsen's dramas and a pithy summary of the new significance attributed to the word 'catastrophe'. A catastrophe is no longer the result of a causal chain of actions at the end of a play; it is the start of the play now and impacts on every narrative logic. Modern dramas begin when the dead awaken and become aware of their death, as the title of Ibsen's play suggests. And it is no coincidence that the title of another of his well-known plays is *Ghosts*.

New grammar of gestures

With the implosive embedding of catastrophe in modern theatre, a new grammar of gestures developed on the stage too. However diverse their nature may be, they are all ways of dealing with the loss of gestures. The art of the silent film, expressionism, surrealism, constructivism, modern dance, as well as the fascination for exoticism, primitivism, Orientalism and, on another level, fascism and communism are likewise ways of forgetting, suppressing, remembering, glorifying, substituting, negotiating or perverting the loss of gestures. They are a search for a language of gestures that resists interiority and the psychologization of the portrayal of mankind.

We do not need to dig deep into the history of the former Soviet Union and the relationship between the arts and communist ideology to see that the biomechanics of Meyerhold (1874–1940) and the doctrine of social realism were two different answers to the loss of gesture, two different attempts to construct a new grammar of gestures determined by the working conditions in an industrial environment. However, the revolutionary artistic potential of Meyerhold's biomechanical anatomy was completely lost in the perverted idealization and ideologization of the working body in social realism. And what the Nazi ideology called *Entartete Kunst*, or degenerate art, was nothing but an acute artistic awareness of the final loss of gesture. The brutal collective discipline of the fascist military gesture was a catastrophic blindness to this loss.

Two figures in particular were crucial to the development of the post-war grammar of gestures: Antonin Artaud (1896–1948) and Bertolt Brecht (1896–1956). In their works, written during the interwar period, Artaud and Brecht explicitly examined the possibility of catastrophe. Economic chaos, the crisis of democracy, the rise of fascism and the threat of war form the unequivocal background for the thinking of both Brecht and Artaud. Their work contains the most ambitious attempts in modern theatre to formulate an answer to the loss of gesture. Both Brecht and Artaud radically rejected the dramatic paradigm of the theatre because it led almost exclusively to a focus on the individual psychology. Their motivation, like that of the movements listed above, was the conceptual creation of a new human being.

The works of Artaud and Brecht revolve like concentric circles around two concepts, the 'hieroglyph' and '*gestus*' respectively. *Gestus* and the hieroglyph represent the two fundamental, radical or revolutionary gestures in modern theatre. Two scenes, both of which are associated with the two concepts, continued to haunt the later (post)modern and (post)dramatic theatre as ghost scenes, not least because they confront catastrophe full on, although in a completely different way. Before going into the concepts of hieroglyph and *gestus* in Platel's and Sieren's work, I will take a closer look at these ghost scenes.

The stake and the street scene

The first (ghost) scene is the image that Artaud describes at the end of his essay 'Theatre and Culture', the actor as a victim being burnt at the stake, signalling through the flames – bodily agony.

> Furthermore, when we speak the word 'life', it must be understood we are not referring to life as we know it from its surface of fact, but to that fragile, fluctuating centre which forms never reach. And if there is still one hellish, truly accursed thing in our time, it is our artistic dallying with forms, instead of being like victims burnt at the stake, signalling through the flames.[8]

Artaud referred to this signalling as hieroglyphs. Several references come together in the concept of hieroglyph: the almost geometric movements of the Balinese dancer, dream logic, the grammar of silent films, as well as the uncontrolled and crazy movements of the plague victim. Artaud invests the hieroglyphs with a knowledge that is neither rational nor discursive and with an intensity that has an immediate effect on our consciousness without any verbal or intellectual intervention. For Artaud, language and thought had become perversions of themselves and were no longer capable of communicating the fundamental 'cruelty' of life. Artaud's work is one of the most powerful articulations of the above-mentioned crisis of representation and language as an expression of life. It is the victim, burning to death at the stake giving the sign of life, for whom Artaud is looking. In his first letter about cruelty he formulates this aporetic dialectic, this revolution of life and death, very clearly:

> Such cruelty is above all lucid, a kind of rigid control and submission to necessity. There is no cruelty without consciousness and without the application of consciousness. It is consciousness that gives to the exercise of every act of life its blood-red colour, its cruel nuance, since it is understood that life is always someone's death.[9]

The second fundamental scene of modern theatre is Brecht's famous street scene. Describing how an accident (a catastrophe) happened, a man not only describes what actually happened but also how the accident happened and how it could have been avoided. This was how Brecht wanted to make theatre. The *gestus* – because that is what the street scene is about – is stripped of all unnecessary details and brings the past, present and future together in one transparent sign. *Gestus* is anything but superficial imitation of reality; rather it delves into a hidden social and political truth.

Like Artaud's hieroglyph, Brecht's *gestus* differs fundamentally from the ordinary everyday gesture. Both *gestus* and the hieroglyph are intended to grasp a truth and a vitality that exists below or beyond the surface of the fact. The volte-face that Brecht sought was based on dialectical materialism, while Artaud's volte-face was almost metaphysical. Artaud wanted to create not only a new consciousness but also a new body (a 'body without organs') and a new cosmology. Artaud's hieroglyph and Brecht's *gestus* were both revolutionary gestures, steeped in the desire for a volte-face, for the exposure of a lie, the desire to reveal what had previously been invisible (cruelty and dialectic). Whether or not belief in this type of revolutionary gesture has completely disappeared is now open to discussion, but it is a fact that traces of Artaud's and Brecht's gestures are widely evident in postmodern theatre. Or, to put it differently, they continue to 'haunt' postmodern theatre.

Mundus corpus

Nonetheless, Jean-François Lyotard had a point when he said that he still saw Western nihilism at work in Brecht's and Artaud's ideas. He summarized the nature of Western theatre succinctly with his statement, 'To hide, to show, that is theatricality.' It is the Freudian fort/da principle that Lyotard criticizes in Western theatre. Theatre is always presence/absence. A theatrical sign always represents something else. That something else is ultimate reality, which is absent, while the sign (which is only a substitute) is present on the stage. For Lyotard this is the blueprint of Western theology and metaphysics. He finds traces of this thinking in Brecht and Artaud. In Lyotard's opinion, Artaud's hieroglyph is another grammar and syntax for silencing the morbidly libidinous body. And Brecht's *gestus* shows only how a particular scene could or should have been another. In other words, instead of going beyond the traditional concepts of Western theatre, Artaud and Brecht perpetuate them (although not without pushing them to their metaphysical and political limits). Lyotard pleads, therefore, for an 'energetic' theatre, a theatre of 'intensities' instead of 'intentions'.

In recent decades, the body, with its singular and irreducible materiality – its 'intensity' – has become the focus of the theatre, though without taking up a fixed or central position. In performances, the body is decentred again and again. The French philosopher Jean-Luc Nancy put it like this: 'The body is the unity of a being outside itself.'[10] In his essay 'Corpus', from which this quotation comes, Nancy refers to our world as a '*mundus corpus*':

> There was cosmos, a world of distributed places, given by, and to, the gods. There was *res extensa*, a natural cartography of infinite spaces with their master, the conquistador-engineer, a place-taking lieutenant for vanished gods. Now comes *mundus corpus*, the world as a proliferating peopling of [the] body['s] places.[11]

A world of bodies

So, where is this all too brief and too rapid historical sketch taking us, with respect to the two scenes from *Bernadetje* described above? Both the falling of the drunken boy and the bumping of the dodgems is about the shift from *gestus* to hieroglyph, from a 'social' to an almost 'sacred' gesture, from sober prose to intense poetry, from intentionality to intensity, from expressive physical pop music to the sublime spirituality of Bach. But the shift is never final. It is not about the *Aufhebung* of the first term into the second. It is about the space in between where we already have a notion of pure physicality – the body stripped of its social significance and of its sublime potential as well.

In his study of postdramatic theatre, Lehmann also points to the shift from the dramatic '*agon*' (conflict) between characters to the 'agony' (suffering) of the postdramatic body. That body – that world of bodies – becomes more and more fundamental in Platel's more recent work. Between *gestus*, which links dance to the social reality, and hieroglyphs, which are the signature of the sublimation of the body, flesh appears as an ever more compelling presence, with its tics, its symptoms, its singularity, its maladjustment and its nakedness. In *Gardenia* (2010), Platel works with a group of older transsexuals and transvestites who move in the socially undefined zone between men and women. His major choreography *C(H)ŒURS* (2014) opens with this text, 'Vous voyez / Ce que je suis c'est / Ce n'est absolument rien / Et je n'ai rien à dire là-dessus / Rien / Bon, mais, c'est tout / Qu'est-ce que vous voulez / Que je vous dise d'autre?' ('You see / What I am is / Is absolutely nothing / And I can't do anything about it / Nothing / Well, that's how it is / What else do you / want me to say?). While the text is being read, a dancer stands with his back to the public, his head hanging, so that he appears not to have a head. Above his shoulders only his two hands are visible, slowly removing the dress he is wearing and baring his body. It is an image that shows the body in its pure physicality, its materiality signifies its history and memory, its desire and suffering.

What we call postmodern theatre – and that includes Platel's work – bears the traces of the inevitable (and necessary) 'failure' of Artaud's and Brecht's gestures. To reuse Ibsen's title in a somewhat unconventional manner, it is in the aftermath of the 'death' of these two types of gesture that postmodern theatre awakens.

Notes

1. Hans-Thies Lehmann (2006) *Postdramatic Theatre*, trans. Karen Jürs-Munby, London and New York: Routledge, 96.
2. Lehmann, *Postdramatic Theatre*, 117.
3. Giorgio Agamben (2000) *Means without End: Notes on Politics*, trans. Vincenzo Binetti and Cesare Casarino, Minneapolis, Minn.: University of Minnesota Press, 'Notes on Gesture', 1.
4. Agamben, *Means without End*, 2.
5. Agamben, *Means without End*, 1.
6. Agamben, *Means without End*, 1.
7. Agamben, *Means without End*, 2.
8. Antonin Artaud (1958) *Theatre and Its Double*, trans. Mary Caroline Richards, New York: Grove Press, 13.
9. Artaud, *Theatre and Its Double*, 102.
10. Jean-Luc Nancy (2008) *Corpus*, trans. Richard A. Rand, New York: Fordham University Press, 133.
11. Nancy, *Corpus*, 39.

References

Agamben, Giorgio (2000) *Means without End: Notes on Politics*, trans. Vincenzo Binetti and Cesare Casarino, Minneapolis, Minn.: University of Minnesota Press.

Artaud, Antonin (1958) *Theatre and Its Double*, trans. Mary Caroline Richards, New York: Grove Press.

Lehmann, Hans-Thies (2006) *Postdramatic Theatre*, trans. Karen Jürs-Munby, London and New York: Routledge.

Nancy, Jean-Luc (2008) *Corpus*, trans. Richard A. Rand, New York: Fordham University Press.

11

Choreic Gesture

Virtuosic Angularity, Alterkinetic Dance in Platel's *Out of Context – for Pina*

Kélina Gotman

Voyez la joie d'une femme qui peut dire de sa rivale: Elle est bien anguleuse! [See the joy of a woman who can say of her rival – Is she not rather angular!][1]

The form of this chapter is also to query form: it fits and starts, it repeats, it swerves, it gestures: it is all grace, and it is monstrous, awkward, halting; it falters. Thus the chapter is rhythmically unstable, it aims with the material extended throughout to tease and twist the plasticity of concept being offered: that of the alterkinetic, that of the choreic, the notion that shape – in dance, in the movement of rhythm, of body – is a vital and pulsating mass, quivering and quavering; that to render it clean, that to make it linear, is also already to enter it into an economy of productive rationalism, of efficiency; that what les ballets C de la B do with the work in question here – *Out of Context – for Pina* – is to render an homage to a woman stifled by convention, a woman who made of this terror a virtue. Terror is not quite right: this is an anxious stumbling, and at the same time in working with the aesthetics, the politics, of the near-fall, the seizure of grace and away from grace, what Bausch like Platel does, and what I find myself quarrying here is a manner of being with the work of 'figuration': the rendering of (mis)shape, the syntactic work of undoing how language works, inhabiting critical space at the borderland, on the cusp of a chasm.

What context? Surplus affect, faltering gesture in Platel's homage to Pina

If Pina Bausch has come to epitomize a hyper-modern feminine hysteria as theatricalized affective surplus, an homage to her will one way or another return to the aesthetics and politics of surplus; excess, spillage; social awkwardness; control and its loss; as well as standards of normalcy, beauty and the gestural and affective constrictions of the socio-theatrical everyday.[2] In *Out of Context – for Pina* (2010), Alain Platel and les ballets C de la B merge club moves and amateur pop songs with the dyskinetic movements his dancers attempt awkwardly, at times gracefully, often humorously, to imitate. Platel suggests that he sourced his gestural syntax in the so-called hysterias of the nineteenth century, in doing so imitating a range of neuromotor disorders long associated with chorea, the neurological disorder most closely likened to dance (*chorea* is Latin for 'dance'). His own dancers stripped to their underwear, twitched and jerked their bodies, at first to a nearly embarrassing degree, until some audience members left (on the night I attended, at the Théâtre de la Ville in Paris). These were virtuosic professionals replicating movement disorders with a masterful ability to quote the wobbling and the arching, the tensing and the crisping of all the ataxias, choreas and dyskinesias of the medical repertoire. As I experienced the show, the ethics of it all were at first unclear: was this an enlightened approach to gestural alterity or a relatively offensive appropriation? A nervous laugh rippled through the audience as techno beats intensified, spurring on the dancers who began performing an ever wider range of dyskinetic-like techno and hip-hop moves. They were now popping and krumping, with microphones in their hands (and mouths), inexpertly singing fragments of pop songs. As the show progressed, the passage from choreic to club moves and back again increased in fluidity, and the slightly uncomfortable feeling from the start – that we were watching a too-sleek performance of disability – dissolved into what can only be described as sheer movement. This for me was Platel's stroke of choreographic genius. The poorly sung musical riffs (including 'Aisha' and 'Nothing Compares to You') were familiar and funny, not least for the comic poverty of their execution, which highlighted the dancers' vulnerable selves, selves not professionally trained in song. Tense arches of the back, rapid movements of the head, sharply curved elbows and clawed hands were folded back into the head-bopping and body-popping of electronic music and late-night ecstasy parties, with their own striations, to offer a bizarrely remixed universe of order and disorder, normalcy and abnormality, party moves and the crispations and tensions of neuromuscular disorder. By the end of the night, I didn't know what was up or down, so-called able-bodied, disabled, marginal or virtuosic. The beauty of the choreic gestures gained a new relief juxtaposed with popular dance moves from the past twenty or thirty years. In this space, for a while, there was no normal: not on the surface, though one could not help but remember that the dancers did all this with control, out of choice, and that the audience watching this was for the most part likely on the side of the neurologically 'normate'. In spite of the work's title, here the dancers and audience were all in a particular – safe and contained – context: the theatrical stage and darkened auditorium before it; in that context, the dancers, who were trained and able-bodied, were free from the sort of everyday abuse 'hysterics' of the past or neuro-atypicals of the present may suffer.[3]

Yet what I argue in what follows is that the virtuosity of this performance of slippages between 'choreic' and 'club' moves situates discourse on disorder – and specifically, in this case, on 'disabled' performance – in an altogether different realm to that more familiar from discussions of disability studies, theatre and dance; that what Platel's work to my knowledge uniquely does, with this piece, is to interrogate the political aesthetics of choreic gesture in a dance context where the playful toggling between movements of the head, arms, legs, torso and fingers more often recognizably dyskinetic on the one hand, and popular forms of party dance on the other, suggests a reorganization of our aesthetic categories – and that this is political. Following Caroline Levine, 'forms' are politics. Arguing against the notion that consideration of form is separate from political commitment, she writes, 'It is the work of form to make order. And this means that forms are the stuff of politics.' 'Form', she suggests, 'always indicates an arrangement of elements – an ordering, patterning, or shaping'.[4] Rather than posit form as mere abstraction, or mere shape, ahistorical and void, she suggests that attention to hierarchy, network, whole and rhythm, exemplarily enables analysis of the way bodies – individual and social – come to be ordered and constrained, deployed and accounted for. I suggest this manner of reading formal organization is properly choreographic. What I suggest is that political choreography takes place not only in the socio-political realm (as social choreography or choreopolitics) but also intra-corporeally; and that consideration of the way gestural languages migrate and translate also constitutes a political project attentive to gestural entanglements that have the potential to show other gestural relations, to reorganize the shapes of gestural power and control, particularly as these play out onstage – a privileged site for seeing shape, and for contemplating 'beauty' as ultra- or hyper-normality, as an axis of desire.

What Platel does with *Out of Context*, I argue, is stage the rearticulation of medico-popular and balletic form – to show misformations not as grotesque, as curiosity, only, but slipping into a gestural economy of beauty, mundanity and the everyday. What I suggest is that the production does this through a subtle epigenetic structure: a manner of unfurling or unfolding gesture by starting with apparently 'simply' neuromotor disorder gestures, recognizable and awkward to audience members, and progressively juxtaposing these with and subtly flowing between equally recognizable club moves to arrive at a vision of future gesturality: a manner of seeing and saying gesture that is egalitarian, in which there is no longer 'order' or 'disorder'. The notion of epigenesis I touch upon briefly derives from Catherine Malabou's philosophy of epigenetics, in which she suggests that transformations take place on a continuum, each point serving as a new ground zero; thus, the notion of origin dissolves into a perpetually unfurling arrival. Translated to the choreographic stage, this concept allows us to imagine the futurity of gesture in a spatio-temporal now, in which neither 'origin' (history) nor 'biology' has precedence over 'culture'.[5] The notion of monstrosity unravels. Specifically, with Platel's work in *Out of Context*, concepts of grace and gestural taboo are reordered so that we find ourselves at once amused and perplexed; confusion as to how to 'read' or to interpret the gestures wins out over any attempt to fold our reading of the gestures into an economy of display or charity. What is preserved, moreover, with this work, and serves as a further point of political provocation, setting this slightly to the side of important work in 'disability' theatre and dance, is the cultural economy of the professionally trained dancer. In this sense, the work argues simultaneously for an acceptance of virtuosity, a refusal to refuse it, contra the economy of real or simulated amateurism characteristic of what may be termed the non-dance or anti-dance paradigm – inheritors of the Judson Church school of 'mundane' dance theatre, non-dance sought to undo virtuosic dance and disperse it into discourse; to query the institutions and perceived tyrannies of classical training. With theatricalized disability dance, as in the staged displays of 'disability' in recent work by Jérôme Bel, which I will touch on very briefly below, disability dance activism becomes a freak show of another sort, troubling audience expectation without offering an alternative. I argue that Platel's work promises another way forward: a gestural show that spectralizes medical, 'disorderly', virtuosic, balletic and popular dance moves in a radical gestural horizontalization without apology for the dancing craft. This suggests a politico-aesthetic gestural spectrum that is inclusive and crafted; and a gestural porosity that invites reflection on the politically and socially construed and conserved (arguably policed) awkwardnesses of angles and curves, swerves and jerks characteristic of neuromotor disease as well as racialized club culture: the cultures of somatic control that keep choreic and popping bodies generally out of sight. Although hip-hop cultures are celebrated far more so than choreic bodies – there is no properly 'choreic' culture yet – the resonances between these codes belies a far longer history of interpenetration between neuromotor 'disorder' and hyper-modern cabaret, film and performance such as *Out of Context* touches on. I examine the interrelation of racialized and neuromotor gestural 'disorders' elsewhere and will not rest on this genealogy further here.[6]

Out of Context, however, I argue may be seen as a plea for fêting the beleaguered institutions of theatre and dance at a time of neoliberal retrenchment as well as far more directly a plea for extending the movement vocabulary of dance to the para-classical, even while this work inhabits the contemporary dance-theatre stage. Rather than refuse theatricality or dance technique, *Out of Context* employs technique to query form. The work, thus, can be situated at the choreographic cusp of a genre of new formalism, which takes the aesthetics and politics of an art work to inhabit a crafted space of visual and rhythmic re- or de-hierarchization. In particular, what I have elsewhere described, following cultural theorist Hillel Schwartz, as a modern preference for the smooth curvilinearity of 'torque' (as an axial rotation or twist), comes vividly to be reconfigured, as we are no longer either presented with persuasive, torque-like curvilinearity or machinic mutiple purism and the straight line but a deliberately irregular – perhaps neo- or hyper-baroque – set of twists, jerks, striations, hiccups, extensions, flexions and turns.[7] This is not to say that one or another genre of choreographic gesture – whether relatively 'pure' or hyper-composite – is in any absolute sense more desirable (and it is up for question whether *Out of Context* gestures are composite or rather whether they may tend towards the homogeneously 'pure' in the general dissolution of gestural genres that takes place, in the eventually shared rhythmicity and alterkinesthetic display of playful irregularity); but that in showcasing gestures in disarray – choreic, club gestures – Platel with *Out of Context* invites us to bring another genre of semi-embarrassing and inelegant everydayness to the theatrical stage. This – as Pina Bausch had done – refigures embarrassment and elegance, at once preserving the category of the elegant, perhaps (we are, after all, watching virtuosic performance work in an elegant opera house), while para-categorically querying and queering it – performing a gestural swerve.[8]

Thus, *Out of Context* plays anarchically with the sort of gestural plasticity that Malabou describes of post-dialectic Hegelianism: with an understanding of 'dialectic' away from strict opposition and towards a concept or figure of perpetual transformation. The plasticity of gesture, as I describe it here, suggests an alterkinetic regime of the arts within which gestural categories are not mapped and not ultimately mappable onto other (non-aesthetic) categories, such as medical disorder, but for the duration of the work inhabit a tender space of aesthetic autonomy; what's more, in this space of (relative) aesthetic autonomy, the status of the art work – of the dance-theatre piece – suggests another affective and aesthetic order, within which genre categories dissolve. The modest idealism of this work is thus of course political, just as it refuses a sort of 'democratic' representationalism that I consider typically requires and thus reinforces the categories it is ostensibly meant to be transcending (as in Bel's work alluded to);[9] that to 'show' disability is also to preserve it, whereas to reproduce and simultaneously to revise, to alter, to smudge, to slip between genres of order and disorder and thus also to refuse their strict reification offers on the contrary a temporary space of gestural (dis)attunement, a temporary – aesthetic – autonomous zone within which, anarchically, gestural systems are in a spatio-temporal tangle. This play of inspiration rather than representation, this situating oneself alongside one's learned body – ecstatically – enacts an aesthetic destructuring; it unsutures the body from its hierarchies and harmonies, from its working organs and its functionalities, it re-anatomizes dance and medical, as well as social disorder; it demedicalizes and depathologizes gesture without any direct or didactic reference to the particular body being (un)done. At the same time, moreover, this work inhabits a playful space of gestural undercommonality: club moves that are typically racialized, marginalized, set alongside the freakish, the monstrous, and the choreic emerge in the undercommons as presented in the bright light of the theatrical common space.[10] In this way, we have with *Out of Context* dancers who are intensively trained, and it is this training that enables a highly controlled chaos of disorientatingly juxtaposed moves; motion appears onstage thus as vibrant and pre- or post-ordered gestural life, a choreographic space of theatrical de- and re-semiotization. We find ourselves breaking gestural syntax down. This utopic space, within which gestural semantics and histories are undone, is a dreamlike space of confusion: the dancers enact their roles as instruments of gestural plasticity, and that is their political, cultural power and their craft. This is not a democratic zone of representation of others for others but of unbridled desire for union, for exploration, a vulnerable and in certain respects a terrifying attempt to re-embody – a temporary teetering, a coming off one's axis, a careful *déhanchement*.

Ecstasy

In this sense, *Out of Context* embodies ecstasy, it enacts the choreographic outreach that 'outreach' work rarely imagines: it aims to set itself out of itself through mimetic doubling, through copying, owning, disowning; finding oneself alienated from a body that knows what is disorderly or no. Thus, the work stages a structure of corporeal and choreographic transcendence and the immanent setting of oneself (one's dancer's body) alongside a regular body, a regular context, a manner of moving in the street and onstage. What Platel experiments with thus resonates with a long history of overlap between movement 'disorders' characterized by tremors and twitches, spasms and falling, including epilepsy, chorea, myoclonus (characterized by sudden jerks, twitches and seizures), and Tourette's syndrome, and the ecstatic visions of epileptics and non-epileptics whose 'seizures' have alternatively been described across geographic and linguistic territories as disorderly and shamanic at once, and in alternation. It is never entirely clear, in the history of the 'seizure', what is to be cured or what is curing. All these moves have been recuperated here and over decades into a rave-and-club culture paradigm, reappropriating the ecstatically bacchanalian.[11] What Platel and les ballets C de la B wilfully do thus is to play in this indeterminate genealogical and cross-discursive zone, this space within which ecstasy is mundane and medicalized, popular and religious; the work conflates club pop, 'ecstatic' raving and spasmodic neuromotor disorder, so that we are confronted onstage with crafted heterogeneity that enables us to move with and perhaps in a small way to begin to move beyond the sorts of divisions posited as imbricated here (the medical, the cultural, the aesthetic). This means that while *Out of Context* plays with aesthetic rearticulation – literally as I have suggested rearticulating the body towards extreme angularity and smooth curvature, thus also genealogically rearticulating contemporary dance and dance theatre away from predominantly smooth and straight lines and simultaneously away from the hyper-discursive dance theatre of the conceptual dance paradigm of the 1990s – it also does this in a manner that opens up the possibility of a further spectralization of dance-theatre, a further expansion of the range of movement types, gestures and vocabularies we may find onstage. The broadest possible spectrum – what I am calling here an alterkinetic aesthetics – involves slow and fast, controlled and uncontrolled, abled and disabled – presented onstage not for what these movements 'represent' of the political spectrum of abilities or body types, but aesthetically, through rapid juxtaposition and intermingling – gestural elision – dissolving borders between normal and abnormal so that even this juxtaposition eventually, as in my experience of the show, becomes moot. This conjugation of sameness and difference politically and philosophically undoes dialectic as I am suggesting, to inhabit plasticity, a manner of seeing dialectic as always embedded in structures of metamorphosis; similarly, the epigenetic model Malabou sees in philosophical and critical structure, I have suggested, invites us to think movement towards futurity in which every pole, every moment is a present that is constituted of its own past and future, that serves as its own crucible. In this view, *Out of Context* arguably inhabits a moment, a space of opening, a possibility for reconfiguration and metamorphosis within which order and disorder interchange and, epigenetically, move on. There is no 'abnormal' gene, no static place from which disorder is understood; disorder, like order, is always on the move. This is not to say that we do not need provisionally, at times, to see and to query the contours of each, or that a concept like 'order' or historical context is not also useful; but in muddying, twisting and curving the borderland between these, another linguistic space opens up – perhaps a bilingual or a multilingual space, one that suggests bodies moving may be ordered and disordered at once; that this *frontera* is partial, imperfect, a gesture, an invitation and also a moment of aesthetic and social translation.

What I am arguing, then, is not only that *Out of Context* brings our attention to choreic gesture – to the twists and tensions of the back, the rolling of the eyes and stretching of the neck characteristic of various neurological disorders – but also that this attention wrestles with and perhaps reshapes existing concepts of beauty and achievement, rather than elude or reject them. Benjamin Wihstutz provocatively suggests that Jérôme Bel's *Disabled Theater* (2012) – in which members of the Theater HORA collective in Zurich, all of whom have self-described cognitive disabilities, are invited to stand onstage, present themselves, do a dance, then bow – 'is a political piece not because the actors prove to the audience that even they are capable of doing things, but because the form itself bids farewell to this idea of achievement'. But, as I am suggesting, Platel's work begins with the possibilities achievement affords. For Wihstutz, by '[a]bandoning extravaganza and virtuoso performance, Bel's theatre articulates and implements an equality and in-difference of the aesthetic, which remains on this side of the achievement principle'.[12] Achievement, for Wihstutz, is a function of neoliberal economics, a performative alienation, a perpetual 'I can'. This is true, and important. Yet I am arguing that here Platel's work shows a way provocatively to inhabit virtuosity; that even within the 'achievement' paradigm, choreographic craft has the potential for a moment to rearticulate and reconfigure – to perform a gestural, theatrical *détournement* with regard to – movement, arguably the very fabric and rhythm of our everyday lives. With *Out of Context*, we find the embrace of relative virtuosity not necessarily aligned with neoliberal achievement but with the sort of aesthetic autonomy that avant-garde theatre critic John Roberts argues still has the potential to disrupt or at the very least to irritate and to worry it.[13]

What's more, Platel's nod to hysteria's great choreographic *raconteuse*, Pina Bausch, a woman for whom social awkwardness, sadness, femininity, became another sort of virtue, an ambivalent social everyday, suggests an attempt further to rearticulate social performativity in terms of another genre of mundane gesture – gesture that is mundane and yet also exceptional, strange, particular, as 'hysterical', choreic, disordered; in this transformation and translation of everyday complexity into choreographic art, in this gestural cultivation of a genre of playful angularity and part-strange, part-familiar spasmodicism characteristic of popular late-night party moves; in this embrace of the arch and the shudder and the popping and the twitch, within a regime of choreographic control, what takes place we find is a provocatively masterful display of technique deployed for the purposes of aesthetic and affective reconfiguration. Dance in this work appears vulnerably, yet also unabashedly present to us to see as (mere) form. In seeing form, we see, radically, just to the side of 'neurotypical' or 'neurodiverse' disorder and identity. Platel's political aestheticism thus fundamentally embraces a sort of choreographic formalism as a way of rejecting the post-Judson rejection of virtuosity and thus rehabilitating the dancer's craft, a craft we may further argue is anything but socially tyrannical if executed with care.

What's more, within a broadly neoliberal paradigm, this radical openness to technique – once again, away from the anti-dance paradigm of the 1990s, the deconstruction of dance into discourse – burrows a tunnel out of anti-theatrical and choreophobic prejudices that set the choreographer as conceptual auteur, away from the dancers themselves, who may be 'merely' a stand-in or amateur. Platel's *Out of Context* is therefore also a genre of institutional critique and a cultural and institutional politics, a plea to recognize dance as an art and craft, even as – or perhaps all the more so as – 'non-dance' gestures have the potential to infiltrate and transform it.

After atypicality

Platel drew inspiration for *Out of Context* from his work as a special-needs educator for children with motor difficulties.[14] Philosophically, this practice of blurring boundaries between normal and abnormal, neurotypical and atypical, coheres with what Erin Manning calls minor gesture – a term she deploys in connection with autistic perception.[15] So while Manning thinks with autism to imagine a form of seeing and understanding that eschews the clear fixity of form – autistic perception, she shows, arrives gradually into form from washes of colour and motion – my sense of alterkinetics is that it breaks down the border between classical and popular gesture, high and low culture, disease and health, order and disorder. In inhabiting an expansive grey zone in the borderland, alterkinetic gesture finds a full spectrum of movements that roguishly toggles between 0 and 1, normal and abnormal, rapid shifts perceptibly, then nearly imperceptibly thwarting any attempt to pin one gesture down to hysteria or chorea and another to 'culture'. So between nature and culture, disease and dance, we are in and out of 'context': the context for elegance, for the theatre, for cultivating dancing away from the everyday, falters.

Platel's dancers, in their deliberate spectralization of gesture towards the alterkinetic, perform a space eliding divisions between voluntary and involuntary movement. Thus the (in)visibility of involuntary gestures – choreas and other motor irregularities – is troubled, troubling in turn the language and space of 'disability'. Indeed, the question of visibility is paramount in disability theory: Ann Cooper Albright, for instance, has argued that for 'disabled' dancers, the stage is a radical space within which the disabled body, normally occluded from view, collides with the genre of visual availability assumed by performers.[16] Disability Studies in this light has strategically positioned 'disabled' performance in terms of the deliberate recuperation of visibility, the claiming of visual space, the capacity for saying: I am here; I am visible now. What Platel's work does with *Out of Context*, however, that I find so compelling alongside this is also to show that regimes of visibility may be played out; that, as we also find, in the process, the notion of disability (motor disorder) itself is queried within a fault line. This does not mean the choreographed body has absorbed motor disorder, or that all pain is excised from the stage or audience space. Of course one could argue that Platel might have gone a lot further and worked more overtly with 'abled' and 'disabled', 'choreic' and 'neurotypical' bodies as well as with les ballets C de la B performers; yet what I am arguing is that this work provokes, more than anything else, in this case, the question of aestheticization as such: because these are basically 'able-bodied' dancers – at least in appearance (how do we know whether one or more dancers is not, invisibly, also epileptic, for example?) – the shudder of appropriation of gestural irregularities renders the political risks associated with representation all the more present and, I argue, offers this work with gesture all the more potent politically as an act of solidarity precisely because of the tender and awkward space of (mis)representation.

Of course, arguably, nothing is at stake here but the language of choreography: 'beauty' is queried, virtuosity is queried, and in the process, the institutions of dance and of dance theatre are queried as well. While not an exclusive aim – the work on some level fails conclusively to make a case for chorea's intrinsic beauty, for example, or to render its everyday difficulty and pain (this is not a documentary or a didactic show) – nevertheless, the parameters of contemporary dance in the early twenty-first-century shift. After the experiments of Judson Church and the 'exhausted' anti-dance paradigm that André Lepecki described of late-twentieth-century dance theatre, we find ourselves with *Out of Context* in a space of acting out, a hysterical space, a Bauschian space, where gestural heterogeneity exceeds the body politic; we see gesture representing, and failing to represent, identifiable groups onstage: thus, we have a genre of playful and unnerving gestural anarchy, a refusal of identity politics or representationalism. We have an act of dance theatre that inhabits an institutional space just as it queries a recent history of dance theatre and beyond this, a manner of ordering, organizing and hierarchizing gesture as such.

As I have noted, what was so striking in *Out of Context – for Pina* formally was how the dancer's gestures appeared for a time in the most awesome sense merely as bodies moving, such that the worlds of neurology and medicine, movement disorders and hysteria, ability and disability, ballet and club culture dissolved. This is not to suggest that Platel sought to make ethical judgements about neuromotor or neuromuscular disorder or normalcy with the show, but that the conflation and reconfiguration of voluntary and involuntary movements presented what I am calling an alterkinetic space within which ambivalent gesture rewrote the language of the contemporary stage. What Platel shows with this is an expanded realm of aestheticized gesture in a play of choreic alterity reflecting the viewer's gaze straight onto an image of disorder

Figure 11.1 Romeo Runa (front) and Emile Josse, Hyo Seung Ye, Elie Tass, Kaori Ito and Ross McCormack (background) during rehearsals of *Out of Context – for Pina* in dance studio S3, Ghent 2010. © Chris Van der Burght.

Figure 11.2 Mélanie Lomoff, Elie Tass, Romeu Runa and Mathieu Desseigne Ravel during rehearsals of *Out of Context – for Pina* in dance studio S3, Ghent 2010. © Chris Van der Burght.

and distortion, just as this figure of distortion gradually, over the course of the show, begins to appear no longer distorted at all. At stake is not the representation of chorea, or any other 'disorder', but the politics of representation as such. Ecstatically, we stand outside these bodies out of context, looking in.

Catastrophic proliferation: In the shadow of de la Tourette

Platel's *Out of Context* may be seen as a work sitting in a long line of performances probing – and theatricalizing – not only 'hysteria' but medicalized gesture in a more expansive sense. This is gesture that, as in Bausch's work, pertains banally to the everyday, though it is – pertinent for the question of visibility and representation – typically tucked out of sight. In this optic, disorderly everyday motion such as chorea is classified as ill and as such also as socially undesirable, painful because impossible to wrap into a work (an economic productivity) paradigm, and thus taboo. What cannot be controlled, in this optic, must be alienated. Translated into the language of philosophy, choreic gesture signals the failure to mean smoothly (to signify, to signal, to be eloquent): movement is mapped onto discourse and its aporias, its ostensive failures, as well as its productive potential for transformation. Giorgio Agamben, reading neurologist Gilles de la Tourette's writing on spasms, tics and jerks in *Étude sur une affection nerveuse caractérisée par de l'incoordination accompagnée d'écholalie et de coprolalie* [*Study on a Nervous Condition Characterized by Lack of Motor Coordination Accompanied by Echolalia and Coprolalia*] (1885), highlights what he describes as the 'catastrophic' 'proliferation' of gestures in Tourette's syndrome, long allied genealogically with epilepsy and chorea (or chorea minor, as a neuromotor disorder often found in young children, involving the involuntary dance-like movement of the limbs).[17] 'Patients can neither start nor complete the simplest of gestures', Agamben notes. 'If they are able to start a movement, this is interrupted and broken up by shocks lacking any coordination and by tremors that give the impression that the whole musculature is engaged in a dance (chorea) that is completely independent of any ambulatory end.'[18] The 'catastrophe' Agamben describes is characterized by what he sees as purposeless gesture, gesture without end; gesture that appears to be going nowhere – that cannot complete itself. Significantly, this 'catastrophe' looks like dance: dance with no destination.

Agamben draws his analysis of choreic gesture from the novelist Honoré de Balzac's observations on gait, extending the notion of purposelessness to social gaucherie. This reading centres on what Balzac calls '*virvoucher*', a sort of coming-and-going motion, circulating around someone, stopping and starting, buzzing around them like a bee or, allied to this, *virmoucher*, buzzing like a fly, without any apparent purpose.[19] In Balzac's view, this buzzing is typically feminine: he describes women at times jutting their arms and legs out, laughably so. What's more, those who *virvouche* (or *virmouche*) are annoying, in this analysis. They must be sent out into the fields so that they do not 'break' one's head or one's furniture through these awkward gestures. (Balzac uses the expression *casser la tête*, literally to break the head.[20])

Women, first and foremost, are liable to gestural spillage, gestural excess, in this portrait; like children, also long described in terms of gestural awkwardness, the seemingly uncontrollable, automatic motion of chorea positions them against the rational and efficient gesture of 'modern' (usually white) man.[21] Even Picasso's recuperation of angularity at the turn of the twentieth century, allying gestural syncopation to jazz, preserves a measure of nostalgic primitivism, although aesthetically, the modernist shift his work enacts can be seen as a close forerunner to the alterkinetic translation I am suggesting taking place in Platel's work, among others, in dance. Although this move hinges on aesthetic ambiguity, still within the space of this ambiguity, another imaginary can be played out that has the potential to redraw aesthetic lines.

What arrests my attention thus is the apparent purposelessness of choreic gesture, which comes to appear pathological (in Tourette's description) or bothersome (in Balzac's) on account of its 'queer' excess – excess that appears too feminine, too queer, reprising Jana Braziel and Kathleen LeBesco's analysis, inasmuch as feminine and queer bodies appear to walk, eat, talk and gesture too much;[22] they are always apparently excessive relative to their 'context', to the space around them, and within which they move. This is why they are – normatively – confined to the home or to the closet, kept out of sight. Yet such gestural excess, in Agamben's formulation, is nearly describable as dance cast as the (purposeless) aesthetic excess towards which movement tends. As I am arguing, this is where its 'pure' aestheticization on the stage allows us to shift the framework – the context – and thus to experience at least for an evening the alternative rhythmicity and (anti-)flow of chorea. Whether this confirms the normative and the normate is another question; I am arguing that alterkinetics deliberately transforms gestural alterity in a stage space radically opening up gesture to transformation, aesthetically and politically. This anarchic refusal to conform to norms of beauty, grace, normalcy and taboo is arguably all the more provocative as it deliberately inscribes alterkinetic work into a practice of trained concert dance.

Indeed, when recuperated into choreography, gestural excess has the potential to signal an expansive vocabulary – alongside smooth, curvilinear and comparatively predictable motion – redrawing the boundaries of what constitutes normal (or 'beautiful') movement. The angularity and unpredictability of Tourette's syndrome, chorea, and other gait or neuromotor 'disorders' causing individuals to fall, shake, wave or jolt their limbs, understood in terms of an alterkinetic aesthetic, amplifies the scope of choreographic (and unchoreographed) movement to encompass regular and irregular motion. Alterkinetic gesture, which includes smooth as well as jagged gesture, teeters on either side of an aesthetics and politics of control characteristic of military and balletic motion long (though ambivalently) associated with state power. These alterkinetic modalities thus work at an angle with and alongside Plato's celebration of Pyrrhic or war dances, with their rhythmic regularity; the alterkinetic participates in the 'Bacchic-type' dances Plato decried, those which appear to imitate drunkenness or ecstatic rapture; those that teeter and fall into syncopes: hiatuses, suspensions of movement and breath.

By resituating choreography on either side of the 'control' border, questioning the shape of virtuosic mastery, alterkinetic aesthetics help us rethink the relationship between agency and unintentional motion, and the pathologization of the latter, its typical excision from dance. Even spontaneous, 'natural' movement, prized by Isadora Duncan, or the improvisatory strategies of the Judson Dance among others, typically embrace smooth and controlled (though seemingly mundane) movement, over the striations, ruptures and rifts of the choreic body prey to its daily fits and starts. This choreic, 'hysterical' body spills out of itself, out of its own context, as one may say with Platel and with Pina. The alterkinetic body is nearly socially illegible: it eschews the clean lines and classical fluidity that balletic and contemporary conceptual dance similarly espouse, as well as the pathologizing stamp of the (perpetually reinforced) everyday medical and identitarian gaze. The alterkinetic is everyday gesture; it is only bumpily, at times uncontainably, so. And it has not had a serious place in theatrical dance; a place beyond mere quotation, a function that places a particular body onstage to be seen, but does not translate this motion into others, rather maintains a divide and thus perpetuates the distinction between order and taboo.

Out of the closet: Another form of grace

It would be too easy to chastise Platel for failing to offer what dancers and companies such as described by Albright have done, opening up the stage to variously 'abled' bodies. That would be to miss the point of this choreographed, stylized work, which is doing something else. Where companies working with 'disabled' performers seek to shift the public perception of skill and broaden the visible spectrum of bodies onstage,

Platel does so primarily from within classical and contemporary dance languages that emphasize form, rhythm, motion and control in particular ways. As such, he seeks to expand gestural vocabularies that stretch at the edges of comparatively more institutionalized dance within the establishment of contemporary dance theatre. As I have suggested, this heralds a shift away from the last new dance paradigm that typically refused the grandiloquence of highly skilled movement and the supposed tyranny of technique. With the alterkinetic mode, whether from within or without the world of 'abled' and less-'abled' performers, the parameters of what shape and rhythm motion can take shift. Movement itself is not good or bad; rather, the alterkinetic aesthetic undermines any hierarchy of gestural or body types. What I am calling the alterkinetic emphasizes gesture at the limits of choreographable movement, refiguring, while ostensibly disfiguring, various bodies in motion.

This may herald a new sort of formalism or post-formalism, an aesthetics after the straight line or the smooth curve, reconfiguring 'grace' in the old etymological sense of good will. This heightened, heterogeneous range of movements offers a twist to the political aesthetic dyad that pits symmetrical beauty against asymmetrical monstrosity, technique and virtuosity against the mundane or the amateur, structure against incoherence, control against loss of control, and voluntary against involuntary motion, instead opening up a conversation on the relationship between orderliness or harmony and unrest, and a reconfiguration of the possibilities afforded by dance as a particular gestural craft.

Another everyday/exhausting exhaustion: After anti-dance

The exhausted anti-dance paradigm of the past twenty years – characterized by the work of Jérôme Bel, Xavier Le Roy and others, for whom dance began to vanish into the idea, a disappearing present, as Lepecki has noted, perpetually without a past – has stood alongside artists such as Platel working within a vividly kinematic and at times hyperkinematic rhythm and vocabulary.[23] According to this latter mode, there is and never was anything to be eschewed in mastering dance technique or a dancing body; dance does not all have to be failure, inhibition or impotence. Rather, in what I am describing as the alterkinetic aesthetic, a whole range of movement vocabularies and intensities may be fair play, from the fast-paced to the still or the haphazard. It is as if dance and dance theatre were turning back on themselves and an important moment of refusal of virtuosity to reaffirm and re-embrace variegated gestural vocabularies onstage, to reaffiliate gesture with the complex rhythmicity of everyday life: the angularity of surprise, the striations and smoothnesses of 'normal' (rather than normalizing, controlled or controlling) locomotion.

Medicine is arguably the ultimate repository of gestural 'abnormality'. In this sense, the juxtaposed, occasionally integrated, realm of movements that alterkinetic aesthetics present suggests an expanded and messy concept of the everyday, passing through contemporary anti-dance to arrive at a heteroclite figure of the conjugated virtuosic and mundane. Yet, paradoxically, this mundanity is not easy: choreic movement presents real challenges every day.

Disorders of motion, recuperated and heightened in dance, offer the antithesis to the sort of contemporary choreographic work that Lepecki describes as being still or silent. Hypomania involves muscle spasms and psychomotor agitation; chorea describes involuntary, jerky movements of the arms, legs and/or face; and myoclonus brings a sudden contraction of the muscles. Not all necessarily occur with speed or intensity; these gestural hiccups can be halting as well. But these movements, when framed and reconfigured onstage, offer a gestural irregularity that goes against classical symmetry – and its postmodern rejection. At the same time, these movements quote, while transforming, the language of 'hysteria', and the hysterical body of the nineteenth-century ballets romanticized, as Felicia McCarren has argued, in the madness of Giselle (a ballet that also stages the monomaniacal impulse, the obsessive fixation on a singular thing, like dance, such as nineteenth-century psychiatry imagined of the medieval dancing plagues and other instances of affective and gestural surplus).[24] Instead, dancers and choreographers borrowing from dyskinetic gestural vocabularies move dance along into a choreographic space where everyday disorders of motion come to be seen otherwise, reframed, out of context, possible nearly to perform on account of something between curiosity, grace, virtuosity and spectacular action, reframing feats that defy the neurotypical body's learned mechanisms, staging thus the more vulnerable, unwilled loss of motor control. All this, wrapped into an expanded field of 'dance', begs us to ask once again what dance is and what it can be.

To the side of disorder(s)

This chapter has situated my reading of Platel's *Out of Context* in a chasm: an awkward space just to the side of work by individual 'disabled' performers such as Jess Thom (a.k.a. Tourette's Hero), and long-established companies including Candoco and Amici, which work with abled and 'dis'-abled dancers – men and women who were born with or developed a range of neuromotor alterities, from Tourette's syndrome and ataxia (a condition that inhibits muscular coordination) to myoclonus.[25] In Platel's work, we find gesture onstage that is almost, but not quite like these. With Platel, arcs of the back, jerks, twitches and spasms are replicated, explored, by perfectly 'able'-bodied dancers, for whom mobility poses none of the everyday challenges confronted by these other dancers. The difficulties inherent in such a reading are many: what hierarchies of normality and control appear in setting alongside one another representations of neuromotor alterity? What discourse on 'truth' emerges when comparing performances by 'really' otherly abled bodies and those that are not 'really' otherly abled – those that are, by all appearances, neurotypical? How would the discourse on theatrical reality play out, if we hypothesized that some of Platel's dancers may actually be neuro-atypical, only it is not apparent (as mentioned earlier, someone suffers from epilepsy, for example, a condition only visible in the isolated event of a seizure)?

In focusing on Platel's work with this piece, treading a tender line between representations of neuro-alterity and the 'real' performance of visible neuromotor disorders onstage, I have sought to suggest that we find, perhaps paradoxically, in the aesthetic repetition and transformation presented by this choreography, a form of aesthetic spectralization: an expansive shift in gestural language which, rather than trade in stillness or excess, banality or balletic virtuosity, recuperates a different order of polymorphic gesture in the everyday. This polymorphism explores all the tensions, waves and spasms of neuromotor alterity as well as other forms of spasmodic everyday movement among minor club and popular dance genres including trance dance and the popping and krumping of hip hop, themselves indirectly continuing a long line of performative recuperations of movement disorders, unwittingly allying themselves with the 'abnormal' medical body. Already in the nineteenth century, so-called epileptic singers performing in Parisian cabarets recuperated the gestures of 'hysterical' syncopes popular from demonstrations by Jean-Martin Charcot's 'hysteria' and 'hysteroepilepsy' patients, whose motions he put onstage at the Salpêtrière hospital for a broad array of audience members – artists, writers and medical students – to enjoy and learn from.[26] The popularity of viewing alternative corporeal gestures, then, is not new; what I hope to be suggesting is that the recent turn – if we may call it that – towards alterkinetics closes a persistent gap between freak show, identity politics (in the form of community and disability art), and high art (including contemporary dance and ballet), as well as between the discursive, conceptual dance of the past twenty-five years and the extension of the 'democratic' spectrum in contemporary dance theatre that goes beyond supposedly elitist theoretical discourse without further thinking the specifically aesthetic question of representations of motor alterity onstage.

The chapter has thus been arguing that the polymorphic space of gestural recuperation that Platel's work showcases – when viewed alongside an efflorescence of new works by and with neuro-atypical dancers and theatre artists – expands the kinaesthetic regime of the arts, allowing us to rethink representations of gestural ownership, agency and alterity.[27] I have been calling this expanded realm alterkinetic: it embraces the smooth and the spasmodic, the sudden and involuntary, as well as the carefully controlled and precisely executed *rond de jambe*, the mathematically symmetrical *port de bras* that makes of the arms a textbook curve. I use the term 'alterkinetic' in contrast to the distinctly medicalized term 'dyskinetic' (disorder of motion) to signal a performative and aesthetic recuperation of dyskinetic gestures in concert dance and dance theatre. In this view – we may call it, as I have suggested, hyper-baroque – simplicity has relatively little special purchase; irregular rhythmicity is no more nor less suspect than rhyme; and the syncope (the sudden fall or temporary hiatus, the suspension of breath) is part and parcel of a regime of consciousness that may be interrupted, visibly or not, at any time. Of course, this expanded realm of aesthetic experimentation is informed by and may even be said to exploit the corporeal possibilities afforded by a body 'in control', one that can deftly manipulate the borderline between apparently voluntary and involuntary motion; one for which aestheticized figures of order and disorder are wilfully imbricated, the part each limb plays onstage carefully meted out. Yet what I am arguing is that by experimenting with an expanded realm of gesture that includes movements typically classed as 'disordered' or 'disabled' and gestures proper to the minor forms of club or pop dance and ballet, the alterkinetic regime of the arts has the potential radically to shift the contemporary dance-theatre spectrum which, toggling between a balletic and anti-dance prejudice, brought contemporary dance virtually to a standstill in the past decades. Characteristic of the polarized 1990s to 2000s non-dance paradigm, dance (and dance theatre), in the wake of the Judson Church project of the 1960s, positioned a certain brand of quiet mundanity (sitting on a chair and talking, for example) against the supposedly oppressive virtuosity of modern technique and ballet, as 'dance' threatened nominally, even playfully, to disappear into the aporetic space of discursive failure. With the explosion of polymorphic, polyvalent gestures characteristic of the alterkinetic landscape, a resurgence of movement orders and disorders appears onstage that is neither strictly classical in its virtuosic minimalism and romantic narrativism nor strictly baroque in its curvatures and proliferation of lines; nor is it 'against' or 'with' dancing as a technique and a craft; but presents instead a plastic space of discursive para-regimentation, one that operates a *détournement* of the anti-balletic prejudice.

Although this modest shift will require revision in turn, if its potency as a toggling space between 'normal' and 'abnormal' gesture undoes the distinction (a tall order for any aesthetic practice!), for now the alterkinetic suggests an elastic space of normative reconfiguration that is open and affirmative: not only a zone of gestural inclusion, but one that circumvents – deliberately muddies and blurs – visible distinctions between virtuosic and banal, ability and disability, and thus also between the super, the para and the infra-human. In this view, we are all more or less merely moving: there is no up or down, right or wrong, aesthetic or inaesthetic action. More importantly, there is no gesture that does not have an equal right to the stage.

I am arguing that the partial appearance of alterkinetic gestures onstage thus constitutes a zone of gestural intensity, an area of theatrical framing within which a tangle of encounters and readings takes place, moving our ideas about the body's twists and turns. Alterkinetic gestures do not only describe the recuperation of imagined monstrosity, pathology, heresy or dissidence into dance but enact the cross-pollination of gestures, seismically shifting whole spheres of our kinaesthetic imagination. In this sense, the history of choreic gesture is choreopolitical as well as it is choreographic, concerned with the border between (in this case bodily) normality and abnormality, what Georges Devereux has described as the definitive borderline in the science of mind.[28] What's more, alterkinetic gesture takes this borderline further into the heightened realm of normalitivity that concert dance represents: that which gives form to beauty and to the good.

Alterkinetics after Foucault

What I am calling alterkinetic thus draws from the movement vocabularies of medicine and the life sciences, club culture, cultures of display and freak shows, to reclaim the broadest possible spectrum for gesture in dance and dance theatre. This shift, exemplified in Platel's *Out of Context*, describes a performative landscape that is heterogeneous and polymorphic. Rather than focusing on the figure of the amateur, the aesthetics of not-dance, or an existential aporia barring the performer from engaging in a lost Atlantis of balletic worlds past, I am suggesting the alterkinetic turn in Platel's work as reconfiguring movement, theatre and dance in a politically and ethically, as well as an aesthetically expanded field. This shifts the choreographic project away from a rhetorical undoing of classical technique and its supposed elitism towards a polysemic and heteroglossic gestural language borrowing as much from neurology and medical science, ballet and hip hop, as the cognitive stage or choreographic lab.

In refusing the segregation and self-segregation of identity politics and the social embarrassment or self-imposed closeting and enclosure that neuro-'atypicals' experience every day, alterkinetic aesthetics propose to move the borderline of transgression onto the stage. This view aims to further what Michel Foucault has identified among late medieval and early modern religious heresies as articulating a perpetually emergent 'system of transgression', series of borders not exactly coinciding with illegality or criminality, revolution, monstrosity or abnormality, but with acts of denunciation and delimitation that carve out ever-shifting spaces of judgement.[29] So whereas there is still a long way to go before audiences with Tourette's syndrome, for example, such as Jess Thom, are readily allowed into the audience at a show, for fear they will disrupt other audience-goers and performers, the gestural representation of dyskinesia helps a little bit to move aesthetic literacy along and thus one can hope to participate in a broader reconfiguration of our modes of seeing and our co-habitations of space. This understands the space of the stage to be a heightened zone for negotiating everyday gestural politics: it takes the *theatron* in the strongest sense as a seeing-place, one that denounces or on the contrary reframes, highlights and arguably also transforms particular manners of moving, speaking and gesturing, respectacularizing corporeal forms. This is not sufficient, of course, but it invites for a while the question what it means to be human in shared motional space; to engage in the plasticity of an ever-shifting gestural dialectic, a zone of gestural indeterminacy. If we may imagine spasms and twitches alongside all-night dance, we may give a little more space to the choreic man or woman on the bus, in the street; we may hop-step together. This is a fantasy; it is a leap of the imagination, a falling into a gulf; but if we don't dream now, then when?

So as not to conclude: Gesture after Dionysus

Against (and alongside) what Schwartz has called torque – smooth, predictable, curvilinear motion arising in the nineteenth and early twentieth centuries from graphology and modern dance to architecture – I have read Platel's *Out of Context – for Pina* as an homage to Bausch's perpetual tribute to dancing at the borderline between control and uncontrol, voluntary and involuntary; as well as to a poetics of 'hysteria' cast as affective and gestural surplus.[30] Platel's work thus indicates a turn, a space, occupying neither disability theatre nor virtuosic ballet with its typically smooth and efficient lines, but a playful, irreverent examination of 'normalcy' in the body onstage, mixing medicalized gesture with everyday dance, virtuosic and amateur. This alterkinetic aesthetic, hovering between professional replication and tentative exploration, has the potential to shift the boundaries of what we see as stage-worthy, something directly to look at (rather than that from which to avert one's gaze). With *Out of Context*, the tic, the stumble, the fall, the spasm, the convulsion and the apparent disorder of gesture normally characterized as dyskinetic shifts the contemporary dance-theatre landscape away from the 'exhausted' dance paradigm – characterized by a refusal to move, silence and stillness presenting dramaturgies of failure, discursive choreo-ontologies – to a heightened, ecstatic affirmation of everyday articular life. Such alterkinetic dance borrows from the choreographic gestures of neurodegenerative conditions such as chorea and epilepsy, as well as from club and pop moves, rearticulating the body's social regimens in an expanded field of movement, a polymorphic landscape that repositions the smooth and the striated, the stiff and the angular, the lilting and the swift alongside one another as equally workable 'beauties', objects of desire and contemplation. Constituting an alternative, non- or even para-normative gestural language, this unruly choreography heralds an expansive dance theatre at the edges of choreographic repeatability, calling forth reproductions and reperformances of the voluntary and involuntary, coordination and its loss. This is not mere representation; movements aligning themselves with dyskinetic gesture rather shift the pathological border, presenting an expansive kinaesthetic regime that recuperates and also transfigures gestural articulacy, going over the no-fly zone between repetition and transformation, with the potential to overturn the gendered and racialized standards of smooth, controlled, poised and supposedly articulate – torque-like – beauty and grace.

The ironies are many: as I have noted, these dancers deliberately perform gestures that for many in everyday life are not willed, not even (perhaps) wanted; but aligning this work with the minor gestures (in Manning's terminology) of everyday motion across the neurological spectrum enables us – all – potentially to reimagine the spectacular, the monstrous and the taboo. In Manning's terms, the minor gesture describes a reaching-towards that undoes the primacy of agency and the tyranny of individuation, twin terms she notes overdetermine culturally entrenched notions of the self as a wilful, controlled and purposeful being. With alterkinetic aesthetics, we find a genre of re-individuation, rearticulating the Dionysian myth of dance as ecstatic transformation in the margins of nominally civilized life. With alterkinetics, embodied by Platel's dancers, gestures may be as central as they are peripheral, performing, aesthetically, a para-normative gestural *détournement*. The *détournement* is at once aesthetic and political: gestures are not only recuperated and represented, made visible otherwise; they are also moved into a sphere – the ultimate sphere – out of which they had been barred, that of the most beautiful thing, dance meant to capture, even to rarify (to make sublime) natural corporeal life.

Notes

1   Honoré de Balzac (1853) *Théorie de la démarche*, Paris: Eugène Didier, Éditeur, 58.
2   An earlier version of this chapter appears in 'Epilepsy, Chorea, and Involuntary Movements Onstage: The Politics and Aesthetics of Alterkinetic Dance', *About Performance*, 11 (2012): 159–83. For a provocative treatment of cognate questions and issues in Jérôme Bel's recent work, see, for example, Sandra Umathum and Benjamin Wihstutz (eds.) (2015) *Disabled Theater*, Zurich and Berlin: Diaphanes. The problems raised by Bel's work differ markedly from those I treat here, as he

works onstage with 'disabled' performers in *Disabled Theater*; nevertheless, questions provoked by the de- or re-aestheticization of the stage space in connection with 'disabled' moves – often involuntary, shaking or angular gestures not normally associated with the classical, curvilinear grace of ballet or the equally clean but rearticulated control of even the most 'everyday' modern dance – remain shared.

3   Men and women with so-called movement disorders – involuntary, often repetitive gestures described of psychiatric conditions such as hypomania and, more often, of neuromotor disorders involving tics, spasms and myoclonus – typically have difficulty performing regular and controlled muscle movements; fluidity is continually at stake. These disorders can be enormously distressing and are very common: Parkinson's disease alone affects in the order of 127,000 people in the United Kingdom. See https://www.parkinsons.org.uk/content/about-parkinsons (accessed 13 September 2016). While disability dance companies including Candoco and Amici develop their own alterkinetic vocabularies that shift the range of available movements and figures of beauty or virtuosity in theatrical space, conditions such as Parkinson's have also become the focus of public-engagement projects among neurotypical classical and modern dance companies including the Mark Morris Dance Group, whose Dance for Parkinson's Disease brings dance 'back' to those who suffer from Parkinson's and related motor disorders. A further iteration of the present work would explore movement disorders in dance in relation to old age. See http://markmorrisdancegroup.org/community/Dance-for-PD (accessed 13 September 2016). The English National Ballet operates a similar scheme, at http://www.ballet.org.uk/learning/dance-parkinsons/(accessed 13 September 2016).

4   Caroline Levine (2015) *Forms: Whole, Rhythm, Hierarchy, Network*, Princeton, NJ: Princeton University Press, 2–3.

5   See esp. Catherine Malabou (2014) *Avant demain: Épigenèse et rationalité*, Paris: Presses Universitaires de France.

6   Kélina Gotman (2018) *Choreomania: Dance and Disorder*, Oxford: Oxford University Press.

7   Gotman, *Choreomania*; Hillel Schwartz (1992) 'Torque: The New Kinaesthetic of the Twentieth Century', in Jonathan Crary and Sanford Kwinter (eds.), *Zone 6: Incorporations*, Cambridge, Mass.: The MIT Press, 71–127.

8   Not all dances that I am calling alterkinetic replicate (in order to co-compose) all the dyskinesias of the medical repertoire. Juxtaposition and cohabitation also enable collaborative research into alternative forms of movement. In Wayne McGregor's *AtaXia*, premiered at Sadler's Wells in 2004 and performed by McGregor's company Random Dance, Sarah Seddon Jenner, a woman suffering from ataxia, performed alongside the other dancers. This was staged in the context of a collaborative research project with Scott deLahunta at Dartington College, and researchers in experimental psychology, computing, cognition and brain science across the United Kingdom and France. In contrast to Random Dance's normally ultra-sleek movement vocabulary, McGregor sought in this project 'to make a piece about disorder, about being uncoordinated'. His initial questions were, 'How can you make a highly skilled body be genuinely uncoordinated?' and 'How could we set up interventions or confusions that would prevent the dancers from being able to exercise the facilities they're trained in?' In Catherine Hale (2004) 'The Science of Making Dances', *Dance Gazette*, 2: 16–19. On *AtaXia* and the Choreography and Cognition project, see http://www.choreocog.net/ataxia.html (accessed 13 September 2016). See also Petra Kuppers (2007) *The Scar of Visibility: Medical Performances and Contemporary*

Art, Minneapolis, Minn.: University of Minnesota Press, 178–81. The carefully crafted performance of un-coordination presented by McGregor's dancers offered moments of disorientation and kinetic loss such as those experienced by those with ataxia and other neuromotor disorders. These choreographed movements were informed by the company dancers' experimentation, in a laboratory setting, with control and loss of control, experimentation then integrated into the choreography throughout. In performance, the contrast between stereotypically controlled and non-controlled moments was jarring, breathtaking in its precision, and troubling for the muscular dispossession the gestures represented. But, except for Jenner, this was a representation. The movements were both real and fabricated: acts of gestural mimesis evoking a dyskinetic world. As such, this piece staged the drama of ballet: bodies inhabiting classical technique, coordination and control, crafted to be rhetorically set free. If the conflict was never quite reconciled, inasmuch as the piece suggested (often without enacting) controlled disorder, it also opened up an aesthetic – specifically, what I am calling an alterkinetic – approach to ataxic and dyskinetic movement through classically shaped bodies, seeking not so much the *informe* (or formless) as what I am calling the syncopated movement of the alterkinetic, or *alter-forme*, a form not intrinsically abnormal but socially, historically and culturally determined to occupy that space. In performing (and significantly in performing with) ataxia, these dancers resisted an aesthetic strategy of recuperation or mere framing; the piece situated itself between being and becoming – an epigenetic space – troubling the discourse on and depiction of monstrosity and its mere aestheticization. Although this does not entirely rid us of the spectral problem of an injection of alterity into a majoritarian body politic – the problem André Lepecki poses of black bodies imagined again and again to infuse the limp white corpse with sexually charged vitality, an almost animal life force – it nevertheless helps us think of the politically cogent potential of juxtaposition and relative, temporary blurring to reconfigure the shape of the aestheticized dancing body, and thus too the 'natural' state it is meant admirably to exemplify – as *la belle nature*, nature rendered beautiful. André Lepecki (2006) *Exhausting Dance: Performance and the Politics of Movement*, London and New York: Routledge, 109.

9   Scott Wallin astutely articulates this complicated paradox, in 'Come Together: Discomfort and Longing in Jérôme Bel's *Disabled Theater*', where he writes of the show's 'normative setup of disability', one with which 'neurotypical audiences simultaneously identify and lament because of the gulf it opens up between spectators and actors'; he writes, 'because the show's structure introduces the actors as passive, isolated, authentic subjects whose main purpose is to be gazed upon', the show ultimately represents 'a very safe space where spectators can feel that they are engaging with disabled people even though the experience is rudimentary and predicated on a lack of familiarity and requires the discomfort of social distance that many normate people yearn to repair'. Scott Wallin (2015) 'Come Together: Discomfort and Longing in Jérôme Bel's *Disabled Theater*', in Sandra Umathum and Benjamin Wihstutz (eds.), *Disabled Theater*, Zurich and Berlin: Diaphanes, 61–80. This characterization coheres with my own experience of Bel's work with 'disabled' performers in *The Show Must Go On* and *Gala*. Although it is beyond the scope of this chapter to pursue the comparison further, provocative writing on disability performance in a context of contemporary European dance theatre has emerged in connection with this piece, and I refer to this literature in passing. It is worth noting that the critical context within which I situate the present discussion centres

on a European dance theatre paradigm informed by the non-dance movement of the 1990s; for a longer discussion of cognate works outside Europe, including Rita Marcalo's 'epileptic' performances and Québécois choreographer Marie Chouinard's performance of medicality, see Gotman, 'Epilepsy, Chorea'.
10 Gotman, *Choreomania*.
11 Gotman, *Choreomania*.
12 Benjamin Wihstutz (2015) "' ... And I Am an Actor": On Emancipation in Disabled Theater', in Sandra Umathum and Benjamin Wihstutz (eds.), *Disabled Theater*, Zurich and Berlin: Diaphanes, 35–50, at 44.
13 John Roberts (2015) *Revolutionary Time and the Avant-Garde*, London: Verso.
14 See Hildegard De Vuyst (2010) '*Out of Context – For Pina*: Introduction'. Available at http://www.lesballetscdela.be/fr/projects/productions/out-of-context-for-pina/info (accessed 20 August 2019).
15 Erin Manning (2016) *The Minor Gesture*, Durham, NC: Duke University Press.
16 See Ann Cooper Albright (2001) 'Strategic Abilities: Negotiating the Disabled Body in Dance', in Ann Dils and Ann Cooper Albright (eds.), *Moving History/Dancing Cultures: A Dance History Reader*, Middletown, Conn.: Wesleyan University Press, 56–66, at 57.
17 For a discussion of this intertwined genealogy, and Agamben's remarks on choreic gesture, see Gotman, *Choreomania*.
18 Giorgio Agamben (2000) 'Notes on Gesture', in *Means without End: Notes on Politics*, trans. Vincenzo Binetti and Cesare Casarino, Minneapolis, Minn.: University of Minnesota Press, 48–59, at 50.
19 Balzac, *Théorie de la démarche*, 57.
20 Balzac, *Théorie de la démarche*, 57.
21 See, for example, Felicia McCarren (2003) *Dancing Machines: Choreographies of the Age of Mechanical Reproduction*, Stanford, Calif.: Stanford University Press. See also Gotman, *Choreomania*.
22 Jana Evans Braziel and Kathleen LeBesco (2005) 'Performing Excess', *Women and Performance: A Journal of Feminist Theory*, 15 (2): 9–13.
23 Lepecki, *Exhausting*, 124.
24 See Felicia McCarren (1998) *Dance Pathologies: Performance, Poetics, Medicine*, Stanford, Calif.: Stanford University Press; Gotman, *Choreomania*.
25 Since 1980, Amici Dance Theatre Company has been among several companies pioneering work 'integrating able-bodied & disabled artists and performers'. See http://www.amicidance.org/about/amici-dance-theatre-company (accessed 13 September 2016). See also Candoco Dance Company, at http://www.candoco.co.uk (accessed 13 September 2016). Performance-maker Jessica Thom has written vibrantly about living with Tourette's in *Welcome to Biscuit Land: A Year in the Life of Touretteshero* (London: Souvenir Press, 2012) and on her blog, http://www.touretteshero.com/ (accessed 13 September 2016).
26 On epileptic singers, see especially Rae Beth Gordon (2003) 'Natural Rhythm: La Parisienne Dances with Darwin: 1875–1910', *Modernism/Modernity*, 10 (4): 617–56, at 626ff; Rae Beth Gordon (2001) 'From Charcot to Charlot: Unconscious Imitation and Spectatorship in French Cabaret and Early Cinema', *Critical Inquiry*, 27 (3): 515–49, at 534 ff.
27 This is a slightly different but related understanding of gesture to that posited by gesture theorists in the past decades; according to Carrie Noland, gesture signals a kinaesthetic experience of the body's capacity to act in the world. Gesture signifies

agency as well as experience. For Deirdre Sklar, gestures reinscribe and transform ideology every day, as we repeat but also reconfigure gestures learned in particular social circumstances (waving, clapping, etc.). See Carrie Noland and Sally Ann Ness (eds.) (2008) *Migrations of Gesture*, Minneapolis, Minn.: University of Michigan Press.

28 Georges Devereux (1977), 'Normal et anormal (1956)', in *Essais d'ethnopsychiatrie générale*, trans. Tina Jolas and Henri Gobard, Paris: Éditions Gallimard, 1.

29 Michel Foucault (2001) 'Les Déviations religieuses et le savoir médical', in *Dits et écrits*, vol. I: *1954–1975*, eds. Daniel Defert and François Ewald with Jacques Lagrange, Paris: Gallimard, 652–63, at 652.

30 Schwartz, 'Torque'.

References

Agamben, Giorgio (2000) 'Notes on Gesture', in *Means without End: Notes on Politics*, trans. Vincenzo Binetti and Cesare Casarino, Minneapolis, Minn.: University of Minnesota Press, 48–59. First published 1996.

Albright, Ann Cooper (2001) 'Strategic Abilities: Negotiating the Disabled Body in Dance', in Ann Dils and Ann Cooper Albright (eds.), *Moving History/Dancing Cultures: A Dance History Reader*, Middletown, Conn.: Wesleyan University Press, 56–66.

Balzac, Honoré de (1853) *Théorie de la démarche*, Paris: Eugène Didier, Éditeur.

Braziel, Jana Evans, and Kathleen LeBesco (2005) 'Introduction: Performing Excess', *Women and Performance: A Journal of Feminist Theory*, 15 (2): 9–13.

De Vuyst, Hildegard (2010) '*Out of Context – for Pina*: Introduction'. Available at http://www.lesballetscdela.be/fr/projects/productions/out-of-context-for-pina/info/ (accessed 20 August 2019).

Foucault, Michel (2001) 'Les Déviations religieuses et le savoir médical', in *Dits et écrits*, vol. I: *1954–1975*, edited by Daniel Defert and François Ewald with Jacques Lagrange, Paris: Gallimard, 652–63.

Gordon, Rae Beth (2001) 'From Charcot to Charlot: Unconscious Imitation and Spectatorship in French Cabaret and Early Cinema', *Critical Inquiry*, 27 (3): 515–49.

Gordon, Rae Beth (2003) 'Natural Rhythm: La Parisienne Dances with Darwin: 1875–1910', *Modernism/Modernity*, 10 (4): 617–56.

Gotman, Kélina (2012) 'Epilepsy, Chorea, and Involuntary Movements Onstage: The Politics and Aesthetics of Alterkinetic Dance', *About Performance*, 11: 159–83.

Gotman, Kélina (2018) *Choreomania: Dance and Disorder*, Oxford: Oxford University Press.

Hale, Catherine (2004) 'The Science of Making Dances', *Dance Gazette*, 2: 16–19.

Kuppers, Petra (2007) *The Scar of Visibility: Medical Performances and Contemporary Art*, Minneapolis, Minn.: The University of Minnesota Press.

Lepecki, André (2006) *Exhausting Dance: Performance and the Politics of Movement*, London and New York: Routledge.

Levine, Caroline (2015) *Forms: Whole, Rhythm, Hierarchy, Network*, Princeton, NJ: Princeton University Press.

Malabou, Catherine (2014) *Avant demain: Épigenèse et rationalité*, Paris: Presses Universitaires de France.

Manning, Erin (2016) *The Minor Gesture*, Durham, NC: Duke University Press.

McCarren, Felicia (1998) *Dance Pathologies: Performance, Poetics, Medicine*, Stanford, Calif.: Stanford University Press.
McCarren, Felicia (2003) *Dancing Machines: Choreographies of the Age of Mechanical Reproduction*, Stanford, Calif.: Stanford University Press.
Noland, Carrie, and Sally Ann Ness (eds.) (2008), *Migrations of Gesture*, Minneapolis, Minn.: University of Michigan Press.
Schwartz, Hillel (1992) 'Torque: The New Kinaesthetic of the Twentieth Century', in Jonathan Crary and Sanford Kwinter (eds.), *Zone 6: Incorporations*, Cambridge, Mass.: The MIT Press, 71–127.
Thom, Jessica (2012) *Welcome to Biscuit Land: A Year in the Life of Tourette's Hero*, London: Souvenir Press.
Umathum, Sandra, and Benjamin Wihstutz (eds.) (2015) *Disabled Theater*, Zurich and Berlin: Diaphanes.
Wallin, Scott (2015) 'Come Together: Discomfort and Longing in Jérôme Bel's *Disabled Theater*', in Sandra Umathum and Benjamin Wihstutz (eds.), *Disabled Theater*, Zurich and Berlin: Diaphanes, 61–80.
Wihstutz, Benjamin (2015) '"… And I Am an Actor": On Emancipation in Disabled Theater', in Sandra Umathum and Benjamin Wihstutz (eds.), *Disabled Theater*, Zürich and Berlin: Diaphanes, 35–50.

12

Staging the Precarious

Vulnerability and Sexual Identity in Alain Platel's *Gardenia*

Miriam Dreysse

The performing arts have increasingly engaged with the concept of precariousness, as it has been defined by Judith Butler in her essay collection *Precarious Life* as a fundamental vulnerability of the human subject.[1] Theatre, performance and contemporary dance showcase that which is beyond the norm, the Other – different bodies, precarious subjects, unsecured identities. In the ailing bodies of Socìetas Raffaello Sanzio, Christoph Schlingensief's disabled performers, or Christoph Marthaler's characters who seem to have fallen off the face of the earth, theatre reveals the fragility of the images we use to understand the world and ourselves. There are always things that remain excluded from these images but that still have the power to disrupt them, by inscribing them with ambivalences and contradictions. Most particularly in dance, which in ballet still subscribes to an extreme regime of standardizing and disciplining the body, the individual's vulnerable, digressive, precarious body takes centre stage. In the works of Xavier Le Roy, Jérôme Bel or Meg Stuart, imperfect bodies, deformative and fragmented movements, contortions and contractions question dichotomies such as beautiful–ugly, male–female or normal–abnormal. They capitalize on precariousness as a departure from the norm, an in-between space where unsecured identities can exist.[2]

Often the presence of such other, vulnerable bodies is connected to a questioning of representability: 'How can I represent subjects without either reproducing accepted norms or situating these subjects outside such norms, thus contributing to their exclusion?' Put differently, to what extent can an aesthetic of precariousness question representation itself and its corresponding mechanisms of normalization and exclusion? The question of precariousness hence also becomes a question of representation. I will explore this question of precariousness and the potentials and conditions of its representation in *Gardenia*, a performance that Alain Platel created in 2010 with his les ballets C de la B and in collaboration with Frank Van Laecke.[3] In this performance, nine people take the stage, seven of them transvestites or transsexuals aged between sixty and seventy years old. They are former colleagues of the transsexual actress Vanessa Van Durme, who gave Platel the idea for the piece, and who joins them onstage. I will combine an observation of the staging of *Gardenia* with a reading of Butler's *Precarious Life*.[4] How can theatre and dance bring us to be, in Butler's words, 'wakened to the precariousness of the Other's life'? To what extent can it become a language that 'communicates the precariousness of life that establishes the ongoing tension of a non-violent ethics'?[5]

The precariousness of the life of the Other

Drawing on Emmanuel Levinas, Butler develops the concept of an ethics that is built on the understanding of the precariousness of the life of the Other. She posits a fundamental vulnerability of the human being that is constitutive of humanity itself: 'a common human vulnerability, one that emerges with life itself'.[6] This existential precariousness of human life is due to the dependency of each individual on the other, on the 'disposition of ourselves outside ourselves'.[7] The subject does not experience itself as a closed-off unit but is constituted through being addressed by the other. It is therefore essentially dependent: '[W]e are not only constituted by our relations but also dispossessed by them as well.'[8] When contact is unsuccessful, our existence reveals itself to be precarious, but even successful contact dispossesses the subject to an extent, as it can never completely control it.[9] We are doubly dependent on and endangered by the Other: it constitutes us, but is also capable of injuring, even destroying, us.

The precariousness of existence is understood to apply to all people, albeit to different degrees. Human beings' vulnerability – their humanity – is subject to normative and mediatized conditions, which can partially or entirely exclude certain individuals from the realm of humanity, for instance for political reasons.[10] For Butler, the question of how to represent precariousness is crucial, for it is 'in the domain of representation where humanization and dehumanization occur ceaselessly'.[11] She seeks to develop forms of representation that restore the humanity of those who have been dehumanized in such a way. More than simply an 'entry of the excluded into an established ontology', for Butler it is about an 'insurrection at the level of ontology, a critical opening up of the questions, What is real? Whose lives are real? How might reality be remade?'[12]

Gardenia's precarious identities

The people onstage in *Gardenia* represent precarious identities on several levels. They embody the concrete social precariousness of a non-heteronormative sexual identity, which is insecure in a very real, everyday sense: marginal, limited to a very specific set of social functions, or excluded from society entirely. Moving between traditional images of femininity and masculinity, they play with bodily and clothes-related signifiers of both genders as well as the unnamed space between them, thus refusing the binary choice of accepted gender and identity norms. What is more, they are old, which adds a further level of precariousness, as elderly bodies are usually given visibility in our contemporary media society only to promote the idea of fitness – in other words, only if they radiate youthfulness.[13] In other words, these transvestite or transsexual performers bring the fundamental vulnerability of the human subject to the stage.

As the curtain opens, nine people stand on the square, empty stage, all of them in grey suits: a younger woman and a young man, the actress Vanessa Van Durme and six elderly gentlemen looking perfectly ordinary in their everyday clothes. Van Durme walks to a microphone centre stage, gives a slow rendition of 'Somewhere Over the Rainbow' and then explains the theatrical situation we find ourselves in: the cabaret *Gardenia* is closing and presents its final performance.[14] She thanks the audience for its loyalty and calls for a minute of silence to remember those who died during the forty years that the cabaret existed.

Then, with an air of grandiosity, she introduces the cabaret's artists. The only people to step forward, however, are the elderly men, who come to the front and stand in a line. The glamour of the announcement is undermined by the ordinariness of these distinctly unglamorous men in grey suits. They do eventually raise their arms, receiving an imaginary ovation, but the gaze they direct into the audience is melancholic. Throughout the performance, this state of melancholia appears to be an element of how they present themselves in the roles they play. According to Butler, melancholia, like dehumanization, arises from being prohibited to grieve, for grief is the acknowledgement of loss. Prohibiting grief is a political instrument of exclusion from the realm of humanity, as Butler says in *Precarious Life*. In earlier works, she interprets 'heterosexual melancholia' as an effect of denied grief for the object of love of the same sex. Drag, Butler observes, allegorizes this heterosexual melancholia, or a 'set of melancholic incorporative fantasies that stabilize gender'.[15] *Gardenia* makes grief explicit and stages drag, as will become clear in the following, not as a stabilization of sexual identity but as both means and effect of a brittle identity that fluctuates between male and female, desire and grief, and between the symbolic, imaginary and real body.

Language troubles and tableaux vivants

Several times during the performance, a recording of Joseph Beuys's 1969 work *Ja Ja Ja Ja Ja, Nee Nee Nee Nee Nee* is played. It is an endless monologue that plays with phrases in the vernacular that do not mean very much, troubling the notion of language as identity-building. 'Yes' and 'no', this fundamental binary opposition, is robbed of its exclusivity and becomes mere material for vocal play, similar to how the signs of binary gender identity become material for play and ambiguity in the course of this performance. In between 'yes' and 'no', using 'yes' and 'no' as material, *Gardenia* develops role-play that questions the coherence of identity as a concept, opening up spaces in which the vulnerability of the lives of others can be perceived.

Two particular scenes in *Gardenia* are very telling in this context. In a first scene, the performers come together for a series of tableaux vivants, which they hold for several seconds before they unfreeze and regroup. They centre around three of the performers, who sit on chairs in the centre of the stage, looking into the audience to create the impression of photographic portraits. The first tableau evokes businessmen in distinctly masculine poses: men in suits, wide stances, arms crossed or hands thrust into pockets. These are stereotypical gestures, made unfamiliar by the freeze and the isolation from any kind of narrative context. They are thus exposed as 'poses' in the sense of artificial role-play, of symbolic constructions of selfhood. Only Van Durme is wearing high heels underneath her suit, adding a visual irritant to the homogeneous group portrait.

The tableau then re-forms into new constellations. At the same time, everybody begins to undress, so that for the next freeze, some have half removed their jacket, one shoe, or their tie. The act of undressing is done deliberately, orderly, matter-of-factly. The tableaux capture moments in mid-movement, resulting in slapstick-like images, those of trousers half pulled down, chequered underpants, bare legs and socks showing, and so on. In marked contrast to this everyday and asexual way of undressing, the act of looking out into the audience during the freezes implies a more knowing, deliberate kind of posing. The suits are further removed, and women's clothes begin to appear, colourful dresses with flowers, and as the process of undressing continues, the poses also become more feminine: clasped hands, a tilt of the head, knees pressed together, a knowing smile, doe eyes. But these poses, too, are soon unfrozen and the process of undressing continues as matter-of-factly as before.

The sequence of tableaux captures the 'in-between' on two different levels: for one, the freeze frames the act of undressing as a momentarily undefined state of gender identity, locking it into position and offering it up for scrutiny. It is an act seldom performed in public, a private, intimate moment of nakedness and undecidedness. This is an in-between moment between two roles, between the male and female, private and public, ordinary and staged body. Second, an in-between space opens up on the level of representation, as the frozen poses disrupt the flow of representation as well as the represented identities. By suspending the performance, disrupting it with a freeze, the entire modus of a closed system of representation is put into question. The tableau vivant highlights the act of performing by disrupting the continuity of play and revealing it to be staged, denaturalizing the representation of bodies and exposing the constructedness of body images. Accepted value judgements on concepts such as 'natural' (or true) and 'artificial' are thus put to the test, together with the understanding of representation itself as a reflection of reality: 'The reality is not conveyed by what is represented within the image, but through the challenge to representation that reality delivers.'[16]

Disruption also opens up a space for that which lies beyond representation: for the performers' physical bodies, always present regardless of their role, and their vulnerability, which would have remained hidden in the context of a closed representational system. Butler believes that humanity defies representation, only revealing itself once representation fails: 'For representation to convey the human, then, representation must not only fail, but it must show its failure. There is something unrepresentable that we nevertheless seek to represent, and that paradox must be retained in the representation we give.'[17]

Gardenia contains such failures of representation, questioning the very idea that identity can be represented. As the performance progresses and the masculine clothes continue to be removed, the poses that the performers strike increasingly resemble icons of female stars well known from stage and screen. At the same time, the tableaux become more fluid, so that the impression of group portraits begins to fade. The figures seem isolated, as they are not held together by formal unity or any kind of narrative context. Above all, they seem unfinished in a very concrete sense. The colourful dresses have not been done up properly, zippers are left open, straps and sleeves are hanging off shoulders, bodies are caught in mid-movement appearing dishevelled or strangely twisted. The costumes do not create complete identities but rather fragments of imaginary body images, unsecured and incomplete. It is precisely in this incompleteness, in these gaps, that the precariousness, vulnerability and fragility of identity and self-image are revealed.

Moments of in-betweenness are particularly suited to conveying the precarious situation of the individual subject. Conflicting signifiers create an ambiguity that eludes identification. Gesa Ziemer characterizes vulnerability as a 'concept that is not based on dichotomies' and defies categorization.[18] Vulnerability is therefore 'located in the gaps, in-between formation and deformation, in-between rational and sensual forms of thinking and perceiving, in-between theory and practice'.[19] In this respect vulnerability can also be thought of as a way of questioning accepted dichotomies and opening up gaps in the first place. Even as we see the dancers striking recognizable poses, the disparate elements from which they are composed combine femininity and masculinity, the everyday and the theatrical, private and public, so that unity is never in fact achieved. The montage of conflicting signals does not simply alienate but creates an in-between space that defies identification and opens up new ways of looking at bodies and individuals beyond dichotomic categorization.

Figure 12.1 Danilo Povolo in *Gardenia*, 2010. © Luk Monsaert.

Figure 12.2 Vanessa Van Durme and Richard Dierick in *Gardenia*, 2010. © Luk Monsaert.

The gaze into the audience

During the entire scene (and almost the whole performance), the performers are looking directly at the audience. This gaze into the auditorium takes into account the spectators' gaze, which becomes an essential part of the performance and is reflected upon as an act of looking. Body images and identities are always effects of production and reception, and it follows that spectators are necessarily involved in the creation of norms and formations as well as the production of body and gender images. Here, the spectators are made aware of their involvement in the constitution of humanity by having their gaze turned upon them, appealing to each individual's sense of responsibility. Other forms of media usually address the spectator as somebody situated outside the realm of representation, as Butler explains, 'It is precisely as the unrepresented viewer, the one who looks on, the one who is captured by no image at all, but whose charge it is to capture and subdue, if not eviscerate, the image at hand.'[20]

Unlike the electronic or print media to which Butler here refers, theatre is defined by the co-presence of spectator and performer and thus enables a (self-)reflective analysis of the point of view of the spectator and their involvement in the production of the image.

Being exposed, a state that Butler defines as an existential condition of the individual subject, is a fundamentally theatrical situation. Onstage one exposes oneself to the gazes of others, the spectators, and in the process one puts oneself in jeopardy, for one relies on their approval, their affirmative gaze. Conventional narrative theatre creates a closed system of illusion that hides this fact, or protects performers from this vulnerability. But when the closed system is prized open by theatrical means such as disruption or direct address, the moment of exposure is brought to the fore again and the performers' vulnerabilities and pleas for affirmation are revealed. The reverse gaze as a form of direct address communicates the precariousness of the life of the Other. It also makes it possible for the spectator to experience their own body as the Other – as a spectator, I put myself on the line to a certain extent by accepting the address of the other and the performance as a shared enterprise. I become aware of my own responsibility for the performance.

Swapping in-between roles

I would now like to turn to another scene in *Gardenia*. It contains a swapping of roles between performers by theatrical means – not in the sense of an illusionistic transformation into a different person but as a series of costume changes that produce different potential identities without ever arriving at one that appears intrinsic or true.

The performers, in men's clothes at first, walk across the stage in straight lines, from one side to the other, back and forth, now and then looking into the auditorium. Here and there, isolated dance movements are added. Some of them retreat to a dressing table in the background of the stage and begin to put on make-up or jewellery before returning to their walks slightly altered: wearing a glittering earring or colourful eyeshadow, which disrupts the unity of the image. As the scene progresses, the performers continue to change their appearance. Someone appears onstage with a wig, others return topless, a jacket is removed to reveal a red bra, trousers come off and stockings are put on. The costumes are fragmentary and process-oriented, highlighting how gender identity is constructed from outward signals and performative acts. This becomes even more obvious as the only biologically female woman onstage also participates in this construction of gender – she, too, dresses up as a woman, constructs herself as a woman through signals and performative acts. Gender reveals itself to be a culturally constituted function not bound by biological conditions.

Like the earlier scene, this one frames moments of in-betweenness: between female and male, between yes and no (Beuys's 'Ja' and 'Nee'), between body and sign. In this in-between space, the individual subjects appear in all their vulnerability and formlessness, unsecured and open to injury in the naked state between masculine and feminine clothing. Nevertheless, these moments of insecurity are also moments of openness and opportunity. Everything is possible. The performers are as assured and confident in their state of ambiguity as when they are in full costume. During the in-between periods highlighted by the production, the state of unfixedness puts the individual subjects centre stage in all their ambivalence and multisidedness.

As the production focuses on the unsecured space between genders, we notice how diverse the performers are. There is no normative ideal body; tall slim bodies encounter thin ones with sunken chests as well as small, fat and strong bodies. Most of them are old. Next to straight, slim, muscular legs we see crooked or fat legs, unsteady on their feet. Hierarchies and categorizations are avoided. Whether perfect diva or plump elderly man, all present themselves to the audience equally, joyfully play with different signals and identities, assertively return the audience's gaze, and thus draw our attention back to the norms and pre-established ideas that constitute, assess and in- or exclude our own bodies and those of others.

The ageing body

It takes approximately twenty minutes for all performers to be dressed entirely as women, wearing glittering evening gowns, high heels, wigs, make-up, jewellery and handbags. But even then, there are aspects that jar. Judging by conventional standards of beauty, some of them are too tall, too small, too fat or too old. In fact, the point of the exercise is not to create a perfect illusion or to embody a different gender entirely but rather to play with different identities in an open-ended game. The ageing body in particular is a body in process. And this focus on the process is what the body shares with theatre – all bodies are essentially ageing bodies, bodies that grow older even as the performance progresses, while they see and are being seen. Theatre allows us to experience bodies ageing onstage as well as to connect with our own bodies in the process of ageing. The ageing body is testament to the precariousness of human existence, for it is in the middle of an ongoing process, fundamentally endangered and on the very borders of representability.

In conventional narrative theatre, the representation of elderly people is achieved through illustrative signals such as costumes and props, hairstyles, make-up, posture and movements. These signs show how closely the state of 'being old' is bound up with culturally and discursively conditioned ideas. At the same time, the limitations of such stereotypical signs in portraying the reality of what it means to be old are obvious.[21] In *Gardenia*, by contrast, the wrinkles, sunken chests, hanging shoulders, unsteady feet and wobbles appear as realities invading the illusion. Even if some of the performers are near perfect in their embodiment of the role, their real age creates a fissure that allows the vulnerability of the physical body to shine through. In theatre and particularly in dance it is unusual to see older bodies, old skin, exposed onstage, so the prominence of older bodies in *Gardenia* questions representational conventions and reveals normative ideals as tools for exclusion of the Other, of subjective and imperfect bodies. By presenting older bodies onstage, the production also reveals the precarity of the theatrical situation as a shared process. Spectators are confronted with the realities of the ageing body as something that is relevant to us all. At the same time, they are invited to question their own position. Is it permitted to invade the intimate space of these vulnerable bodies by looking at them? Their fragility draws attention to the voyeurism inherent in the act of looking and thus critiques the position of the spectator and the theatrical situation as a whole.

Gesa Ziemer writes that 'the stage is the space of vulnerability par excellence, as those who stand onstage open themselves up to scrutiny live in front of an audience'.[22] Here, the basic vulnerability of those who expose themselves to the spectators' gaze is highlighted even further through the use of performers with imperfect bodies. We see old bodies – not beautiful by conventional standards – that nevertheless seek the limelight and confidently oppose their exclusion from the norm. They demand the right to be the subjects of their own representation, bringing their own, very real, vulnerability into play. This vulnerability, exemplified by the visibility of old, naked skin, emerges in those moments when they do not embody roles or characters, when identities become fluid and the narrative breaks down. 'Personification that claims to "capture" the human being' risks a loss of humanity, according to Butler.[23] In *Gardenia*, the individual performers resist such personifications (in the sense of a complete characterization) by disrupting the formations of identities, by framing moments of in-betweenness, and by revealing how different roles are performatively constructed. They thus create disjunctions that run counter to the trends of unification and standardization. 'The human is indirectly affirmed in that very disjunction that makes representation impossible, and this disjunction is conveyed in the impossible representation.'[24] It is precisely in the gaps of representation – the moments when representation fails – that human vulnerability and thus humanity itself appears. By staging the vulnerable, the production objects to normative forms of representation, questions the order of representation and awakens us to the precariousness of existence not just of others but also of our own.

Acknowledgements

This text first appeared in *Sicherheitslos. Prekarisierung der Künste und ihre Geschlechterverhältnisse*, ed. Kerstin Brandes, Linda Hentschel and Miriam Dreysse, *FKW, Zeitschrift für Geschlechterforschung und visuelle Kultur*, 53 (2012): 96–107.

Notes

1 Judith Butler (2004) *Precarious Life: The Power of Mourning and Violence*, London: Verso.
2 On bodies in the work of Le Roy, Bel and Stuart, see Gerald Siegmund (2006) *Abwesenheit: Eine performative Ästhetik des Tanzes*, Bielefeld: Transcript.
3 *Gardenia*, directed by Alain Platel and Frank Van Laecke, stage by Paul Gallis, music by Steven Prengels. Cast: Gerrit Becker, Griet Debacker, Andrea De Laet, Richard 'Tootsie' Dierick, Timur Magomedgadzjeyev, Danilo Povolo, Rudy Suwyns, Vanessa Van Durme, Dirk Van Vaerenbergh.

4 Katharina Pewny has to be credited with productively introducing Butler's concept of precariousness to German theatre scholarship. Her study is fundamental to the analysis of precariousness in contemporary theatre: Katharina Pewny (2011), *Das Drama des Prekären: Über die Wiederkehr der Ethik in Theater und Performance*, Bielefeld: Transcript Verlag.
5 Butler, *Precarious Life*, 139.
6 Butler, *Precarious Life*, 31.
7 Butler, *Precarious Life*, 25.
8 Butler, *Precarious Life*, 24.
9 Butler, *Precarious Life*, 130.
10 Using the modes of representation of US media after 9/11 as an example, Butler shows how certain people, by being branded as 'evil', are excluded from the domains of grief, compassion and, finally, humanity.
11 Butler, *Precarious Life*, 140.
12 Butler, *Precarious Life*, 33.
13 See Carolin Bergert and Thomas Koch (2008) 'Die Entdeckung der Neuen Alten? Best Ager in der Werbung', in Christina Holtz-Bacha (ed.), *Stereotype? Frauen und Männer in der Werbung*, Wiesbaden: Springer, 155–75.
14 With this narrative, Platel alludes to the documentary *Yo soy asi* (NL, 2000) by Sonia Herman Dolz about the closure of a drag club in Barcelona.
15 Judith Butler (1993) *Bodies That Matter: On the Discursive 'Limits of Sex'*, London and New York: Psychology Press, 179.
16 Butler, *Precarious Life*, 146.
17 Butler, *Precarious Life*, 144.
18 Gesa Ziemer (2008) *Verletzbare Orte: Entwurf einer praktischen Ästhetik*, Zurich and Berlin: Diaphanes, 103, 111.
19 Ziemer, *Verletzbare Orte*, 107.
20 Butler, *Precarious Life*, 143.
21 See Miriam Dreysse (2010) 'Wie spielt man Altsein? Theatrale Darstellungen des Altern(n)s', in Sabine Mehlmann and Sigrid Ruby (eds.), *'Für dein Alter siehst du gut aus!' Von der Un/Sichtbarkeit des alternden Körpers im Horizont des demographischen Wandels*, Bielefeld: Transcript Verlag.
22 Ziemer, *Verletzbare Orte*, 107.
23 Butler, *Precarious Life*, 144–5.
24 Butler, *Precarious Life*, 144.

References

Bergert, Carolin, and Thomas Koch (2008) 'Die Entdeckung der Neuen Alten? Best Ager in der Werbung', in Christina Holtz-Bacha (ed.), *Stereotype? Frauen und Männer in der Werbung*, Wiesbaden: Springer, 155–75.
Butler, Judith (1993) *Bodies That Matter: On the Discursive 'Limits of Sex'*, London and New York: Psychology Press.
Butler, Judith (2004) *Precarious Life: The Powers of Mourning and Violence*, London: Verso.
Dreysse, Miriam (2010) 'Wie spielt man Altsein? Theatrale Darstellungen des Alter(n)s', in Sabine Mehlmann and Sigrid Ruby (eds.), *'Für dein Alter siehst du gut aus!' Von*

der Un/Sichtbarkeit des alternden Körpers im Horizont des demographischen Wandels, Bielefeld: Transcript Verlag, 235-52.

Pewny, Katharina (2011) *Das Drama des Prekären: Über die Wiederkehr der Ethik in Theater und Performance*, Bielefeld: Transcript Verlag.

Siegmund, Gerald (2006) *Abwesenheit: Eine performative Ästhetik des Tanzes*, Bielefeld: Transcript Verlag.

Ziemer, Gesa (2008) *Verletzbare Orte: Entwurf einer praktischen Ästhetik*, Zurich and Berlin: Diaphanes.

13

tauberbach, a Diagrammatical Reading

The Body between Self and Language

Piet Defraeye

In a 2011 interview with dance dramaturg Guy Cools, Alain Platel comments on one of his major inspirations: marginality and difference in the physical, psychological, as well as social realm. Coming from the interventionist and hands-on world of orthopaedic therapy, he fully realizes that 'the body takes over when you are not able to talk about certain things anymore'.[1] Platel and his collaborators around les ballets C de la B have explored physical, psychological, and social marginality through the medium of dance with an unparalleled commitment and sensibility. In what follows, I will focus on *tauberbach* and pursue what I call a diagrammatical reading, burrowing into its paradigms, syntax and compositional grammar. As with many of Platel's works, this production reveals a remarkable dichotomy between on the one hand its epic scope in *mise en scène* – with a cast of six and an imposing set – and on the other hand, a surprising degree of intimacy. This dichotomy is paralleled with an embrace of an almost pure and silenced physicality, that foregrounds a choreography of minute and meticulous detail in the tradition of Anne Teresa De Keersmaeker, and at the same time allows for a considerable role for language, which acquires a narrative and/or commenting function. In other words, there is a paradox at work in *tauberbach*: large-scale versus intimacy, pure dance versus theatricalized narrative. What we witness is a physicalized and self-referential dance, but also a continuous commenting role for language. Platel's particular use of a chorus – dancing, singing, as well as spoken discourse – contributes to this tension between outside and inside, between language and self, between community and individual. Add to this the external references and inspirations for the piece – a documentary on schizophrenia, a choir of deaf singers, an interest in entomological adaptation – and the impetus for a diagrammatical reading becomes clear. In my pursuit of these different grammars, I follow certain trails while losing others, bumping into dead ends, and marvelling in clearings, all the while mimicking the spectator's voyage of discovery and exposure.

Tauberbach premiered at the Münchner Kammerspiele in January 2014. The title is somewhat enigmatic. On the surface, it could refer to a quaint village somewhere in southern Germany (*Bach* is German for 'brook'), or the name of a stream where pigeons congregate (*die Tauber* refers to male pigeons). When we dig deeper, we find out that les ballets C de la B's *tauberbach* refers to *Deaf Bach*. The piece is set in a derelict and incongruous stage landscape of industrial lifts and discarded clothes.[6] While colourful and enigmatic in its design, it presents a stark habitat for the ensemble of six performing artists. The overwhelming dimensions of this theatrical landscape, as well as the bizarre soundscape that supports (or resists?) the choreography, seem to lessen the might and self-control of these moving bodies. The impression we have is one of a primeval world, weirdly populated with a peculiar fauna that is often closer to insect than human, yet produces deeply moving tableaux of strife as well as concord. With immediate access to an expansive and multicoloured assortment of apparels, the dancers change their appearance similar to chromatophoric frogs. Limbs become entomotomic extensions that grasp spasmodically from inside a pile of old clothes, lips morph into percussion instruments for stridulation and crepitation. Joints click uncomfortably, amplified through a microphone. Necks produce startling flicks initiating mating romps; and at least one of the dancers, Romeu Runa, seems to have, like some tettigoniid crickets do, joints and spines on different parts of his body that allow curbs and backbends that would snap the spinal column of most mortals.

> Frogs are notorious as an invasive species, and with these migrations often come phenomenal consequences in terms of environmental upturns. Brazilian frog specialist Felipe Toledo mentions impacts like 'the introduction of foreign lethal pathogens … acoustic niche overlap with native species … changes in local food webs … and noise pollution'.[2] Invasive groups must adapt or, as is often the case, must overcome serious handicaps to persist. One such frog species, which made it to Fernando de Noranha, a paradise archipelago just off the Atlantic coast at the westernmost tip of Brazil, has largely lost its functional eyesight. Most of these Cururo toads, as the species is called, have now changed from active foraging to 'sit-and-wait predators' and locate 'their prey by means of tactile stimuli exclusively'.[3] Together with his team, the same scientist recently discovered that both the bright yellow-coloured Pumpkin toadlet and the small carrot-coloured Pitanga toad (both of the Brachycephalus genus) are now deaf. In their habitat of the neotropical rainforests of southern Brazil, the males continue to produce their cricket-like sounds – 'two to six minute pulsing buzzes'[4] – as a mating call to attract females. The only problem is that sonic communication between the two is impossible, and the need for a mating call is, well, moot. The male apparently can't even hear its own chirping noise.[5] What makes it even odder is the fact that both species are brightly coloured so that the noise, futile as it is, may actually be a dangerous magnetizer for predators. However, the latter should think twice, if the bright colour is not enough of an aposematic warning sign: subcutaneously, these frogs are able to release a dozen or so paralytic poisons. Better to keep at a distance and not make a meal out of it.

Figure 13.1 Romeu Runa, Elsie de Brauw, Ross McCormack, Bérengère Bodin, Elie Tass and Lisi Estaras during rehearsals of *tauberbach* in dance studio S3, Ghent 2013. © Chris Van der Burght.

The dance production was received as a 'triumph',[7] 'nothing short of extraordinary',[8] 'a successful explosion of thought-provoking ideas and profound imagery'.[9] Reviewing a Berlin performance, Peter Laudenbach praises *tauberbach* as 'anthropological research that focuses on man, this rare animal'.[10] Along the same line, Silvia Stammen calls it a school for primary seeing that makes us watch the world anew: 'Alain Platel allows us to observe as on the First Day';[11] and Katja Schneider avows: 'You could look at each of these dancers forever.'[12] Geert Van Der Speeten concludes after seeing a Paris performance, 'The coarse poetry of Platel's dance theatre has rarely been so sharp and profoundly touching as in this small masterpiece.'[13]

Although *Theater Heute* proclaimed *tauberbach* the production of the 2013–14 season, critics did have reservations about the implied nihilism,[14] confusing dramaturgy,[15] and 'overextended' sequences.[16] Mark Monahan was most pronounced in his overall rejection of what he calls Platel's 'over-familiarity of tropes … and tiresome schtick'.[17]

Similar to Gertrude Stein's landscape writing, *tauberbach* seems modelled not on any specific narrative but rather on an erratic but self-generating landscape; we watch a formation that is continuously in relation, 'one thing to the other thing' and 'any detail to any other detail' as Stein puts it observingly.[18] Our role as spectator is not one of implication but instead as the observer and student of its relations. We enter its ecology, not the other way round, or in Stein's words: 'the landscape does not have to make acquaintance. You may have to make acquaintance with it, but it does not with you.'[19] We remain observers of what becomes a somatic process, without being part of it. *Tauberbach*'s scenography works in tandem with the music, the performers, their movements and their sounds, presenting a landscape that is continuously impacted and morphing by a variety of impulses that contribute to a specific ecology, which we observe and try to understand in all its different grammars. This stunning performance landscape offers a rich point of departure: a truck-full of old clothing spread out on the stage. Multicoloured dishevelled and visceral, the hotchpotch stirs up echoes of a stinking rat-plagued landfill. But the striking limitation to clothing-only also sets in motion associations with visits to Holocaust sites. We hear a fly buzzing around our ears. The sound is not going to go away until just before the very last sequence of the ninety-minute production. With the same animated convolutedness of the droning fly sound, there is a stir, here and there, in the piled-up clothes. We see a lump moving in the medley of clothes. An arm emerges, a head surfaces from another batch. Humans? Do they hear the fly? Where are we? More of these creatures emerge, some of them collecting clothing. The sounds of pigeons flapping their wings join the buzz of bluebottle flies. 'You hear that?' says a woman onstage, immediately followed by a loud imperative: 'ARE YOU LISTENING?!' We feel directly addressed and implicated as an audience, but it is also the cue for the other bodies onstage to burrow back underneath the bundles of clothes. The woman, Dutch (theatre) actress Elsie de Brauw, steps up to a dangling microphone and splutters something that sounds like Portuguese, interrupted by a slap on the forehead and a self-chastizing 'STAY IN CONTROL!' The latter is echoed by a male voice toning in from somewhere not locatable. De Brauw continues in Portuguese ('PTG' she calls her dialect), sliding into a deafening guttural scream in which she is joined in a one-upmanship by the amplified male voice, only to have the yelp-fest abruptly broken off by a violent slap on the microphone and the heavenly strings of the solemn andante movement of J. S. Bach's *Violin Concerto* BWV 1041. The popular melody is almost immediately challenged in an overlay of cacophonous off-key choir sounds, imploringly yelping. An accordion chimes in, and Elsie de Brauw sets in motion both aluminium lighting trusses that span the stage, and now go stoically up and down. For a short instance, the entire stage becomes alive, a teeming pen of frenzied and wild activity. We witness a burst of rhythmic explosion: it seems like the animals spring from their burrows, clothes fly through the air, the machine-like trusses respond laconically, with the dancers hanging on them, falling down, jumping back into the pillowy mounds of clothing. The sounds we hear are both alienating and comforting. This first part ends as abruptly as it started with the male voice again initiating a peculiar exchange with Elsie de Brauw: 'Shortage of food'.

> Meanwhile, in another part of Brazil, in an altogether different biotope, there are no frogs croaking away. In Rio de Janeiro's suburb of Duque de Caxias, Jardim Gramacho,[20] the world's largest garbage dump, is teeming with so-called catadores, garbage pickers. Officially closed since 2012, a couple of thousand catadores continue to live off the landfill through selling recyclables. One of these never witnessed the (controversial) closure – although it was through her that the site acquired notoriety. Estamira Gomes de Sousa (1941–2011) lived in the nearby favela for decades and was the subject of the two-hour-long documentary *Estamira* (2004) by Marcos Prado.[21] Through the focus on 'a socially subaltern, physically abused, and mentally ill woman',[22] the film also comments on bigger questions of ecology, public health, psychiatric treatment, sexual abuse, and even theological queries.

While *tauberbach* presents a richly textured dance performance, this description of the show's 5½-minute-long overture is an apt summary of its dramaturgy. A woman, Elsie de Brauw, somehow belongs in a derelict world of refuse. She loudly voices her relentless attempts to find structure in the chaos that surrounds her ('Stay in control!'), and does so in what sounds like shards of English and Portuguese quotations, which are equivocated by a male voice. Is it a voice in her head? Her echo? An overseer? Her therapist? Or a bigger structuring force? A soft-spoken God? Or perhaps just a theatrical prompter for action? At any rate, the Voice provides inspiration as well as resistance. Her resolute answer to the 'Shortage of food' is that 'There's enough food to make spaghetti.'

The woman is surrounded by five dancers, her fellow *catadores*, whom she mostly observes and sometimes interacts with. The dancers' movements are motivated and supported by a strange amalgamation of sounds, a mixture of classical Bach, Platel's fallback composer. This is presented not only through recorded strings and organ but also as an unusual accordion interpretation, and sometimes in live a cappella song. The soundscape has a quasi-continuous overlay of insect sounds of buzzing flies and flapping birds, and the humming electrical sounds of the two overarching trusses.

Strangest of all is the dissonant disharmonious choir that comes back time and again. The *tauberbach* world has a particular ecology, so much is clear; and as the production moves along, it becomes overwhelmingly clear that these characters we watch feel at home and belong in this world. They have adapted wonderfully to the laws of this ecosystem and established a peculiar somatic practice among each other and in this physical setting. As much as Elsie de Brauw has developed a structuring vocabulary to engage with her tattered world, the dancers, like those dislocated toads in the Brazilian forests, or the deaf Polish choir youth, have acquired a communication system with their own physical vocabulary of corporeality, rhythms, gestures, choral synchronicity and contra-points, copulation games, costuming and disrobement, tribal

> We zoom in on Estamira's physical environment of the landfill and her shack, and on her social environment of fellow catadores and her daughter and son. Both of these environments are overwhelming and contribute to the viewer's rationalizing picture they feel they need to make in response to the mental constructions in the mind of this quasi-prophetic figure. I agree with Nicola Gavioli that there are moments in the documentary where 'the operation verges on romanticizing mental illness as an overwhelming poetic furore engaged in a struggle against the universe'.[23] The camera catches Estamira's oracular pronouncements in her raging perlocutionary intensity. Somehow they resonate as urgent calls for action, and deeply insightful, yet troubling comments on the state of the planet. Their rhetorical and poetic force in her own version of Portuguese spills over in the English subtitles. 'There are no innocent people anymore' could be a straight quotation from one of the gods in Brecht's *Der gute Mensch von Sezuan*. And it seems ultimately the gods themselves that are the main target of Estamira's wrath as she rages about a 'filthy god ... a rapist god ... an all usurping god ... a home-wrecking god'.

body-painting and puzzling vocal utterances. This is not a world of failure, though in many ways it is an ecology in which failure plays on a level field with success and accomplishment. The performance we observe presents itself as a somatic organism, in which growth and decline, inhaling and exhaling, absorption and secretion are equally important, and are mere appositions, without any hierarchy.

Marcos Prado's documentary film on *Estamira Gomes de Sousa* was Alain Platel's main inspiration for *tauberbach*, and his dramaturgical point of departure.[25] Elsie de Brauw impersonates the Brazilian woman, diagnosed with schizophrenia, and just as in Prado's film, the paradox between her own solipsistic existence and the relentlessly expository nature of her interventions is hard not to experience as a voyeuristic privilege. Her aggressive and intimidating language, echoed in the garbage aesthetics of the piles of clothes, results in an abject affect. Many of the dancers' movements break with taboos and notions of conventional beauty and thus add to this overall affect of abjection. The use of Bach music constitutes a potential contrast with this abjection, but Platel's choice for a Polish deaf-choir rendition of some of the key musical support certainly echoes the overall abject aesthetics of *tauberbach*, also on a musical level. Interestingly, this sound inspiration also came to Platel filmically in Artur Żmijewski's documentaries. While the choir selections by Platel and his music editor Steven Prengels are exclusively from Jan Maklakiewicz's *Kyrie*, the Polish composer's music is certainly part of a Bach tradition, which is further enhanced by Prengels's artful mixture and overlay of J. S. Bach selections, as is the case in the opening section elaborately described above.

Music critic Julian Cowley comments on the deaf-choir music of Żmijewski's *Singing Lesson (I and II)* as an experience that drives 'a jarring wedge into the comfort

A continent away, the Polish artivist Artur Żmijewski assembles a group of deaf youngsters to have them sing religious music. In his documentary film Singing Lesson 1 (2001) he has a group of alumni of Warsaw's Deaf-Mute Institute sing Jan Maklakiewicz's *Kyrie* from the Polish Mass (1944) in the front nave of a Warsaw church. The result is a disturbing, cacophonous rendition, breaking all the conventions of sacral music. The contrast between the disharmonic sounds of the ad-hoc choir and the organ piping out a wonderfully melodious piece of liturgical music cannot be more estranging. With the suffering loin-clothed crucified Christ as background to the choir, the suppliant pleading of the *Kyrie*'s 'Have Mercy' is an excruciating exercise: tremendously moving and unbearable at the same time.[24] In 2002, Żmijewski repeated the intervention using excerpts from Bach cantatas with a group of hearing-impaired youngsters at the Thomaskirche in Leipzig, the city where Bach was a cantor. Żmijewski had the youth accompanied by a professional mezzo-soprano and a chamber baroque orchestra with organ. It is a transcendent experience for the participants – disabled singers and professionals alike – as well as for us, the listeners, and it certainly fractured the tradition of marvellous Bach productions at the very church where Bach was buried. Both *Singing Lessons* were made into short docufilms and screened at various occasions.

zones and complacencies that enable us to live with a sense of harmoniously ordered reality'.[26] His observation could have been a summarizing response to Alain Platel's *tauberbach*. Jarring it certainly is. It is hyper-real in its embodied reality, and while there is an elementary sense of structure, it is mostly its anarchic disorder that constantly guides us in our apperception. We are acutely aware that *tauberbach* presents a world 'free from the normative regularities', not just of 'the listening world' but also of the visual and visceral world we witness onstage. Cowley concludes his Żmijewski review musing on the etymology of the word 'absurdity'. In muscology, it typically refers to dissonance and lack of harmony. Its Latin origins, *absurdus*, connect it with perversity and incongruity, but also, Cowley reminds us, with 'out of deafness' and senselessness. *tauberbach* is certainly not senseless, though its sense must be found beyond the habitual 'superficial congruence and surface coherence'.[27]

It has become clear that *tauberbach* has its own idiosyncratic ecosystem. We certainly do not witness just a madhouse, driven by lack of meaning and lack of structure. For sure, Platel presents some typical features of how we conventionally understand schizophrenia, with the typical aggressive dispositions, the hearing of voices, the abjection expressed in lack of hygiene, and offensive gestures and manners. Already in 1908, the Swiss psychiatrist Eugen Bleuler, who coined the term 'schizophrenia', emphatically denied the causal link with auditory hallucinations. Schizophrenia for him implied not a 'split personality, as is often thought, but a disconnect among psychological functions such as thinking, memory, and perception'.[28] In *tauberbach*'s ecosystem, as in most ecological displacements, the disconnect becomes the condition to reconnect. Platel's compositional syntax is one of associative and pivotal conjunction as well as disengaging and unravelling apposition. It is an aesthetic approach that renders imagery reminiscent of the mind-blowing pictures of Hieronymus Bosch. At the very least, the strategy works in an emancipatory way: the characters onstage, as well as the spectators in the auditorium, are encouraged not to censor but instead to embrace the vocal and physical turns and tribulations of the exploration. It is a strategy that seems eerily similar to Dutch psychiatrist Marius Romme's non-judgemental and non-hierarchical approach in allowing schizophrenic patients to be at peace (at various degrees) with the voices they do sometimes hear and to cope with them, instead of stigmatizing them. This 'has helped', according to Daniel Smith, 'spawn a new "cognitive" approach to hallucinations'.[29]

Tauberbach does not primarily invite cognitive responses – though they are certainly part of the matrix. Instead, the focus here is on affect, which is a result of the entire cauldron of de Brauw's assertive iteration, the dancers' gestures and postures, the vast repository of clothing, and the music and sounds from which the whole production emanates. The live sounds from the four microphones that hang onto the stage in quadrangle formation add an authentic source to the rest of the soundscape. About three-quarters into the show, Elsie de Brauw, dressed this time in a yellow polyester raincoat, is flanked at the microphone by French dancer Bérengère Bodin. 'The storm was inside me', says de Brauw – an iteration that sixty minutes into the production has become abundantly obvious. Both respond by producing live sounds: the friction of the polyester coat is boosted by the microphone as an actual squall, to which she adds the sharp popping of the opening snap-buttons of her coat. The interior emotional force is echoed in Bodin dispassionately snapping her finger and wrist joints into the same microphone. The sound of popping cartilage is certainly uncomfortable, but coming from the trained dancer itself, it also reminds us of vulnerability. The matching of the physiologically based sounds of the dancer's joints and the technically based sounds of de Brauw's synthetic coat creates an uncanny echo. This short scene is abruptly cut by a loud whistle, immediately followed by the slightly swithering organ pipes and, yet again, the imploring prayer of the deaf *Kyrie* solo. Bodin dances solo – though the other four dancers form a gestural chorus behind her upstage, while de Brauw looks on silently from stage right. Bodin's dance is meticulous and exhausting, and is one of failure. Commenting on the opening night in Munich, Silvia Stammen sees it as a dance in '*somnambuler Selbstvergessenheit*' or a somnambulic reverie.[30] With spasmodic gestures and a beseeching gaze, she continuously falls down, as we listen to the suppliant disharmonies of a deaf soloist. One solo meets another solo. One failure accompanies another. Together, it is an incredibly synchronous achievement.

What stands out in Bodin's short dance is not only the repetitive falling down and getting up but also her enigmatic spasmous and seemingly uncontrolled gesturing. Throughout Platel's piece, it is these kinds of gestures that contribute to the alienating dynamic of much of the aesthetic. Strangely, and working in tandem with some of the familiar music, it is mostly this puzzling gestural language that invites us to take part in *tauberbach*'s peculiar ecology, because we acutely acknowledge this language as a system – part of a certain discourse – that we must respond to, but are unable to immediately recognize and comprehend.

Thirty years ago, well before Ryanair tourism and Trump politics, Giorgio Agamben wrote on the destruction and deprivation we suffer from as authentic experience has become hardly possible. The daily numbing through simulation, fake, mass, surveillance and derivation, on just about all levels of engagement and consumption, makes effectively genuine experience *a priori* impossible. Agamben references Benjamin's commentary on tactical choices we continuously make versus genuine experiences we enter into: everything is strategy in function of pre-schemed outcomes, from kindergarten to post-career pension. He painfully reminds us that as 'modern man has been deprived of his biography, his experience has likewise been expropriated'.[31] In a peculiar addendum, Agamben also laments the loss of a meaningful gestural practice as a further sign of this loss of experience. The middle class has lost its gestural capacity and gestural language (and he sees the obsession with cinema as further proof of an obsession with precisely that loss). Referring to Terentius Varro's *Lingua Latino*, Agamben situates gesture 'in the sphere of action' although gesture does not make, nor does it act or represent. Gesture is 'neither production nor enactment'. It opens 'the sphere of ethos as the most fitting sphere of the human'.[32] Authentic gesture inevitably refers to what Emmanuel Levinas captures as 'the face of the other' and therefore implies an ethical intervention. Although it may not be understood, or it may not be welcomed, it can simply not be refused. In its 'destitution and nudity – its hunger', the other cannot remain deaf to its appeal.[33] Gesture sets in motion an ethical dynamic because it is the ultimate embodiment of a primordial discourse that cannot be refused.

While neither Agamben nor Levinas write about dance, it is in the encounter with a dance piece like *tauberbach* that we are reminded of the power of gesture as a depository of originary experience and ethical encounters. In its poiesis, the piece certainly brings into being something that did not exist before, but it also presents us with an epiphanic recognition on all levels of the mind and senses. *Tauberbach*, in its entire onstage duration, constantly generates new and changing relationships between its inhabitants (and undoubtedly also with its audience). At the same time, they also illuminate the ethical dimension of gesture. Although the six performers deal plenty with power, their relationship in the world of *tauberbach* is one of ethos: it is one of fellow character, not of rivalry. What we observe is certainly not a calm symbiosis but an organic somatic togetherness. Levinas' famous trope of a non-allergic disposition towards the face of the other is useful to fully capture our own disposition towards the world of *tauberbach*. The apperception by the characters of their own world, as well as our apperception of their world sets in motion 'a non-allergic relation with alterity, towards apperceiving desire – where power, by essence murderous of the other, becomes, faced with the other and "against all good sense", the impossibility of murder, the consideration of the other, or justice'.[34] *Tauberbach* displays a non-allergic world. While there is lots of anger in its affective energy, there is mostly, as in all dance, the affect of desire: the desire to discover, to move, to dance, to sing, to encounter, to rise and fall: the desire to breathe, the desire to live; the desire for affirmation. After a short triadic exchange between de Brauw, the Argentinian dancer Lisi Estaras (in PTG/Portuguese) and the Voice (in English), the New Zealand dancer and voice artist Ross McCormack joins de Brauw at the microphone and evokes dripping water with his lips and tongue, and with gestures. Certainly in *tauberbach*'s trash-dominated ecology, water seems a rare commodity. The imaginary water promptly flows over de Brauw's hand, arm, and then cascades over her entire body, which willingly churns along in McCormack's arms, all the while continuing to generate his water sounds through the microphone. The two figures remain stationary on the stage; the duet is supported by the prelude of Bach's contrapuntal *Suite #4 for Solo Violoncello* (BWV 1010), one of the most technically demanding of the suites. What develops in front of us is a perfect example of Levinas' non-allergic but obligatory engagement with the other. In the movement immediately following, and while Bach's cello concerto continues as a jagged cascade, de Brauw remains the object of desire, this time in a duet with Portuguese dancer Romeu Runa. Here too, the pair remains stationary, and Runa's reptilian movement is a constant flow of gestures and postures. His relentless flicking of parts of his body reflects the arpeggio of the music, and reads like an anthropoid pre-copulatory ritual. Sweaty, sullied and grimy, the two do not touch. Agamben's observation on Aby Warburg's photo dance archives comes to mind: gesture as 'a crystal of historical memory' is freed here from its crystalline structure in the face of the other.[35] The two-minute segment onstage has become experience, and by the cello's final coda in an uplifting E flat – 'a triumphant conclusion'[36] and 'splendid resolution'[37] of sub-dominant into dominant tone, Carl Schachter calls it – the mating match has fully evolved into ethos: they finally touch in a gentle kiss.

Many dance aficionados will refuse to see Romeu Runa's spastic movements as artful dance language. Indeed, Platel's dance dramaturgy – 'animal-like actions which are both ridiculous and grotesque' – has met resistance because of what is seen as 'outrageous and indignant spectacle', only aimed at 'being shocking'.[38] Platel himself, as quoted in *tauberbach*'s programme for de Singel's 2014 production, responds confidently: 'Always these spastic goings-on, I sometimes hear. When I endure with this kind of movement language, it is not because I want to get underneath people's nails, but simply because I want to express something with it.'[39] Clearly, the dance dramaturgy of *tauberbach* is a continuation of dance research initiated by earlier productions, including *pitié!* (2007), *Out of Context – for Pina* (2010), and *C(H)ŒURS* (2012). What is called 'bastaarddans' is rarely a representational kind of dance but instead presents the whole gamma of functional and dysfunctional muscle tension, including spasms, cramps and convulsions that are often associated with mental and physical disorders.[40] What is evoked here is a poetics of failure, as an aesthetic response to the ineffability of much of the human condition, though at the same time, it also exposes unknown capacities of the body. It is a dance dramaturgy that never reveals everything but instead relies on inference,[41] leaving the spectator with what Lise Uytterhoeven calls 'an active labour of understanding'.[42]

About halfway through *tauberbach*, immediately following a particularly challenging trio rendition of Maklakiewicz's *Kyrie*, with the dance ensemble downstage performing a mechanical machine-like response to it, the incessant buzz of a fly comes back to the fore. Ross McCormack steps to the microphone and carefully unfolds something from a paper wrap. It is a rare moment of mime in the production. He holds the thing in his right hand, only to suddenly release it, and promptly joins the buzzing fly sound now live in the microphone. The fly is now purportedly live onstage, but it is mostly the extraordinary bravura of McCormack's voice wizardry that gets our admiration. From the buzzing fly sound, his voice transitions into a stammer and gradually into a persistent auctioneer's rant, which is picked up in a loop by the sound system and deformed through slowing down and speeding up. As if in a centrifuge, Mc Cormack has no choice but to respond to the rhythm and is pulled from one side to the other, in alternating slow motion and high speed. It is a virtuoso movement sequence that lasts for six minutes and only finishes when the breathless dancer goes back to the microphone to mime catching the fly back into the paper wrap. Virtually every reviewer of *tauberbach* mentions the segment. What Platel serves us here comes close to a lesson. The virtuoso aspect of both voice and movement is simply said: awesome. Yet, the deformation of sound is not that different from Żmijewski's deaf choir, which we respond to as failure, since it contrasts with the prescribed score of the music and how we want to hear it. There is no other moment in *tauberbach*, and perhaps in Platel's entire oeuvre, where success and failure are so syntagmatically interwoven. As much as we recognize and admire the dazzling auctioneering cattle rattle, we have no problems with its failure whether in stutter, in unkept rhythm, or failing physical follow-up. McCormack's success is his failure with the language and the movement. If this segment were not embedded within the ecosystem of *tauberbach*'s world – right in the middle of the production as it turns out – it could easily be waved off as a bit of humorous slapstick. As the Voice admonishes loudly 'STAY IN CONTROL!', the sequence is closed by a complete black-out, a rare feature in Platel's work. Immediately following, we observe a short tableau of two naked pairs hanging from their wrists, metonymically whipped with black paint on their backs and buttocks, while de Brauw pleads: 'I want peace in my life. NO MORE SUFFERING!' and announces: 'I am going to dance. I warned you, you dirty dog!' As we hear the soft organ version of Bach's *Fantasia und Fugue* (BMV 944),[45] with its silky but restless modulation, what we witness can best be described as frolicking stage gambols and exhausting failed dance, overlaid with de Brauw's occasional screaming, and the off-stage Voice's predications: 'Permanent Problem!'

Tauberbach's relentless foregrounding of failure is strenuous for the audience too, as it plays on all levels and certainly undermines the autarchic meaning-making of the absent master-narrative. Christel Stalpaert's observation on another work is applicable here: as we work through the interpretative challenges of trauma and mental and physical (dis)order in Platel's work, this 'embodied poetics of failure also entails an ethical perspective; it dismantles the differential distribution of precarity at work in a unilateral master-narrative'.[46] Or, to say it with a succinct Deleuzianism: 'Experiment. Never interpret.'

As in many of Platel's creations, there is plenty of religious referencing in *tauberbach*; with the use of Bach-inspired cantatas and choir music, religion is never far away. 'Asked if he's religious, [Platel] doesn't hesitate to answer "yes"', writes Renate Klett.[47] Not incidentally, his first creation in 1985 was called *Stabat Mater*, and in more recent productions, including *vsprs* (2006) and *pitié!* (2008), religious music remains a point of departure. His fascination for religious sensitivity and sacral music comes from a desire to focus on 'the inside much more than … the outside' which seems particularly accessible to him in the vocabulary of disability.[48] It is interesting to read Platel's comment on Estamira's passionate language and her idiosyncratic dialect in Prado's film: he compares it to telephoning with God (*tauberbach*), though equally interesting is the fact that her manifold blasphemic pronouncements from the documentary did not make it to Platel's stage production. Also important is the fact that the dance dramaturgy hardly ever produces blatantly religious imagery, notwithstanding an ephemerally held crucifixion posture, a short Lazarus moment, or a rather acrobatic ascension bit. Apart from the situational echo of Hieronymus Bosch paintings, some of the dance

---

A fly is not always just another buzzing fly. The Fonseca seed fly, or Botanophila fonsecai, is one of the rarest insects on our planet. The year before *tauberbach*'s premiere, D. Gibbs suggests in his report for Scottish Natural Heritage that its sole habitat is a 2.5-square kilometre narrow stretch of dunes just north of the small town of Dornoch and south of Embo on the edge of the Scottish Highlands alongside the North Sea. It likes the 'bare sand and accreting foredune'[43] where the capitula of ragwort (Senecio vulgaris) seems to be a rare deposit for their larvae, its numbers dwindling drastically over the past three decades. A US billionaire, who made his fortune in the greeting-card business, has been campaigning for permission to build a golf link on the northern end of the dunes, stretching into the fly's habitat. If approved, it will bring well-heeled tourists to the area, and add more millions to the billions. But it will also most likely mean the end of the Fonseca fly,[44] just one of over 100,000 fly species worldwide. Do we care if we cannot hear this particular buzz any longer?

iconography (and Carlo Bourguignon's lighting!) is reminiscent of El Greco's religious paintings, with their typical gestural and facial focus. And yet, *tauberbach*'s iconic world is emphatically profane, and any religious connotation is mostly induced by the choice of music. Oliver Sacks famously reminds us of the power of music, how it 'can pierce the heart directly; it needs no mediation'.[49] In *Musicophilia* he gives an extraordinary account of how some music is almost irresistible as a prime mover for some disabled patients. While in *tauberbach*, there is plenty of incentive for the ensemble to engage in their frenetic leaps and turns, the *primum mobile* function is less prominent. Instead, the function of the religious music is more akin to the Greek *kinoumenos kinei*, or the unmoved mover. In and of itself, the music is just part of *tauberbach*'s complex soundscape; however, its impact is one of an internal sounding that goes deeper and deeper. It may not be universal, but at least with an audience for whom Bach's cantata *Jesu der du meine Seele* means something else than a pleasant jingle at a hockey game, the affect of the music is considerable. Undoubtedly, even for our post-religious theatre audiences, it is the kind of music of which Oliver Sacks concludes that although 'it has no power to represent anything particular or external ... it has a unique power to express inner states of feelings'. Considering what actually is (re)presented on the stage in *tauberbach*, it is also the kind of music that 'makes one experience pain and grief more intensely, it brings solace and consolation at the same time'.[50]

Jesu der du meine Seele, also known as BWV 78, is a consolation cantata for the sick, for four voices. Bach followers recognize the melody from the first measure. It is known as an example of a perfect four-part chorale setting for SATB (soprano, alto, tenor and bass). In contrast to much of the music that is often repeated throughout *tauberbach*, Platel only uses it once, immediately following Bérengère Bodin's somnambulistic solo. All six performers, vulnerably attired in their underwear, stand looking at each other, distributed throughout the stage, and, after a short tone indication from the organ, softly sing the almost-300-year-old song a cappella. With their fragile untrained voices, they do so quietly, hesitantly and failingly. It lasts only one minute. Not enough to let this quietest fragment of the entire production do its interiorizing and stilling work, since, towards the end, the deaf choir takes over the soundscape, and we get yet another blast from Maklakiewicz's *Kyrie*, to which the dancers promptly execute a crashing choreography of collapse and shaking in response to the wailing choir. We are afraid that Lisi Estaras is going to shake out her brains. The contrast between the two segments cannot be greater, but it demonstrates the almost insufferable interiorizing effect (and affect) of *tauberbach*. What we witness is an internal sounding of existence, *tauberbach* presents us with an endoscopic picture of the human condition.

As with all endoscopies, the inside must, in the end, become outside. So it goes with *tauberbach*; as it moves to its exit, its soundscape changes to a decidedly more profane tone. The folksy nature of Bach's jiggy *Violin Concerto* (BWV 1041) initiates a mad carnivalesque celebration. The tall Belgium-born Elie Tass leads his co-dancers on a savage Dionysian revelry that shifts between indigenous rain dance and sexual bacchanalia; all the while with Romeu Runa, dressed in a black pinafore dress, performing a feral blitz-scouring of the stage, clothes flying through the air. It is party time, and therefore, clearly, anti-theological. It is surely the point where the theatre's apron protects the audience as the moat in the zoo. We cannot see the dancer from the dance, the centrifugal forces have taken over. Exhausted, and failing more than ever, they are circularly led by Bach's *Orchestral Suite No. 3* that initiated *tauberbach* in the very beginning, but now mixed with the innocent tone of children's voices. It is a journey in slow motion – a final demonstration of virtuoso muscular control – till all six squat on the stage in a tight circle. It is a manifest moment of yet another kind of soma, leaving behind the chaos, the deaf voices, the Voice, the buzzing fly that suddenly stopped, the sacral music, the sweat and grime, the contortions, and, most remarkably, leaving behind J. S. Bach. They hesitantly – and failingly – sing a well-known opera song, *Soave sia il vento* from Mozart's *Così fan tutte*, a title that implies we are all in the same boat, although Platel's reference certainly broadens the original's implied gender. Amidst the onstage debris, the three women and three men form an imperfect and precarious a cappella choir. Clearly, they have not arrived. *Tauberbach*'s endoscopic journey's end is a point of departure, in the form of a wish:

> Soave sia il vento
> Tranquilla sia l'onda
> Ed ogni elemento
> Benigno risponda
> Ai nostri desir.
> [May the wind be gentle,
> May the wave be calm,
> May every element respond
> Benevolently to our desires.]

Acknowledgements

With thanks to Guy Cools, David Grammit, Stefano Muneroni, Lin Snelling, Christel Stalpaert, Luk Van Den Dries, Louise Chardon, Ann Verhaert, and Lut Defraeye for their help with procuring video archives, their Bach prowess, their help with translations, their thoughts and edits, and their stimulating company at Platel events. Thanks also to my graduate research assistant, Mahmoud Khosrowparast, for initiating the research.

Notes

1 Guy Cools (2016) *Imaginative Bodies:. Dialogues in Performance Practices*, Amsterdam: Valiz, 144.
2 J. Toledo and F. Toledo (2015) 'Blind Toads in Paradise: The Cascading Effect of Vision Loss on a Tropical Achipelago', *Journal of Zoology*, 296 (3): 167–76, at 167.
3 Toledo, 'Blind Toads in Paradise', 170.
4 Christie Wilcox (2017) 'Lovestruck Toadlets Can't Even Hear Their Own Flirting', *Gizmodo*, 21 September.

5   For a CBC radio documentary on the scientific discovery, go to http://www.cbc.ca/listen/shows/as-it-happens/episode/14118920, a Canadian website where you can listen to the actual mating call.
6   The trope of discarded clothing has been used quite often in theatrical and dance production, including by Platel himself, for instance in his *vsprs* (2006) production, with a laundry mountain of white undergarments. Two years before *tauberbach*'s premiere, French choreographer Thierry Malandain presented a strikingly similar stage picture in *Une dernière chanson* (2012). The set, with its abundance of clothes, served as a depository for drawing costumes, props and dance support. Set on music by Vincent Dumestre, and with its overall folksy and often comical disposition, *Une dernière chanson* has a very different overall feel.
7   Rebecca Galloway (2015) 'les ballets C de la B returns to Montreal with *tauberbach*', review, *Bachtrack*, 31 May. Available online at https://bachtrack.com/review-tauberbach-ballets-c-de-la-b-transameriques-montreal-may-2015 (accessed 20 August 2019).
8   Laura Cappelle (2014), '*tauberbach*', review, *Financial Times*, 29 January, 9.
9   Rosamaria Cisneros (2014) 'Tenets of Nihilism from les ballets C de la B: Alain Platel's *tauberbach*', review, *Bachtrack*, 13 April. Available at https://bachtrack.com/review-ballets-c-de-la-b-tauberbach-london-apr-2014.
10 Peter Laudenbach (2014) 'Müll und Würde', *Der Tagesspiegel*, 3 March: 'einer anthropologischen Forschung, die dieses seltsame Tier, den Menschen, betrachtet'. All translations in the text are mine, unless otherwise indicated. Original quotations in footnote.
11 Silvia Stammen (2014) 'Jenseits von Gut und Schön', *Theater Heute*, 55 (3): 12–13, at 13: 'Alain Platel lässt uns schauen wie am Ersten Tag.'
12 Katja Schneider (2014) '*tauberbach*', review, *Zeitschrift für Ballett, Tanz und Performance*, 3: 8–11, at 10. 'Jedem dieser Tänzer könnte man ewig zusehen.'
13 Geert Van Der Speeten (2014) 'Een vuilnisbelt vol brute poëzie', *De Standaard*, 28 April: 'Zelden was de brute poëzie van Platels danstheater zo helder en zo fundamenteel aangrijpend als in dit meesterwerkje.'
14 Cisneros, 'Tenets of Nihilism from les ballets C de la B'.
15 Graham Watts (2014) 'les ballets C de la B – *tauberbach* – London', *Dancetabs*, 13 April. Available at http://dancetabs.com/2014/04/les-ballets-c-de-la-b-tauberbach-london/ (accessed 20 August 2019).
16 John O'Dwyer (2014) 'Dramatic, Unsettling Performance from les ballets C de la B', *Seen and Heard International*, 10 April. Available at http://seenandheard-international.com/2014/04/dramatic-unsettling-performance-les-ballets-de-la/ (accessed 20 August 2019).
17 Mark Monahan (2014) 'Dance Master Who Needs to Change His Tune', *Daily Telegraph*, 9 April.
18 Gertrude Stein (1935) *Lectures in America*, Boston, Mass.: Beacon Hill, 125.
19 Stein, *Lectures in America*, 122.
20 The name Jardim Gramacho fits in an eponymous tradition of having geographical names refer to previous local historical residents or landowners. It apparently refers to João Pereira Lima Gramacho who was a sugar-cane farmer in the area at the end of the eighteenth century. See http://gramachosdobrasil.blogspot.ca/2011/05/jardim-gramacho-duque-de-caxias-rj.html (accessed 20 August 2019).

21 *Estamira*, dir. Marcos Prado, Rio de Janeiro, Zazen Produções, 2004.
22 Nicola Gavioli (2016) 'Mythicizing Disability: The Life and Opinions of (What is Left of) Estamira', in Beth E. Jörgensen and Susan Antebi (eds.), *Libre Acceso: Latin American Literature and Film through Disability Studies*, Albany, NY: State University of New York Press, 191–208, at 194.
23 Gavioli, 'Mythicizing Disability', 196.
24 Żmijewski's *Singing Lesson 1* can be viewed at http://ubu.com/film/zmijewski_singing.html (accessed 20 August 2019).
25 *Estamira*, dir. Marcos Prado.
26 Julian Cowley (2011) 'Rev. of *Singing Lessons*', *The Wire*, 334 (December): 64.
27 Cowley, 'Rev. of *Singing Lessons*', 64.
28 Daniel B. Smith (2007) *Muses, Madmen, and Prophets: Rethinking the History, Science, and Meaning of Auditory Hallucinations*, New York: Penguin, 60.
29 Smith, *Muses, Madmen, and Prophets*, 77.
30 Stammen, 'Jenseits von Gut und Schön', 13.
31 Giorgio Agamben (1993) *Infancy and History: On the Destruction of Experience*, New York: Verso, 15.
32 Agamben, *Infancy and History*, 154.
33 Emmanuel Levinas (1979) *Totality and Infinity: An Essay on Exteriority*, Dordrecht: Springer, 495.
34 Levinas, *Totality and Infinity*, 105.
35 Agamben, *Infancy and History*, 152.
36 Carl Schachter (1994) 'The Prelude from Bach's *Suite No. 4 for Violoncello Solo*: The Submerged Urlinie', *Current Musicology*, 56: 54–71, at 55.
37 Schachter, 'The Prelude', 68.
38 Roger Salas (2012) 'The Public versus Platel', *Ballet 2000*, 230: 45–6, at 46.
39 'Altijd dat spastische gedoe, hoor ik soms. Maar als ik op die bewegingstaal doorga, is dat omdat ik er iets mee te vertellen heb, niet omdat ik ermee op de zenuwen wil werken.'
40 Hildegard De Vuyst (2014) 'Though This Be Madness Yet There Is Method in 't (*Hamlet* II.2)', dramaturgical notes in *tauberbach* production programme.
41 Ryan Platt (2010) 'Human Failure and Humane Exhaustion: The Passion of Alain Platel', *PAJ: A Journal of Performance and Art*, (T94), 32 (1): 90–6, at 92.
42 Lise Uytterhoeven (2011) 'Dreams, Myth, History: Sidi Larbi Cherkaoui's Dramaturgies', *Contemporary Theatre Review*, 21 (3): 332–9, at 339.
43 D. Gibbs (2013) 'Survey and Ecology of *Botanophila fonsecai* Ackland (*Diptera, Anthomyiidae*), a seed-fly endemic to Scotland', Scottish Natural Heritage Commissioned Report No. 618, 15.
44 Chris Baraniuk (2018) 'The Billionaire Versus the Fly', *The Verge*, 16 January. Available at https://www.theverge.com/2018/1/16/16892904/not-coul-links-scotland-golf-course-mike-keiser-conservation (accessed 20 August 2019).
45 The online archival documentation of les ballets C de la B identifies BWV 944 as 'Sechs Kleine Präludien' (of which there really are only five).
46 Christel Stalpaert (2015) 'Towards an Embodied Poetics of Failure', *Performance Research*, 20 (1): 56–71, at 57.
47 Renate Klett (2006) 'Nothing Happens, and Yet Everything Does', *Theater*, 36 (1): 162–5, at 164.

48 Alain Platel and Lou Cope (2010) 'Looking Inward, Outward, Backward and Forward', *Contemporary Theatre Review*, 20 (4): 418-20.
49 Oliver Sacks (2007) *Musicophilia*, New York: A. Knopf, 301.
50 Sacks, *Musicophilia*, 300-1.

References

Agamben, Giorgio (1993) *Infancy and History: On the Destruction of Experience*, London and New York: Verso.
Baraniuk, Chris (2018) 'The Billionaire Versus the Fly', *The Verge*, 16 January.
Cappelle, Laura (2014) '*tauberbach*', review, *Financial Times*, 29 January.
Cisneros, Rosamaria (2014) 'Tenets of Nihilism from les ballets C de la B: Alain Platel's *tauberbach*', review, *Bachtrack*, 13 April.
Cools, Guy (2016) *Imaginative Bodies: Dialogues in Performance Practices*, Amsterdam: Valiz.
Cowley, Julian (2011) 'Review of Singing Lessons by Artur Żmijewski', *The Wire*, 334 (December): 64.
De Vuyst, Hildegard (2004) 'Though This Be Madness Yet There Is Method in 't (*Hamlet* II.2)', dramaturgical notes in *tauberbach*.
Estamira (2004), dir. Marcos Prado, Rio de Janeiro, Zazen Produções.
Gavioli, Nicola (2016) 'Mythicizing Disability: The Life and Opinions of (What Is Left of) Estamira', in Beth E. Jörgensen and Susan Antebi (eds.), *Libre Acceso: Latin American Literature and Film through Disability Studies*, Albany, NY: State University of New York Press, 191-208.
Galloway, Rebecca (2015) 'Les ballets C de la B returns to Montreal with *tauberbach*', *Review Bachtrack*, 31 May.
Gibbs, D. (2013) 'Survey and Ecology of *Botanophila fonsecai* Ackland (*Diptera, Anthomyiidae*), a seed-fly endemic to Scotland', Scottish Natural Heritage Commissioned Report No. 618.
Klett, Renate (2006) 'Nothing Happens, and Yet Everything Does: The Theater of Alain Platel', *Theater*, 36 (1): 162-5.
Laudenbach, Peter (2014) 'Müll und Würde', *Review Der Tagesspiegel*, 3 March.
Monahan, Mark (2014) 'Dance Master Who Needs to Change His Tune', review, *Daily Telegraph*, 9 April.
Levinas, Emmanuel (1979) *Totality and Infinity: An Essay on Exteriority*, Dordrecht: Springer.
O'Dwyer, John (2014) 'Dramatic, Unsettling Performance from les ballets C de la B', *Seen and Heard International*, 10 April.
Platel, Alain, and Lou Cope (2010) 'Looking Inward, Outward, Backward and Forward', *Contemporary Theatre Review*, 20 (4): 416-20.
Platt, Ryan (2010) 'Human Failure and Humane Exhaustion: The Passion of Alain Platel', *PAJ: A Journal of Performance and Art* (T94), 32 (1): 90-6.
Salas, Roger (2012) 'The Public versus Platel', *Ballet 2000*, 230: 45-6.
Schachter, Carl (1994) 'The Prelude from Bach's *Suite No. 4 for Violoncello Solo*: The Submerged Urlinie', *Current Musicology*, 56 (January): 54-71.
Schneider, Katja (2014) '*tauberbach*', review, *Zeitschrift für Ballett, Tanz und Performance*, 3: 8-11.

Smith, Daniel B. (2007) *Muses, Madmen, and Prophets: Rethinking the History, Science, and Meaning of Auditory Hallucinations*, New York: Penguin.
Stalpaert, Christel (2015) 'Towards an Embodied Poetics of Failure', *Performance Research*, 20 (1): 56–71.
Stammen, Silvia (2014) 'Jenseits von Gut und Schön', review, *Theater Heute*, 55 (3): 12–13.
Stein, Gertrude (1935) *Lectures in America*, Boston, Mass.: Beacon Hill.
Toledo, J. and L. F. Toledo (2015) 'Blind Toads in Paradise: The Cascading Effect of Vision Loss on a Tropical Achipelago', *Journal of Zoology*, 296 (3): 167–76.
Uytterhoeven, Lise (2011) 'Dreams, Myth, History: Sidi Larbi Cherkaoui's Dramaturgies', *Contemporary Theatre Review*, 21 (3): 332–9.
Van Der Speeten, Geert (2014) 'Een vuilnisbelt vol brute poëzie', *Review De Standaard*, 28 April.
Watts, Graham (2014) 'Les ballets C de la B – *tauberbach* – London', *Dancetabs*, 13 April.
Wilcox, Christie (2017) 'Lovestruck Toadlets Can't Even Hear Their Own Flirting', *Gizmodo*, 21 September.

14

Schizophrenia and Resistance

On *tauberbach*

Jeroen Donckers

Figure 14.1 Elsie de Brauw and Romeu Runa in *tauberbach*, Münchner Kammerspiele, Munich 2014. © Chris Van der Burght.

Dear Mr Platel,

Please allow me to write this letter to express my gratitude for the performance of *tauberbach* which I saw on 19 December 2015 at the NTGent city theatre in Ghent for the fourth and probably last time. I am especially grateful for its warm after-effects. At the same time, this letter is an attempt to understand the emotional turmoil this performance generates with a psychotherapist, for this is my profession.

How to speak about what cannot be told? How to speak about those things that were unable to find their way to speech? And considering *tauberbach*, how to speak about a dance performance that unveils genuine but inexpressible traces of thoughts, feelings and memories? The answers that I might imagine are drifting back and forth between Wittgenstein's decisive 'Whereof one cannot speak, thereof one must be silent' and the ethical resolution of Freud's unconscious, 'Of that what cannot be spoken of, one has to speak.' The body speaks in so many ways; there are so many things that cannot be told or have no wish to be heard. This performance has managed to uncover traces of things that remain undiscussed, undisclosed in our daily lives, things that have been set aside, have been numbed or are waiting patiently for a rare moment of recognition. In a performance such as *tauberbach*, they find themselves heard without having to speak.

This performance touches upon the idea that there is so much more than just speech and silence; many words can be found in silence, just as deafness can be part of a conversation. To speak can be the right approach. To be silent just as well. But there are so many more possibilities to express oneself besides speech and silence; in movement, in dancing, in approaching the other, in leaving the other behind, in lust, eroticism, in touching, watching, biting, groping or kicking, in fucking.

Perhaps both Freud and Wittgenstein were underestimating the vital power of the body – of a communication that does not express itself in words, of a communication that distances itself from words. To refuse to be fooled by words, to refuse to be trapped in this sealed bag of human communication.

Mister Platel, this performance has made me realize that it is (nearly) always possible to exist, and to exist in a right way: this is called life. Estamira (played by Elsie de Brauw), the protagonist in *tauberbach*, is a destroyed but living woman. People are born into, or end up in a variety of situations that may deprive them from their possibility to exist, situations that complicate their existence by denying it. Different material and psychological needs play a part in this process (that often stretches across generations), and these create circumstances in which a child can be born without even being acknowledged. The relationship between a parent and a child may be one in which the child's existence is denied, either through all sorts of brutalities or through the absence of any meaningful encounter between them. And yet, despite this frustration, there is always a life to be lived, a life that contains a source of authentic living despite the incompetence and the pathological condition that the individual suffers.

'They were always my parents, but they have not adopted me', were the very first words of a psychotic girl during our first therapy session [1] She had come all the way from the French-speaking part of the Flemish Ardennes to Ghent. There is no use in trying to express this better than she did. She felt she had not been adopted in life, a fact that was not due to ill will or intentional malice, but simply to incompetence. To end up on a garbage dump, schizophrenic, constantly balancing the staggering line between the inside and the outside world, between delusion and reality, between inner thoughts and paranoid voices, between desire and destruction, between the rush and the high of the body and the need for serenity, silence. Schizophrenia, psychoses, autism and so on are not so much entities as they are ways of living, as are all our daily neuroses. The difference lies in the price that has to be paid for each way of living; that of a schizophrenic in general is immensely higher. Maybe one could say that the price that has to be paid for so-called normality is equally immense, but at the same time we are rewarded for it, and thus it becomes less obtrusive.

Just as every other human being, the schizophrenic is a sponge that inhabits a certain environment and is shaped by the reflection of this environment. Without a concrete tangible, perceptible, audible and visible human surrounding, no human being can emerge. We are born a sprig, absorbing everything that surrounds us. Gradually we separate, we differentiate, we are compelled to detach ourselves from the trunk we were grafted on, but we feel an imperative resistance to initiate an individual life. Is it possible that the schizophrenic feels the urge to resist in a premature stage? Before they are rooted even? Maybe the way they are treated (or mistreated), the way they are loved (or not loved) fails to provide the significance that is indispensable to initiating individuality? Maybe this is not about love or desire but about mere existence? Is this word 'schizophrenia' not a description or a denial of the desperate attempts of human beings to retain their sanity, to install a somehow endurable barrier to shelter them from the madness of what surrounds them? Is it not a reflection of this madness and a barrier at the same time? One just as much as the other, as we are all just as much our surroundings as ourselves. Is the gap between normality and schizophrenia wider than that between the trunk we were grafted on and the moment of the unavoidable separation?

The schizophrenic reflects and self-protects, but at such an early stage and so intensely that he cannot recognize the outside world and thereby loses the ability to become a consistent individual. There can be no consistent inner world without a consistent outer world. The more vulnerable the inner world is, the more threatening the outside world is experienced. And conversely: the less we are acknowledged by the outside world, the more we are forced to reflect this by denying the existence of this outside world. The more we deny this world, the more ephemeral we become. Are we not constantly both, 'we' just as much as the schizophrenic?

Your performance, *tauberbach*, displays the schizophrenic other, but at the same time it displays us; it discloses our inner self. And this feels good: it feels good to me not just to watch the other onstage but to find my inner self through this other. I become just as much one as the other. *Tauberbach*, to me, is an incredible window and a mirror at the same time. I just like the way that the people I listen to as a therapist also grant me the possibility to listen to myself, and that the children I take care of, who suffer from so-called behavioural or emotional problems, grant me the possibility to take care of myself.

The resistance of the schizophrenic is a resonance of the denial they themselves are part of, a denial of their own grounding and grounded subjectivity. This resistance comes at a price as this grounded sense of subjectivity is lost in the process of attempting to attain it. The schizophrenic remains in anticipation of the moment that someone will arrive and approach them differently, someone who can hear what is said without having to distort words or to attach a certain significance to them. Someone who can hear the words of Estamira (Elsie de Brauw), the words that carry so much truth. But none of these truths generate any meaning, nor do they generate a meaningful consistency: neither in relation to Estamira herself, nor in relation to the outside world. Schizophrenia and dance in a Greek tragedy, as if she were the result of a one-night stand between antique figures Tiresias and Cassandra, the blind clairvoyant and the woman who forecast the future but was never heard. A blind prophet among the deaf and dumb. The way you let them sing Bach together!

When watching the performance for the fourth and last time, it became a meaningful entity, without being reduced to one particular meaning. Before, the performance was a flood of impressions to me: chaos, the swinging to and fro between excitement and serenity, between isolation and togetherness. Eventually, the show became increasingly passionate, more sexual, harsher and more tender at the same time. Only this last time I perceived what I saw on the stage as part of one experience: the dancers, the actress, all became part of the experience of one and the same character. There is Estamira, but everybody else is part of Estamira, and perhaps what we see is not the interplay between Estamira and the others but just one experience.

The same goes for Elsie de Brauw's text. The words that I heard the first three times but that I perceived as screams, cries, moaning and muttering, became more clear and prominently present – not by adding meaning but just by being more present. Maybe de Brauw's acting became more powerful? Maybe it is because I had the opportunity to watch it over and over again?

As a choreographer, you are the engineer of these intense experiences: the sensory tides that slowly find a safe haven, a haven of coherence, of consistency, without losing their energy, their lust. You provide the time and space to slowly let these impressions settle, one after the other. You provide a frame for the schizophrenic energy, both lustful and destructive, both imperative and fatal, to find a shape of its own, to descend, to be born. I presume you have not only succeeded in doing this on stage and for the spectator but also for the actress and dancers that are co-creative in this process.

This is what this performance brings me: the thought that the schizophrenic process, that might well be a universal human process, can settle in such a way that its destructive, fatal character can subside, that the anticipated revolt chooses another route and finds opportunity instead of defence.

I think that human beings are inclined to search for those living conditions that allow them to relive the ancient break lines, the primitive fears; to look for situations that do not adequately correspond to our primitive dependence on our environment. I am more and more convinced that this is something we all do. Not because we are driven by a fatal urge to relive the same pain over and over again but because we are driven by a sense of hope: the hope to experience something different this time, to experience a different kind of encounter, to be able to actually do something different other than surrendering passively to an impotent, non-emancipated other. I truly believe that the return to that point where we were left behind holds a tremendous source of lust for life.

A schizophrenic woman can thus be forced to roam a garbage dump, to eke out her life there, maybe because this garbage dump somehow resembles the way she was brought into this life – resembles it sufficiently and differs from it as well. Can we say such a thing, Mr Platel? There she hears her truths, screams out her truths. She finds her daily bread and gets swallowed by her daily rambles, of which we, as spectators of *tauberbach*, are allowed a temporary glance, until we dare to put an end to it, until we dare to applaud.

Maybe we applaud to reinstall the old break lines, to make the characters dancers and actors again, to become spectators again. If we failed to do that and were to remain there, a part of it, a scenario like that of Lars Von Trier's *Idiots* would become highly probable.

Again, the performance was a true pleasure to watch, each and every time. For me, as a spectator, it opened the curtain that keeps closing, the curtain of our normal everyday lives that we have collectively shut so that we are not confronted continuously with the unbearable nakedness of human life, that of others and our own. The same goes for dependence, our own dependence, which continuously stares us in the face as an uneasy but inevitable invitation. It is an invitation that we cannot uncritically accept, as it jeopardizes our own existence.

I cannot be like Fernand Deligny, the French artist/thinker/pedagogue who was able to fully accept the invitation of his autistic fellow man, to really live with them, far away from the spoken world. I think I would be unable to accept a similar invitation, but I am happy to find it knocking at my door, to have the opportunity to open it. The performance was important for me because of its determination to open the curtain and offer the spectator the opportunity to be face to face, eye to eye and ear to ear with a human being. The human being onstage is performing the human being on the garbage dump, with the body language of an infant, a newborn baby, overwhelmed but fulfilled as well. The human being onstage is also performing the human being in the audience, what we see and what we are, what we see and become throughout the performance. How the human being reaches us, all the way from the stage (the garbage dump), and how we, overwhelmed and fulfilled, become human for a short while, always only as much as possible.

Our daily hectic world of efficiency, evidence-based lifelong learning, competences, management, return, protocols and a lot more newspeak has very little consideration for many things, but most of all it ignores the human condition. The government, our society, our politics that refuses to stay in touch with our humanity is now based on rules, meetings, protocols and policies, and thereby completely loses faith in its own virtue. This might very well be a contemporary form of schizophrenia. We must all deal with an environment that is prior to our own existence. In a sense we must all refuse this environment, refuse to adapt to it. We must all find our way between adaptation and resistance.

This is the reason why resistance is imperative to becoming a human being, to remaining human. *Tauberbach* displays a resistance that bears no defence, as it is a resistance that defies nothing, that accuses nothing, that does not contest any other human. There is no enemy. *Tauberbach* shows a resistance that is the resistance of life itself, of the life that wants to be lived and it does exactly that, fully, without looking behind, without other concerns, without resentment, without the need to be applauded. Becoming itself, moving as itself, speaking as itself. By being genuine. Not enforced to be authentic, but genuine. Not fighting anymore, not trying to convince, not waiting for approval. But instead speaking as it comes, dancing as it happens, writing without trying to be academic. Accepting the roots as they are, accepting the environment as it is, and to live. To resist without a fight. The happiest resistance of them all, the most contagious of them all, is life that lies at its own origin, together with all the pain, the hunger, the exhaustion and the disturbance that it can bring. *Tauberbach* displays a human being that positions itself in this world, alongside another human being, and another. Or, to put it in Deligny's words, the human being as a verb, one of your major sources of inspiration.

> être là
> être cet être là
> qui est avec un autre
> et un autre
> alors il te faut être là
> tout simplement
> et faire ce que tu as à faire
> verbe vivant que tu es
> et dont l'enfant n'est ni le sujet
> ni le complément
> mais le compagnon

Just like the deaf are singing Bach, I try to write these words. They express and translate something that they are unable to hear but have experienced in a different way. The way they sing the Bach they cannot hear, echoes the Bach that I know but leaves me speechless as well. I have no immediate words for what I have experienced during *tauberbach*, and am in that way at least partially deaf, but I have tried to describe what the performance has done to me and inside of me – not as an explanation or an interpretation but as a resonance, with the hopeful intention to return something to you, Mr Platel.

Thankfully and cordially yours,
Jeroen Donckers

Note

1   'Ils ont toujours étés mes parents, mais ils m'ont pas encore adoptée.'

Part Four

Politics

15

Mourning a Europe in Crisis

les ballets C de la B's *En avant, marche!* (2015)

Lourdes Orozco

Les ballets C de la B's *En avant, marche!* (directed by Alain Platel and Frank Van Laecke) was seen in London on 16 and 17 June 2016, a few days before the country voted to leave the European Union after forty-four years of membership. The production had already been touring internationally for a year before its arrival at the capital's most reputed dance stage (Sadler's Wells), which has become a regular home for Alain Platel's les ballets C de la B since the early 1980s. In their visits to the UK, the company always brings up a reminder of the dance and theatre work that goes on in the Continent and the visible split between dance and music genealogies – as well as programming and other infrastructural issues – between mainland Europe and the UK. Platel's work, firmly rooted in Belgium, is born out of the 1980s Flemish avant-garde also known as the 'Flemish Wave'. As such, he is considered by English theatre scholars to be part of a group of theatre, dance and performance practitioners that converge and populate the stages of Europe and the USA with work that was characteristically pushing the boundaries, that was genre-defiant and that embraced innovation and experimentation.[1] From this genealogical perspective, Platel's choreographic work also builds on a longer European tradition of avant-garde and experimental art that links directly with the European avant-garde movements of the late nineteenth and early twentieth centuries. These are themselves indebted to forms of theatrical and cultural representation that date back to the medieval and Renaissance periods. The latter can be seen particularly in Platel's choice for music from that period as stimuli for his dance and theatre work and his collaborations with musicians and composers, such as Steven Prengels and Fabrizio Cassol amongst others, who work mostly within the context of old music. The large number of Platel's productions that have been born out of or are an homage to European classical music and its musicians – *Requiem pour L.* (2017) and *Wolf* (2003), to Mozart; *tauberbach* (2014), to Bach; *C(H)ŒURS* (2012), to Verdi and Wagner; and *vsprs* (2007), to Monteverdi; to name but a few – testifies to Platel's clear and incontestable embeddedness in a particular European musical and cultural tradition.

In this contribution, I reflect on what 'Europe' means for Platel and how this idea of Europe feeds and shapes his work. I want to do this mainly by looking at the sources, themes and performance histories that are central to Platel's choreographic work. I focus particularly on the London production of *En avant, marche!* because I believe that the production offers an opportunity to explore the complexity of the European project. Furthermore, the specific socio-political moment in which it was performed exposes the connections but also the disconnections between mainland Europe and the UK. In what follows, I explore how *En avant, marche!*'s 'Europeanness' functioned in these particular London performances in June 2016 as a both a bridge and a wall between the UK and Europe materializing, in some ways inadvertently but in others knowingly, the tensions between these geopolitical territories. I demonstrate that the piece did this by investigating music and community and the relationship between the two. Community and music both frame and propel the production forward, co-creating a piece that simultaneously mourns and celebrates the idea of Europe through the metaphor of brass bands.

In this chapter, I will firstly explore how the idea of community/communities and its/their formations functions within the performance, referring to notions such as toleration, civility and participation. The specific context in which the show was performed in London will enable me to question these concepts and their role in shaping particular understandings of community in relation to the Brexit vote and the relationship between the UK and mainland Europe.

Second, given the centrality of brass bands within the piece, I will focus on music as a mediator, or perhaps even intermediator, of these relationships. I want to think of brass bands as a musical vehicle for highlighting and transcending geopolitical and cultural borders. In the show, Platel and Van Laecke use music and the brass band as builders of community cohesion and as drivers with transformative potential which, most importantly, remain active relentlessly through time.

Staging communities: Civility and toleration

The curtain raises and presents the performance space. A backdrop of a copper-coloured wall split by a central door and a set of asymmetrical windows frame an almost empty stage. Only visible are some scattered chairs, musical instruments and a couple of microphones. No specific geographical location is suggested, no particular time. The audience knows from the programme notes that, for this performance, les ballets C de la B will be joined by a local brass band. However, there is no sign of them onstage, only their instruments are on display.

The company is well known in London for its intergenerational, multinational, multicultural, multilingual and multiracial profile. Since its formation in 1984, it consists of a small group of regulars and an intermittent group of ad-hoc collaborators, ranging in age, race and nationality. Because of this fluctuating composition, the audience sitting in the Sadler's Wells auditorium does not really know who les ballets C de la B will be today. They do not know who the dancers, actors, musicians are; what they will look like; where they will be from; how old they will be. The slow opening scene and the anticipation produced by the empty stage allows for all this thinking to take place and for the audience to imagine what they will see, before they see it.

The diverse identity of the company is also transferable to the show. The piece is presented as theatre, musical theatre, brass-band concert, dance, dance theatre and opera at the same time. In her review for the performance in Edinburgh in 2015, Lyn Gardner already identified the multifarious nature of the show: 'A production that swoops between high and low culture and combines concert, theatre and dance in one category-defying package, this is a show about community that places a community band – the Dalkeith and Monktonhall Brass Band – at its sweaty, brimming heart.'[2]

This willingness to escape genre classification unsettles audience expectations, once again. There will be music and probably dancing, but there is no hint of a plot in the programme notes, no story, not even a theme. Knowledge of the company's previous works will not help either, as every piece unveils a different aesthetic, a different engagement with its material, a different set of questions for the audience to consider, and an articulation of a diverse set of theatrical and choreographic vocabularies. The empty stage that the audience is invited to scrutinize for a few minutes before the first performer appears onstage allows the audience to reflect on the long list of unknowns that Platel has purposely created for the show. It is also a time built for pre-emption and pre-judgement, for the audience to imagine what they will see before they see it based on the little that they can see, and on the previous knowledge they have on the show, the company and the venue. Knowledge that will either materialize or dissipate as the show begins.

A few minutes after the curtain rises, a man comes onstage dressed in his brass-band uniform, dragging his feet and a chair slowly across the stage and carrying an old tape player. He coughs and has a dishevelled look. His beard and hair are messy. He also has a large plaster over his throat, possibly the signs of a tracheostomy. He plugs in the tape player, reaches for his cymbals and prepares for his performance. As the music begins to play in the tape player and the man waits for his cue, I am convinced that he is a member of the local brass band. I am sure that he is from North London, that he sounds like a local, and that he has never been on the stage of Sadler's Wells before. I think I can feel nervousness in his performance, which I base on all of my preconceptions about what actors, dancers and musicians look like, and how they behave (or should behave) onstage. My judgements around what people who play in small local brass bands look like come into play too, and they are aligned with my preconceptions around his national and cultural identity. I read his beard and dishevelled look and his large belly as signs of English eccentricity. I assume his role in the show is minimal, but he has been asked to open it, and I imagine the excitement and the pressure that he must feel being part of a show by this internationally acclaimed company who he has not heard about previous to this collaboration.

However, as the scene unfolds, I realize that I am completely wrong, that the man is in fact the actor Wim Opbrouck, who performs the main role in the production *En avant, marche!* He plays the cymbals, the trombone, sings opera, dances, and speaks and sings in four different languages. He is, like all the other performers in this piece, a constant surprise. In *En avant, marche!* everything is a surprise. Narratives are initiated randomly and end abruptly without resolution; dancers are disguised as musicians and musicians as dancers; instruments are played in conventional and unconventional ways; singing and shouting are performed side by side. Anything could and does happen. Reviewers of the show have highlighted the chaotic nature of the piece and its 'category-defying' intentions. In her review for *The Guardian* newspaper, for instance, Lyn Gardner refers to the show's messy nature by stating that 'to be honest, it's not always entirely clear what is happening' and 'you never know quite where to look'.[3] The piece is an invitation to reflect on established understandings of identity and on the preconceptions and prejudgements that come with it. It does so by presenting a constant reimagining of personal and community identities, a continuous fabrication of random connections, encounters and associations. This unceasing pushing and reconsidering of established concepts and boundaries that directly relate to personal identity (what one is and one is not); national identity (what it means to be Flemish in relation to what it means to be Belgian, British, European) and to genre (tragedy, comedy, dance, theatre, brass-band concert) enables Platel and Van Laecke to produce a frame for the piece within which its main questions must be considered openly and fluidly. Fluidity is, in fact, central to the piece and constitutes the core demand that *En avant, marche!* asks of its audience. The piece offers a representation of contemporary life that is chaotic, unexpected and unpredictable and where non-linear narratives, erratic behaviours and random encounters are the norm.

I want to reflect for a moment on what this particular chaotic way of representing has enabled Platel to do in former performances. In my analysis of Platel's *Wolf* (2003), I observed how the use of animals onstage echoed the fragmented, unpredictable and chaotic nature of contemporary life.[4] Also, the animal onstage embodied the fears borne out of a Europe in crisis, a Europe that has lost a sense of unity due to the loss of tradition: 'Europe has gradually lost its national identity, its ideas of family and religion. There is undoubtedly a lack of points of reference, and all this has made for a void and thus for fear.'[5] Fear – represented by the onstage presence of dogs on the loose – had created an opportunity for state control which materialized in what Beck and Giddens termed the 'risk society': a society primarily concerned by the risks brought about by technological development.[6] I observed that the dogs in *Wolf* were an invitation for the audience to embrace that fear and thus to participate in an illusory challenge to the risk society and its control mechanisms.

Similar to the dogs in *Wolf*, chaos drives and defines *En avant, marche!* The piece revolves around a central character: a trombone player performed by Opbrouck, who, the audience soon finds out, is dying of epithelioma (an abnormal growth in his mouth that is cancerous). Platel and Van Laecke build a community around this character, which is based on Luigi Pirandello's short play *L'Uomo dal fiore in bocca* (*The Man with the Flower in His Mouth*, 1922). The group of random people accompanies the trombonist in his journey towards death. This provides an opportunity for Platel and Van Laecke to explore community formations built on forms of toleration and civility that are particular and specific to liberal societies in amidst of a perceived moment of crisis. In *En avant, marche!* the crisis is embodied by both the dying trombonist and the community that surrounds him, echoing those perceived losses that have produced,

Platel thinks, the collapse of European identity/identities. The central dying character relies on music, and especially music from the European classical tradition, and on the community that surrounds him (the local brass band, the core band, the majorettes) to carry him through at a point when he and, arguably, them have lost a sense of identity that can only be reclaimed by their membership to the community/communities (the brass band, the stage) that they belong to.

The questions that are central to *En avant, marche!* are already contained in the opening scene, and they relate heavily to identity. Who is this man? Where is he from? What does he do? These questions return every time a new performer enters the stage and will dissipate as the audience gets to know them as individuals but also as they become a community. Opbrouck's old trombone player, Chris Thys's and Griet Debacker's middle-aged majorettes, the core wind and percussion band, the local brass band. They are the characters and performers that inhabit the stage and, for about ninety minutes, form unexpected relationships, burst into unforeseen confessional monologues, show the audience their ugliest and most vulnerable side. As a community, they are bounded to the stage and bonded by forms of civility and toleration that, as Derek Edyvane explains, are key to maintaining core social structures in contemporary liberal societies. As Edyvane suggests,

> civility essentially embodies the acknowledgement of society with others, not just in the minimal sense of the acknowledgement that we share space, but also that we share a problem. It is bound up in the conviction that finding a way of living together is not just my problem or your problem, but a problem we share.[7]

Figure 15.1 The Heroes Band and cast of *En avant, marche!* at Sadler's Wells, London, 2016. © Wim Piqueur.

The characters of *En avant, marche!* not only share the space in this sense but they also have in common a being together for themselves and for the other in the face of a common problem that is specific – the death of the trombonist, the decay of the old majorette – but is also, and most importantly, about the problem of living together.

In what follows, I explore how this idea of a tolerant and civil community in *En avant, marche!* is an attempt to disarticulate the discourse of fear that is associated with the loss of identity, and thus of tradition, that Platel remarks is central to contemporary Europe. This fear has seen the growing state control mechanisms through self-policing, self-censorship, dependence on certain methods of prevention and protection such as insurance policies, etc., that are features of Beck and Giddens's 'risk society'.

Opbrouck's character, moments after his cymbal solo, asks the members of the local brass band the very same questions that members of the audience have, potentially, asked themselves about him. Once the local band enters and occupies their place on the stage, Opbrouck moves towards them and randomly asks them for their names, where they come from, what they do for a living, what they do in their spare time. This is a significant moment in the piece, as Opbrouck not only introduces the band to the audience but also places importance on its individual members as their names, their hobbies, their day jobs are announced. This is not just a local band but a band made of people who have lives that continue off the stage, lives that signal to other lives – their children, their friends, their colleagues, their neighbours – slowly creating a web of interconnections that makes apparent that individuals are part of large social networks and that they can neither be completely singularized nor totally homogenized.

In his two articles on civility – 'Toleration and Civility' and 'The Passion for Civility', both published in 2017 – Derek Edyvane, working within the theoretical framework of political sciences in the UK, argues that community formations in contemporary liberal societies are held together by a shared experience of civility and toleration. For him, these two terms need to be differentiated as, while they are both 'typically experienced as rewarding', they do differ in the role they play in gelling communities together.[8] For Edyvane, toleration is the practice of understanding and accommodating diversity, and civility is the sense of rights and responsibility that individuals feel for belonging in a community. These rights include the responsibility to tolerate the other in order to make the community function.[9] In his article, Edyvane spends some time challenging Samuel Scheffler's idea that civility and toleration are more likely to arise when a shared sense of authority is experienced – a sense of authority, Scheffler explains, that is comparable to the sense shared by siblings in relation to parental authority.[10] This is why, Edyvane explains, Scheffler bases his notion of toleration and civility on religious belief, since a common experience of religion is the sense of a community bonded by a shared belief in a higher, superior and often authoritarian being.

Platel's sense of a Europe in crisis, which he sees as an outcome of the loss of tradition produced by the collapse of institutions such as the family and structured religion, might mean, following Scheffler's framework, that there is no room for community formation or that those communities are weakened because they cannot be built on a shared sense of civility and toleration. If, as Judith Shklar argues, the kinds of government that societies live under shapes the kinds of friendships and communities that are formed, what remains to be seen is what kinds of communities can be built in what Platel perceives to be a Europe in crisis.[11]

However, I want to argue that in *En avant, marche!* Platel and Van Laecke propose a different form of community. The community surrounding Opbrouck's character is established not as a response to a perceived form of collective oppression or authority but built on civility and toleration which have grown as part of the everyday life experiences and synergies of its members. Civility and toleration in contemporary liberal societies, as Edyvane suggests, need not grow out of a shared moral ground. Instead, 'cultures of liberal freedom are more conducive to forms of solidarity in which moral agreement or the shared experience of subjection to moral authority are less fundamental'.[12] He explains this by attributing the potential of bonds of basic concern to modern personal friendship:

> We see this clearly enough in the case of modern personal friendship. The fuel that ignites and sustains such friendships is only seldom the fuel of moral consensus or a sense of a shared predicament provoked by subjection to normativity (or some other kind of authority). It is much more often a host of quotidian shared interests and shared pursuits: college attendance, dog ownership, tennis, TV shows, baking. Of course, such shared interests and pursuits might reflect deeper, underlying shared values, but equally they might not, and they are usually sufficient on their own to ground and sustain bonds of basic concern irrespective of moral differences.[13]

In *En avant, marche!* the members of the community are linked by their membership to the brass band, their shared interest and passion for music. They form a cohesive community that is able to support its members at times of crisis. They do not respond to normativity but instead produce their own rules and accept them as functional to keep the community alive. Their lives might be chaotic, unexpected and unpredictable, but they represent unity at moments of fragmentation.

Soon after the opening scene, Wim Opbrouck's character explains to the audience the nature of his disease and what that means for his musical career accompanied in the background by the wind sounds of the core musicians onstage. When they stop playing at the dramatic revelation of his imminent death, he shouts at them to continue playing, to continue with the music. He considers this bond in music to be an important support, particularly in difficult times.

En avant, marche! trusts in music to erase national boundaries by drawing from a variety of musical sources, popular and exclusive, well known and less well known, national anthems and popular songs. It presents music as anchored in a territory but not bound to it and as a united energy that enables these individuals and communities to continue marching on together, regardless of their differences and the singularity of their personal tragedies.

Halfway through the performance, the dying trombonist performs a dialogue with an imaginary Giuseppe Verdi and asks him if the band could play him a march – 'only a little march …?' he asks sheepishly. He then proceeds to mimic playing the trombone, making his struggle visible, while making the instrument's sound with his tightly closed

Figure 15.2 Gregory Van Seghbrouck, Wim Opbrouck, Griet Debacker and KMV De Leiezonen at NTGent, Ghent 2015. © Chris Van der Burght.

lips. A few metres to his left, performer Griet Debacker, dressed in a gold majorette outfit, begins to softly spin her baton and cries. The various communities that inhabit the stage, united as one, are presented as the driving force for both the characters and the piece itself. As the trombonist struggles to play and the majorette cries, they both begin a slow march first on the spot and then across the stage. Gradually, they are joined by the core wind and percussion band and by a second majorette (Chris Thys) who instead of a baton carries a flag on her shoulder. They all march around the stage. They march, march and march on. They march as a united force that will go forward in spite of their circumstances.

In this scene, the characters represent the possibility of an idea of community that is built not on shared moral values and/or beliefs but instead on a shared experience of music, on the simple act of doing something together. Following Edyvane, civility performs the important role of signalling towards a society.[14] I believe that in *En avant, marche!* Platel – who is suspicious of community cohesion in contemporary Europe – trials a form of community formation that, with its basis on civility, signals towards a functional society. This is a society that pulls together when it perceives imminent threats and crisis – the death of Opbrouck's character, the tragic love life of the old majorette. As Mark Brown states in his review of the Edinburgh production, the show believes that brass bands 'are fascinating mini-communities which swim against the tide of atomization and individuation that characterizes Western societies in the twenty-first centuries'.[15] The brass band serves as a platform to gel the community together as well as being a vehicle for its expression.

In what follows I explore the role that music and the brass band have in the piece, particularly in relation to the idea of Europe and its significance in the current state of affairs between Europe and the UK.

Brass bands and European identity: Forward, forward and marching on

The focus on society in *En avant, marche!* is clear from the outset. The production is based on people's stories, on people telling stories – verbally or otherwise – about people, about themselves, about the relationships they build with one another and about them as part of their communities. In the programme notes, the show is described as being Van Laecke and Platel's approach to

> the world of music clubs as a 'miniature society' in its own right: a collective of very different individuals who try to keep to one and the same marching direction. An arrangement that is kept as well as possible, sometimes by trial and error, and as such is a metaphor for our society as a whole.[16]

Alain Platel has talked about the show in these terms too, discussing how the piece might in fact be about Belgium and about its people. The show was inspired by a 2012 exhibition, curated by Huis van Alijn, Ghent's folklore museum, focusing on music clubs (brass and other wind bands) which 'have been part of the social and cultural life for decades'.[17] The exhibition featured a collection of objects and photos and also produced a book 'containing both new portraits of musicians and majorettes and black & white pictures from the archives'.[18] Both the book and the exhibition were entitled *En avant, marche!* The link with Belgian folklore is clear.

The Flemish flavour is also clear in Platel's *En avant, marche!* Three well-established Flemish actors (Griet Debacker, Wim Opbrouck and Chris Thys) feature in the performance. Dutch and various Flemish dialects are spoken, music from the Flemish classical repertoire is played and, perhaps more evidently, the local tradition of the brass band occupies a central role in the piece. The core wind and percussion band that is part of the production cast and tours the piece internationally is a representation of the traditional 'fanfare orchestra', an adaptation of the British-style brass band that was born in the Netherlands and Belgium in the mid-nineteenth century. It is part of the military band tradition, although fanfare orchestras were mainly civil with the exception of some bands that were formed by veterans in both countries. It is a type of brass band that includes instruments such as trumpets and saxophones that produce a distinctive sound differentiating them from British-style brass. All these different elements produce a distinctive 'Flemish' feel in the piece.

However, the piece also presents connections and shared European traditions onstage. Europe is present in the production's music, its languages (Spanish, Italian, French and English are spoken), in its literature (Pirandello's text is a blueprint for the show's main character), its dance (clearly rooted in contemporary avant-garde dance genealogies) and, most importantly, in its choice to position centrally the European brass-band heritage and repertoire. The fanfare orchestra plays side by side a local British-style brass band, highlighting not only the transformation, the differences, but also the connections. In the show, the Flemish and British brass bands both bring to mind an industrial Europe, a Europe that cherishes tradition. Perhaps most importantly, the brass band presents an idea of a multinational Europe that is united by its cultural heritage. A music and a cultural formation that crosses borders and that, like the communities I explored earlier in this article, resists homogenization but is intrinsically linked to wider forms of cultural expression.

In the London production, the band chosen to join les ballets C de la B was the Heroes Band, a local band from the City of London borough, which is part of the organization In Support of Help for the Heroes which raises funds to help veterans and army personnel from the UK involved in national and international conflict. The connection with the city's history of brass bands and their military association was clear from the outset. In the Edinburgh performances, for instance, the company was joined onstage by the Dalkeith and Monktonhall Brass Band, and a related event inspired by the production, entitled *Fanfare (A Fanfare for the Festival City)*, emphasized the link between the Dutch and Scottish brass traditions. The free community event aimed to 'tap into one of the most enduring symbols of Scotland – the beloved brass band' and 'called on the Scottish Brass Band Association to harness the enormous forces of Scotland's brass bands by presenting a day of free outdoor performances' in order to 'share the joy and passion of the live brass band in a coordinated community experience'.[19]

In the London performance of *En avant, marche!* the local British band is, on the one hand, the largest group of people onstage, playing the central musical number throughout the show. Their uniforms highlight their unity, as well as their moving together in and around the stage. However, they are at times confused, mixed up, with the core Flemish band. At points they all wear the same band uniforms (actors, dancers and musicians) signalling towards a kind of integration. In this way, the show facilitated a conversation between a strong symbol of the nations' cultural tradition and identity across a seemingly borderless continent. It is a form of community formation that exists outside shared moral values and it is the fact of 'doing something together', as I mentioned earlier, that produces that cohesion. However, the brass band is also a cultural signifier that links countries across Europe – both southern and northern – foregrounding their differences but also establishing their commonalities. Brass-band traditions are well established in countries such as Spain, Italy, Germany, France and also countries in Eastern Europe. In that sense, *En avant, marche!* also brings to mind Platel's perceived loss of European identity.

There was something particularly poignant about the *En avant, marche!* performance in London in June 2016, just a few days before the UK voted to formally leave the European Union after forty-four years of membership. On the stage of Sadler's Wells, London, a show defined by its internationalism, multilingualism, multiculturalism – a genre-defying show that draws on the European musical canon of the eighteenth and nineteenth centuries and is framed by the cross-European cultural tradition of brass – produced a peculiar experience. The show, which explores the idea of collaboration, community, cohesion, resilience, poses interesting questions to the city and the country of which it is the capital. It produces, knowingly and unknowingly, a reflection on the country's future within Europe, its past and present relations with the Continent, and its future place within it. At one point in the performance, going completely off script, Opbrouck addressed the London audience directly: 'Fuck Europe, uh? What is going on here?' The show quickly positioned itself within the immediate socio-political context as if the themes of unity, collaboration, dialogue and community cohesion that are at its core were severely undermined by the looming Brexit referendum that was to happen in the country some days after.

In the referendum that took place on 23 June 2016, British citizens could vote on the country leaving or staying part of the European Union, radically transforming – even before its outcome was known – the country's relationship with Europe. The idea that it was possible for the country, which had joined the European Economic Community in 1973, to cut its ties with the Continent, if not geographically at least politically and economically, became a reality, and a definite shift in self-perception for the country and its inhabitants – British-born and otherwise – took place. The Leave narrative had been fundamentally based on a traditional and static form of national identity, claiming a true meaning of Britishness based in the past, in history, in tradition. It presented Europe as divided between those who want to have overall control of the UK (its borders, its economic and political systems) and those who want to invade it (embodied by the current refugee crisis). Europe was presented as a place where the UK does not belong, claiming a difference that makes the country unique and therefore in need of separation. This separatist discourse fitted well with the geographical distance that already had significance in the country's self-perception of its relationship with mainland Europe.

In terms of the theatre industry, this distance is clearly felt. Only a few cities in the UK are part of the international festival circuit, and the locations for European theatre within the country are, while increasing and diversifying, still limited. London, Glasgow, Manchester and Edinburgh, and the main annual and biannual festivals that some of these cities hold, are primarily the places where European theatre, mostly pan-European co-productions and collaborations, can be seen. European City of Culture or UK City of Culture awards are also intended to make those European connections and are often opportunities for artists to come to the UK that would not otherwise step on British soil. Sadler's Wells, perhaps one of London's most international stages, and LIFT, the London International Festival Theatre, are two of these locations where audiences can watch European co-productions by established and emerging European companies. Questions around how this visibility (of European theatre in the UK and of UK practitioners in Europe) will be affected by the socio-economic and political changes that Brexit will bring remain unanswered, and it is not my intention to speculate about them in this essay but rather to consider how a show like *En avant, marche!* exposed the fragility of these relations when the results of the Brexit referendum, while still to come, were clearly felt by the majority of the British population.

It is important to consider the interrelations that a performance like *En avant, marche!* produces and the questions it raises in this context. Its intentions cannot be underestimated if the continuing interest demonstrated by Platel to articulate national and cultural identity through his work with les ballets C de la B is taken into account.

The programme notes also reveal the international dimension of the show, presented as a venture produced by les ballets C de la B in Ghent (Belgium) in collaboration with regional and national theatres, cultural organizations and festivals across ten countries, nine of which are European (France, Italy, Spain, Croatia, Australia, Luxembourg, Austria, Germany, Switzerland, Belgium). It is not surprising then that the home for the production in the UK is LIFT (the London International Festival Theatre), a biannual festival of theatre that takes place in the city during the month of July and that has become one of the few opportunities to watch international theatre companies in the country.

The company's multicultural, multi-ethnic, multilingual and multigenerational make-up, its ongoing collaboration with practitioners and companies across the world though their programme Co-laBo, the multinational and the multiple sources of their funding (private and public) has to be understood side by side this interest in border crossing and in their belief in cross-cultural and cross-national collaborations.

In *En avant, marche!* the brass band, literally but also metaphorically, symbolizes the Continent's multinational identity, its constant struggles with membership and cohesion and, above all, its capacity to march on regardless. The show unfolds around a solid but also, and paradoxically, a minimally sketched central narrative: that of a musician who, due to epithelioma, cannot play his instrument (the trombone) anymore and is instead relegated to playing the cymbals. The piece presents his various struggles with the illness through his continuous cough, his inability to sing, the invisibility of the instrument, which is mimed by the musician but never held, the changing of his dressing and cleaning of his injury and his deliriums. Around him, a core group of musicians, playing a set of wind instruments and percussion, and two women dressed in majorette outfits, perform a series of routines involving dance, playing music, reciting poems, singing. They cry, they fight, they laugh, they love, they reminisce, they watch and are watched, they listen.

Opbrouck's direct address to the audience immediately was a sign of the astonishment felt across some European countries at the UK's willingness to leave the EU. However, it was also a provocation, an opportunity to reflect on how these clear cultural links will be transformed by the drafting and the implementation of the policies to come and the future of UK–Europe relationships. *En avant, marche!*'s engagement with the idea of a Europe in crisis, embodied in the representation of a dying musician who is kept going by music and his community of musicians, seemed even more real at a point when the UK was in the cusp of beginning a process of cutting ties with the Continent.

This key moment was followed some moments after by the dying trombonist's performance of 'God Save the Queen'. Accompanied by the rest of the music ensemble and the local band, and aided by the two ageing majorettes, the delivery of this anthem was somehow fraught. As he is unable to play his trombone, he instead sings the piece while gurgling on what seems to be warm tea. With this, Platel and Van Laecke deform grotesquely the national anthem while also presenting a form of community resilience embodied in Opbrouck's character and the rest of the musicians and performers that make the difficult delivery of the anthem possible.

Platel and Van Laecke also use the anthem here as a reminder of nation-building, a signalling towards the importance of symbols in the formation of communities.

However, the chaotic context and precarious delivery is far from the grandiose position it occupies in official events of all kinds. The anthem becomes a pagan symbol, a useless and outdated emblem questioned in a context of national disintegration.

The piece closes with another British anthem ('I Vow to Thee, My Country') which follows after a carnivalesque and chaotic fanfare section in which actors, dancers and musicians all dance and sing frenetically. This storm before the calm includes a *pas de deux* featuring Opbrouck and Hendrik Lebon, in which the death of the trombonist appears closer than ever. He falls, is lifted by the band, is given breath by Lebon, falls and is lifted again. He is carried flat in the air by the band musicians, and a funeral march is performed interspersed with his heavy, tired, breathing. A voice coming from off stage, speaks defiantly: 'Very brave, very brave ... is that all you have maestro?' At that point, Opbrouck asks the whole ensemble to get together and to play the final anthem which is perfectly orchestrated and beautifully delivered by the two bands as if to counterbalance his pathetic performance. 'God Save the Queen' is gurgled, but the anthem that culminates the piece is a celebration not of the UK but of homeland in general, of a country that is any country. The origin of the anthem is a poem by European diplomat Sir Cecil Spring Rice, who travelled across the Continent in the years previous and during the First World War acting as a diplomat for the UK in various European countries. In the poem, also entitled 'The Two Fatherlands', Spring Rice refers to two countries: one on the earth and one in heaven to which all people belong and are indebted. As if to move away from the nation, the final musical number in the piece sees the whole ensemble together, dressed in the same band uniforms, their previous singularity now erased.

If, according to José Ortega, civility reflects, 'before all, the will to live in common' and is fundamentally 'an attempt to make possible the city, the community, common life', it is precisely this common goal that keeps the community together.[20] Doing away with shared moral values and both emphasizing and collapsing national borders, *En avant, marche!* invites for a reflection on the art of living together with others. In doing this, the production willingly but also inadvertently tapped into current forms of community disintegration, such as the Brexit vote and the current UK–EU crisis. However, in doing so it demonstrated the cyclical nature of community formation, which, as demonstrated in the show, can be dispersed and brought together again. Edyvane suggests that 'civility essentially embodies the acknowledgement of society with others, not just in the minimal sense of the acknowledgement that we share space, but also that we share a problem'.[21] Opbrouck's direct address to the audience in the context of a performance fundamentally concerned with the idea of Europe and the challenges to this idea seemed to me a reminder of that shared problem. Tackling this problem means to perform connections based in shared cultural traditions, moving beyond national politics, and looking for answers in the shared concerns of people who bring these traditions to life.

Notes

1   Peter Boenisch and Lourdes Orozco (2010) 'Editorial: Border Collisions: Contemporary Flemish Theatre', *Contemporary Theatre Review*, 20 (4): 397–404, at 397.

2   Lyn Gardner (2015) '*En Avant, Marche!* Edinburgh Festival Review: Mortality Take with a Brimming Heart', *The Guardian Online*, 25 August. Available at https://www.theguardian.com/stage/2015/aug/25/en-avant-marche-at-edinburgh-festival-review-mortality-tale-with-a-brimming-heart (accessed 21 August 2019).
3   Gardner, 'Review'.
4   Boenisch and Orozco, 'Editorial: Border Collisions'.
5   Platel in Lourdes Orozco (2010) 'Never Work with Children and Animals: Risk, Mistake and the Real in Performance', *Performance Research*, 15 (2): 80–5, at 81.
6   Ulrich Beck (1992) *Risk Society: Towards a New Modernity*, London: Sage; and Anthony Giddens (1999), 'Risk and Responsibility', *The Modern Law Review*, 62 (1): 1–10.
7   Derek Edyvane (2017) 'Toleration and Civility', *Social Theory and Practice*, 43 (3): 449–71; available at http://eprints.whiterose.ac.uk/114997/1/Toleration%20and%20Civility%20FINAL.pdf (accessed 2 September 2019). Page numbers are from the self-archived PDF document, at 22.
8   Edyvane, 'Toleration and Civility', 8.
9   Edyvane, 'Toleration and Civility', 9.
10 Samuel Scheffler (2010) 'The Good of Toleration', in *Equality and Tradition*, Oxford: Oxford University Press.
11 Edyvane, 'Toleration and Civility', 12.
12 Edyvane, 'Toleration and Civility', 16.
13 Edyvane, 'Toleration and Civility'.
14 Derek Edyvane (2017) 'The Passion for Civility', *Political Studies Review*, 14 (3): 344–54.
15 Mark Brown (2015) '*En Avant, Marche!* King's Theatre, Review: Self-indulgent', *The Telegraph*, 25 August.
16 les ballets C de la B, '*En Avant, Marche!*' Available at www.lesballetscdela.be/en/projects/productions/en-avant-marche/info/ (accessed 21 August 2019).
17 les ballets C de la B, '*En Avant, Marche!*'
18 les ballets C de la B, '*En Avant, Marche!*'
19 Edinburgh International Festival, 2015
20 In Edyvane, 'Toleration and Civility', 21.
21 Edyvane, 'Toleration and Civility', 21.

References

Beck, Ulrich (1992) *Risk Society: Towards a New Modernity*, London: Sage.
Boenisch, Peter, and Lourdes Orozco (2010) 'Editorial. Border Collisions: Contemporary Flemish Theatre', *Contemporary Theatre Review*, 20 (4): 397–404.
Brown, Mark (2015) 'Edinburgh 2015: *En Avant, Marche!* King's Theatre, Review – Self-Indulgent', *The Telegraph*, 25 August.
Cools, Guy (2001) 'Intercultural Storytelling: A Voyage around the Theatre World of Alain Platel', *Parachute: Contemporary Art Magazine*, 102: 102–13.
Edyvane, Derek (2017) 'Toleration and Civility', *Social Theory and Practice*, 43 (3): 449–71. Available at http://eprints.whiterose.ac.uk/114997/1/Toleration%20and%20Civility%20FINAL.pdf (accessed 2 September 2019).
Edyvane, Derek (2017) 'The Passion for Civility', *Political Studies Review*, 14 (3): 344–54.

Gardner, Lyn (2015) '*En Avant, Marche!* Edinburgh Festival Review: Mortality Take with a Brimming Heart', *The Guardian Online*, 25 August. Available at https://www.theguardian.com/stage/2015/aug/25/en-avant-marche-at-edinburgh-festival-review-mortality-tale-with-a-brimming-heart (accessed 21 August 2019).
Giddens, Anthony (1999) 'Risk and Responsibility', *The Modern Law Review*, 62 (1): 1–10.
Klett, Renate (2006) 'Nothing Happens, and Yet Everything Does: The Theater of Alain Platel', *Theater*, 36 (1): 162–5.
Orozco, Lourdes (2010) 'Never Work with Children and Animals: Risk, Mistake and the Real in Performance', *Performance Research*, 15 (2): 80–5.
Platel, Alain, and Lou Cope (2010) 'Looking Inward, Outward, Backward and Forward', *Contemporary Theatre Review*, 20 (4): 416–20.
Scheffler, Samuel (2010) 'The Good of Toleration', in *Equality and Tradition*, Oxford: Oxford University Press, 312–36.

16

Troubled Pasts and Presents, Differential Futures

Alain Platel's Choreopolitics with les ballets C de la B

Christel Stalpaert

Over the years les ballets C de la B has developed a choreographic oeuvre that also testifies to a sincere social and political commitment. Since 2001, the company regularly visits the Occupied Palestinian Territories (mostly Ramallah). In 2006, this results in a collaboration between les ballets C de la B, KVS (Koninklijke Vlaamse Schouwburg – Royal Flemish Theatre) and the A. M. Qattan Foundation (AMQF), a private charity dealing with culture and education that mainly operates in Palestine. In November 2004, Alain Platel travels to Palestine with five dancers for a workshop with young local artists. In his report, Alain Platel observes the following about the dance company El-Funoun:

> The company presents itself as a modern Palestinian company that has its roots in traditional Palestinian dance. Decades of isolation prompted it to seek collaboration with European artists ... I feel this has resulted in a curious tension. Although the Palestinian dancers are confronted with new ideas, challenging formats and processes, their aim is not just to imitate ... This causes an awkward tension in the young dancers, who, on the one hand, are inspired by new ideas and wish to experiment, and on the other wish to remain true to their heritage and traditions.[1]

In August 2007, members of the KVS and dancers of les ballets C de la B travel to Palestine for a summer workshop with young potential performing artists. Koen Augustijnen and Rosalba Torres Guerrero (from les ballets C de la B) and Hildegard De Vuyst (at the time working as a dramaturg at KVS) work together for the first time. The collaboration results in the dance production *Badke* (2013). Together with a group of young Palestinians with various backgrounds, they explore the curious tension between folkloristic and contemporary dance and the entanglement of dance with (political) issues of identity, nation and nationality.

The team adopts Platel's open, process-based way of working. Everyone involved in the creative process has a voice in developing the performance. In *Badke*, this means that all performers have agency (and hence responsibility) in the way they are represented. Hildegard De Vuyst calls this the shared 'intellectual responsibility of a piece'.[2] This responsibility has not so much to do with having intellectual authority over something or someone in support of a creative process nor with having good judgement or fine taste in artistic choices. This responsibility should rather be understood as a response-ability, that is, as the ability to respond to the different constituents (including both ideas and people) that come with a networked mode of creation.[3] As such, the Palestinian dancers share a creative space in which they perpetually explore, negotiate and reinvent every move they make. This allows for a constant negotiation with and *déplacement* of existing clichés of 'Palestinians' dancing from within the performers' particular bodies-as-archives. The dancers inevitably bring along their particular (troubled) pasts and presents on the stage, but none of the performers 'owns' a dance technique, a choreographic phrase or a dance movement. Sharing the creative space also means sharing and appropriating each other's moves. As such, the performers mess up and accumulate diverse dance styles, tackling any clear-cut identity or national(ity) that accompanies a dance style. The positions the performers hold are 'multiple, complex, and in some cases, even contradictory'.[4] The result is a highly energetic, stylistically diverse experience, displaying a profound passion for life with differential futures, despite the troubled pasts and presents.

This open, process-based way of working is also at stake in *Coup Fatal* (2014), for which Alain Platel collaborated with thirteen musicians and dancers from Kinshasa, and with composer Fabrizio Cassol and countertenor Serge Kakudji, with whom Platel also collaborated for *pitié!* (2008). For *Coup Fatal*, the performers did not only have agency in co-creating a performance that moved beyond clichéd thinking about the Congolese as being poor, exploited and sick. The Congolese musicians appropriated several European baroque themes and rearranged them with their musical traditions. They do not merely imitate or adjust themselves to an operatic style that is imposed on them. They give a profound twist to the baroque fragments by Monteverdi, Bach, Handel, Vivaldi and Gluck they encounter while also exchanging among themselves the diverse dance and music traditions that are inscribed in their bodies-as-archives.

An important issue in the creation process of both performances is the shared responsibility in creating a common ground and understanding for dealing with existing clichés about notions of identity, nation and nationality. What are the limits in making jokes about cliché representations of 'the Palestinians' and 'the Congolese' in order to point at clichéd thinking in a society? The open, process-based way of working as such also entails a choreopolitics in the sense that it opens up opportunities 'to move politically',[5] 'as expressions of freedom'.[6] Whereas politics as we know it is usually connected with the rhetoric effectiveness of the spoken word and with the realm of the discussable, these performances are political precisely because they outwit the confidence that sides with eloquent speech in conveying a clear message, and with the rhetoric of the spoken word in populist propaganda.

This contribution unravels the choreopolitics at work in the different, yet related works of *Badke* and *Coup Fatal*. The choreopolitics of les ballets C de la B operates on three levels. First, on the level of the creation process, the choreographer (Augustijnen or Platel) is less concerned with controlling, channelling and directing movements in a confined space, following his preconceived idea. He engages in an open, process-based co-creation with bodies possessing their own particular archives of dance techniques, dance movements, tics and habits. Second, allowing these (sometimes vulnerable) bodies to move in particular ways calls for a displacement of clichéd thinking about bodies moving through time and space. The perpetual exchange and appropriation of dance movements calls for a redistribution of habitual and legitimate ways of moving. Virtuosity and beauty subsequently acquire another dimension. Performance scholar Rebecca Schneider would say that the performers' skill lies in their 'ethics of gestural response-ability', rethinking relationality as 'something that always already anticipates and perpetually reinaugurates possibilities for response'.[7] On a third, conceptual level, the choreopolitics of les ballets C de la B also tackles (political) issues concerned with notions of identity, gender, nation and nationality that are attributed to moving bodies. Probing the paradox in the constructed cultural divide between 'high' and 'low' culture, between 'tradition' and the 'contemporary', between 'victim' and 'terrorist', between 'colonized' and 'colonizer', *Badke* and *Coup Fatal* render the spectator perplexed, in the sense of stuttering in perception. The performances leave us at times lost for words, as we have to let go, not only of dominant or clichéd societal meanings and preconceived notions of race, age and gender but also of the ideological positions of post-colonial or gender studies.

The choreopolitics at work with les ballets C de la B inaugurates a new mode of political and post-colonial thinking that is not stuck in or paralysed by the troubled past or present but that provides space for imagining differential futures specific to but not limited or overdetermined by these troubles. In both *Badke* and *Coup Fatal*, the performers' bodies-as-archives testify to an ever-expanding and ever-shifting encounter between so-called 'high' and 'low' culture, the 'traditional' and the 'contemporary' and between different dance styles. Dancing through their complex bodies-as-archives, the performers of both *Badke* and *Coup Fatal* co-create the past, the present and the future, with the spectator as their accomplice.

Troubled pasts and presents

In *Coup Fatal*, some elements refer to the Democratic Republic of Congo's (DRC's) decades of human misery. The giant stage-curtains, created by visual artist Freddy Tsimba, are made from discarded bullet casings from the DRC's civil wars. Dancers steam through the golden string of bullets, taking the stage, and percussionists playfully use them like a drummer's chimes, but they are nevertheless a constant reminder of the violent past (and present) that the performing bodies in a way carry with them. In their stubborn presence, these bullet casings testify to the constant threat of violence in DRC and Kinshasa. DRC's post-independence history counts several civil wars between 1998 and 2003, but armed groups continue to fight for power, natural resources, or because of ethnic differences. Handel's popular concert piece 'Lascia ch'io pianga' or 'Let Me Weep' sung by countertenor Serge Kakudji powerfully resonates with a grieving over the losses through war.

The garish suits in which the performers appear in the second part of the show also refer to a cry for freedom in a region that is scarred by armed conflicts. The extravagant yellow tweeds, the colourful silk scarves and socks, the kilts … are inspired by the elegant and immaculately dressed Congo dandies who stroll the most poverty-stricken areas in Kinshasa. The Sapeurs, as they are called, belong to Le SAPE or La Société des Ambianceurs et des Personnes Elégantes (The Society of Tastemakers and Elegant People). Their history reaches far back into the troubled past of slavery and colonialism in Congo, as these Congo dandies build upon a long history of African dandies, with roots in the times of slavery in the eighteenth century. European seigneurs gave their slaves 'proper' costumes so that they would fit better into their luxurious surroundings. Wearing 'European' designer clothes as such echoes the erasure of a 'black' identity. However, this is only one side of a very complex issue. Some Sapeurs are very proud of having created their own 'extravagant' style, celebrating the abolition of the slave trade, appropriating European fashion standards. They consider it a cultural form of resistance against colonial regime. Moreover, Congolese dandies proudly associate elegant style with a respectful and considerate attitude towards others. Despite the brutality and horror that they experienced during slavery and three civil wars, they profile themselves as outspoken non-violent persons. As such, they inspire people with their motto to drop the weapons, to work and to dress elegantly. From this perspective, dandyism is associated with a resistance to disappear in the anonymous crowd. Claiming that (personal) style is something completely different than being a dedicated follower of fashion, dandies claim their own, nonconformist paradigm of courtesy. It is associated not only with copying 'European' elegance and style but also with humour and independence.

The question remains how independent you can be if you live in poverty but aim to be dressed in the most expensive European tailoring. The reality of the Congolese dandies' poor living conditions is very inconsistent with the image they want to uphold. They have to spend a fortune on the most expensive designer brand accessories – Gucci, Prada, Dior – while their average annual income is among the lowest in the world. And yet, posing for photographers, on waste belts and ruins, these Congolese dandies point exactly at the sinister cruelty of our global world economy in capitalist times. While DRC has the potential to be one of the richest countries in Africa, because of its rich natural resources, it still remains at the bottom of the Human Development Index, scoring very low on items such as income, education and health.[8] This has to do with governmental corruption but cannot be dissociated from a long history of colonialism and European imperialism, as well as current international policies.

When the Congolese musicians dress up as Sapeurs, they wear playful variations of designer clothes, such as a 'fancy' dress made of ties. Rather than merely celebrating an extravagant style, they point at the ambivalence of the image. They give the sapeur a twist, and this makes me wonder about the tensions between 'colonizer' and 'colonized', between 'high' and 'low' culture. Why do Sapeurs dress like this? Why do they prefer to buy a designer suit rather than a piece of land? Do they really acquire status and power

Figure 16.1 Bouton Kalanda, Russell Tshiebua and Costa Pinto during rehearsals of *Coup Fatal* in KVS, Brussels, 2014. © Chris Van der Burght.

through their carefully constructed *imago*? Do they want to escape an African identity and culture that has been considered 'low' or even 'bestial' throughout colonial history? Or do they resist a colonial discourse by appropriating it? Are Congolese dandies merely imitating European aristocratic lifestyle or do they mock colonial culture? Are they a victim of capitalism or do they resist capitalism by choosing not to buy land and to die in debt? The performers in *Coup Fatal* probe these questions rather than providing an answer to them.

Appropriation and negotiation in process-based co-creation

Much like Sapeurs are taking pleasure in appropriating (and probing) European aristocratic dress codes, the Congolese countertenor Serge Kakudji became a very skilled singer in the 'high' culture of opera. Already as a child in his native Lubumbashi, he dreamt of becoming an opera singer. Participating in workshops and contests at a young age, the self-taught singer caught the attention of the Congolese choreographer Faustin Linyekula and was engaged to sing Mozart (excerpts from *Requiem*) in *Dinozord: The Dialogue Series III* (2006). Touring with this production brought him to Brussels, Belgium and other European cities.[9] When he returned home, he ended up composing and performing his own opera in 2006. *Likembe Opera*, the first opera in Swahili, debuted in 2007 in Lubumbashi.

Alain Platel met Kakudji and engaged him for a key role in *pitié!* in 2008, which was based on the *St Matthew Passion* by Bach. It is precisely Kakudji's ambivalent identity and his position in between cultures that drew Platel's attention. Balancing 'between his African culture and that of the West which he had appropriated', Kakudji escapes superficial, clichéd thinking and develops an interesting dialogue with heterogeneity.[10] Also, by casting Kakudji as the figure of Jesus in Bach's *St Matthew's Passion*, Platel made a statement, as this is a role usually not attributed to a young black singer with little 'official' opera experience. Co-composer Fabrizio Cassol delivered the score and transformed and rearranged the story of Christ's passion in close consultation with Platel. He describes their collaboration as very open: 'our previous collective projects had already strengthened our mutual understanding and trust, which enabled me to anticipate what he would do', he says.[11]

Cassol focused on the mother's pain with regard to the inevitable sacrifice of her son, a non-existent part in the original. The sacrifice of Christ is split up in two, resulting in three lead singers, consisting of a soprano for the mother (Claron McFadden, Laura Claycomb and Melissa Givens), an alto/mezzo for one child (Cristina Zavalloni, Maribeth Diggle, Monica Brett-Crowther) and a countertenor for the other child (Serge Kakudji). The orchestra consisted of Aka Moon, a Brussels jazz band, and Magic Malik, a French jazz-flute player who embodies 'written and unwritten traditions, both Western and African'.[12] Instruments ranged from saxophone, trumpet, cello and violin to fender bass, bouzouki, accordion, drums and other percussion instruments. As such, the composition itself embraces a wide range of styles and traditions. Cassol explains:

> I did not want a homogeneous cast of baroque voices for the vocal ensemble. I wanted voices that could vibrate, which is not in the baroque tradition. I wanted various qualities which could be mixed: opera, baroque, African and contemporary. Which means that the singers are very different from one another, and that although they are all 'characters' they allow themselves to be mixed.[13]

The African context played a role in the composition. However, the score for *pitié!* mainly took shape in close consultation with Platel, not in co-creation with the musicians and the dancers. As Cassol was already working on *pitié!* while on tour, the music was not created in parallel with the dance (as was the case with, for example, *vsprs*). The musical proposals were delivered to the musicians to perform and delivered at the start of the creation process with the dancers.

A more open, co-creative process is at stake in *Coup Fatal*, in which Kakudji took on a more active role. The musical proposals were not delivered to the musicians and the dancers beforehand but took shape in co-creation. It was in fact Serge Kakudji and Paul Kerstens, at the time working with Jan Goossens to develop the Congo trajectory of the KVS, who had started the *Coup Fatal* project in the context of the Connexion Kin festival in Kinshasa in 2010.¹⁴ Fabrizio Cassol joined the team in the subsequent festival editions, and Alain Platel also travelled to Kinshasa to work with the musicians. Thirteen musicians from Kinshasa, guitar player Rodriguez Vangama and composer Fabrizio Cassol together engaged with the repertoire of various baroque composers. Kakudji himself selected the arias to be performed. Several European baroque themes by Monteverdi, Bach, Handel, Vivaldi and Gluck were messed up and rearranged. As John Lewis observed in *The Guardian*:

> A Monteverdi overture becomes a duet for hi-life guitar and thumb piano. A Bach prelude is elegantly arranged for likembes, balafon and xylophone. A Handel piece is played on flamenco guitar. Operatic arias by Vivaldi and Gluck are sung by Serge Kakudji in a startlingly androgynous countertenor, while the band's percussionists lay down fiendishly complex polyrhythms.¹⁵

The musicians rearranged baroque music along their musical traditions. However, they were also probed to expand their habitual ways of playing and moving. Alain Platel asked the musicians to play their instruments upright, not seated in a concert formation, as they were accustomed to doing up until then. During the creation process in the KVS, when the composition was ready, Platel further engaged with the musicians as dancers, assisted by dancer Romain Guion. Platel positioned the two

Figure 16.2 Tister Ikomo, Angou Ingutu and Serge Kakudji during rehearsals of *Coup Fatal* in KVS, Brussels, 2014. © Chris Van der Burght.

backing vocals in the forefront and allowed them to explore their dance qualities. He also detected Tister Ikomo among the musicians, who, apart from playing the xylophone, also turned out to be a gifted dancer at the ballet dance group Arumbaya. This resulted in Ikomo's solo behind the curtain of bullets, with his ever-curling back turned to the audience.[16]

Instead of categorizing musicians according to the instruments they played, Platel encountered bodies-as-archives that could perform more than they appeared to. Rather than delving into an 'African' musical and dance tradition, the co-creation in *Coup Fatal* hence started from the presence of bodies possessing their particular archives of musical skills, movement habits, tics and dance techniques. These bodies primarily tell the story of particular, individual histories that are nevertheless (always) intertwined with social and political histories.

In that sense, the open creation process of *Coup Fatal* is similar to that of *Badke*, a production of KVS and les ballets C de la B with Palestinian dancers. *Badke* assembles a group of ten Palestinian dancers from different home locations: Galilee, Jerusalem and Ramallah. They all have a different relation to 'home', 'tradition' and 'dance'. The performers hence possess very different bodies-as-archives, but they nevertheless share a Palestinian identity. Two dancers are refugees from families who have lived in Askar Camp for several generations, a Palestinian refugee camp located on the outskirts of the West Bank city of Nablus. Two other dancers are Israeli-Palestinians; they are Israeli citizens who identify as Arab or Palestinian. Others come from Jerusalem or the West Bank. Together with Koen Augustijnen, Rosalba Torres Guerrero and Hildegard De Vuyst, the dancers co-create a performance in which the traditional dance of *dabke* encounters new proposals, vocabularies and ideas from hip hop, circus, contemporary dance, capoeira, etc.

Some of the dancers were acquainted with or trained in *dabke*, an Arab folk dance. Some were not familiar with the particular stamping of the feet, the circle dance motifs and the line dance motifs and started learning the Arab folk dance during the rehearsal process from each other. However, the *dabke* body movements were not merely copied, they were exchanged, appropriated and corporeally acculturated in particular bodies-as-archives. The same happened with other dance phrases, tapped from the very different and very diverse dance trainings of the performers, ranging from hip hop to circus, capoeira, kickboxing and martial arts. These movements were exchanged and appropriated among the dancers, sometimes with the help of YouTube videos.

Dabke served as a common ground for a group of dancers having a sense of community with a diasporic people.[17] The recognizable folk dance movements offered a connecting image of a homeland, while the never-ending corporeal acculturation of movements, dance techniques, habits and tics in their very diverse bodies-as-archives connected the dancers, as a community, with numerous other parts in the world. No movement was 'owned' or 'possessed' by any body, hence any solid (national) identity was avoided. *Badke* is therefore not a 'Palestinian' performance. It is a very diverse gathering of bodies-as-archives, testifying to a particular relation to what is considered a traditional folk dance, displaying an ever-growing corporeal acculturation of dance techniques coming from diverse contexts across the world.

Ambivalence in corporeal acculturation

As Lepecki observed, the body constantly gathers techniques, movements, habits, bits and pieces of repertoire that are being stored in a body-as-archive for later use.[18] Even when Palestinians had to leave behind their home and their material belongings, their bodies-as-archives travelled with them, wherever their wanderings led them. In *Badke*, the performers display the diverse ways in which the Arab folk dance of *dabke* has been inscribed into or appropriated by Palestinian bodies along generations, time and history. From a dance studies perspective, the displayed elements of folk dance are 'a useful synecdoche for the complex web of relations that link performers to particular subjectivities, histories, practice, and to each other'.[19] This points at the power of dance and performance as 'a social force, as cultural poesis, as communication infrastructure that makes identity, solidarity and memory sharable'.[20] Or, as Celeste Fraser Delgado and José Esteban Muñoz would put it: 'identification takes the form of histories written on the body throughout gesture', in this case dance movements.[21] In performing the shared (or appropriated) embodied memories of traditional *dabke* dance, the performers in *Badke* acknowledge the potential of shared (embodied) memory to 'promote an ethics of caring among communities of memory'.[22]

However, the presence of Arab folk dance elements in *Badke* should not be regarded as a melancholic aesthetic, merely communicating a longing for a lost home, for 'memory's point of origin'.[23] *Badke* moves beyond this melancholic aesthetic as the performers do not dwell in a melancholic dead end. Through the exchange and appropriation of very diverse dance techniques they explore their very diverse and ever-accumulating corporeal dance archive to come to terms with the reminiscences of a dispersed 'Palestinian culture'. They move on, beyond a melancholic desire of belonging. They creatively and energetically engage with the losses and burdens of the pasts and presents in order to generate new opportunities for the future. This creates a curious tension, from the perspective of the performer as well as the spectator. In an interview, Samaa Wakeem, dancer and actress in *Badke*, explains how, while travelling abroad, she saw different things which opened up her mind and which she tried to incorporate. This was not an evident thing to do, however, considering her strong sense of community with Palestinians:

> When you are trying to use this 'new' language and to mix it with your narrative, the rehearsal space becomes a very sensitive place: how to use *dabke* in your dance, but without getting in conflict with people who think that *dabke* is a resistance, and that you cannot play with it? But sometimes, you have to provoke people so that they hear and see you.[24]

During the creation process of *Badke*, there was a certain hesitance to transform the *badke* idiom. Atta Khattab, for example, has a close connection to the *dabke* folk dance tradition. He started taking *dabke* classes at the age of six, at the Popular Arts Centre's School of Dabke. Later, he joined El-Funoun's Youth Troupe, a dance troupe that was established as a politically conscious act in 1979, to maintain our identity as Palestinian people'.[25] Teaching *dabke* in several parts of the world, he passed on his father's legacy to a new generation of young dancers. To him, the connection that is the hardest to establish is that with the Palestinian community. In an interview for theatre journal *Documenta* he explains:

> Dancing was hence not something just to enjoy; it was something to defend yourself, something to connect yourself with an identity, with your land. This still is what we are doing now in El-Funoun: how to make art as a tool to communicate with your society and to make the people there find a space to dance and rethink their situation.
>
> I think art in our particular situation in Palestine should really be a tool to connect the people in the political situation there. It shouldn't be a bubble, in which you separate yourself from your society, and that you're enjoying as an individual. This is a discussion, you know, even in Palestine, but I think my responsibility, as an artist, is how I can really bring people together.[26]

At the same time, Atta Khattab also acknowledges the importance of expanding the boundaries of his body-as-archive and of opening up to other dance experiences:

> For me, it's a front that I fight. But at the same time, the identity for me as an individual, as an artist or as a people, wouldn't be created without also connecting with people and artists around the world ... If I want to extend the boundaries of my body and my experience, I should also communicate with artists and on an artistic level, without forgetting the political and the social level. You are not dancing outside the system. Every time we work on a performance, we reflect on these things.[27]

When Atta Khattab refers to the importance to 'reflect on these things', he refers to the important issue of a shared responsibility in the creation process of *Badke*, which entails a constant questioning and negotiation with the performers on the way they are represented as 'Palestinians' in the performance. This means questioning any construction of an identity through dance.[28]

> So, for example, in *Badke*, when a guy leads the line of the dance, and he says to the dancers what they should do, the following questions inevitably rise: Who is that guy? What does he represent in the bigger picture? What if the line refused this guy to lead them? This is a question of the political, social and even economic inside the dance.[29]

This constant negotiation and displacement concerns not only dance traditions and dance sequences but also cliché representations of places and people. What are the limits in making jokes about cliché representations in order to point at clichéd thinking in a society? When the Palestinians are imitating a shooting and eliminating themselves, they play with the cliché representation of themselves as terrorists. In working towards these dance sequences, there is a lot of reflection on how much one can push the limits in addressing clichés.

In constantly exploring and negotiating new ideas in co-creation, and in encountering challenging formats and creative processes, the performers in *Badke* explore their shared yet individual histories along their complex and ever-expanding corporeal (music and dance) archive. In using their body as a living archive, the performers adopt a dynamic understanding of 'body', 'dance' and 'archive', hence activating the body as 'an endlessly transformational archive'.[30] The performers in *Badke* do not dance what is considered the 'genuine' or 'original' *dabke*, performed in social gatherings such as weddings or other joyous occasions. They testify to the complexity of interconnections between 'traditional' and 'experimental' music and dance motifs, with their diverging and converging dance trainings and techniques. These interconnections are often displayed in one and the same dance sequence, and in an accumulative way, as in an assemblage. As such, we see dancers holding hands, forming a semi-circle, stamping their feet, in synchronized movement, sometimes one dancer heads the line, dividing his attentive gaze between the audience and the other dancers. The rhythmic stomping initiates a capoeira *chute* (kick) or *bananeira* (handstand), a change of pace or a sudden slowing down gives way to a hip-hop downrock.

But there is more. In an email conversation, Hildegard De Vuyst recalls how the performers of *Badke* took part in an intense two-day dance workshop with the Congolese ballet dance group Arumbaya during the festival Connexion Kin in Kinshasa in 2015.[31] After this workshop, their body awareness had changed considerably. It resulted in including the middle part of the body (hips, bottom) in a folk dance that is all about the upper part of the body (shoulders and arms), and the lower part of the body (knees and feet), with the upper part communicating a connection to others and the lower part communicating a connection to the land. De Vuyst calls this a displacement in an otherwise comfortable, common appropriation of dance movements. With the bum dance, the performers explored in a way an as-yet-unexplored territory in their body-as-archive. Each dancer made a short bum movement of four counts. They taught their moves to one another, and they were glued together in one choreographic phrase. De Vuyst remembers how a lot of this bum stuff looked like premature Michael Jackson, but it became a powerful statement. Infusing the *dabke* dance with the middle part of the body of course has a sexual connotation, bringing in the delicate sex and gender issue in Palestine. Samaa Wakeem, performer in *Badke*, testifies to the sexual taboos in Palestine:

> But how much can you push the limits? … talking about women who have sex before marriage. A lot of young women are doing this in Palestine and it's not a big issue anymore, but you're not supposed to talk about it. There is a small bubble of artistic people who broke the taboos. But to talk about it in the performance, before an audience …[32]

Instead of cultivating a 'pure' or 'authentic' *dabke* dance style, *Badke* explores what I call a dance technique of corporeal acculturation. In the process of 'acculturation', a multiple entity is maintained.³³ It entails the accumulation of different cultural entities and is opposed to the process of integration, a process that demands from human beings to disappear as 'other' and to become one with 'us'. Integration entails 'usurpation, the process of annihilation, and hence the vanishing as a differentiated entity'.³⁴ The complex layering of *Badke*'s folk dance with other dance techniques such as hip hop, circus, contemporary dance, capoeira, etc., displays an assemblage of dance techniques, each of them connected with personal memories and diverse notions of cultural identity. The corporeal acculturation of the bum dance into the *dabke* idiom further expands habitual ways of moving and dancing. From a choreopolitical perspective, this entails an open or unbound mode of dancing, not excluding any aesthetic or movement possibilities. In displaying a very diverse set of dance and performance skills, the performers in fact move beyond categorization in dance, embracing and expanding all styles available in their body-as-archive.

As Andrew Hewitt has pointed out in *Social Choreography*, choreography is the modality through which dance reflects 'a way of thinking about social order'.³⁵ Dance studies have revealed how folk dance serves a state's bio-politics by developing a spectacle of nationhood. Folk dance and folk music as such also regulate a disciplined body, assessing social, cultural and political developments within the nation. The way that folk dance turns into a system of obedience, or choreopolice as Lepecki would put it, is exemplified in the mass spectacles of the Sokol movement that have been performed throughout Eastern Europe. The manipulation of individual bodies through mass configurations disseminated spectacles of nationhood and desired to constitute supra-ethnic identities. Mass-choreographed festivals such as *slets* were performed to constitute a pan-Slavic identity, aiming at uniting all Slavic people. This is choreopoliced movement, 'as any movement incapable of breaking the endless reproduction of an imposed circulation of consensual subjectivity, where to be is to fit within a prechoreographed pattern of circulation, corporeality, and belonging'.³⁶

On the other hand, dance practices not only perpetuate but also contest national and antagonist groundings in the quest for identity.³⁷ The dancing body 'displays the intrinsic diversity that composes each citizen-body' and hence can surpass the strictures of the dance technique that align bodies with authority.³⁸ In 'playing' with not only the traditional *dabke* dance motifs but also with the hip-hop, circus, capoeira, kickboxing and martial-arts techniques, the performers point out that however 'monumental', however rigorously drilled into generations, dance techniques are not 'static' and 'forever'. They depend on dancing bodies, which keep them in motion and play, and whose freedom consists in the possibility of refashioning them along personal bodies, histories and desires.³⁹ Moreover, breaking with traditional codes, the dancers allow for uncertainty, discomfort and displacement in the open creation process. They constantly rebel and accept, reject and confirm, erase and repeat, isolate and accumulate bits and pieces of their body-as-archive in an astonishing swiftness. This calls for another perspective on notions such as beauty and virtuosity.

The beauty and virtuosity of response-ability

In *pitié!* Serge Kakudji became the 'star' of the performance, with *The Guardian*, among others, describing 'the golden tracery of his voice ... offering us a glimpse of the sublime'.[40] Rather than looking at the 'sublime' beauty of Kakudji's voice, defining his virtuosity in terms of perfection in his execution of a Western opera piece, I would like to touch upon the notions of beauty and virtuosity in terms of response-ability. What particularly strikes me in *pitié!* in this context is that Bach's *St Matthew's Passion* is not regarded as a religious piece that idealizes suffering. Bach's music is traditionally considered as having a morally uplifting function. It predominantly relies on overwhelming emotions, beauty and virtuosity for communicating suffering as an idealized concept. Fate gives people the courage of endurance in suffering. An important difference with this perception of Bach is that 'Fabrizio exposes the innermost part, the "guts"'.[41]

The excellence of the dancers and musicians in *pitié!*, *Coup Fatal* and *Badke* articulates another kind of virtuosity and beauty than the acrobatic movement in the circus, seeking perfection, stretching human capacities to overcome gravity forces. These dancers' virtuosity has nothing to do with perfection, harmony, nor with the effectiveness of how a dance movement is executed. It has everything to do with the courage to connect with the other, with the swiftness of moving within the different registers of acculturation in the body-as-archive on the one hand and with the skill of response-ability, in the sense of accounting for the ability to respond in the attachment with an other, on the other hand. This demands a new mode of relationality towards fellow dancers. Virtuosity and beauty acquire a different dimension through the skill of response-ability, rethinking relationality as 'something that always already anticipates and perpetually reinaugurates possibilities for response'.[42]

Whereas Alain Platel used to work with 'amateur' dancers and non-professionals in his early choreographic works, he increasingly works with talented professionals in his more recent work. The critique that this leads to a virtuoso spectacular is an unjustified criticism. Platel himself is very reluctant towards this form of virtuosity; 'all that remains is its value as a spectacular, where it serves no other form of expression'. He regrets that this spectacular notion of virtuosity refrains the dancers 'from using their potential', censoring themselves for new opportunities.[43] It is true that very skilled professional performers often display their virtuosity, affirming the importance of personhood and self-centredness. However, it is precisely the passing on of movement material in the creative process that prevents performers from settling in the comfort zone of virtuosity and skill. The passing on of movement material entails a constant risky search through appropriation and displacement. The beauty and virtuosity lie precisely in the dancers' courage to constantly reconnect with fellow dancers' material, tapping movement material from 'others' and inscribing it in their own body-as-archive. This passing on of movement material is not the same as imitating moves or choreographic phrases; Platel describes it as a movement 'going through the wringer of other bodies'; 'it becomes distorted and changed so that it no longer expresses the particular identity of one thing or another'.[44] The dancers and performers cannot simply excel in confident, intentional moves or targeted actions because a bonded agency with other bodies-as-archives is at work. These moves are courageous explorations as they entail hesitant gestures of the unknown that demand the courage to think the yet unthought.[45]

When in *Coup Fatal*, the compositional elements with the likembes, the balafon and the percussionists' complex polyrhythms support the so-called 'traditional' element in the score, the performers are easily coined as the cliché of 'the young, gifted and black', hence circulating in a short-circuited vision on beauty and virtuosity. As such, the musicians are merely associated with the traditions of their Congolese home country. From this perspective, the Congolese musical elements serve as 'a synecdoche for the complex web of relations that link performers to particular subjectivities, histories, practice, and to each other'.[46] However, during the creation process, Fabrizio Cassol precisely threw in the cliché of 'the young, gifted and black' in order to negotiate and displace with the performers the representation of this clichéd thinking about 'the virtuous Congolese'.

Critical moves beyond belonging

The ways in which the performers in *Coup Fatal* and *Badke* deal with the burdens of pasts and presents is with a blunt playfulness and humour. In *Coup Fatal*, the dancers steam through the giant stage-curtains, made from discarded, brass bullet casings from the DRC's civil wars, and percussionists playfully use them like a drummer's chimes. They might be burdened by a colonial past, but they refuse to be determined by it. When the backing vocals Russell Tshiebua and Boule Mɔanya come to the forefront and are moving around like monkeys or gorillas, they choose to consciously play with a colonial representation of themselves. They push the limits of clichéd thinking about 'the' Congolese as uncivilized, poor, exploited or sick. In this moment, they instil 'agency' in people's representation. A similar agency is at work in the performers' broadly-smiling display of seducing, bumping and grinding as Sapeurs, dressed in colourful designer clothes. These performers embody the persistent belief of the possibility to move forward despite the troubling past and present.

However, *Coup Fatal* is not mere feel-good fun. These playful dance movements remain 'critical moves'.[47] As such, the Nina Simone song, 'To Be Young, Gifted and Black', indeed does not 'belong' to the Congolese, just as little as it belongs to 'us'. As Hildegard De Vuyst recalls:

> It belongs to them in just the same way as it belongs to us: through channels of globalization. But it's coming from a different context and injects a different layer of meaning: the political fight for equal rights in black America, transported to the opera houses in Europe. Where the audiences are applauding the young, gifted and black on stage, but [there are] very little young, gifted and black in the audience, or in the regular opera repertoire, or in the conservatories etc., etc. It's where *Coup Fatal* gets part of its edge.[48]

The giant stage-curtains with the bullet casings remain onstage, as a stubborn reminder of the burdened past that persists within the post-colonial present. However, it does not persist in the present as an 'over-determining or specifying legacy, but as the ground from which differential futures emerge in unpredictable, unforeseeable and ever new ways'.[49] *Coup Fatal* performs 'both the burden of the past and the possibility of a new beginning'.[50] It is not a denial of racism, but the 'recognition that racism does not define and exhaust all the "creative" potential of race'.[51]

Here the choreopolitics of Platel with les ballets C de la B sides with contemporary post-colonial author-thinkers such as Erwin Jans, Édouard Glissant, Antonio Benítez-Rojo, Wilson Harris, Mohammed Dib and Adrian Johnson who follow the reasoning of Achille Mbembe. Mbembe observed that the word 'post-colonial' should be systematically replaced by 'post-colony', thereby indicating that 'the' post-colony is, in fact, many post-colonies, and the position one holds in that place is 'multiple, complex, and in some cases, even contradictory'.[52] People should not be convinced of one Truth, or a univocal moral message, but instead possibilities should be created for developing a perpetual dialogue with heterogeneity. In current post-colonial thinking, Rick Dolphijn points out that moralism is replaced by an ethical call for accountability.[53]

This becoming-post-colonial does not imply that the colonial past should be neglected. On the contrary.[54] By moving away from a fixation on the colonial past, differential futures can be imagined from an experimental engagement with the present. *Coup Fatal* and *Badke* do not only evolve from a catastrophic past but above all inaugurate unpredictable encounters and constantly shifting linkages with social bodies, including the spectator's. The experience of the dancers and performers may well be informed by a burdened past, but they are no longer determined by it. In *Badke*, the incorporation

Figure 16.3 *Badke* in KVS Brussels, 2013. © Danny Willems.

of *dabke* material similarly does not bring back – be it imaginatively – a lost home but creates a new acculturated community. By dancing through the complex time knots in their bodies-as-archives, the performers co-create the future, with the spectator as their accomplice. This also accounts for the percussionists' complex polyrhythms supporting the so-called 'traditional' element in the score of *Coup Fatal*. After all, if (music or dance) technique is an archive,[55] then the question of the (dancing) body-as-archive is not, we repeat after Derrida, 'a question of the past … It is a question of the future, the question of the future itself, the question of a response, of a promise and of a responsibility for tomorrow'.[56] In other words, *Badke* and *Coup Fatal* are not only directed towards a burdened past and present, the performance is also engaged with 'differential futures'.[57]

Ethical implications of response-ability

Contemporary cultural identities are hybrid and can no longer be strictly defined according to national origin or other types of inherent belonging. They are, rather, constituted by 'the intricate and extensive web of relationships that different individuals and groups establish in their daily practice and in their imaginary enactments'.[58] Identity is a constant becoming, based on relation rather than on affiliation, blood ancestry and land. This demands a kind of openness towards otherness, in the sense of encountering the 'other'.

In exploring another mode of relationality onstage, *Coup Fatal* and *Badke* are a test case with world-making potential for new relational identities. The spectators are engaged in a conceptual swiftness in encountering the other in wonder, in the sense that they also have to open up towards several possible meanings, relations and identities. The performances not only probe 'to rethink relation' but also to 'rethink it in order to relate anew'.[59] Common sense fails to acknowledge otherness on the basis of easily recognizable external features such as race, gender or age. The mirroring attitude of common sense and clichéd thinking is often reductive as far as 'mapping' the other is concerned. When we look for superficial characteristics of the other, such as form, function or kind, we annex the 'other' and capture them within clichéd thinking. We capture otherness within preconceived notions and identities, within superficial representation, as a touchstone for our own so-called 'clear-cut' but reductive identity. In *Coup Fatal* and *Badke* we experience a shock to thought, probing us to reconsider our own mechanisms of oppositional and stereotypical thinking. The 'other' cannot simply be thought as opposing 'us'. The comfort of oppositional thinking is gone. In this ontological instability, a co-creative relation might emerge, in which the spectator experiences a 'co-emerging I and Non-I prior to the I versus other'.[60] As such, the consistent openness in Platel's choreopolitics with les ballets C de la B also tackles (political) issues concerned with notions of identity, gender, nation and nationality. *Pitié!*, *Coup Fatal* and *Badke* are not political in their message, nor in the 'identities' they stage nor in the feelings the performances invoke concerning social, political or moral questions. The performances unfold heterotopias rather than utopias, with differential futures to emerge.

This is what I also tell the dancers: don't forget to live; weigh up the importance of what you are doing; bring things into focus, even in a negative way if you have to, so that you don't live a blurred life.[61]

Acknowledgements

I would like to thank Hildegard De Vuyst for her dramaturgical notes on the creation process of *Badke* and *Coup Fatal*. Her valuable comments triggered my thoughts in writing this article.

Notes

1. Alain Platel (2007) 'Diary'. Available at http://www.lesballetscdela.be/en/projects/les-ballets-and-the-world/palestine/extra/journey-palestine (accessed 21 August 2019).
2. Scott deLahunta (2000) 'Dance Dramaturgy: Speculations and Reflections', *Dance Theatre Journal*, 16 (1): 20–5; see also Christel Stalpaert (2009) 'A Dramaturgy of the Body', *Performance Research*, 14 (3): 121–5.
3. See also Christel Stalpaert (2017) 'Dramaturgy in the Curriculum: On Fluctuating Functions, Dramaturgy as Research and the Macro Dramaturgy of the Social', *Documenta*, 35 (1): 130–58, at 144.
4. Mbembe, quoted in Bruce B. Janz (2012) 'Forget Deleuze', in Lorna Burns and Birgit M. Kaiser (eds.), *Postcolonial Literatures and Deleuze*, Basingstoke: Palgrave Macmillan, 21–36, at 28.
5. André Lepecki (2013) 'Choreopolice and Choreopolitics', *The Drama Review*, 57 (4): 13–27, at 13.
6. Lepecki, 'Choreopolice and Choreopolitics', 16.
7. Rebecca Schneider (2017) 'In Our Hands: An Ethics of Gestural Response-ability', *Performance Philosophy*, 3 (1): 108–25.
8. 'Congo: Human Development Indicators', United Nations Development Programme, Human Development report, 2016. Available at http://hdr.undp.org/en/countries/profiles/COD (accessed 30 August 2019).
9. Kakudji continued to improve his singing skills at the Institut Supérieur de Musique et de Pédagogie in Namur, Belgium, and at the Conservatoire Nationale Régionale de Saint-Maur-des-Fossés with Yves Sotin.
10. Fabrizio Cassol and Hildegard De Vuyst (2008) 'An Interview with Fabrizio Cassol about *pitié!*'. Available at http://www.lesballetscdela.be/en/projects/productions/pitie/extra/an-interview-with-fabrizio-cassol/ (accessed 21 August 2019).
11. Cassol and De Vuyst, 'Interview'.
12. Cassol and De Vuyst, 'Interview'.
13. Cassol and De Vuyst, 'Interview'.
14. Connexion Kin is an annual festival that has taken place in June and July in Kinshasa since 2009, focusing on creation and reflection. Jan Goossens, former director of the KVS describes the festival as follows: 'It is mainly artist-driven, run by a network of Congolese, African and international partners, and has no formal or official political or institutional connections, except with the KVS. Its ambition is to reinforce artists

and their projects, whether they are from Kinshasa, Brussels or other cities, to attract local and diverse audiences, and to connect all of them with more international conversations and dynamics'. Jan Goossens, 'Why KVS in KIN?' Lecture, Experience as Institution, Tate Modern, 29 November 2013, London.

15   John Lewis (2015) 'Coup Fatal Review: Zoot-Suited Spectacular Celebrates Congolese Sapeurs', *The Guardian*, 5 June.
16   I thank Hildegard De Vuyst for the detailed information on the creation process.
17   The word 'diaspora' has multiple uses. I deliberately use the term 'diasporic' here in the more general sense of the ancient Greek word meaning 'to scatter about'. People of a diaspora are hence a scattered population, involuntarily removed from their homeland to places across the globe, spreading their language, their culture and their traditions as they move. The Bible refers to the diaspora of Jews, expelled from Israel. The Jewish Diaspora subsequently came to be used as the historical settlement of the dispersed Jews from Israel across the globe. However, there are countless other examples of diasporic people. The African diaspora, for example, is one of the largest diaspora of Sub-Saharan Africans, resulting from the African transatlantic slave trade. See Patrick Manning (2010) *The African Diaspora: A History through Culture*, New York: Columbia University Press. There also is a Palestinian diaspora; see Helena Lindholm Schulz (2005) *The Palestinian Diaspora*, London and New York: Routledge. I share Lindholm Schulz's vision and that of most recent studies that 'diaspora' becomes a problematic term when it relates to one very unique experience, i.e. the Jewish (*The Palestinian Diaspora*, 8). As such, I also consider the Palestinian dancers in *Badke* as having a strong sense of community with a group of people that experiences the 'enduring condition' of being 'dispersed … to at least two countries in the world' (*The Palestinian Diaspora*, 9).
18   André Lepecki (2010) 'The Body as Archive', *Dance Research Journal*, 42 (2): 28–48, at 34. See also Christel Stalpaert (2011) 'Re-enacting Modernity: Fabián Barba's A Mary Wigman Dance Evening (2009)', *Dance Research Journal*, 43 (1): 90–5.
19   Judith Hamera (2007) *Dancing Communities*, Basingstoke: Palgrave Macmillan, 5.
20   Hamera, *Dancing Communities*, 1.
21   Hamera, *Dancing Communities*, 22.
22   Avishai Margalit, cited in J. Creet and A. Kitzmann (eds.) (2011) *Memory and Migration*, Toronto: University of Toronto Press, 14.
23   Zofia Rosińska (2011) 'Emigratory Experience: The Melancholy of No Return', in J. Creet and A. Kitzmann (eds.), *Memory and Migration: Multidisciplinary Approaches to Memory Studies*, Toronto: University of Toronto Press, 29–42, at 40.
24   Wakeem in Christel Stalpaert (2018) 'A Conversation about Flemish-Palestinian Artists: Connections with Ahmed Tobasi, Atta Khattab, Dalia Taha, Samaa Wakeem, and Christel Stalpaert', *Documenta*, 36 (1): 167–79, at 176–7.
25   Khattab in Stalpaert, 'A Conversation about Flemish-Palestinian Artists', 172.
26   Khattab in Stalpaert, 'A Conversation about Flemish-Palestinian Artists', 172.
27   Khattab in Stalpaert, 'A Conversation about Flemish-Palestinian Artists', 172.
28   See also deLahunta, 'Dance Dramaturgy', 24; and Stalpaert, 'Re-enacting Modernity'.
29   Khattab in Stalpaert, 'A Conversation about Flemish-Palestinian Artists', 172.
30   Lepecki, 'The Body as Archive', 34.
31   Hildegard De Vuyst in an email conversation with Christel Stalpaert, 24 September 2018.
32   Khattab in Stalpaert, 'A Conversation about Flemish-Palestinian Artists', 177.

33　I borrow the concept of acculturation from the Polish philosopher Zofia Rosińska. She introduces the notion in the context of the structural bases of the emigratory experience and defines it as the accumulation of different cultural identities. It is opposed to the process of integration (Rosińska, 'Emigratory Experience', 32).
34　Celeste Olalquiaga (1999) *Megalopolis: Contemporary Cultural Sensibilities*, Minneapolis, Minn.: University of Minnesota Press, xx–xxi.
35　Andrew Hewitt (2005) *Social Choreography*, Durham, NC: Duke University Press, 11.
36　Lepecki, 'Choreopolice and Choreopolitics', 7.
37　Andrée Grau and Stephanie Jordan (2000) *Europe Dancing*, London and New York: Routledge, 4.
38　Randy Martin (1998) *Critical Moves*, Durham, NC: Duke University Press, 21.
39　Hamera, *Dancing Communities*, 4.
40　Luke Jennings (2009) 'You Don't Have to Be Mad to Work Here', *The Guardian*, 8 February.
41　Alain Platel and Hildegard De Vuyst (2008) 'An Interview with Alain Platel about pitié!' Available at http://www.lesballetscdela.be/en/projects/productions/pitie/extra/an-interview-with-alain-platel/ (accessed 21 August 2019).
42　Schneider, 'In Our Hands', 108.
43　Platel and De Vuyst, 'Interview'.
44　Platel and De Vuyst, 'Interview'.
45　Gilles Deleuze's aesthetic of intensities pleads in favour of an art form that forces the spectator to think the yet unthought, an art form that performs 'the hesitant gestures which accompany our encounters with the unknown'. Paul Patton (1997) 'Introduction', in *Deleuze: A Critical Reader*, ed. Paul Patton, Oxford: Blackwell, 1–17, at 8–9.
46　Hamera, *Dancing Communities*, 5.
47　Martin, *Critical Moves*.
48　Hildegard De Vuyst in an email conversation with Christel Stalpaert, 24 September 2018.
49　Lorna Burns and Birgit M. Kaiser (2012), 'Introduction: Navigating Differential Futures, (Un)making Colonial Pasts', in Lorna Burns and Birgit M. Kaiser (eds.), *Postcolonial Literatures and Deleuze: Colonial Pasts, Differential Futures*, New York: Palgrave Macmillan, 1–20, at 15.
50　Freddie Rokem (2000) *Performing History*, Iowa City, Iowa: University of Iowa Press, 2.
51　Janz, 'Forget Deleuze', 31.
52　Mbembe quoted in Janz, 'Forget Deleuze', 28.
53　Rick Dolphijn and Iris van der Tuin (2012) *New Materialism: Interviews and Cartographies*, Ann Arbor, Mich.: Open Humanities Press, 22.
54　Burns and Kaiser, 'Introduction', 13.
55　Hamera, *Dancing Communities*, 6.
56　Jacques Derrida (1995) 'The Time Is Out of Joint', in A. Haverkamp (ed.), *Deconstruction Is/in America*, New York: New York University Press, 14–38, at 36.
57　Burns and Kaiser, *Postcolonial Literatures and Deleuze: Colonial Pasts, Differential Futures*.
58　Olalquiaga, *Megalopolis*, xvi.
59　Kathrin Thiele (2012) 'The World With(out) Others, or How to Unlearn the Desire for the Other', in Lorna Burns and Birgit M. Kaiser (eds.), *Postcolonial Literatures and Deleuze: Colonial Pasts, Differential Futures*, New York: Palgrave Macmillan, 55–75, at 56.

60 Bracha L. Ettinger, cited in Thiele, 'The World With(out) Others', 69.
61 Platel and De Vuyst, 'Interview'.

References

Burns, Lorna, and Birgit M. Kaiser (eds.) (2012) *Postcolonial Literatures and Deleuze: Colonial Pasts, Differential Futures*, Basingstoke: Palgrave Macmillan.

Cassol, Fabrizio, and Hildegard De Vuyst (2008) 'An Interview with Fabrizio Cassol about *pitié!*' Available at http://www.lesballetscdela.be/en/projects/productions/pitie/extra/an-interview-with-fabrizio-cassol/ (accessed 21 August 2019).

Creet, J., and A. Kitzmann (eds.) (2011) *Memory and Migration: Multidisciplinary Approaches to Memory Studies*, Toronto: University of Toronto Press.

deLahunta, Scott (2000) 'Dance Dramaturgy: Speculations and Reflections', *Dance Theatre Journal*, 16 (1): 20–5.

Derrida, Jacques (1995) 'The Time Is Out of Joint', in A. Haverkamp (ed.), *Deconstruction Is/in America: A New Sense of the Political*, New York: New York University Press, 14–38.

Dolphijn, Rick, and Iris van der Tuin (2012) *New Materialism: Interviews and Cartographies*, Ann Arbor, Mich.: Open Humanities Press.

Goossens, Jan (2013) 'Why KVS in KIN?' Lecture. Experience as Institution: Artist Collectives and Cultural Platforms in Africa at Tate Modern, London, 29 November. http://www.kvs.be/sites/default/files/kvs/ConnexionKin_TateModern_JanGoossens.pdf (accessed 20 October 2018).

Grau, Andrée, and Stephanie Jordan (2000) *Europe Dancing: Perspectives on Theatre, Dance and Cultural Identity*, London and New York: Routledge.

Hamera, Judith (2007) *Dancing Communities: Performance, Difference and Connection in the Global City*, Basingstoke: Palgrave Macmillan.

Hewitt, Andrew (2005) *Social Choreography: Ideology as Performance in Dance and Everyday Movement*, Durham, NC: Duke University Press.

Janz, Bruce B. (2012) 'Forget Deleuze', in Lorna Burns and Birgit M. Kaiser (eds.), *Postcolonial Literatures and Deleuze: Colonial Pasts, Differential Futures*, Basingstoke: Palgrave Macmillan, 21–36.

Jennings, Luke (2009) 'You Don't Have to Be Mad to Work Here', *The Guardian*, 8 February.

Lepecki, André (2010) 'The Body as Archive: Will to Re-Enact and the Afterlives of Dance', *Dance Research Journal*, 42 (2): 28–48.

Lepecki, André (2013) 'Choreopolice and Choreopolitics; or, The Task of the Dancer', *The Drama Review*, 57 (4): 13–27.

Lewis, John (2015) '*Coup Fatal* Review: Zoot-Suited Spectacular Celebrates Congolese Sapeurs', *The Guardian*, 5 June.

Lindholm Schulz, Helena (2005) *The Palestinian Diaspora*, London and New York: Routledge.

Manning, Patrick (2010) *The African Diaspora: A History through Culture*, New York: Columbia University Press.

Martin, Randy (1998) *Critical Moves: Dance Studies in Theories and Politics*, Durham, NC: Duke University Press.

Olalquiaga, Celeste (1999) *Megalopolis: Contemporary Cultural Sensibilities*, Minneapolis, Minn.: University of Minnesota Press.

Patton, Paul (1997) 'Introduction', in *Deleuze: A Critical Reader*, ed. Paul Patton, Oxford: Blackwell Publishers, 1–17.

Platel, Alain (2007) 'Diary'. Available at http://www.lesballetscdela.be/en/projects/les-ballets-and-the-world/palestine/extra/journey-palestine (accessed 21 August 2019).

Platel, Alain, and Hildegard De Vuyst (2008) 'An Interview with Alain Platel about *pitié!*' Available at http://www.lesballetscdela.be/en/projects/productions/pitie/extra/an-interview-with-alain-platel/ (accessed 21 August 2019).

Rokem, Freddie (2000) *Performing History: Theatrical Representations of the Past in Contemporary Theatre*, Iowa City, Iowa: University of Iowa Press.

Rosińska, Zofia (2011) 'Emigratory Experience: The Melancholy of No Return', in J. Creet and A. Kitzmann (eds.), *Memory and Migration: Multidisciplinary Approaches to Memory Studies*, Toronto: University of Toronto Press, 29–42.

Schneider, Rebecca (2017) 'In Our Hands: An Ethics of Gestural Response-ability – Rebecca Schneider in Conversation with Lucia Ruprecht', *Performance Philosophy*, 3 (1): 108–25.

Stalpaert, Christel (2009) 'A Dramaturgy of the Body', *Performance Research*, 14 (3): 121–5.

Stalpaert, Christel (2011) 'Re-enacting Modernity: Fabián Barba's A Mary Wigman Dance Evening (2009)', *Dance Research Journal*, 43 (1): 90–5.

Stalpaert, Christel (2017) 'Dramaturgy in the Curriculum: On Fluctuating Functions, Dramaturgy as Research and the Macro Dramaturgy of the Social', *Documenta*, 35 (1): 130–58.

Stalpaert, Christel (2018) 'A Conversation about Flemish-Palestinian Artists: Connections with Ahmed Tobasi, Atta Khattab, Dalia Taha, Samaa Wakeem, and Christel Stalpaert', *Documenta*, 36 (1): 167–79.

Thiele, Kathrin (2012) 'The World With(out) Others, or How to Unlearn the Desire for the Other', in Lorna Burns and Birgit M. Kaiser (eds.), *Postcolonial Literatures and Deleuze: Colonial Pasts, Differential Futures*, New York: Palgrave Macmillan, 55–75.

17

Offspring

Hildegard De Vuyst

It started with a group of friends – extremely talented people who believed that they did not need a formal training in order to step onto a stage, in accordance with the zeitgeist and the spirit of the Sex Pistols. Everyone did everything, unburdened by knowledge or know-how. This resulted in unconventional performances, conducted in living rooms or lofts, in any place the leaderless group had access to. Dirk Pauwels, a member of the legendary Radeis group, who had just converted a former warehouse into a performance space, invited the anarchist lot into the Nieuwpoorttheater in Ghent. The rest is history. But it is seldom told from the perspective of its own transformations.

The company has always claimed it was not 'the Alain Platel company', even though he was the driving force behind each of the company's transformations. The first transformation can be situated at the end of the 1980s. Platel withdraws from the collective les ballets C de la B. He has, so he says, reached the limits of his abilities and the limits of working collectively: the company has relied on his energy, his imagination for too long. The company's trademark is collective work, but in reality Platel's shoulders carry its productions. On the one hand, he wants to recharge, and indulge in the knowledge and expertise of experienced theatre-makers; on the other hand, his move forces others to leave the safe confinement of the collective. Hans Van den Broeck is the first one who rises to the occasion. He creates *How to Approach a Dog* (1992), and later *Everyman* (1994), *(They Feed, We) Eat, Eat, Eat* (1996), *La Sortie* (1999) and *Lac des singes* (2001) with les ballets C de la B, before founding his own performing arts company SOIT (Stay Only If Temporary) in 2002.[1]

While Van den Broeck is taking his first steps as a choreographer, Platel is doing an internship at Eva Bal's Speeltheater and at Kirsten Delholm's Hotel Pro Forma. He creates a duet in the gloomy Abattoirs de Marseille, where he meets dancer Isnelle da Silveira, whom he will marry in 1995. At Het Muziek LOD he begins to work on his first musical theatre projects, together with Dick van der Harst. In the meantime, he has also accepted Dirk Pauwels' offer to reflect on and contribute to a fusion of Nieuwpoorttheater and Oud Huis Stekelbees baptized 'Victoria'.

It is not until November 1993 that Platel returns to les ballets C de la B. He creates *Bonjour madame* (1993), the first performance explicitly bearing his signature. It puts the company on the map. *La Tristeza Complice* (1995) and *Iets op Bach* (1998) continue this development. *La Tristeza Complice* was a coproduction between les ballets C de la B and Het Muziek LOD; it is the culmination of a long collaboration between Alain Platel and Dick van der Harst, resulting in this performance on Purcell with accordions. At the same time, Platel is working with Arne Sierens at Victoria in creating the trilogy *Moeder en Kind* (1995), *Bernadetje* (1996) and *Allemaal Indiaan* (1999).

After *Iets op Bach*, Platel announces a retreat and a production stop, leaving space for others. Koen Augustijnen, active as a dancer in performances by Platel and Van den Broeck since 1991, makes his first dance-theatre production *To Crush Time* (1997), with Hildegard De Vuyst as dramaturg. Critic Pieter T'Jonck recognized 'the style of other les ballets C de la B directors, such as Alain Platel' but also praised Augustijnen for his particular talents in cultivating scenes of so-called 'miserabilism'.[2] There's a prolific outburst of first creations by other ex-dancers of *Bonjour madame* or *Iets op Bach*: by Francisco Camacho, Sam Louwyck, Minne Vosteen and eventually also Sidi Larbi Cherkaoui.

Koen Augustijnen marks a breakthrough in 2004 with *Bâche* (2004) and continues collaborating with dramaturg Guy Cools for *Import/Export* (2006) and *Ashes* (2009).

Christine De Smedt, who danced in *Mussen* (*Sparrows*) in 1991 and created a first solo in les ballets C de la B in 1994, makes her mark with *9×9* (2000) in which she asked eighty-one mostly non-professional performers to participate in a mathematically structured dance piece. Christine De Smedt also collaborated with choreographers such as Eszter Salamon, Mårten Spångberg and Xavier Le Roy.

Figure 17.1 Christine De Smedt, Hans Van den Broeck, Pascale Platel and Koen Augustijnen in *Mussen*, 1991. © Chris Van der Burght.

Figure 17.2 Christine De Smedt in *Untitled 4*, 2010. © Chris Van der Burght.

Following in Augustijnen's and De Smedt's footsteps, Sidi Larbi Cherkaoui seizes his opportunity in 1998. His first choreography (with Hildegard De Vuyst as dramaturg) *Rien de rien* (2000) wins the Special Prize at the BITEF Festival in Belgrade in 2001 and the prize for emerging choreographer in December 2002 at the Nijinsky Awards in Monte Carlo. It marks the beginning of an international career, with *Foi* (2003), *Tempus Fugit* (2004) and others ever exploring 'gestures of cultural difference'.[3]

It is remarkable that artists as diverse as Koen Augustijnen, Christine De Smedt and Sidi Larbi Cherkaoui were all active as in-house choreographer of les ballets C de la B at one time. 'However diverse they are, these three artists managed to successfully circulate their work internationally [there]'.[4] According to Pieter T'Jonck, this is 'proof of the ongoing diversity, liveliness and quality of the Flemish dance landscape'.[5]

While these artists are working on their careers, Platel takes a sabbatical, travels to Palestine and begins a project with London choirs for the opening of the Roundhouse in 2001. Five hundred people sing their hearts out in this project, for which Orlando Gough collaborates with Platel and sixteen participating amateur choirs. Soon after that, Gerard Mortier, at the time intendant of the Ruhrtriennale, convinces Platel to create a new production. *Wolf* (2003), the piece with the dogs, is the baroque capstone of a series about the representation of a multicultural reality.

Les ballets C de la B has transformed into a platform for choreographers, and Platel is just one of them. While he is doing well artistically, continuing long-term collaborations with various dancers, with composers Fabrizio Cassol and Steven Prengels, and director Frank Van Laecke, the rest of the company is sometimes having trouble keeping up. They are relying heavily on the artistic credit that Platel's work has built. For Sidi Larbi Cherkaoui, the platform soon becomes too small, the waiting too long. After a short time at Toneelhuis, he founds his own company Eastman. Lisi Estaras, since 1997 dancer with Platel, steps in.

The inequality within the platform was endangering the stability. Platel used his tried and tested strategy to remove himself from view and bring other artists to the forefront, to confront others and to create space for different initiatives, while at the same time relieving the pressure and responsibility he himself was coping with. In the company's grant application form for the time period 2013–16, the appointment of a

Figure 17.3 Sidi Larbi Cherkaoui and Akram Khan in *Zero Degrees*, 2005. © Tristram Kenton.

new artistic leader is announced. However, this attempt to rethink les ballets C de la B as a platform is impeded by financial setbacks and a critical inquiry by the dance commission.

As a result, the platform was dissolved in 2012, and the organization was trimmed down. The process has not been a painless one, but in the end the crisis has opened up other perspectives for each of the choreographers involved. Estaras, who has choreographed *Patchagonia* (2007), *Bolero* (2009), *The Gaza Monologues* (2010) and *Primero-erscht* (2010), founded her company Monkey Mind. She returned as a dancer in *tauberbach* (2014), while continuing projects with amateurs and disabled persons. After *Badke* (2013), Koen Augustijnen and Rosalba Torres Guerrero continued to work together, and Christine De Smedt found a temporary home in PARTS (Brussels). Les ballets C de la B became the company of Alain Platel.

From a certain distance in time, we can now see that the way dancers used to take the opportunity to create their own work was sometimes based on a partial understanding of the true nature of Platel's collaborative creation. Dancers making their own material (often in response to a question or a stimulus) and acquiring a great sense of autonomy within the process find it hard to return to the position of 'executive' artist. These artists would rather take the risk of making their own work. In that case, Platel's method often served as a starting point, but that does not necessarily result in work of a similar quality. This is because Platel does not simply present the dancer's work; he transforms it in a way that transcends the total sum of its parts. He creates a context within which the materials relate to each other, resonating in a way that, in the end, has little to do with the (dancer's) initial individual starting point. It is this added value, the gently enforced collectivism, that sometimes remains under the radar, even to participating dancers.

Creating material is something different than creating a performance with that material. Not every great dancer is able to lead a project from A to Z. And not everyone who can run one project is able to construct an oeuvre of multiple works. Perhaps the company was focusing too much on looking for the next Platel? And 'the next Platel' always turned out to be a little too small or, in a single case, too big for the organization at hand. Whatever may be the reasons, these experiments and experiences have yielded some beautiful offspring.

It is not just the previously mentioned Sidi Larbi Cherkaoui, currently at the wheel at the Royal Ballet Flanders, who started his career at les ballets C de la B. Platel can also be considered the spiritual father of Peeping Tom by Franck Chartier and Gabriela Carrizo; of Faso Dance Theatre by Serge Aimé Coulibaly, of Siamese (the new name for the structure by Koen Augustijnen and Rosalba Torres) and of Monkey Mind, where Lisi Estaras, Quan Bui Ngoc and Nicolas Vladyslav make work. And this is only a row of formalized structures. Kurt Vanmaeckelberghe (the deaf actor from *Wolf*) continued creating high-quality work; Arend Pinoy; Laura Neyskens with Bollylicious; Lies Pauwels … even composer Steven Prengels is currently working on his first project. Critic Pieter T'Jonck adds to this list of names Lilia Mestre, Mette Edvardsen and Einat Tuchman.[6] And we are probably forgetting a few names. Les ballets C de la B proved a particularly rich source of new choreographic talent. For a man who does not have any children himself, this is a lot of offspring.

In the meantime, les ballets C de la B is really an organization around a single artist. But it is not in Platel's nature, as a man and as an artist, to claim the resources and well-attuned team only for his own benefit. For him, sharing is a fundamental attitude in life – one that does not only extend to the rehearsal process, in sharing content and materials but also to the organization itself: in sharing resources and infrastructure, knowledge and insights, experience and expertise.

Having learnt from the past, les ballets C de la B are now running a residency programme called Co-laBo, a response and proposition of dramaturg Hildegard De Vuyst to meet the needs of the company with the needs of young artists. Selected projects get financial, logistic, technical, administrative and artistic support. Platel proves to be an excellent coach for the work of others. The artistic profiles are very diverse and represent a different kind of conversation, away from the clan-like ties that used to dominate the artistic choices in the past. The body is still at the centre, in all its glory and imperfection, the body-as-archive, the body as battlefield or space for negotiation, and that focus does not exclude language or text. Les ballets C de la B does not prioritize certain forms or movement idioms; there is just as much attention for meta-levels and reflection.

Although the concentration on Platel's work with its international touring could have led to a sort of 'splendid isolation', the residency programme creates new opportunities for connections with the dance field in Flanders and abroad. Young makers have the chance to enter the programme, coming straight from dance schools, from the nearby KASK–School of Arts, or as a result of international encounters in Congo or Palestine or elsewhere. This will allow les ballets C de la B to root itself again within the Flemish performing arts scene, without giving up its position as citizen of the world. With his retirement looming on the horizon, it is clear that Platel will withdraw once again from the organization – maybe less of his own choice this time – and that les ballets C de la B are facing another transformation. But it is also clear that Alain will always play a part in whatever comes up next.

Notes

1   The Norwegian choreographer, dancer and performance artist Mette Edvardsen was a performer in several performances by Hans Van den Broeck and assisted director/choreographer on *Lac des singes* before she started developing her own work.
2   Pieter T'Jonck (1997) 'Danstheater op de vuilnisbelt', *De Standaard*, 7 November 1997.
3   Jeroen Peeters (2000) 'Gebaren van culturele differentie', *Financieel-Economische Tijd*, 15 October.
4   Pieter T'Jonck (2009) 'Hedendaagse dans in Vlaanderen 1993–2009', in Charlotte Vandevyver (ed.), *Dans in Vlaanderen (Concertgebouwcahier)*, Ghent: Borgerhoff & Lamberigts, pp. 11–27, at 20.
5   T'Jonck, 'Hedendaagse dans in Vlaanderen 1993–2009', 19.
6   T'Jonck, 'Hedendaagse dans in Vlaanderen 1993–2009'.

References

Peeters, Jeroen (2000) 'Gebaren van culturele differentie', *Financieel-Economische Tijd*, 15 October.

T'Jonck, Pieter (1997) 'Danstheater op de vuilnisbelt', *De Standaard*, 7 November.

T'Jonck, Pieter (2009) 'Hedendaagse dans in Vlaanderen 1993–2009', in Charlotte Vandevyver (ed.), *Dans in Vlaanderen (Concertgebouwcahier)*, Ghent: Borgerhoff & Lamberigts.

Index

Abbate, Caroline 101
Agamben, Giorgio 10–11, 149–50, 164–5, 196–7
Aka Moon 235
Albright, Ann Cooper 7, 22, 27, 162, 166
Allemaal Indiaan 5, 10, 63, 87, 136–7, 146, 252
alterkinetic 10–11, 23, 26–7, 29, 155, 159–72
A. M. Qattan Foundation 230
Anezin, Marie 52
Anzieu, Didier 124, 128, 130
appropriation 12, 156, 162, 232, 234, 237–9, 240–2
Arendt, Hannah 3
Artaud, Antonin 10, 64, 86, 145, 151–4
Arumbaya 237, 240
assemblage 240–1
Augustijnen, Koen 62, 230, 237, 252, 255

Bach, Johann Sebastian 4, 8, 21, 71, 79–80, 102, 123, 138, 140, 148, 153, 190, 193–5, 197, 199–201, 209, 211, 215, 231, 235–6, 242
Badke 230–2, 237–46
Baricco, Alessandro 10, 137–9
Barthes, Roland 124
bastard dance (*bastaarddans*) 12, 126, 198
Batash, Ido 10, 50, 119, 126–7
Bausch, Pina 5, 32–3, 35, 49, 63, 145, 148, 155, 158, 161, 163–4, 171
Because I Sing 28
Beck, Ulrich 218, 220
Béjart, Maurice 2, 34
Bel, Jérôme 158–9, 161, 167, 178
Bellon, Michael 100
Benjamin, Walter 5, 37, 54, 63, 196
Berger, John 7, 27, 72, 77–8, 82–3
Bernadetje 5, 8, 10, 63, 87–96, 145–8, 153, 252
Bernadette of Lourdes 88–9

The Best Belgian Dance Solos 20
Besuelle, Claire 9
Beuys, Joseph 180, 184
Bleuler, Eugen 195
Blickregie 5, 22
Blom, Philip 39
Bodin, Bérengère 118, 121–2, 195–6, 200
body-as-archive 24, 231–2, 237–43, 245, 256
Bonjour Madame, comment allez-vous aujourd'hui, il fait beau, il va sans doute pleuvoir, etcetera 4–5, 19–20, 36, 53, 62–3, 252
Borch-Jacobsen, Mikkel 91
Bosch, Hieronymus 195, 199
Bourguignon, Carlo 200
brass band 12, 216–27
Braziel, Jana 154
Brecht, Bertolt 8, 10, 37, 53–4, 64, 93, 96, 145, 151–4
Butler, Judith 11, 178–86

Camacho, Francisco 252
Cassol, Fabrizio 28, 40, 47, 100, 140, 215, 231, 235–6, 243, 254
Charcot, Jean Martin 10, 149, 169
Chekhov, Anton 150
Cheng, François 116
Cherkaoui, Sidi Larbi 20–1, 63, 253–5
C(H)OEURS 8–9, 28, 39, 99–114, 138–9, 153, 198
choreopolice 3, 241
choreopolitics/choreopolitical 3–5, 8, 12–13, 157, 170, 230–2, 244–5
Clapton, Eric 8, 138
Co-laBo 1, 226, 256
collaborative dramaturgy 48
Congo 232–3
Connexion Kin festival 236, 240
Cools, Guy 1, 4, 189, 252
corporeal acculturation 237–8, 240–1

corporeal space 7, 27, 72, 83
Coup Fatal 12–13, 47, 140, 231–7, 242–5

dabke 237–41, 245
Debacker, Griet 219, 222–3
de Balzac, Honoré 165
De Brauw, Elsie 70, 192–9, 207–9
De Bruyckere, Berlinde 9, 39, 116, 118
decentred dramaturgy 4, 52–3
Defraeye, Piet 11
De Keersmaeker, Anne Teresa 2, 34, 62, 64, 136, 189
de la Tourette, Gilles 10, 24, 75, 149, 160, 164–6, 168, 171
Deleuze, Gilles 29
Delgado, Celeste Fraser 238
Deligny, Fernand 10, 210–11
Demuynck, Dorine 48
Derrida, Jacques 245
De Smedt, Christine 62, 252, 255
De Somvielle, Charlotte 13
détournement 11, 161, 170–1
dEUS 28
Devereux, Georges 170
Devriendt, Mirjam 14
De Vuyst, Hildegard 1, 3, 5, 9, 13, 36–42, 49–55, 230–1, 237, 240, 243, 252–3, 256
Diaghilev, Sergei de 149
Dietrich, Marlene 8
Dion, Céline 8, 138
displacement (*déplacement*) 122, 129, 231–2, 239–42
Dolphijn, Rick 244
Donckers, Jeroen 11
dramaturgy of the skin 115–16, 119
drastic 101, 105, 112–13
Dreysse, Miriam 11
Duncan, Isadora 149, 166
Duras, Marguerite 9, 100, 108–9
dyskinetic (dyskinesia) 11, 24, 26, 34, 156–7, 168–9, 171–2

Eckersall, Peter 39
Edyvane, Derek 219–22, 227
El-Funoun 230, 238–9
emoterror 136–7, 141
En avant, marche! 12, 47, 215–29
energetic theatre 7, 27, 71–2, 83, 153
Estaras, Lisi 10, 40, 48, 197, 200, 254–5

Etcetera 136–7
Etchells, Tim 23, 38

Fabre, Jan 2, 34, 62, 64
Flemish Wave 2–3, 136, 215
Foster, Susan Leigh 115
Foucault, Michel 170–1
Freud, Sigmund 11, 94, 152, 207

Gardenia 4, 11, 23, 140, 153, 178–86
gestus 10, 151–3
Giddens, Anthony 218, 220
Gielen, Pascal 2
Gluck, Christoph Willibald 236
gnostic 101, 112–13
Goossens, Jan 236
Gotman, Kélina 10, 26
Gough, Orlando 253
Green, André 86
Grimonprez, Johan 20, 34
Grossman, Evelyne 130
Guerrero, Rosalba Torres 230, 237, 255
Guion, Romain 118–19, 128–9, 236

Handel, George Frideric 233, 236
Heroes Band 224
Herr, Sophie 124
hieroglyph 10, 151–3
Hoghe, Raimund 32
Hewitt, Andrew 241
Huis van Alijn 223

Ibsen, Henrik 150, 154
Iets op Bach 4–5, 8, 19–21, 34, 53, 63, 95–6, 100, 102, 138–9, 252
Ikomo, Tister 237
Irigaray, Luce 9

Jackson, Michael 240
Jameson, Frederic 93
Jans, Erwin 10, 244
Judson Church 157, 161, 163, 166, 170

Kakudji, Serge 13, 231, 233–6, 242
Kear, Adrian 8
Kerstens, Paul 236
Khattab, Atta 238–9
Kinshasa 231–3, 236, 240
Klett, Renate 28, 73, 75, 199

Knowles, Ric 37
Krott, Severine 138
KVS (Koninklijke Vlaamse Schouwburg) 28, 138, 230, 236–7

Lacan, Jacques 91, 93–4
Laermans, Rudi 2, 9, 136–8, 140
Laplanche, Jean 93–4
La Tristeza Complice 4–5, 7, 19–20, 22–4, 36–7, 53, 63, 73, 76–9, 81–2, 138, 252
LeBesco, Kathleen 165
Lebon, Hendrik 227
Lehmann, Hans-Thies 7, 22, 27, 71, 74–5, 83, 146, 153
Lepecki, André 3, 26, 36, 163, 167–8, 238, 241
Le Roy, Xavier 167, 178, 252
Lessing, Gotthold Ephraim 54
Levinas, Emmanuel 11, 179, 196–7
Levine, Caroline 157
Linyekula, Faustin 235
LOD Muziektheater 36, 62, 251–2
Lomoff, Mélanie 40–1, 50
Lotz, Wolfram 29
Louwyck, Sam 29, 63, 252
Lyotard, Jean-François 71, 152–3

McCarren, Felicia 168
McGormack, Ross 197–8
Madonna 139
Maes, Francis 8
Maeterlinck, Maurice 150
Magic Malik 235
Mahler, Gustav 39, 47–50, 121–6
Maklakiewicz, Jan 194, 198, 200
Malabou, Catherine 157–8, 160
Manning, Erin 162, 172
métissage 12, 35, 125
Meyerhold, Vsevolod 151
micro- and macro-dramaturgy 5, 34, 39, 54
minor gesture 162, 172
Moeder en Kind 5, 10, 63, 87, 146, 148, 252
Monteverdi, Claudio Giovanni Antonio 8, 40, 100, 138, 215, 231, 236
Mortier, Gerard 8, 99, 102, 253
Mozart, Wolfgang Amadeus 8, 99–100, 102, 111, 138, 201, 215, 235
Mpanya, Boule 47, 123–5, 243
Mudra 2

Muñoz, José Esteban 238
Museum Dr. Guislain 24
musical dramaturgy 7, 9, 28, 49, 111, 125–6

Nancy, Jean-Luc 81–3, 153
new dramaturgy 35
nicht schlafen 9, 14, 39, 42, 47–50, 52, 115–31
Nietzsche, Friedrich 126
Nieuwpoorttheater 62, 251
Noeth, Sandra 54
Nussbaum, Martha 9, 137–9

Opbrouck, Wim 217–23, 225–7
Orozco, Lourdes 12
Ortega, José 227
orthopaedic therapy 189
Out of Context – for Pina 4, 10, 23–6, 32–3, 138, 140, 155–72

Palestine 12–13, 28, 138–9, 230, 239–40, 253, 256
PARTS 2, 255
Pauwels, Dirk 251, 255
Pecková, Dagmar 126
Peeters, Jeroen 34
Perón, Evita 139
Phlips, William 36
Picasso, Pablo 165
Pirandello, Luigi 218, 223
pitié! 4, 7, 13, 24–5, 73–4, 79–83, 138, 198–9, 231, 235, 242, 245
Platel, Pascale 20, 34
Plato 166
Platt, Ryan 80, 83
postdramatic theatre 10, 22, 38, 74–5, 146, 153
Prado, Marcos 192, 194, 199
precarious/precariousness 4, 11, 25, 178–86
Prengels, Steven 42, 47–9, 71, 99–101, 123–4, 194, 215, 254–5
Prince 8, 90, 138
Profeta, Katherine 37–8
Proust, Marcel 149
Purcell, Henry 36–7

Radeis 251
Rancière, Jacques 3–4, 11

Ravel, Maurice 8
Rekto:Verso 138
Rembrandt 7, 72
response-ability/responsibility 8–9, 13–14, 23, 29, 34, 39, 54, 63–4, 73, 83, 87, 91, 96, 127, 183–4, 220, 231–2, 239, 242–3, 245–6
Rigaglia, Dario 119
Rilke, Rainer Maria 149
risk society 218, 220
Roberts, John 161
Romme, Marius 195
Rosas 35
Rossell, Lazara 139
Runa, Romeu 10, 26, 190, 197–8, 200

Sachs, Hans 103–4, 106–7
Sacks, Oliver 200
Salamon, Eszter 252
Sapeurs 12, 233–4, 243
Scarry, Elaine 26
Scheffler, Samuel 220
schizophrenia 11, 189, 194–5, 208, 210
Schmidt, Daniel 195
Schneider, Rebecca 232
Schwartz, Hillel 158–71
Shklar, Judith 220
Sierens, Arne 2, 10, 63, 87, 90, 136, 145–6, 252
Simone, Nina 243
Sklar, Deirdre 83
Solnit, Rebecca 83
sonorous dramaturgy 7, 47
Spångberg, Mårten 252
Stabat Mater 199
Stalpaert, Christel 1, 13, 29, 54, 199
Stein, Gertrude 191
Strauss, Richard 123
Strindberg, August 150
Stuart, Meg 178
stuttering 4, 12–13, 28–9, 198, 232
Szondi, Peter 150

Tass, Elie 119, 121, 128, 200
tauberbach 7, 11, 69–71, 138–40, 189–201, 206–11, 215, 255

Thom, Jess 168, 171
Thys, Chris 219, 222–3
T'Jonck, Pieter 2, 34–5, 136, 252–3, 255
Trenscényi, Katalin 5, 20
Tshiebua, Russell 47, 119, 123–5, 243
Tsimba, Freddy 232
Tuchman, Einat 139

Uit de Bol 28
unruly dramaturgy 5, 34
Uytterhoeven, Lise 198

Valéry, Paul 130
Vandekeybus, Wim 2, 34, 64
Van den Broeck, Hans 62, 251–2
Vandenhouwe, Jan 99
van der Harst, Dick 36–7, 251–2
Van Durme, Vannessa 179–81
Vangama, Rodriguez 236
van Gehuchten, Arthur 24
Van Kerkhoven, Marianne 5, 35, 39
Van Laecke, Frank 178, 215–16, 218, 221, 223, 226, 254
Varro, Terentius 196
Verdi, Giuseppe 8, 28, 39, 99–112, 139, 215, 221
Verniers, Roel 136
Victoria 62, 87, 148, 251–2
Vivaldi, Antonio 231, 236
Vosteen, Ghani Minne 21, 63, 252
vsprs 4, 24–5, 28, 39, 53, 100, 105, 138, 140, 199, 215, 235

Wagner, Richard 8, 28, 39, 99–107, 109, 111, 139, 215
Wakeem, Samaa 238, 240
Warburg, Aby 197
Wihstutz, Benjamin 161
Witness 21–3, 27, 29, 73, 75, 78–9, 82–3, 95–6
Wittgenstein, Ludwig 207
Wolf 8, 34, 99–100, 102, 138, 215, 218, 254–5

Ziemer, Gesa 182, 186
Żmijewski, Artur 194

www.ingramcontent.com/pod-product-compliance
Lightning Source LLC
Chambersburg PA
CBHW050342230426
43663CB00010B/1953